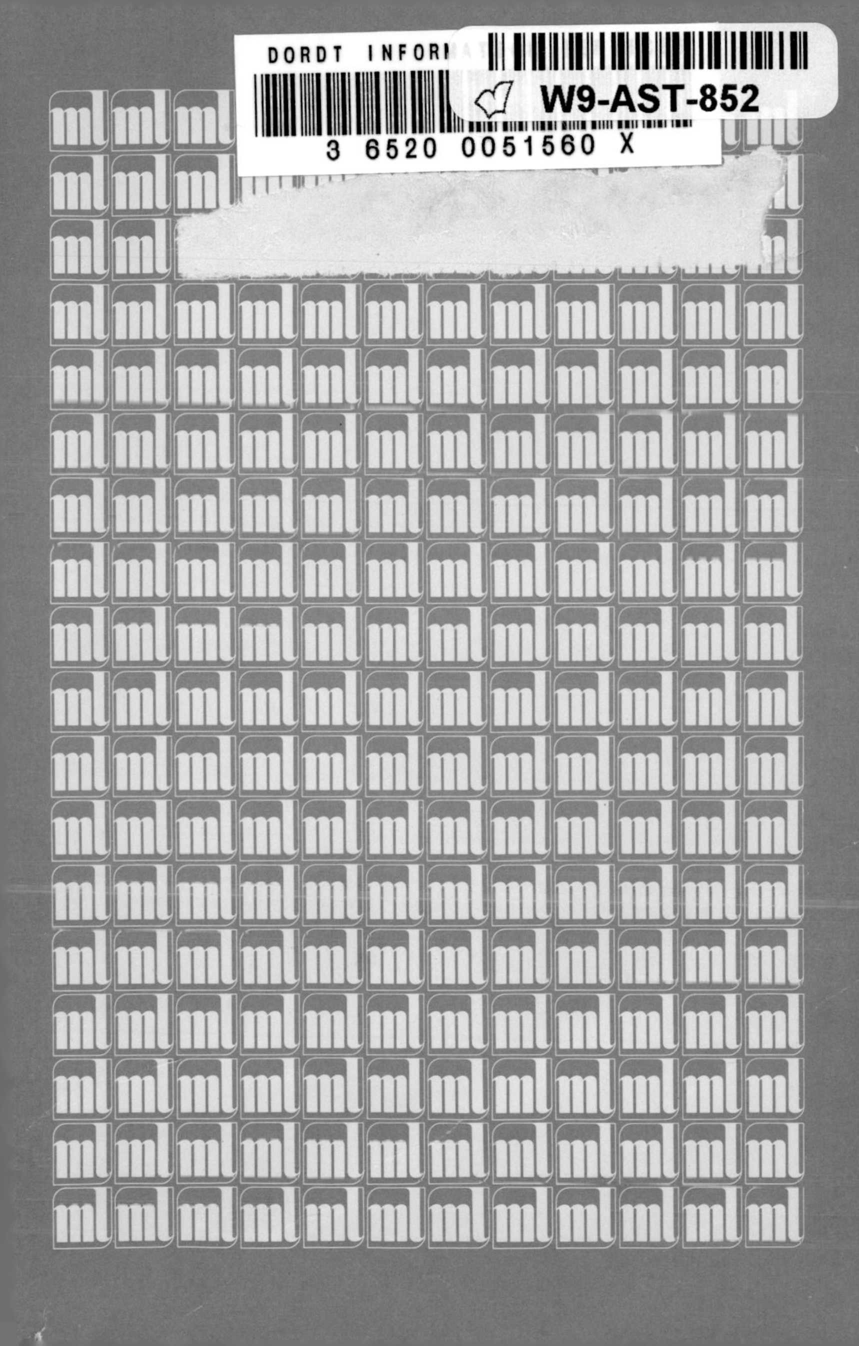

THE MODERN LIBRARY

OF THE WORLD'S BEST BOOKS

The World's GREAT OPERAS

THE WORLD'S
GREAT OPERAS

John Tasker Howard

NEWLY ENLARGED EDITION

The Modern Library • New York

 Published
in New York by Random House, Inc.,
and simultaneously in Toronto, Canada,
by Random House
of Canada, Limited.

Library of Congress Catalog Card Number: 59–10911

Random House IS THE PUBLISHER OF *The Modern Library*

BENNETT CERF • DONALD S. KLOPFER

Manufactured in the United States of America by H. Wolff.

To

RUTH, AMY *and* JOAN

CONTENTS

CONTENTS

APPENDIX

A BRIEF BACKGROUND

Opera as a form of entertainment has its roots in the tragedies of ancient Greece, in which music was an integral part. The theatrical performances of ancient Rome also used music. In the Middle Ages drama became the property of the Church, and it was then that the principle of modern opera was developed. Practically no play was performed without some kind of music, not only as an accompaniment for the action, but also for the expression of the text. In the liturgical dramas the words were sung or intoned.

One of the early attempts at writing what we would call an opera was made by a group of musicians and literary men at Florence in the last decade of the sixteenth century. These men met at the house of Count Bardi and planned a form of performance which would revive the methods of Greek tragedy. Their discussion resulted in a drama on the legend of Daphne and Apollo. The poetry was written by Ottavio Rinuccini and the music was composed by several musicians, principally by Jacopo Peri. Only a few fragments of the music have been preserved, composed by Jacopo Dorsi, but the words are still in existence. In 1600, Peri and Rinuccini collaborated on another opera, *Euridice*. The music for this work was printed, and it is therefore the first known opera that has survived in complete form.

These early Florentine operas consisted mostly of recitative, supported by rather colorless harmonies provided by a small orchestra. As in the Greek drama, the voice parts adhered closely to the natural rhythm of the words and phrases, and little attempt was made to write distinctive melodies for the singers. Claudio Monteverdi (1567–1643) was the first musician to bring successfully into opera the full resources of the art of music. In his *Orfeo* (1607) and *Arianna* (1608) he achieved dramatic characterization through truly expressive recitative, and through more colorful and melodious arias and set pieces. A large orchestra for that day (twenty-six players) provided a background that was rich and varied harmonically. Only a fragment of *Arianna* is preserved today, but the score of *Orfeo* is still extant, and while it is something of a museum piece, it may still be considered a masterpiece because of its broad musical continuity and for its effective use of the basic principles of dramatic composition.

One of the important events in the history of opera was the opening of the first public opera house at Venice in 1637. This was the Teatro S. Cassiano and it housed productions of works by Monteverdi, Francesco Cavalli (1602–1676) and Marc' Antonio Cesti (1623–1669). The operas of Cavalli and Cesti catered to the public taste by providing light, popular, melodic arias, by including comic and burlesque situations in the action, by using lavish stage productions, and by employing a larger number of characters and more complicated plots in the librettos. The purely musical effects became less subtle and the accomplished soloist began to be the leading feature of the performance. Thus the early Venetian operas established the form as a public entertainment, rather than as a private diversion for royalty and the aristocracy. They also developed a standardized musical style and form of libretto, and they exerted a strong influence on the growth of opera in France and Germany.

In France opera was an outgrowth of the ballet. By the middle of the seventeenth century France had perfected two forms of entertainment—the classical tragedy and the ballet. The composer Jean-Baptiste Lully (1632–1687) took certain features of each of these forms, and by adding the spirit of the pastorale (a dramatic performance based on an idyllic plot) combined them into a distinctive type of opera. This was distinguished from the early Italian school by a greater emphasis on dramatic elements; by subordination of music to the text; by a greater use of instrumental music; by introduction of short, simple songs instead of elaborate, florid arias; by having the action carried on by recitative; by the important place given to the ballet; and by the use of elaborate scenery. The type of opera perfected by Lully was continued by Jean Philippe Rameau (1683–1764) and by other French composers.

In England the early operas were developed from the masque. The *Venus and Adonis* (ca. 1685) of John Blow (1648–1708) was called a masque but was actually the first opera given in England. The outstanding figure of this period was Henry Purcell (ca. 1659–1695), whose *Dido and Aeneas* (1689) is still considered a masterpiece even though it is more or less a museum piece today. It combined such features of early French opera as dancing and instrumental numbers, with typically English melodies and truly original music.

Germany developed no characteristically German form of opera until late in the seventeenth century. For almost a century its operas were written mostly by Italian composers at German courts or by native composers who were satisfied with composing in the Italian style to Italian texts. The chief German opera composer of this period was Reinhard Keiser (1674–1739). He is supposed to have written 120 operas, but only eighteen of them have been preserved.

The first half of the eighteenth century saw the development of what is known as "Neapolitan" opera, so-called because most of those who developed it worked in Naples. Sometimes the term is used for operas which are tuneful and have simple harmonic accompaniments, but actually it is applied to works which vary considerably in their technical structure. The so-called Neapolitan operas were written in all countries, by native as well as by Italian composers.

Alessandro Scarlatti (1659–1725) is generally credited with founding the Neapolitan school. He composed some 114 operas of which none is available in any modern edition. Scarlatti was followed by a group of minor composers, but most importantly by the German-born Georg Friedrich Handel (1685–1759) who learned to write Italian operas in Italy and produced his most significant operas in London from 1711 to 1740. These works are not produced as operas today, but musical selections from many of them have proved immortal as concert pieces or songs—particularly the aria from *Serse* which is universally known as the *Largo*.

Even though the Neapolitan operas vary considerably in details of style, there were certain traits which characterized the majority of the early specimens. They were generally written in three acts, with characters and plots drawn from classic history or legend. The scenes were divided into two parts, the first presenting the action and the second the effect of the action on the characters—showing the expression of their feelings, their reflections, or their resolves. Thus the libretto would consist of an alternation between action and reflection, the first accompanied musically by a recitative and the second forming an aria. There was little written for chorus, and the orchestral accompaniment was given a secondary role. As the aria grew to be the principal center of interest, a vocal technique was developed which led to the "bel canto" tradition. Literally this term may be translated "beautiful singing," but it specifically denotes the eighteenth-century Italian style of aria which emphasized brilliance of execution and beauty of tone, rather than dramatic expression.

One of the reasons for the operas of Scarlatti and Handel being forgotten today is that their scores called for the use of male sopranos, for which tenors are not adequate substitutes. These *castrati* were used first, not in the theatre, but in the churches of Italy where it was difficult to find good boy sopranos. For almost two centuries all the hero roles in Italian operas were sung by these male sopranos.

After a time the conventions of opera became so rigid, and the singers who were the main attraction became so arrogant and overbearing, that efforts were made to reform the abuses, in France as well as in Italy. The leader in the reform movement was Christoph Willibald Gluck (1714–1787), who succeeded in subordinating music to the drama and making it a medium for expressing the meaning of the text, and in discarding superfluous ornaments in the vocal parts. Most important, he combined the various elements of an opera into a more integrated whole. Two of Gluck's operas were composed to Italian librettos (*Orfeo ed Euridice,* 1762, and *Alceste,* 1767), while the others were based on French texts and were designed for production in Paris. Gluck used many of the features that characterized the French operas of Lully and Rameau—large choral and ballet scenes, a greater flexibility of form and structure, and a greater simplicity of both subject and treatment.

The dominant figure of the late eighteenth century was Wolfgang Amadeus Mozart (1756–1791), the Austrian who composed masterpieces of Italian and German opera. In his early *Idomoneo* (1781) Mozart showed that he had the dramatic sincerity of Gluck but far greater musical craftsmanship and a new conception of the sensitiveness of the orchestra. In *Die Entführung aus dem Serail* (1782) Mozart tried to break away from the widespread tradition that opera must be written in Italian by setting a German libretto. *Die Entführung* is therefore important in being the first German comic opera by a great composer. The Court at Vienna continued to demand its opera in Italian, so Mozart composed next an opera based on an Italian version by Lorenzo daPonte of the French Beaumarchais's play, *The Marriage of Figaro* (1786). This proved to be a tremendous advance in the development of opera. The music vividly characterizes the action of the play and typifies the characters and their emotions, and the orchestra is an equal participant in the performance, contributing independently to the dramatic outline. In his next opera, *Don Giovanni* (1787), Mozart again used an Italian libretto by daPonte, and once more showed his genius for subtlety of characterization through music, and for masterful integration of vocal and orchestral mediums. In his comedy scenes he perfected the comic ensemble and finale, and adapted the classic symphonic style to his ensemble finales. After *Don Giovanni* Mozart composed the very light *Cosi Fan Tutte* (1790) in which the music is far superior to daPonte's libretto, and then in his last opera, *The Magic Flute* (1791), again used a German text. This work has been termed the first great work of music to be composed for the humbler classes of society, because it was written not for a grand opera house, nor for a royal or wealthy patron, but for a theatrical manager in Vienna who produced it in a theatre where it enjoyed a continuous run of nightly performances. It is generally assumed that the plot of *The Magic Flute* has Masonic significance. It is rather complicated and to some listeners altogether absurd and unconvincing. Mozart's music for the opera is itself so convincing that the action seems logical.

Although the works of Gluck and Mozart, and the *Fidelio* (1805) of Ludwig van Beethoven (1770–1827), are classified as French, Italian, and German operas, they are essentially international works, and were composed in a universal, rather than a nationalistic, idiom, regardless of the language of their texts. The early nineteenth century marked the birth of several national schools in opera, particularly in Italy, France, Russia and Germany. In Italy the composers carried on the bel canto tradition of the Neapolitan school, starting with Gioacchino Rossini (1792–1868), Gaetano Donizetti (1797–1848) and Vincenzo Bellini (1801–1835). Although Rossini is represented in modern opera houses only by his comic opera, *The Barber of Seville* (1816), he had a genius for writing both in the grand, or heroic, manner, and in comic vein. He followed Mozart in his symphonic use of the orchestra, and the overtures to many of his thirty-eight operas are still widely used as concert pieces. Donizetti's works are somewhat superficial and showy, and were designed primarily to display the vocal abilities of singers. Bellini had a fine gift for melody, but his orchestrations are thin, and the principal interest of his works is provided by the singers.

The Rossini–Donizetti–Bellini triumvirate was followed by Giuseppe Verdi (1813–1901). In Verdi's early works–*Rigoletto* (1851), *Il Trovatore* (1853), *La Traviata* (1853), and others–the tuneful Italian opera with melodramatic plots, popular melodies, and florid operas reached its highest peak. Later, starting with *Aida* (1871), and culminating in *Otello* (1887) and *Falstaff* (1893), Verdi achieved a greater continuity of expression and a closer union of vocal and instrumental agencies. He still maintained the Italian tradition of bel canto and the expressive use of the singing voice, but he composed works of greater significance and substance. In these later works Verdi was unconsciously influenced by Wagner, and he also benefited from collaboration with the poet-composer Arrigo Boïto (1842–1918), who supplied him with the librettos of *Otello* and *Falstaff*. Boïto was a man of great intellect and culture, and as a composer wrote the music as well as the text of his opera *Mefistofele* (1868).

The outstanding figures in early nineteenth-century France were Daniel-François-Esprit Auber (1782–1871) and Giacomo Meyerbeer (1791–1864). Both of them composed what may be termed political operas, following the example of Rossini's *Moïse* (1827) and *William Tell* (1829). Auber's *Masaniello* (1828) deals with the uprising of the Neapolitan people against the Spanish rulers in 1647, and a performance of the opera at Brussels in 1830 is credited with starting the rising of the Belgians against the Dutch king. Meyerbeer's *The Huguenots* (1836) and *Le Prophete* (1849) are based on political differences and strife between religious groups. Both Auber and Meyerbeer exerted a great influence over the course of French grand opera for a long period. Their works, and those of Jacques Halévy (1799–1862) used every resource of the form—chorus, ballet, elaborate scenery and staging, and a large orchestra.

Side by side with the development of French "grand" opera was the growth of the *opéra comique,* a term which means literally comic opera, but which came to designate works which were often based on tragic, rather than comic, subjects. Originally an *opéra comique* was one which had spoken dialogue as well as musical numbers, but it gradually grew into a type of lyric drama in which the music was almost continuous, such as the *Faust* (1859) of Charles Gounod (1818–1893), *Mignon* (1866) by Ambroise

Thomas (1811–1896), *Carmen* (1875) by Georges Bizet (1838–1875), *Lakmé* (1883) by Léo Delibes (1836–1891), and the operas of Jules Massenet (1842–1912).

Russia developed a nationalist school of opera in the first half of the nineteenth century, starting with *A Life for the Czar* (1836) by Mikhail Glinka (1804–1857). This was followed by Glinka's *Russlan and Ludmilla* (1842) which was so filled with Russian folk-songs and the spirit of the Russian people that the aristocrats called it the "music of coachmen." The chief Russian nationalist composer of opera was Modeste Moussorgsky (1839–1881), whose *Boris Godounov* (1874) is one of the great masterpieces of all times. It combines pageantry and drama in a compelling manner, and its music, derived from a background of Russian folk-music and the modal style of the Greek Catholic Church, is of great originality and dramatic power. The Russian tradition was further developed through the nineteenth century by Alexander Borodin (1833–1887) and Nicolas Rimsky-Korsakoff (1844–1908). The operas of Peter Tchaikowsky (1840–1893) are romantic rather than nationalistic.

The opera of early nineteenth-century Germany was the romantic opera, and was part of the romantic movement not only in music but in all the arts and literature. It has its background in the German *Singspiel,* a serious or comic play with music. Since it originally had spoken dialogue, the *Singspiel* was related to the French *opéra comique* and the English ballad-opera. The early German romantic operas usually glorified the German homeland and culture, and often used folklike melodies along with conventional opera arias. Most of the subjects of the romantic operas were drawn from national legend or folklore. Supernatural agencies were accepted as a means for developing the drama, and natural as well as supernatural phenomena of nature were essential elements in the plots.

One of the earliest composers of German romantic opera was Ludwig Spohr (1784–1859). Spohr's operas are seldom performed today but they were popular through the entire nineteenth century. As late as 1885, in *The Mikado,* W. S. Gilbert wrote of the music-hall singer who for punishment must attend a series

> Of masses and fugues and "ops"
> By Bach interwoven
> With Spohr and Beethoven,
> At classical Monday Pops.

Today Spohr is completely overshadowed by his colleague Carl Maria von Weber (1786–1826), who was a leader in the romantic movement, and who established the fundamental traits of German romantic opera with *Der Freischütz* (1821), *Euryanthe* (1823), and *Oberon* (1826). Musically, Weber advanced the principle of unity in opera, with a balanced relationship between music, action, and text, and he developed the art of colorful instrumentation in the orchestra.

The type of romantic opera achieved by Weber was continued in Germany by such composers as Heinrich Marschner (1798–1861), whose *Hans Heiling* (1833) presents both supernatural and human characters, and even by *The Flying Dutchman* (1843) of Richard Wagner (1813–1883). Wagner continued to the end of his life as a romanticist. Musically his work was the culmination of the romantic period, but his great contribution to the stage was his perfection of the music-drama, a super art-form in which all the arts are combined, none of them for its individual contribution alone, but rather for its effect on the whole production. The voices of the singers are considered as instruments of the orchestra, not for solo display but as parts of the entire ensemble. Separation into formal divisions of recitatives, arias and set pieces is avoided as consistently as possible. The orchestral music is continuous throughout each entire act, and does not come even to a temporary conclusion at the end of definite episodes or scenes.

In *Der Ring des Nibelungen,* a cycle of four music-dramas (1869–76), Wagner built his entire musical structure from so-called *leit-motifs,* short themes or motives each identifying a character, an emotion, or some object connected with the drama. These *leit-motifs* recur, sometimes varied or developed, in accordance with the recurrence in the action of the subjects they identify. Wagner himself never announced the meaning of any of his *leit-motifs,* their identification and labeling were left to students and writers who have waged many controversies over their exact significance.

Wagner was his own poet and librettist, but it is as a musician and composer that he has had the greatest influence. For a full half-century the influence of Wagner was so great that the works of the majority of later composers were Wagnerian in some respect—in a conception of harmonic progressions, in the use of the orchestra, or in some idiom associated with him. In the few exceptions to this influence, the composers were definitely and consciously anti-Wagnerian, and refused to accept Wagner's theories.

The most notable of these was the Frenchman, Claude Debussy (1862–1918), who took Moussorgsky's *Boris Godounov* as his ideal, rather than the music-dramas of Wagner. In *Pelléas et Mélisande* (1902) Debussy applied impressionist idioms to opera and actually achieved the Florentine ideal of making music an unobtrusive, though atmospheric, support for poetry. The German, Richard Strauss (1864–), on the other hand, continued the classic-romantic style of Wagner, with continuous melodic lines and uninterrupted orchestral accompaniment. In two of his operas, *Salome* (1905) and *Elektra* (1909), Strauss went far beyond Wagner in seeking bold and brutal realism. In *Der Rosenkavalier* (1911) he returned to a classic-romantic type of comedy and composed one of the greatest comic operas since Wagner's *Die Meistersinger* (1868). *Der Rosenkavalier* is ranked by many critics as the equal of Rossini's *The Barber of Seville* and Mozart's *The Marriage of Figaro*.

The Italian reaction to the music-drama was the growth of the realistic, or *verismo* school, dealing often with contemporary subjects and situations and attempting to depict life as it exists. Pietro Mascagni (1863–1945), with his *Cavalleria Rusticana* (1890), Ruggiero Leoncavallo (1858–1919) with *Pagliacci* (1892) and *Zaza* (1900), and, most important of all, Giacomo Puccini (1858–1924) with *La Bohéme* (1896), *Tosca* (1900), *Madame Butterfly* (1904), and *The Girl of the Golden West* (1910), exemplify this movement. In France, Gustave Charpentier (1860–) followed the same principles in his opera *Louise* (1900), which deals with life among the working people of Paris.

Puccini did away with any remaining distinction between the French sentimental *opéra comique* and "grand" opera. His realism is romantic in the sense that it is generally sentimental, but his tragic endings, rather than being tragic in the classic sense of the term, seem to delight in a realistic portrayal of physical as well as mental anguish. Puccini possessed a magnificent technical craftsmanship. His operas are not only appealing to lay music lovers, they are accepted as masterpieces by musicians.

Modern opera after Strauss, Debussy and Puccini has

perhaps produced no towering masterpieces to compare with those that still dominate the repertories of the world's major opera houses, but there have been a number of interesting developments, some of which may bring a new vitality to the lyric stage. It is inevitable that composers have used modern idioms in their operas just as they have in their works for the concert hall. Thus, shortly after the first World War, the Austrian Alban Berg (1885–1935) used the atonal idiom of his teacher Arnold Schoenberg (1874–1951) to present the problems of his psychopathic hero *Wozzeck* (1925). Schoenberg himself wrote an opera that he did not finish. He composed the music of only the first two acts of his *Moses and Aaron* and when the work was finally performed three years after his death the third act was only a short scene with spoken dialogue. The composer believed that his work was too difficult ever to be performed. He was almost right, for the production that was given in Zurich required months of preparation. The chorus had 320 rehearsals.

Igor Stravinsky (1882–), who has shared with Schoenberg the distinction of being the world's two leading innovators, returned to the field of opera with *The Rake's Progress,* a work that offers marked contrast to his earlier *Le Rossignol* (1914).

Following Debussy, many composers have composed operas in the sensuous, atmospheric medium of Impressionism, yet *Pelléas et Mélisande* remains the only true masterpiece among Impressionist operas. As recently as 1957 the French composer Francis Poulenc (1899–) produced his *Dialogues of the Carmelites,* a work imbued in Impressionist atmosphere but lacking the unity that tied *Pelléas* into an integrated whole. Another French-born composer who has composed modern operas is Darius Milhaud (1892–), whose *La Pauvre Matelot* (1926) and *Cristophe Colombe*

(1928) have been followed in recent years by *David,* first produced at La Scala in Milan in 1955. Milhaud has been resident in the United States for a number of years, as has the German-born Paul Hindemith (1895–). Hindemith has been one of the leaders in the so-called Gebrauchsmusik movement. The term is translated "music for use" and designates works composed for specific purposes, in Hindemith's case operas for children and school groups. He has, however, composed a number of full-length operas, notably *Mathis der Mahler* (1938) and the recent *Die Harmonie die Welt* (1956).

In Central Europe the most recent contemporary opera composers are the Swiss-born Gottfried von Einem (1918–), whose *The Trial* was produced at the City Center in New York in 1953, and the German Werner Egk (1901–), whose *The Irish Legend* was given at Salzburg in 1955.

The leading Soviet composer, Dmitri Shostakovich (1906–), has been concerned principally with symphonic works, but his opera *Lady Macbeth of Minsk* (1934) has been heard in countries other than Russia. Official indictment, in the form of an article in *Pravda* condemned the work as theatrically vulgar and "musically formalistic." The older Serge Prokofieff (1891–1953) produced operas more consistently than has Shostakovich. His *The Love for Three Oranges* (1921) is still widely performed, and in his later years he added to his list *The Flaming Angel,* first produced posthumously in 1954, and the earlier *War and Peace,* based on Tolstoy's novel. *War and Peace* was first produced in Leningrad in 1946, and then in revised and shortened form in 1953. In 1955 Americans saw it on television, performed by the NBC-TV Opera Theater.

England has produced a composer who seems to have the ability to integrate music and drama in highly effective fashion. This is Benjamin Britten (1913–), who first attracted attention with his vivid *Peter Grimes* (1945). Other works have followed in quick succession—*The Rape of Lucretia* (1946), *Billy Budd* (1951), *Gloriana* (1953), and *The Turn of the Screw* (1954). Other contemporary English composers of opera are William Walton (1902–), whose *Troilus and Cressida* was first produced in 1954, and the Australian-born Arthur Benjamin (1893–), whose *The Tale of Two Cities* was introduced in 1953.

In America the first quarter of the century produced works that were creditable but did not seem to meet the demands of the operatic stage. Two operas by Deems Taylor (1885–) had their day at the Metropolitan in New York (*The King's Henchman* in 1927 and *Peter Ibbetson* in 1931) but they were for the most part delightful mixtures of the idioms of Wagner and Puccini. In *The Emperor Jones* (1933) Louis Gruenberg (1884–) composed highly appropriate music for Eugene O'Neill's play, but it was not effective enough to dispel the feeling that the play did not need music. Other works, like Howard Hanson's (1896–) *Merrymount* (1934), seemed handicapped by their librettos.

In the late 1930's a new figure appeared in America who seemed to have inherited from his Italian ancestors everything that is required to produce integrated, effective operas. The Italian-born Gian-Carlo Menotti (1911–) came to this country in his youth to study and has lived here ever since. Menotti writes his own librettos and has a sense of theatre combined with a knowledge of the dramatic values of music that results in works that are musically valid and theatrically true to life. Although his first work, *Amelia Goes to the Ball* (1937), was a typical opera bouffe, some of his later works are tragedies of the *verismo* school, so vivid that several critics have declared that Menotti has inherited the mantle of Puccini.

Others of the more recent American composers who have shown ability to write effectively for the operatic stage are Norman Dello Joio (1913–), Vittorio Giannini (1903–), Carlisle Floyd (1926–), and Samuel Barber (1910–). There is also the older Douglas Moore (1893–), whose *The Devil and Daniel Webster,* first produced in 1939, has had many subsequent productions, and whose *Ballad of Baby Doe* (1956) has been featured for several seasons in the repertoire of the New York City Opera Company.

Several developments in this country have helped to encourage the composition of opera. The New York City Opera Company at the City Center has been able to be more experimental than has its neighbor, the Metropolitan, or the San Francisco and Chicago opera companies, and has produced many contemporary works. The growth of opera workshops and local production groups throughout the nation has also provided an incentive to young composers. These producing units, mostly in universities and conservatories, are constantly in need of short operas, particularly those that may be produced with limited resources. Television, too, has welcomed new operas, and on occasion has commissioned them from contemporary composers.

A glance at the Menotti operas in this book will show that only two of them were produced at the Metropolitan. Of the others, one was commissioned for radio and another for television and several were performed in Broadway theatres where they were given extended runs. The latter is true of George Gershwin's (1898–1937) *Porgy and Bess* (1935), a genuine folk-opera even though it derives from Broadway. We may very well find a typically American form of opera developing from the commercial theatre, as well as the opera workshops, rather than from the large opera houses, of which we have so few in America.

Musical comedy in this country has grown rapidly in the past twenty-five or thirty years. The light, frothy, girl-and-music shows have become operettas that have many of the elements of grand opera. Perhaps they are outgrowths of the old German *Singspiel,* but the integration of music into the dramatic framework that one finds in the musicals of Richard Rodgers (1902–) and Oscar Hammerstein 2nd (1895–) is certainly a valid art form. Jerome Kern (1885–1945) paved the way for this development with *Showboat* (1927), and a genre has been produced that includes not only the works of Rodgers and Hammerstein but those of the late Kurt Weill (1900–1950), and of Frank Loesser (1910–). *My Fair Lady* (1956), an adaptation of George Bernard Shaw's *Pygmalion,* by Frederick Loewe (1904–) and Alan Jay Lerner (1918–), and *West Side Story* (1957) by Leonard Bernstein (1912–), are recent examples of this continuing tradition.

The World's
GREAT OPERAS

THE OPERAS

L'AFRICAINE

Giacomo Meyerbeer

Sometimes known by its Italian title, *L'Africana* (*The African*), this opera by Giacomo Meyerbeer was composed to a libretto by Eugene Scribe. It was Meyerbeer's last opera and was completed just one day before his death, May 2, 1864. It was first produced at the Grand Opéra in Paris, April 28, 1865.

The principal characters are:

DON PEDRO (*Bass*), president of the Portuguese Royal Council
DON DIEGO (*Bass*), member of the Royal Council
INEZ (*Soprano*), daughter of Don Diego
VASCO DA GAMA (*Tenor*), officer in the Portuguese Navy, in love with Inez
GRAND INQUISITORE (*Bass*)
SELIKA (*Soprano*) } slaves taken captive by Vasco
NELUSKO (*Baritone*) }

The action of the opera occurs in the sixteenth century, and its plot deals with love and conquest and the search for treasure in newly discovered continents. Inez, the heroine, is betrothed to Vasco da Gama, an admiral who has been gone for more than two years on an expedition of exploration and conquest. As the curtain rises, Inez is discovered with Anna, her attendant, in the Royal Council Chamber at Lisbon. Inez is worried about Vasco, for she has had no word from him. Her father, Don Diego, comes to tell her that she must forget Vasco. According to a message just received, Vasco and all his followers have perished in a shipwreck. Moreover, Inez has been chosen by the King to marry Don Pedro, president of the Royal Council. The sudden appearance of Vasco denies the rumor of his death. He and two captives, Selika and Nelusko, were survivors of the disaster, and he has returned to ask the Council for funds and ships for another expedition. If he can persuade the captives to show him the route to their native land, he will rival Columbus in discovering a continent of vast riches. Several members of the Council are impressed with Vasco's claims, but his scheming rival, Don Pedro, overrules them. Vasco loses his temper and reviles the Council, and is thrown into prison for his insolence.

The second act is laid in the prison. Vasco lies asleep while Selika, the slave, is singing of her love for him. Nelusko is about to stab the sleeping Vasco. Selika is the Queen of her people, and Nelusko must avenge her honor by killing the man who took her captive. He shows by his actions that he too is in love with Selika, his Queen. Selika saves Vasco by waking him. When Vasco and Selika are alone, Vasco persuades Selika to tell him of the route to her native land. In gratitude he embraces her just as Inez and Don Pedro enter. Don Pedro accuses Vasco of being unfaithful to Inez. Vasco denies the charge and makes Inez a present of Selika as her personal slave. Inez tells Vasco that she has obtained his release from prison, and Don Pedro reveals that the price Inez has paid for Vasco's freedom is her marriage to him, Don Pedro. Don Pedro also announces that he has obtained for himself the backing of the Council for an expedition to discover the native land of Selika and Nelusko.

The third act shows Don Pedro's ship. Nelusko is at the wheel. He has offered to guide Don Pedro and is treacherously steering the ship toward a hidden reef. Vasco, following on another boat, comes aboard to warn Don Pedro of his danger, but Don Pedro does not trust Vasco and has him thrown into chains. The ship is then attacked by Indians, kinsmen of Selika and Nelusko. They come aboard and capture the Portuguese.

The fourth act shows the Temple of Brahma on the beautiful island which is Queen Selika's homeland. The people are hailing her return and the High Priest of Brahma insists that she order the execution of the entire Portuguese crew. She refuses to include Vasco in the order, and to save him she declares that she is married to him. Vasco, entranced by the beauties of the island, is delighted. He sings the aria *O Paradiso*, and in gratitude to Selika announces his willingness to be her husband. The Brahman rites of marriage are about to be performed when Vasco hears Inez singing in the distance. His old love for Inez awakens and he tries to go to her.

Act Five is laid in the garden of Selika's palace. Selika, realizing that Vasco still loves Inez, is about to have Inez executed. When Inez is brought before her she relents and magnanimously helps Inez and Vasco to escape. After they have gone Selika inhales the deadly fumes of the mancanilla tree. Nelusko finds her dying and he too ends his life by breathing the poisonous fragrance.

§)&(§

AÏDA

Giuseppe Verdi

Giuseppe Verdi composed *Aïda* at the invitation of the Khedive of Egypt. It was first performed at the opening of a new opera house in Cairo, December 24, 1871. The plot was originally sketched out in prose by an Egyptologist; then it was translated into French verse by Camille du Locle and into Italian by Antonio Ghislanzoni. The action is set against a background of wars between the Egyptians and Ethiopians. The cast includes:

THE KING OF EGYPT (*Bass*)
AMNERIS (*Mezzo-soprano*), his daughter
AÏDA (*Soprano*), an Ethiopian slave
RADAMES (*Tenor*), an Egyptian, Captain of the Guard
RAMPHIS (*Bass*), high Priest of the Egyptians
AMONASRO (*Baritone*), King of the Ethiopians and father of Aïda

The first act is laid in the palace at Memphis. As the curtain rises Ramphis, the high priest, is telling Radames that he, Radames, has been chosen to lead an expedition against the Ethiopians who have recently invaded Egypt. Radames declares that if he defeats the enemy he will lay his laurel wreath at the feet of the lovely Ethiopian slave, Aïda. Then he sings the opera's most famous aria, *Celeste Aïda.* As he finishes his song, Amneris enters. She is the daughter of the Egyptian King, and is in love with Radames. She suspects that Radames is in high spirits because he loves Aïda, but he explains that he is happy because he has been chosen to lead the Egyptians. When Amneris sees Radames gaze on the beautiful slave, Aïda, she becomes even more suspicious. At this point the King formally appoints Radames commander of the Egyptian forces. Aïda is torn between conflicting emotions. She loves Radames and wants to rejoice at his victory, but she is an Ethiopian and her father is the King of the Egyptians' enemies. The scene changes to the Temple of Phtha, where Ramphis and the priestesses dance. They consecrate Radames and pray for the success of the campaign.

The second act opens in the private apartment of Amneris. The battle against the Ethiopians has been successful and Amneris is being dressed by her slaves for the victory festival. When she is alone with Aïda she announces that Radames has been killed in battle and in this way tricks the slave into admitting her love for him. Then Amneris tells Aïda that she has deceived her and that Radames is alive. She further warns Aïda that she herself loves Radames.

The second scene of Act Two shows the plaza of Thebes, where the conquering army parades in pomp and majesty with its captives and booty. Amonasro, the Ethiopian King, is among the prisoners, and he manages to warn his daughter Aïda not to reveal his rank. He announces to the Egyptians that the Ethiopian King was killed in the battle. The Egyptian King tells Radames to name his own reward and Radames asks that the captives be freed. In spite of the protests of Ramphis, the high priest, the wish is granted, and all the prisoners are set free except Amonasro and Aïda, who are held as hostages. The King then announces that his daughter, Amneris, shall marry Radames, and that the young warrior will be the heir to the throne.

The third act is laid on the banks of the Nile, with the Temple of Isis in the background. Amneris is praying that Radames may not only be her husband but that he will really love her. Aïda enters, followed by her father, and as the two talk in secret, Amneris hides in the background and listens. She hears Amonasro, the father, persuade Aïda to beg Radames to fly with her to Ethiopia and to reveal to her the route by which the Egyptian army will again attack the Ethiopians. Radames enters and Amonasro hides. Aïda is successful in persuading Radames to elope with her. Then she asks him about the route they will take for their flight. From this information the eavesdropping Amonasro is able to learn where his forces can best attack the Egyptians. He comes from his hiding and invites Radames to join the Ethiopians. Radames is not ready to become a traitor, but while they are arguing, Amneris comes forward and accuses Radames of treason. The hero is disgraced and taken prisoner, while Amonasro and Aïda escape.

The fourth act opens with the trial of Radames. He is found guilty and is sentenced to be buried alive. Amneris offers to have him pardoned if he will renounce Aïda, but he refuses. The final scene shows the burial dungeon. Over it, on an upper level, is the Temple where the priests and priestesses dance in the execution ceremony. Radames enters the dungeon and as the tomb is sealed, he discovers Aïda, who has stolen into the tomb to die with her lover. Above, the repentant Amneris makes a futile attempt to open the passageway. She kneels, and chants a prayer while the priests and priestesses sing an incantation.

§)&(§

ALCESTE

Christoph Willibald Gluck

Gluck's *Alceste* was first produced at the Burgtheater in Vienna, December 26, 1767. Its libretto was adapted by R. de' Calzabigi from Euripides' tragedy, which was first performed at Athens in 438 B.C.

The characters include:

ADMETOS (*Tenor*), King of Pherae
ALCESTE (*Soprano*), his wife
THE HIGH PRIEST (*Bass*)
APOLLO (*Baritone*)

In the first act the people of Pherae in Thessaly have flocked to the temple of Apollo to pray for the life of their King, Admetos, who is very ill. The High Priest declares that the King will not live unless one of his subjects will die in his stead. The people are terrified and run from the temple. Alceste, the King's wife, is left alone in her grief. She vows that she will sacrifice her own life to save her husband.

The second act is laid in the King's palace. Because Alceste has offered herself as a sacrifice the King has recovered. He does not know that it is Alceste who must die. When he forces from her the admission that she is the one who will make the sacrifice, he begs the gods to strike him, their intended victim. Alceste prays to the gods to prevent Admetos from dying.

In the third act Alceste approaches Hades. As she comes to the gate she finds Admetos. He has followed her so that he may challenge the gods to take his wife from his arms. Apollo appears. He praises Admetos for his courage and returns to him his wife Alceste. The couple returns happily to earth.

§)&(§

ALESSANDRO STRADELLA

Friedrich von Flotow

By a curious, hair-line distinction, Friedrich von Flotow's opera *Martha* is regarded as a "grand" opera, and his earlier *Stradella* is considered an operetta, or a "light" opera. Musically and dramatically there does not seem to be enough difference in type to warrant such distinction. *Stradella* is seldom performed in modern times in its entirety, but its overture is a favorite concert piece. The libretto of the opera was written by W. Friedrich. It was first given as a play with music by several composers at the Palais Royal Theatre in Paris, February 4, 1837. On December 30, 1844, it was given at Hamburg in revised form as *Alessandro Stradella,* with the music exclusively by von Flotow.

The cast includes:

ALESSANDRO STRADELLA (*Tenor*), a singer
LEONORA (*Soprano*), his sweetheart
BASSI (*Baritone*), Leonora's guardian
MALVOLIO (*Baritone*) } assassins
BARBARINO (*Baritone*) } assassins

The action occurs in early nineteenth-century Venice and Rome. The first act shows the outside of Bassi's home on one of the canals in Venice. Stradella, a famous singer, is in love with Leonora, but her guardian, Bassi, plans to marry her himself. Stradella serenades Leonora from his gondola, and a band of carnival masqueraders helps the couple to escape.

The second act shows Stradella's house near Rome. He and Leonora are about to be married, and they are joined by a gay wedding party which accompanies them to the marriage ceremony. On their return they are confronted by Malvolio and Barbarino, hired assassins whom Bassi has sent to kill Stradella. Stradella sings for them and they are so entranced by the beauty of his voice that they refuse to kill him.

The third act again shows Stradella's house. Bassi raises the price he had originally offered for Stradella's murder and the assassins promise to try again. When Stradella returns he rehearses a "Hymn to the Virgin" which he is to sing in public the next day. Again the murderers are so touched that they cannot kill him, and Bassi himself is moved to forgiveness. He gives his blessing to the marriage of Leonora and Stradella.

§)&(§

AMELIA GOES TO THE BALL

Gian-Carlo Menotti

Gian-Carlo Menotti, an Italian-born American composer, supplied his own libretto for his one-act opera, *Amelia Goes to the Ball*. The work was first produced April 1, 1937, at the New Amsterdam Theatre, New York by the opera department of the Curtis Institute. On March 3, 1938, it was presented by the Metropolitan in New York.

The principal characters are:

AMELIA (*Soprano*)
THE HUSBAND (*Baritone*)
THE LOVER (*Tenor*)
THE CHIEF OF POLICE (*Bass*)

The scene is laid in Amelia's boudoir in Milan during the 1890's. As Amelia is dressing for a ball her husband comes in with a letter Amelia has written to her lover. The husband demands the name of the lover, and Amelia strikes a bargain. She will tell her husband who her lover is if he will promise to take her to the ball. The husband agrees, and Amelia tells him that the lover is the man in the apartment upstairs. The husband grabs a pistol and goes upstairs to find the lover. Fearing that she will be cheated of going to the ball, Amelia signals a warning to her lover who lowers himself by a rope and comes into the boudoir. He suggests that he and Amelia elope, but because of the ball she puts him off until next week. The husband returns and finds the lover in his wife's boudoir. He tries to shoot but his pistol jams. A fist fight is threatened, but the two men decide to sit down and talk things over. Each becomes interested in the other's point of view, and the conversation becomes so friendly that Amelia is sure she will miss the ball if her husband and lover talk so much. She is so exasperated that she seizes a vase and breaks it over her husband's head. The unlucky man falls to the floor unconscious, and Amelia's screams bring the neighbors and the police. Amelia accuses her lover of being a burglar who attacked her husband, so the lover is taken to jail and the husband to the hospital. Amelia weeps so loudly that the chief of police is touched and tries to comfort her. He tells her that she still has her jewels and that her husband is not badly hurt. But it is not for her husband that she is crying. She sobs to the police chief that there is no one to take her to the ball. The chief becomes gallant, and offers her his arm. He will be glad to escort her.

As they depart the chorus of neighbors sings the moral of the story—if a woman sets her heart on going to a ball, to the ball she will go.

§)&(§

L'AMICO FRITZ

Pietro Mascagni

The libretto of Pietro Mascagni's *L'Amico Fritz* was written by P. Suardon (a pseudonym for N. Daspuro), who based it on a novel by Erckmann-Chatrian. The opera was first produced at the Teatro Costanzi in Rome, October 31, 1891.

The cast includes:

SUZEL (*Soprano*), a farmer's daughter
BEPPE (*Soprano*), a gypsy
FRITZ (*Tenor*), a rich bachelor
DAVID (*Baritone*), a rabbi

The opera has for its hero Fritz Kobus, a rich bachelor, a friend to all, and especially kindly to those who live on his estates. To date, he has not loved any maiden enough to want to marry her. The first act is laid in the dining room of Fritz's house where Fritz is talking to the Rabbi, David. The Rabbi is asking Fritz to advance a dowry for a young couple about to be married, and he offers to provide the security for the loan himself. Fritz agrees, though somewhat grudgingly, for he is beginning to tire of seeing others marry. David tells Fritz that he will yet find a wife, and just as Fritz is laughingly protesting, Suzel enters bringing flowers from her father's farm. With her flowers and her song she offers Fritz the best wishes of the springtide, and an invitation from her aged father to visit them. Beppe, the gypsy, joins the group and sings a song of love and spring. Talk of love begins to wear on Friend Fritz, but the Rabbi again prophesies that he will soon marry. Fritz offers one of his vineyards as a wager that he will not. The Rabbi then predicts that Suzel will soon find a husband.

The second act shows the farm of Suzel's father. As the curtain rises, Suzel is picking cherries for Fritz. They gaze at each other and sing of spring, of cherries, of flowers, and of love. For the moment the references to love are impersonal. Fritz leaves and David, the Rabbi, enters. By persuading the girl to recite to him the biblical story of Eliazur's finding a wife for Isaac, he learns that Suzel is really in love with Fritz. Having gained this information, the match-making Rabbi interviews Fritz. By telling Fritz that he has found a husband for Suzel, the Rabbi learns that the confirmed bachelor is in turn in love with her. Fritz is violently opposed to Suzel's marriage and is so disturbed that he returns to town.

The third act is laid in Fritz's house, where he is longing for Suzel. Beppe the gypsy comes to him and sings a song he has composed to console him. As Beppe leaves the Rabbi enters. He tells Fritz that Suzel is indeed to be married to a handsome, rich young fellow, and that her father will come today for Fritz's approval. Fritz declares that he will not give his permission, not knowing that the Rabbi intends that Fritz himself shall be the bridegroom. Nor does Suzel know who her husband is to be, and she comes to Fritz and begs him to withhold his permission. Fritz and Suzel discover that each loves the other, and the thoughts of springtime which they have been scattering impersonally are gathered up and sung for each other's benefit. David, Beppe, and their friends join them to add their congratulations and their "I told you so's." Fritz tells the Rabbi that he has won the wager and the vineyard, and David promptly gives them to Suzel as a wedding present.

§)&(§

L'AMORE DEI TRE RE

(The Love of the Three Kings)

Italo Montemezzi

L'Amore dei Tre Re, music by Italo Montemezzi, libretto by Sam Benelli, was first produced at La Scala in Milan, April 10, 1913. The cast includes:

ARCHIBALDO (*Bass*), the aged, blind king of the Barbarian conquerors
MANFREDO (*Baritone*), his son
AVITO (*Tenor*), Prince of Altura
FIORA (*Soprano*), wife of Manfredo, formerly betrothed to Avito before the province was conquered by the barbarians
FLAMINO (*Baritone*), attendant to Archibaldo

The action takes place in Italy during the Middle Ages, after a Barbarian invasion. King Archibaldo has conquered the province of Altura and has received as payment for peace the princess Fiora, who was betrothed to the Alturian prince, Avito. Archibaldo has given Fiora in marriage to his son, Manfredo, and has expected her to be faithful to him. The first act shows a hall in Archibaldo's castle leading out to the terrace. It is shortly before dawn, and the old blind King has been unable to sleep. He has his attendant, Flamino, a former Alturian, bring him to the terrace. A lantern is burning as a signal to Manfredo, his son, who is off at war. Archibaldo suspects that his son's wife, Fiora, is unfaithful. He orders the signal light extinguished, for he has lost hope that Manfredo will return that night. Archibaldo retires and Flamino admits Avito, Fiora's former lover. Avito and Fiora renew the lovemaking of former years. Archibaldo returns, and although Avito escapes, Archibaldo knows that someone has been with Fiora and does not believe her when she explains that she was talking to herself. Trumpets announce the return of Manfredo, who has come to visit Fiora, his wife. Fiora greets her husband coldly and distantly, and Archibaldo is still further convinced of her unfaithfulness.

The second act is laid on the terrace of the castle. Manfredo has been staying at the castle for several days and must now return to the war. As he says farewell to Fiora he begs her to show some sign of affection, and asks that she wave to him with a scarf as he passes through the distant valley. Fiora is touched by his devotion, and even though she cannot really love him she agrees to wave to him. When Manfredo has gone and Fiora's hand-maiden has brought the scarf, Avito returns. Fiora tries to be true to her husband and to deny Avito's love, but as she waves the scarf to Manfredo her arms drop lower and lower. The scarf falls from her hand. Then she turns to Avito and falls helplessly into his arms. Archibaldo interrupts them, and although Avito escapes, the King has heard enough to know that Fiora has again been with her lover. In fury he seizes her by the throat and strangles her. Soon Manfredo appears. He has seen the scarf drop from Fiora's hand and is afraid that she has suffered some accident. His father tells him that he has killed Fiora because she had a lover. Being blind, he was not able to see who the man was. Manfredo cries that there was love stronger than life in Fiora's heart, even though she would not give it to him. He shrinks from his father as the old man takes the girl's body over his shoulder and carries it into the castle.

The third act shows the crypt of the castle where Fiora lies on her bier. Avito comes and weeps over her. He kisses her lips, and gradually becomes ill, for Archibaldo has placed a poison upon Fiora's lips, hoping to trap her lover. As Avito grows weaker Manfredo enters and learns that Avito was his wife's lover. He too kisses Fiora's lips, and when Archibaldo comes to rejoice over his revenge, he finds that his own son has been an added victim of his plot.

§)&(§

L'AMORE MEDICO

(Doctor Cupid)

Ermanno Wolf-Ferrari

Molière's famous play *L'Amour Médecin* is the basis for the libretto of Ermanno Wolf-Ferrari's opera, *L'Amore Medico*. The adaptation was made by Enrico Golisciani. The opera was produced first at the Hofoper in Dresden, with the German title *Der Liebhaber als Arzt,* December 4, 1913.

The characters include:

ARNOLFO, a rich landowner
LUCINDA, his daughter
LISETTA, her maid
CLITANDRO, her lover
FOUR DOCTORS
A NOTARY

The action occurs near Paris, during the reign of Louis XIV in the seventeenth century. The first act shows the garden of Arnolfo's magnificent villa. Arnolfo is receiving the sympathy of his friends for the poor health of his only daughter, Lucinda. When the friends have gone, Lucinda appears, dressed in childish clothes. Arnolfo tries to cheer her by taking her on his lap and giving her toys and trinkets. He cannot rouse her from her melancholy, and finally asks her if it could be that she is in love. She answers: "Yes, Papa!" and Arnolfo is furious. He becomes still more angry when the maid Lisetta declares that all Lucinda needs is a husband. The old man departs in a rage. When he has gone, Lucinda's lover Clitandro is heard outside the garden wall. Lucinda is so moved that she cannot speak, and Clitandro goes away thinking that she does not love him. Lucinda is in despair, but Lisetta tells her to go immediately to bed and hints that she has a scheme for solving the problem. Arnolfo returns and mutters to himself that he must take Lucinda to some distant place where he can keep her as a child. He falls asleep and is soon aroused by the screams of Lisetta, who shouts that Lucinda is much worse and may die immediately. Arnolfo orders his servants to fetch all the doctors in the world. He too starts in search of doctors, and as he reaches the gate he is knocked down by the arriving apothecaries. They gather around him and insist upon treating his injuries. Four doctors arrive, and they too insist on attending to Arnolfo. During the confusion Lisetta escapes, saying that she will bring a doctor she knows about.

The second act is laid in the salon of the villa. The four doctors are having a consultation about Lucinda. Each makes a different diagnosis and prescribes his own remedy. They cannot agree and finally leave, each demanding a huge fee. Lisetta introduces Dr. Codignac, the prince of doctors, who is actually Clitandro, the lover, in disguise. Clitandro examines the patient and declares that she is suffering from an obsession that she must be married. He tells Arnolfo that the only way to cure the malady is to allow the patient to believe that she is married. He suggests that a mock ceremony be performed. He, the doctor, will pose as bridegroom and his secretary can impersonate the notary. Arnolfo thinks this is an ingenious plan and agrees to it. When the ceremony has been performed and Lucinda and Clitandro have disappeared, Arnolfo learns that the secretary was a real notary and that the marriage is genuine.

§)&(§

ANDREA CHENIER

Umberto Giordano

Umberto Giordano's most famous opera was first produced at La Scala in Milan, March 28, 1896. Its libretto, by Luigi Illica, has for its hero the French poet André de Chenier, who lived from 1762 to 1794, and was guillotined during the French Revolution.

The characters of the opera are:

ANDREA CHENIER (*Tenor*), a poet
MME. LA COMTESSE DE COIGNY (*Soprano*)
MADELEINE DE COIGNY (*Soprano*), her daughter
CHARLES GERARD (*Baritone*), servant in the De Coigny household and a revolutionary leader
BERSI (*Mezzo-soprano*), Madeleine's attendant
ROUCHER (*Bass*), a friend of Chenier's
A SPY (*Tenor*)
THE ABBE (*Tenor*)

The first act occurs a few years before the outbreak of the French Revolution. The scene is the ballroom in the Paris chateau of the Comtesse de Coigny. The servants are making the room ready for the arrival of guests, and Gerard shows that he is a revolutionary by singing of the wrongs he and his colleagues have suffered at the hands of their frivolous, fashionable employers. He ends with a warning: "The hour of doom is nigh!" Later he reveals his secret love for Madeleine, daughter of the Comtesse. The guests for the ball arrive and are announced by the major-domo. Among them is the distinguished poet Andrea Chenier, who is silent while his friend the Abbe tells of the unrest in Paris and of the weakness of the King. Presently Madeleine comes to Chenier and asks him to recite some lines of his own, "Some harmless poem," she says, "that might amuse a schoolgirl." Chenier replies with a poem on the wrongs the poor have suffered. The fashionable hostess and guests are horrified, and the Comtesse tries to relieve the general embarrassment by ordering the dancing to begin. Just as she bids the cavaliers to choose their partners a crowd of paupers and beggars led by Gerard bursts into the room. Gerard throws off his livery and boasts that he has admitted the intruders. The footmen easily overcome the invaders and hustle them out, while the Comtesse orders that the gavotte be finished so that "mirth once more shall reign."

The second act is laid in the Café Hottot in Paris, several years later, in 1794. The Revolution is at its height. Chenier, who is seated at a table, has denounced Robespierre and is in disfavor with the Revolutionists. Bersi, Madeleine's maid, sits at another table with a revolutionary spy. She asks whether or not it is true that spies are watching everyone throughout the city. Just then the death wagon rattles by; Bersi hands Chenier a letter, and the spy notes in his book that both Bersi and Chenier will bear watching. Roucher, a friend of Chenier, brings Chenier a passport and urges him to escape from Paris. Chenier refuses, for he is to meet today an unknown lady who has been sending him notes. Robespierre passes outside and Gerard enters. He has become an important figure in the councils of the Revolution. He questions the spy about Madeleine, for now that he is powerful he is eager to possess her. When Gerard leaves the spy hides in the background. Madeleine arrives, throws back her hood and Chenier recognizes her as the young lady who asked him to recite at her mother's ball. The spy also recognizes her, and hurries out to inform Gerard. Madeleine asks Chenier to save her. They realize that they love each other and are about to escape when Gerard returns and tries to drag Madeleine from Chenier. Roucher interferes and takes Madeleine away. Gerard and Chenier fight a duel. Gerard is wounded, and thinking that he will die, tells Chenier that he, Chenier, is on the proscribed list and begs him to save Madeleine. Chenier makes a hurried escape as the mob surrounds Gerard, who refuses to name the man who wounded him.

The third act shows the Revolutionary Tribunal. Gerard learns from the spy that Chenier has been captured and that Madeleine is near by. Hesitatingly Gerard draws up a denouncement of Chenier, and as he signs it and hands it to the spy, Madeleine appears in the doorway. The mob is crying outside for Chenier's execution and Madeleine pleads with Gerard. She offers to give herself to him if he will save Chenier. The mob rushes in and Chenier is brought to the bar. He defends himself and declares he has not been a traitor. Gerard tries to speak for him and declares that the indictment he himself drew up is false. The crowd does not listen and Chenier is led away.

The fourth and last act takes place in the Prison of Lazare. Chenier bids farewell to his friend Roucher as Gerard enters with Madeleine. She has bribed the guard to let her substitute for another prisoner so that she may die with her lover. At the end she and Chenier go together to the guillotine.

§)&(§

ARIADNE AUF NAXOS

Richard Strauss

Hugo von Hofmannsthal wrote the libretto for this one-act opera by Richard Strauss, which was first performed at Stuttgart, October 25, 1912.

The cast includes:

ARIADNE (*Soprano*)
BACCHUS (*Tenor*)
NAIAD (*Soprano*)
DRYAD (*Contralto*)
ECHO (*Soprano*)
ZERBINETTA (*Soprano*)
FOUR CLOWNS

The action occurs on the island of Naxos in ancient times. Ariadne is asleep in a cave. She is filled with self-pity and considers herself lonely and forsaken. Naiad, Dryad, and Echo sing to her so that she will have pleasant dreams. When Ariadne wakes she laments her unhappy state of mind and says that she awaits the coming of death. Zerbinetta comes with four clowns who sing and dance for Ariadne and tell her to be happy and gay. Ariadne scarcely notices them, and they disappear. Naiad, Dryad and Echo announce another visitor, young and handsome. His resonant voice is heard from the distance, and Ariadne says that if this man is Death, he is most welcome. When the visitor appears, he is not Death, but the god Bacchus. He tells Ariadne that he does not bring to her oblivion, but rather the joy of living. Ariadne rushes happily to his arms.

§)&(§

ARIANE AND BLUEBEARD

(Ariane et Barbe-bleue)

Paul Dukas

This opera by Paul Dukas uses a libretto by Maurice Maeterlinck, and it was first produced at the Opéra Comique, Paris, May 10, 1907. The plot concerns Bluebeard's sixth wife, whose courage helped her to escape the fate of her predecessors.

The cast includes:

BLUEBEARD (*Bass*)
ARIANE (*Soprano*), his latest wife
THE NURSE (*Contralto*)
SEYLSETTE (*Mezzo-soprano*)
YGRAINE (*Soprano*)
MÉLISANDE (*Soprano*)
BELLANGÈRE (*Soprano*)
ALLADINE (*Speaking part*)
} Bluebeard's earlier wives

The action occurs in the middle ages. The first act shows a hall in Bluebeard's castle, where Ariane and the nurse hear the angry voices of the mob outside. The people want to save Bluebeard's sixth wife (Ariane) from the fate of the former five. Ariane does not believe that the former wives are dead, and she intends to discover the secret of their disappearance. She has with her six silver keys on which there are no restrictions. There is also a gold key which Bluebeard has forbidden her to use. Each of the first six keys unlocks a vault containing rare jewels which tumble to the floor; first, amethysts; second, sapphires; third, pearls; fourth, emeralds; fifth, rubies; and sixth, diamonds. Inside the vault containing the diamonds is a door with a gold lock. Paying no attention to the protests of the nurse, Ariane opens this door with the gold key. She hears a low, muffled chant, gradually growing louder, and she believes that it comes from the voices of the other wives, imprisoned in a deeper vault. As Ariane is about to enter the inner vault, Bluebeard appears. He rebukes Ariàne for her curiosity, but offers to pardon her if she will quit her search. Ariane refuses and screams as Bluebeard tries to drag her away. The villagers outside hear her and throw stones through the windows. The nurse opens the door and lets the peasants in, but as Bluebeard draws his sword to defend himself, Ariane tells the peasants that he has done her no harm.

The second act shows the underground vault below the castle. Ariane and the nurse find the former wives huddled in a corner, disheveled and in rags. Ariane tries to comfort them but they cannot believe it is possible for them to be rescued. Ariane's lamp is accidentally extinguished and everything is dark. One of the wives, Seylsette, points out to Ariane a distant glow. Ariane finds a trap door, and when she opens it she sees a glass skylight above. Ariane breaks the glass and the wives follow her through the opening.

The third act returns to the hall of the castle. The five wives are standing before mirrors, arranging their hair and decking themselves with the jewels which are still scattered about the room. Ariane is encouraging and helping them. The nurse brings word that Bluebeard is returning, and the women go to a window where they watch him fighting with the peasants. The peasants are winning and are about to throw Bluebeard into the moat. The wives shout to the crowd to spare him. Bluebeard is brought into the hall, where he is at the mercy of his wives. Ariane sends the crowd away and cuts the cords that bind him. Bluebeard revives and is amazed to see himself surrounded by beautiful women. When Ariane bids him farewell he tries to detain her. She refuses, and asks each of the wives if she will come with her. All refuse and say they will stay with Bluebeard.

ARMIDE

Christoph Willibald Gluck

The libretto of Gluck's *Armide* was adapted by Phillippe Quinault from *Gerusalemme Liberata,* an Italian poem of Torquato Tasso. The opera was first produced at the Grand Opéra in Paris, September 23, 1777.

The plot deals with an imaginary eleventh-century episode of the first crusade, and has for its leading male character Rinaldo, a knight in the band of Godfrey of Bouillon. The principal characters are:

HIDROAT *(Baritone),* King of Damascus
ARMIDE (*Soprano*), his niece; a sorceress
ARONT (*Bass*), leader of the army of Damascus
RINALDO (*Tenor*), a knight, leader of the crusaders
ARTEMIDOR (*Tenor*), a crusader
UBALDO (*Baritone*), a knight
A DANISH KNIGHT (*Tenor*)
THE FURY OF HATE (*Contralto*)

The action takes place around Damascus, and the first act shows Armide's palace. Her handmaidens are singing her praises and are reminding her that by her magic spells and her charm she has conquered and rendered powerless all the knights who have come into her presence. Armide complains that all her wiles and magic powers have failed to win the attentions of Rinaldo, the leader of the Christian crusaders. Hidroat, King of Damascus, and Armide's uncle, insists that Armide choose a husband. She declares that she will wed only the conqueror of Rinaldo. Word has come that Aront, leader of the army of Damascus, has defeated the crusaders. A celebration in honor of the victory is suddenly interrupted by the appearance of Aront himself. He is badly wounded, and reports that Rinaldo has freed the captive knights. Aront falls dead as the populace cries for vengeance.

The second act shows a wood near Damascus. Rinaldo is telling Artemidor, one of the knights he has freed, that he, Rinaldo, has incurred the displeasure of Godfrey of Bouillon. He is therefore an exile and will turn his steps independently wherever innocence and justice need his aid. But he is in an enchanted forest which Armide soon transforms into a garden of wonders. Rinaldo falls asleep and is bound by naiads and demons disguised as nymphs. Armide approaches and is about to kill him. When she looks at him closely she falls in love with him and has him carried off to her palace.

The third act is laid in the palace. Armide and Rinaldo are deeply in love but Armide is so ashamed of her weakness that she calls upon the Fury of Hate to deliver her from her passion. Even Hate cannot make Armide forget her love for Rinaldo, and as Hate leaves, vowing never to return, she warns Armide that Rinaldo will escape her wiles.

The fourth act returns to the magic wood. Ubaldo and a Danish Knight are on their way to rescue Rinaldo. Armide tries to stop them but is rendered powerless by Ubaldo's consecrated sceptre. Armide then summons demons in the guise of the knights' sweethearts, but they too are made harmless by the sceptre.

The fifth act returns to the palace. Rinaldo is still in love with Armide, and she entertains him with ballets and tableaux. When she has gone for a moment Ubaldo and the Danish knight appear. Ubaldo's sceptre reminds Rinaldo of his mission. He grasps his sword and bids farewell to Armide. She tries to slay him, but Hate has deserted her and she is powerless. As Rinaldo leaves she orders the demons to set fire to the palace and then she vanishes into the air in a flying car.

AZORA

Henry Hadley

Sub-titled "The Daughter of Montezuma," Henry Hadley's *Azora* was composed to a libretto by David Stevens, and was presented first by the Chicago Opera Company at the Auditorium in Chicago, December 26, 1917.

Its cast includes:

MONTEZUMA II, the Aztec ruler
AZORA, his daughter
XALCA, Prince of Tlascala
RAMATZIN, an Aztec general
CANEK, High Priest of the Sun
CORTEZ, conqueror of Mexico

The action occurs in Tenochtitlan, capital of the Aztecs in Mexico during the reign of Montezuma II, 1479–1520. The first act shows a courtyard before the House of Eagles. Azora, daughter of Montezuma, and Xalca, the Tlascalan prince, are in love with each other. Canek, the high priest, warns Xalca that Azora is betrothed to the Aztec general, Ramatzin, but the warning results only in a love scene between Xalca and Azora, for which Montezuma rebukes Azora. This rebuke is interrupted by the announcement that the Spanish invaders are near, and Xalca is sent against the enemy with the promise that if he is victorious he will be given any reward he may ask.

The second act is laid inside the temple of Totec. Xalca returns from battle. He has won the victory and for his promised reward demands the hand of Azora. Montezuma is furious at such presumption, and declares that on the following day the hearts of the two lovers shall be torn from their breasts.

The third act shows the cavern of sacrifice. Xalca and Azora are bound to the altar. Azora has refused to gain a pardon by marrying Ramatzin. The high priest raises his sword and waits for the sacred sign—a shaft of sunlight coming to rest on the victims. Strange voices are heard outside and Cortez and his officers appear in the entrance. When the shaft of light comes upon the victims, it falls directly upon a white cross. The high priest falls to the ground and Montezuma appeals to his own god Totec for protection. The manifestation of Christian faith prevails and the lovers are saved.

§)&(§

THE BARBER OF BAGDAD

Peter Cornelius

Peter Cornelius himself wrote the libretto for his opera, *The Barber of Bagdad,* and used for his plot a story from the first book of *The Thousand and One Nights*—"The Tale of the Tailor." *The Barber of Bagdad* was first produced at the Hoftheater, Weimar, December 15, 1858.

The cast includes:

THE CALIPH (*Baritone*)
BABA MUSTAPHA (*Tenor*), a Cadi
MARGIANA (*Soprano*), his daughter
BOSTANA (*Mezzo-soprano*), her attendant
NUREDDIN (*Tenor*)
ABUL HASSAN ALI EBE BEKAR (*Bass*), a barber

The action takes place at Bagdad in legendary times. The first act shows an apartment in Nureddin's house, where Nureddin is lying hopelessly ill because of his unrequited love for the Cadi's daughter, Margiana. Bostana, Margiana's attendant, brings word to Nureddin that her mistress will receive him. Nureddin springs from his bed, completely cured. He must be made presentable, so Bostana sends to him the barber, Abul Hassan. Abul Hassan is a garrulous person, interested in horoscopes, and before he will shave Nureddin he must read the lover's future and tell of his own exploits and virtues. According to the horoscope, Nureddin is threatened with misfortune that very day. Nureddin loses his patience and orders his servants to throw Abul Hassan out. The barber draws his razor and drives the servants away, and then proceeds to shave Nureddin. Because of the impending misfortune the barber insists on accompanying Nureddin when he visits Margiana. Nureddin calls his servants and tells them the barber is seriously ill. Then Nureddin escapes while the servants hold the barber on the couch and fill him with medicines.

In the second act Margiana and Bostana are waiting for Nureddin. The Cadi is planning that his daughter shall marry a rich old Selim who has sent a chest of treasures to his prospective bride. When the Cadi leaves in answer to the call for prayer, Nureddin appears and embraces Margiana. The voice of the barber is heard outside, and from inside come the groans of a slave whom the Cadi is punishing for having broken a vase. The barber hears the groans and thinks they are the voice of Nureddin. He cries to the people outside that his friend Nureddin is being murdered. Margiana and Bostana realize that Nureddin cannot escape without being seen, so they lock him inside the treasure chest. When the barber comes with Nureddin's servants, Bostana tells him that Nureddin is in the chest, and orders him to carry it off. The Cadi appears in time to prevent the chest being carried away by strangers, and there is such a noise and tumult in the house that the Caliph comes to see what has caused such a disturbance. The barber accuses the Cadi of having murdered Nureddin and putting the body in the chest. The Cadi accuses the barber of trying to rob his daughter of her treasure. The Caliph orders the chest opened and Nureddin is found inside, seemingly dead. He is revived by Margiana's rose and the Caliph commands that the Cadi hand over the treasure to Margiana in marriage.

§)&(§

THE BARBER OF SEVILLE

Gioacchino Rossini

Gioacchino Rossini showed considerable courage when he composed an opera to *The Barber of Seville,* for it was a setting of the same comedy that his countryman Paisiello had used for an opera with the same title some twenty-five years before. First produced in 1782, the Paisiello work became so popular throughout Italy that when Rossini presented his setting at the Argentina Teatro in Rome, February 20, 1816, it met with the bitter resentment of the opera-loving public. Nevertheless, Rossini's *Barber of Seville* is today a standard item in the world's repertoire, while Paisiello's is long since forgotten.

The libretto of Rossini's opera was adapted by Pietro Sterbini from the first of two plays by Pierre Beaumarchais, both written in the years preceding the French Revolution. The first play, *The Barber,* was written in 1773, and was not produced until 1775 because of royal opposition to a work which poked fun at the aristocracy. Similarly, Beau marchais' second play, *The Marriage of Figaro,* a sequel to the *Barber,* was completed in 1778, but was not permitted to be performed until 1784, when the opposition of Louis XVI to its "dangerous tendencies" was finally overcome.

Both plays are known today chiefly through operatic settings. Five composers made settings of *The Barber of Seville*—Paisiello, Morlacchi, Dall'Argine, Graffigna, and Rossini, while Mozart immortalized *The Marriage of Figaro* with an opera first produced in 1786.

The characters of *The Barber of Seville* are:

COUNT ALMAVIVA (*Tenor*)
BARTHOLO (*Bass*), a physician
ROSINA (*Soprano*), his ward
BASILIO (*Bass*), a music teacher
FIGARO (*Baritone*), a barber
MARCELLINE (*Soprano*)
FIORILLO (*Tenor*), servant to Count Almaviva
AMBROSIO, a notary, servant to Bartholo

The first act opens in the Square at Seville, showing the house of Bartholo. Almaviva is serenading Rosina, and his courtship is made difficult by Rosina's guardian (Bartholo), who himself is eager to marry the girl so that he will have her large fortune. Figaro, the barber, enters to sing the famous aria—*Largo al factotum* "Make room for the factotum." Almaviva asks Figaro how one would meet Rosina, and Figaro advises him to disguise himself as a drunken soldier and thus gain access to her house.

The scene changes to a room in Dr. Bartholo's home. Rosina is writing a letter to Lindoro, a student. This is the name Count Almaviva uses when he writes love notes to Rosina. Bartholo finds Rosina writing and suspects that her letter is addressed to Almaviva. Soon Almaviva appears, disguised as a drunken soldier. He so frightens Rosina's attendant, Marcelline, that she runs to Bartholo for protection. Almaviva manages to see Rosina and to tell her that he is Lindoro. They exchange letters, and when Bartholo demands to see what Rosina has in her hand, she hands him the list of the week's washing. Bartholo orders Almaviva arrested, but when the Count tells the officer his real name, he is released, much to the astonishment of Bartholo and Basilio, the music master, who are accordingly mocked by Figaro.

The second act takes place in the music room at Bartholo's house. Almaviva appears, this time disguised as a music teacher. He announces that he is substituting for Basilio, who, he says, is sick. Bartholo, suspicious, decides to stay in the room with the couple, and orders Figaro to shave him. During this process Rosina and Almaviva plan an elopement, but are interrupted by the coming of Basilio, the real music master. Figaro bribes the real music teacher to feign illness, but Bartholo is not fooled, and he rushes off to find a notary who will draw up a marriage contract between himself and Rosina. When the notary arrives, he too is bribed, and he inserts the names of Almaviva and Rosina in the contract. Basilio and Figaro witness the contract, and Bartholo is outraged until he learns that he will be allowed to keep Rosina's fortune. This arrangement pleases everyone and the curtain falls on a happy ending.

§)&(§

THE BARTERED BRIDE

Bedřich Smetana

Bedřich Smetana's masterpiece is actually a comic opera, but its elaborate musical setting and its colorful pageantry have placed it in the repertory of grand opera. First produced at the Czech Theatre of Prague, May 30, 1866, *The Bartered Bride* represented a renaissance of Czech nationalism. Following the quickly suppressed revolt at Prague in 1848, Smetana had fled to Sweden, where he lived as an exile for ten years. In 1859, when the Italian victories over Austria had lightened the iron handed Austrian rule of the Czechs, Smetana returned to his homeland and joined his fellow-artists in creating works which were filled with the Czech national spirit.

The Bartered Bride, with a libretto by Karel Sabina, pictures a rural Bohemia which is gay and full of sunshine. It makes liberal use of Czech folk-songs and peasant dances, and preserves the folk-spirit of the Bohemian people. The plot tells the story of young Marie, daughter of a farmer whose parents try to force her to marry a stuttering half-wit whose one virtue is that he is wealthy. The cast includes:

KRUSCHINA (*Baritone*), a peasant
KATINKA (*Soprano*), his wife
MARIE (*Soprano*), their daughter
MICHA (*Bass*), a wealthy landowner
AGNES (*Contralto*), his wife
WENZEL (*Tenor*), their half-witted son
HANS (*Tenor*), Marie's sweetheart, and actually the son of Micha by a former marriage
KEZAL (*Bass*), a marriage broker
SPRINGER (*Tenor*), a theatrical manager
ESMERALDA, a dancer in Springer's traveling troupe

As the curtain rises the Bohemian villagers are gathered in front of an inn, celebrating the feast day. As the crowd disperses, Marie and Hans, the young lovers, are left alone. Marie is sad because her parents have planned with the marriage broker that she marry Wenzel, the son of the wealthy landowner, Micha. After Marie's touching love scene with Hans, her parents, Kruschina and Katinka, talk to the marriage broker, Kezal. Kezal tells them that Wenzel will make an ideal husband, and that the only reason he is not there to speak for himself is that he is shy and retiring. Marie interrupts to tell her parents that she will not marry Wenzel because she loves another, but her father insists on arranging matters with Wenzel's father, the wealthy Micha.

The second act shows the interior of the inn, where the peasants are drinking and dancing. Wenzel reveals himself as a simple-minded, stuttering booby. Marie tells him what a terrible life he will have if he marries the girl the marriage broker has selected for him. He will probably be poisoned, Marie warns. Wenzel has never seen Marie before, so he believes her. Kezal, the marriage broker, tries to bribe Marie's lover Hans to give up Marie. Hans pretends to be interested, and forces Kezal to raise the offer to three hundred florins. Then Hans says he will agree to the contract if it specifies that Marie shall marry no one but the son of Micha. Since Wenzel is the only son of Micha that Kezal knows of, the broker thinks he has made a fine bargain. As the contract is formally signed the villagers show their scorn for the apparently mercenary Hans.

The third act returns to the village square. Wenzel is alone, moaning because he must marry a girl who will poison him. A traveling theatrical troupe comes to amuse the townsfolk. Springer, the manager, makes a speech in praise of his numerous attractions, and Wenzel is diverted by the charms of Esmeralda, the tight-rope dancer. Word comes that the performer who was to have played the part of the bear is drunk. Wenzel sees a chance to be closer to Esmeralda, and offers to play the part of the bear. Then Wenzel tells his parents that he will not marry the girl they have chosen. He points to Marie as the person who warned him and says that she would make a better bride. The parents think that this is a happy solution, but Marie asks to be left alone so that she can make up her mind. As she is thinking, Hans enters, as cheery and innocent as if he had never renounced Marie for three hundred florins. Marie reproaches him bitterly and announces to the returning parents and villagers that she is ready to go through with the contract, and to marry Micha's son. Then Hans announces that he himself is a son of Micha by his father's former marriage. Wenzel declares that he is perfectly satisfied with the arrangement and everything ends happily for everyone except the marriage-broker.

§)&(§

BENVENUTO CELLINI

Hector Berlioz

Benvenuto Cellini was the first full-length opera by Hector Berlioz. Its libretto was written by Léon de Wailly and Auguste Barbier and it was produced first at the Grand Opéra in Paris, September 10, 1838.

The cast includes:

BALDUCCI (*Bass*), treasurer of the Pope
TERESA (*Soprano*), his daughter

Berlioz : BENVENUTO CELLINI

BENVENUTO CELLINI *(Tenor),* a goldsmith
FIERAMOSCA *(Baritone),* sculptor to the Pope in the year 1532
POMPEO *(Baritone),* a bravo

The action occurs at Rome in the year 1532 and the plot concerns the creation of Cellini's statue of "Perseus," which is now one of the historic art treasures of Florence. The first act shows the hall of Balducci's palace. Cellini wants to elope with Balducci's daughter Teresa, but the conversation of the lovers is overheard by the papal sculptor, Fieramosca. When Balducci appears, Cellini escapes and Fieramosca is blamed for being an intruder.

The second act occurs in a tavern. Cellini has received from Balducci, the treasurer of the Pope, a sum of money for finishing his statue of "Perseus." Cellini's pupils think the amount is too small and they plot revenge against Balducci. Meanwhile Teresa has agreed to elope with Cellini and has planned to escape during a masquerade. Fieramosca overhears the plot and decides to thwart it. The scene changes to the Colonna Square. Fieramosca and Pompeo arrive, dressed in costumes similar to those worn by Cellini and his apprentice. A fight results in which Cellini stabs Pompeo. Cellini escapes and Fieramosca is arrested for stabbing Pompeo.

The third act is laid outside of Cellini's foundry. Balducci tries to force his daughter Teresa to marry Fieramosca. Cellini is arrested on a charge of murder, and is also charged with not having finished the statue of "Perseus." Cellini thereupon breaks the plaster cast and the crowd sees for the first time the statue he has wrought. All are so enthralled by its beauty that Cellini is pardoned for his misdeeds.

§)&(§

THE BLUE BIRD

(L'Oiseau Bleu)

Albert Wolff

Albert Wolff used Maurice Maeterlinck's poetic fantasy for the libretto to his opera, *The Blue Bird*. The opera was first performed at the Metropolitan Opera House, New York, December 27, 1919.

The principal characters are:

FATHER TYL (*Baritone*), a woodcutter
MOTHER TYL (*Contralto*), his wife
TYLTYL (*Tenor*), } their children
MYTYL (*Soprano*), }
MME. BERLINGOT (*Mezzo-soprano*), a neighbor
BERYLUNE (*Soprano*), a fairy
GRANDMOTHER TYL (*Contralto*)
GRANDFATHER TYL (*Bass*)
LIGHT (*Soprano*)
FATHER TIME (*Bass*)
THE DOG
THE CAT
MILK
SUGAR
NIGHT

The place of action and the time are legendary. The story deals with the age-old search for happiness, in this case embodied in the Blue Bird, and in the discovery that it must be found at home. The first act opens in the woodcutter's cottage, where the children, Tyltyl and Mytyl, are watching the Christmas Eve celebration of rich neighbors across the street. A hunch-backed woman enters, and the children think she is their neighbor, Mme. Berlingot, for she looks very much like her; but no, she is the fairy Berylune, whose daughter is very ill. Berylune asks the children to seek the Blue Bird, for if the little girl can be made happy she will probably get well. Mytyl says that Tyltyl has a bird, but Tyltyl replies that it is his, and he will not give it away. The fairy looks at the bird and says that it is not blue enough anyway. The children will have to go out and look for the bird she wants. The fairy gives Tyltyl a green cap with a diamond. If he turns the diamond in one direction he can see the future; if he turns it the other way around, he can see the past. Tyltyl turns the diamond and everything in the cottage changes. The Dog and the Cat become persons and Bread, Milk, and Sugar come to life. A lamp falls from the table and Light appears as a beautiful, luminous maiden. A knock is heard at the door. Tyltyl turns the diamond back again and the enchantment disappears. Berylune, the fairy, asks who will go with the children on their journey. Only the Dog and Light volunteer. They accompany the children out through the window, and the room is left in darkness. Father and Mother Tyl come in through the door and find that their children are sleeping quietly in their beds.

The next scene is laid in the Land of Memory. Tyltyl and Mytyl find the hut where their grandparents have been living since they left the earth. The children talk with their grandparents and learn that each time the living think of those who have departed, the dead wake up and see those who are thinking of them. Then Tyltyl and Mytyl meet their dead brothers and sisters, who say that they are happier now because they have nothing more to be afraid of. Tyltyl catches a bird that looks blue, but Grandfather Tyl says that he is not guaranteeing anything for the color is not fast. As Tyltyl leaves, he finds that the bird is black.

The second act shows first the Palace of Night. Tyltyl asks Night for the Blue Bird. Night gives Tyltyl the keys to the caverns where the plagues and the evils are kept, but warns him not to open the forbidden door of Destiny.

Tyltyl disobeys, and finds behind the door a beautiful garden filled with gorgeous blue birds. Tyltyl and Mytyl catch whole armfuls of birds, but when they show them to Light, they find that they are all dead.

The next scene shows the Palace of Happiness, where the Luxuries of Earth are having a banquet. When Tyltyl turns the diamond the Luxuries take refuge in the Cave of Mysteries. Then the children meet Happiness and the Joys.

The third act opens in a Graveyard. Tyltyl turns the diamond and the gravestones rise up as a fluorescent light changes the cemetery into the Kingdom of the Future. Here Tyltyl and Mytyl see and talk with the unborn children, and they watch Father Time send out those who are scheduled to be born. Light whispers to Tyltyl that she has the Blue Bird under her cloak. Tyltyl turns the diamond and they escape.

The fourth act shows first the exterior of the woodcutter's cottage. Light and the children have returned, but the Blue Bird has flown away. Light takes leave of the children, the clock strikes, and the children enter the house.

The scene changes to the interior of the cottage. Mother Tyl wakens the children. Tyltyl tells of all that has happened on their journey and the Mother is afraid that he is delirious. Mme. Berlingot calls and Tyltyl thinks she is the fairy Berylune. But this time it is Mme. Berlingot whose little girl is very sick. She would like to have Tyltyl's bird. As Tyltyl gives the bird to Mme. Berlingot he discovers that it is very blue. Soon Mme. Berlingot's daughter runs in, completely cured. The children fondle the bird. It flies away, but Tyltyl calms the children by saying that it will be easy to catch the bird again. Then he addresses the audience: "If any of you should find him, would you be so very kind as to give him back to us? We need him for our happiness, later on."

LA BOHÈME

Giacomo Puccini

Giacomo Puccini's *La Bohème* was first produced at the Teatro Regio in Turin, Italy, January 2, 1896. Its libretto was adapted by Giuseppe Giacosa and Luigi Illica from Henri Murger's novel, *La Vie de Bohème*. The plot is a pathetic little story set against a background of life in the Latin Quarter of Paris, where, to quote Murger's book, the inhabitants are "as abstemious as anchorites when want presses them. But if a little fortune falls into their hands see them ride forth on the most ruinous fancies, loving the fairest and youngest, drinking the oldest and best wines, and not finding enough windows whence to throw their money."

The principal characters are:

RUDOLPH (*Tenor*), a poet
MARCEL (*Baritone*), a painter
SCHAUNARD (*Baritone*), a musician
COLLINE (*Bass*), a philosopher
BERNARD (*Bass*), their landlord
MIMI (*Soprano*), a seamstress afflicted with consumption
MUSETTA (*Soprano*), sweetheart of Marcel, the painter
ALCINDORO (*Bass*), a wealthy Parisian

The first act shows the garret where Rudolph, Marcel, Schaunard and Colline live. It is cold, and Rudolph and Marcel are hunting for fuel for the stove. Marcel is about to break up a chair, but Rudolph finds a manuscript which has been rejected by publishers and he puts that on the fire. Colline comes to tell them he has tried to pawn his books, but nobody wants them. Schaunard, the musician, follows with better news. He has managed to get fuel, money and provisions, so the four lay the table and prepare a generous meal. Just as they are ready to eat, Bernard the landlord comes to demand the overdue rent. They greet him cordially and give him so much wine that he soon forgets his errand and starts telling bawdy jokes. The quartet pretends to be shocked and pushes him out. Then the men decide to celebrate, so they divide the money and three of them start out for the Latin Quarter. Rudolph thinks he had better stay at home and work. Soon there is a knock at the door and Rudolph opens it to find Mimi, a neighbor, asking for a light for her candle. She coughs and faints. Rudolph revives her with some wine and she leaves but soon she returns to look for her key, which she dropped in Rudolph's apartment. Mimi tells Rudolph her name—"They Call Me Merely Mimi." Then she and Rudolph drop to their knees and search for the key. Rudolph finds it and without telling Mimi, slips it into his pocket. Both of their candles go out and their hands meet under the table. Rudolph finds that Mimi's hand is cold, and he sings "Your Tiny Hand Is Frozen." By this time they are in love with each other and they tell of their lives and their struggles. They sing a love duet as they leave to join their friends.

The second act shows a public square in the Latin Quarter. At one side is the entrance to a café. It is Christmas Eve and the four friends are making free with the money Schaunard brought home. They sit at a table in the café and order everything they can think of. Soon an old sweetheart of Marcel's enters. Her name is Musetta and she is escorted by the wealthy Alcindoro. As soon as Musetta sees Marcel, she tries to get rid of Alcindoro. She sends him off to buy her a new pair of shoes. Then she sits down with Marcel and the rest of the party. Presently the waiter presents the bill. The friends count their money and find that they are far short of the amount on the bill, so Musetta tells the waiter to charge it to Alcindoro. Alcindoro returns with the shoes and finds that he has to pay the huge amount of the bill.

The third act is laid at a Customs Gate. Mimi comes to find Marcel, who is working near by. She tells him that she has quarreled with Rudolph and that he has left her. Rudolph enters and Mimi hides. Rudolph tells Marcel of Mimi's consumption, and Marcel tries to keep him quiet so that the hiding Mimi will not hear him. But Mimi has a coughing fit. Rudolph finds her and it is not long before they have patched up their quarrel. As Rudolph takes Mimi in his arms, Musetta enters, and Marcel accuses her of flirting with the rich Alcindoro.

The fourth act returns to the garret. Marcel and Rudolph are at work and soon their two roommates, Schaunard and Colline, come with food for their supper. As they are pretending their meal is a banquet, Musetta enters with Mimi. Mimi is very ill. All except Rudolph go out to pawn their coats so that they may get a doctor for her. Rudolph and Mimi sing of their past happiness and vow that they will never part again. The others return as Mimi dies and the weeping Rudolph kneels beside the cot.

§)&(§

THE BOHEMIAN GIRL

Michael Balfe

Michael Balfe's opera is seldom performed today in its entirety, but it is still widely known through its immortal aria "I Dreamt that I Dwelt in Marble Halls" and the ballad "Then You'll Remember Me." The libretto of *The*

Bohemian Girl was written by Alfred Bunn, who based it on a ballet-pantomime by Vernoy Saint-Georges, entitled *The Gipsy*. Balfe's opera was first produced at the Drury Lane Theatre, London, November 27, 1843.

The cast includes:

COUNT ARNHEIM (*Baritone*), Governor of Pressburg
FLORESTEIN (*Tenor*), his nephew
ARLINE (*Soprano*), daughter of Count Arnheim
THADDEUS (*Tenor*), a Polish exile
DEVILSHOOF (*Bass*), chief of the Gipsies
QUEEN OF THE GIPSIES (*Soprano*)

The action occurs in the environs of Pressburg, Austria, in the eighteenth century, and the first act is laid in the grounds of Count Arnheim's castle. The Count's retainers are ready to accompany him to the hunt, and when he appears with his nephew, Florestein, a foppish young man who is afraid of a gun, he bids an affectionate farewell to his little daughter, Arline. The hunters depart, and Arline climbs a mountain path with her nurse and Florestein. When the stage is cleared Thaddeus appears. He is a Polish exile, and is exhausted from his flight. He is followed by a band of gipsies, led by Devilshoof. They had planned to rob Thaddeus, but instead they persuade him to join their band. Devilshoof gives Thaddeus a ragged gipsy costume and just as Thaddeus has changed his clothes and is mingling with the gipsies, soldiers come to arrest him. At this moment the huntsmen rush in and a trembling Florestein appears to announce that Arline has been attacked by a wild animal. Thaddeus rescues her, and as a reward is invited to a feast. When a toast is proposed to the Emperor, Thaddeus refuses to drink. The crowd threatens his life, but Devilshoof comes to his aid. Devilshoof is thrown into prison, but he soon escapes and kidnaps

Arline. During his flight he is seen by the count and his guests crossing a dangerous precipice with Arline in his arms.

The second act occurs twelve years later. The first scene shows a street in Pressburg, where Arline is sleeping in the tent of the gipsy queen. Thaddeus keeps watch, for he is in love with Arline. Florestein enters and is robbed by Devilshoof and the gipsies. The queen, however, orders them to return all they have stolen, but Devilshoof holds back a medallion which Florestein says is a valuable heirloom. Arline awakens and tells Thaddeus of the dream she has had by singing the famous aria, "I Dreamt that I Dwelt in Marble Halls." Thaddeus tells Arline that it was he who rescued her as a child, but he does not tell her who she is or where she came from. He tells her that he loves her, and their betrothal is celebrated by the gipsies according to their ritual. The gipsy queen is jealous, for she is herself in love with Thaddeus, but Devilshoof makes fun of her.

The scene changes to a fair. Count Arnheim and Florestein appear, and Florestein tries to flirt with Arline. Arline slaps him. The gipsy queen recognizes Florestein as the man the gipsies had tried to rob, and she gives Arline the medallion, knowing that if she wears it, Florestein will see it. Her plot is successful, and Arline is accused of theft. She is arrested and thrown into prison with Thaddeus, who has tried to protect her.

The next scene is laid in Count Arnheim's apartments. A portrait of Arline, painted in childhood, hangs on the wall. The captain of the guard reports the capture of the gipsy girl, who is then brought before the count. Arline protests her innocence, and tells how the medallion was given to her by the gipsy queen. The count believes her but says that he must nevertheless hold her for trial. Arline draws a dagger from beneath her scarf and is about to stab herself. The count seizes her arm and sees on it a mark which stirs his memory. He asks her about it, and she tells how it was made by the antlers of a wild animal from which she was rescued in childhood. Thaddeus, escaping from the guards, rushes into the room; Arline points to him as her rescuer. The count recognizes both of them. He embraces Arline. Devilshoof enters and whispers to Thaddeus that it would be better for him to leave before he is driven away.

The third act shows a large room in the count's castle. Arline, richly clothed, looks sadly at the gipsy dress she has discarded. Devilshoof breaks into the room and begs her to rejoin her old friends. Thaddeus appears at the window and sings the famous ballad "Then You'll Remember Me." He and Devilshoof hide as guests enter. Suddenly the gipsy queen appears and tells the count that Thaddeus is hiding in his house. Thaddeus is found and reveals that he is actually a Polish noble. The gipsy queen orders one of her followers to shoot Thaddeus with her rifle. Devilshoof grabs at the rifle, and in the scuffle the queen herself is shot. When her body is taken away the count gives Thaddeus and Arline his blessing.

§)&(§

BORIS GODOUNOW

Modeste Moussorgsky

Boris Godounow is Modeste Moussorgsky's masterpiece, and the fact that it was the work of a largely untutored genius makes it all the more vital and true to its subject.

Its crudities of structure give it a ruggedness and sincerity that make it truly a folk-opera. The polishings its score has received at the hands of more skilled musicians seem almost an impertinence, even though they iron out many of the rough spots in the complex musical construction.

The opera was first produced in its entirety at the Imperial Opera House in St. Petersburg February 8, 1874. After Moussorgsky's death, Rimsky-Korsakoff attempted to revise the opera. He re-scored the orchestration, omitted several scenes, and changed the sequence of others. It is the Rimsky-Korsakoff version which is performed at the Metropolitan Opera House in New York and few students have been familiar with the original score until its recent publication. Upon studying the original version, some claim that Rimsky-Korsakoff improved it, while others feel that he emasculated it, and that the pure Moussorgsky was more original and more effective dramatically.

Since the various versions present the scenes in different sequence, the order used at the Metropolitan will be followed here. The libretto of the opera was adapted by the composer from an historical play by Alexander Pushkin. The leading character, Boris Godounow, is a privy councilor of the Czar, who has secretly caused the assassination of the Czar's younger brother, Dimitri, the sole heir to the throne.

The leading characters are:

BORIS GODOUNOW (*Bass*)
XENIA (*Soprano*), his daughter
THEODORE (*Mezzo-soprano*), his son
MARINA (*Mezzo-soprano*), daughter of the Voyevode of Sandomir
PRINCE SHOUISKY (*Tenor*)
GREGORY (*Tenor*), a novice, who becomes the pretender Dimitri

VARLAAM (*Bass*)
MISSAIL (*Tenor*) } vagabond monks
PIMENN (*Bass*), a monk and historian
TCHELLAKOV (*Baritone*), secretary of the Duma

At the time of the opera, the Czar has died, and Boris, as regent, pretends that he does not want to assume the throne. Secretly he has given word to his officers suggesting that they urge the people to beg him to accept the crown.

The first scene of Act I shows the square before the Convent where Boris lives. Goaded by the threats of the officers, the people kneel before the Convent and sing their entreaty: "Why hast thou abandoned us?" Then, as part of the scheme, Tchellakov, secretary of the Duma, announces that Boris is unmoved by their plea. He urges them to pray that God may lead Boris to rescue Russia. A band of Pilgrims approaches and comes before the Convent singing their supplication to Boris. The second scene shows a cell in the Convent of Miracles. Pimenn, an old monk who writes a record of all events, tells the novice Gregory that Boris was responsible for the death of the heir, Dimitri. When Gregory learns that he and Dimitri were of the same age, he decides to impersonate Dimitri and spread the report that the heir still lives. In this way, he, Gregory, will usurp his throne. In the third scene, showing the square between the Cathedral of the Assumption and the Cathedral of the Archangels, Boris has at last yielded, and is coming to the Cathedral of the Assumption for his coronation. From the portico of the Cathedral, Prince Shouisky cries: "Long live Czar Boris!" and the populace answers: "Glory to Czar Boris!"

The second act opens in an inn at the Lithuanian border. Gregory, now in the role of the Pretender Dimitri, has escaped from the Convent and appears with the two vagabond monks, Varlaam and Missail. Gregory is trying to cross the frontier and to raise an army. The border guards have been notified of his escape and they look for him at the inn. Gregory eludes them by pointing to Varlaam as the fugitive. The second scene returns to Boris, and shows him with his son and daughter. In a monologue Boris confesses that even though he has reached the height of power, he has no peace of mind. His anxiety becomes panic when Prince Shouisky enters with word that the people have been told that Dimitri is still alive; that they are in revolt, and that Dimitri is now at the Russian border. The terror-stricken Boris asks Shouisky if murdered boys rise from their graves. Shouisky tries to calm Boris, and he tells him that he himself saw the body of the murdered Dimitri. But when he is alone Boris again suffers the agonies of fear and remorse. He sees an apparition of the boy, and he falls on his knees crying: "Lord, have mercy on the guilty soul of Boris!" The scene changes to a garden on the Polish estate of Marina. She is helping Gregory in his pretensions, for she knows that his succession to the Russian throne would advance the interests of Poland. As the scene opens Gregory is waiting for Marina. A banquet is being held inside the palace and Gregory hides as the guests come into the garden and dance a polonaise, singing: "Forward against Moscow!" The guests return to the Palace and Marina joins Gregory. In a duet she urges him to the attack on Moscow and promises him that when he is victorious, she will be his queen.

The first scene of the third act shows a forest where the peasants are taunting a Russian nobleman and a village simpleton. The vagabond monks, Missail and Varlaam, sing a chantlike denunciation of Czar Boris. Gregory is hailed as Dimitri, the lawful Czar. He is accompanied by a procession of troops, and as he passes he promises the people that they will be freed from oppression. As snow begins to fall, the village simpleton is left alone in the forest. He sees in the distance the red glow of the fires the revolutionists have lighted, and he sings: "The foe will come and blood will flow; let thy tears flow, poor, starving people!" The final scene shows the Imperial Palace where the Duma has met to take steps against the Pretender. Shouisky tells the nobles of Boris's secret remorse, and hints at the true cause of Dimitri's death. The consternation among the nobles is interrupted by the entrance of Boris. Although he is at first apprehensive he regains his composure as he mounts the throne. Pimenn, the monk, begs an audience, and tells of an old shepherd who had come to the Convent and had told of a dream in which a childish voice bade him to pray at the tomb of Dimitri. He obeyed and was cured of his blindness. Boris is terror-stricken at this recital and falls in a faint. When he revives he asks to be left alone with his son. He knows that he is dying, and as he bids the lad farewell, he tells him not to try to learn how he gained the throne, but to be a just ruler. As Boris sings his farewell, the bells toll and the people are heard praying for the soul of their sovereign. Boris, growing weaker, cries to the Lord for mercy and forgiveness. As the priests and nobles enter, he revives, and rises to cry: "Hold! I still am Czar!" He falls back again and pointing to his son, says: "Behold your Czar!" With a final murmur of agony and a cry for mercy, Boris falls dead. The nobles stand about with bowed heads as the curtain falls.

Gregory does not appear in the last scene, and it may be assumed that his uprising failed when the facts of the real Dimitri's death became known.

§)&(§

THE CANTERBURY PILGRIMS

Reginald de Koven

Percy MacKaye wrote the libretto for Reginald de Koven's opera, *The Canterbury Pilgrims*, which was first performed at the Metropolitan Opera House, New York, March 8, 1917. The plot is based on Chaucer's tale of the pilgrims en route to Canterbury who assembled in the Courtyard of the Tabard Inn at Southwark, near London, on a late afternoon of April 16, 1387.

The cast includes:

GEOFFREY CHAUCER (*Baritone*), first poet laureate of England
RICHARD II (*Tenor*), King of England
ALISOUN (*Contralto*), the Wife of Bath
MADAME ENGLANTINE (*Soprano*), the Prioress
THE MILLER (*Bass*), one of Alisoun's many suitors

The first act shows the courtyard of the Tabard Inn. Chaucer is much impressed with Madame Englantine, a Prioress who has not yet taken her vows as a nun, and who is on her way to Canterbury to greet a long-lost brother returning from the Crusades. She will recognize her brother by his ring, for it bears an identical inscription to that on her own bracelet—"amor vincit omnia." Alisoun, the wife of Bath, joins the party and is fascinated by Chaucer. She thinks he will make a most satisfactory sixth husband. She soon grows jealous of the Prioress and bets Chaucer that the bracelet is no sister's token, but a gift from a sweetheart. Alisoun insists that Chaucer must marry her if she can get the jeweled talisman away from the Prioress.

The second and third acts are laid respectively in the garden and hall of the One-nine-pin Inn at the hamlet of Bob-up-and-down, on the way to Canterbury. After an involved intrigue, Alisoun, the wife of Bath, secures the Prioress's talisman.

The last act shows the West front of Canterbury Cathedral. All are agreed that Chaucer must pay his forfeit by marrying the wife of Bath, until a man of law interrupts to tell Chaucer that any woman who has had five husbands may not wed a sixth without a special dispensation from the King. The King comes to Chaucer's rescue by deciding that Alisoun may wed again only on condition that her sixth husband shall be a miller. The Miller is delighted, for he has been one of Alisoun's suitors. Chaucer and the Prioress enter the Cathedral in the procession of the Pilgrims. They agree that they will offer the talisman at the shrine and Chaucer repeats the inscription, "amor vincit omnia" ("Love conquers all").

§)&(§

CAPONSACCHI

Richard Hageman

Richard Hageman's *Caponsacchi* (originally entitled "Tragödie in Arezzo) uses for its libretto the play *Caponsacchi by* Arthur Goodrich, which in turn was adapted from Robert Browning's poem *The Ring and the Book.* The opera was first presented in a German translation at Freiburg, February 18, 1932, and at Vienna, March 19, 1935. The original English version was performed at the Metropolitan Opera House, New York, February 4, 1937.

The characters include:

CAPONSACCHI (*Tenor*), a priest
GUIDO FRANCHESCHINI (*Baritone*)

POMPILIA (*Soprano*), Guido's wife
PIETRO (*Bass*) } Pompilia's parents
VIOLANTE (*Mezzo-soprano*) }
POPE INNOCENT XII (*Bass*)
CANON CONTI (*Baritone*)

The action occurs in Italy during the years 1697–8, at Arezzo and in Rome. The prologue shows a court of justice at the Vatican. Count Guido Franceschini is accused of murdering his young wife, Pompilia. He admits the crime but claims immunity under the unwritten law, naming the priest Caponsacchi as his wife's lover. The people outside favor Guido and clamor for his freedom, but the Pope is not convinced of Caponsacchi's guilt. He orders a special hearing and hides behind a curtain where he may hear the testimony and form his own opinion. Guido and Caponsacchi are brought in. Guido boldly admits his guilt and blames his wife and the priest. Caponsacchi, more to defend Pompilia's memory than to clear himself, starts to tell his story and the scene changes to the Carnival at Arezzo, where in flashback fashion Caponsacchi's story is enacted. It starts eleven months earlier, when Count Guido, an old man, has repaired his dwindling fortune by marrying the young Pompilia, a daughter of the wealthy, ambitious Pietro and Violante. Pompilia's father and mother now realize that they have been tricked, and they refuse to give Guido any more of their fortune. Guido plans to murder the parents but is foiled by the handsome priest, Caponsacchi. Guido schemes to entangle the priest in an affair with his wife. He abuses her so flagrantly that she is forced to fly to Caponsacchi for protection. She is pregnant and she begs the priest to help her.

The second act shows Caponsacchi's cell at the Pieve six weeks later. He has been promoted and is about to leave for Rome. Through forged letters Guido has baited Caponsacchi into rescuing Pompilia. The Priest meets Pompilia at her husband's palace and agrees to take her to her parents in Rome. The scene changes to an inn at Castelnuovo. Guido lies in wait for Caponsacchi and Pompilia. Pompilia is exhausted and Caponsacchi carries her to her room. When he returns Guido draws his sword and challenges him. Caponsacchi skillfully disarms Guido, but Guido's friends seize Caponsacchi and are about to put him in jail. Caponsacchi pleads for a trial before the church court at Rome.

The third act shows the Roman home of Pietro and Violante, Pompilia's parents. The church court has found Caponsacchi and Pompilia guilty and has returned Pompilia to her parents. Her child is now two months old. Caponsacchi has been sentenced to an eight-month exile. Guido comes to the house with four of his hirelings. He knows that if the parents and his wife are out of the way, his child will inherit their fortune and he, Guido, will control it. Guido forces Pompilia to watch him murder her parents. Then he throws her to the four men to dispose of. Caponsacchi arrives in time to trap Guido but not to save Pompilia.

The epilogue returns to the Papal Court. Caponsacchi has finished his story. The Pope draws the curtain and steps forward. He is convinced that Caponsacchi has been telling the truth. He sentences Guido for the murder and absolves Caponsacchi.

§)&(§

CARMEN

Georges Bizet

Carmen is Georges Bizet's masterpiece. Its melodious score contains numbers that are easily remembered, and its plot, though tragic, is melodramatic and colorful. In addition, its title-character provides a glamorous role that has been a favorite with the greatest sopranos. *Carmen* was first produced in Paris, March 3, 1875, at the Opéra Comique. It was not admitted to the Grand Opera because it contained a line or two of spoken dialogue. The libretto of *Carmen* was adapted by H. Meilhac and L. Halévy from a novel by Prosper Mérimée.

The principal characters are:

CARMEN (*Soprano*), a gipsy girl
DON JOSE (*Tenor*), a sergeant
ESCAMILLO (*Bass*), a bull fighter, or toreador
MICAELA (*Soprano*), a peasant girl, in love with Don Jose
ZUNIGA (*Bass*), a lieutenant
MORALES (*Bass*), a sergeant
DANCAIRO (*Tenor*) }
REMENDADO (*Baritone*) } smugglers
FRASQUITA (*Soprano*) }
MERCEDES (*Contralto*) } gipsies

The action is laid in Spain, and the first act shows a square in Seville. A cigarette factory is at the right and a bridge at the back. Morales, a sergeant, and others of the soldiers, are talking to Micaela. She tells them that she has come to see Don Jose. She is bringing him money and a letter from his mother. When the guards are changed, Don Jose appears. Morales and Zuniga, a lieutenant, tell him that Micaela is waiting for him. Don Jose tells his friends that he is very much in love with Micaela. It is noon time, and the cigarette girls come from the factory. The belle of the factory and its leading coquette is Carmen, the gipsy girl. When she appears the young men rush to her and surround her. Don Jose, seated on a bench at the side, sees her but is not particularly interested. Carmen sings the beautiful *Habanera,* in which she warns that anyone she loves should beware. When she has finished she sees Don Jose, and dancing close to him, tosses him her bouquet of flowers. As the bell rings she runs back into the factory with the other girls. Don Jose picks up the flowers and remarks that the girl is a witch. Then he looks up and sees Micaela, who has just arrived. Jose hurriedly hides the flowers in his vest and greets Micaela. She gives him the money his mother has sent and a message assuring him that his mother thinks of him night and day, prays for him, forgives and loves him. Micaela also brings a letter which she tells Jose he should read alone, and she leaves him, saying that she will return. Jose declares that he will obey his mother, that he loves and will marry Micaela. He is about to take Carmen's flowers from his vest when there is a commotion in the factory. The girls rush out, crying that Carmen has stabbed another girl during an argument. Zuniga, the lieutenant, arrests the defiant Carmen. She appeals to Don Jose to free her. He refuses, but she flirts with him and tells him that if she escapes she will meet him at an outlying tavern. She suggests that when he is leading her over the bridge, she will give him a push and he must pretend to fall. The plan works, and Carmen escapes.

The second act shows the tavern of Lillas Pastia. Carmen and the gipsy girls are dancing and drinking with Zuniga and Morales. Carmen resists the advances of Zuniga. She dislikes him because he threw Don Jose into prison for helping her to escape. Zuniga tells her that Jose is now free, and Carmen decides to wait for him. From the distance comes the sound of a torchlight procession, and the stirring "Toreador Song" and "March." Escamillo, the famous bull-fighter, is being honored. The crowds enter the tavern and Escamillo sings of his exploits in the bull ring. He spies Carmen and immediately makes love to her. She tells him that she cannot love him now, but that if he wants to wait and hope for her, there is no harm in that. When Escamillo, Zuniga and the officers have gone, the smugglers, Dancairo and Remendado appear. They have a plan to smuggle goods from Gibraltar into the city, and they want the gipsy girls, Carmen, Frasquita and Mercedes, to divert the guards while the men carry the bales through the mountain pass. Carmen will not leave; she is waiting for Don Jose, and soon his voice is heard singing in the distance. The smugglers persuade Carmen to tempt her lover to join their smuggling band. Don Jose enters. He tells Carmen how much he loves her, but his love-making is interrupted by the bugle call which summons him back to his regiment. Carmen tells Jose that if he leaves her he does not love her. She begs him to fly with her, but Jose refuses to desert from the army. Zuniga enters and addresses Carmen affectionately. He orders Jose to leave. Jose, mad with jealousy, refuses, and when the smugglers enter and overpower Zuniga, Jose feels that now he must flee with the gang.

The third act is laid in the wild, rocky, mountain pass which is the principal haunt of the smugglers. After an orchestral entr'acte, the curtain rises and shows Carmen, Jose, the smugglers and the gipsy girls. Carmen's love for Jose is waning, and he calls her a devil. Frasquita and Mercedes are telling their fortunes with cards, and when Carmen joins them she finds that her own future is death. Dancairo and Remendado return from a scouting expedition and announce that there are three guards whom the girls must entertain while the men smuggle the goods to the city. Jose's jealous protests are unheeded and he is left behind, examining the barrel of a gun. Micaela enters, led by a guide. She sings an aria in which she says she is not afraid. She sees Jose but he does not recognize her and nearly shoots her. Escamillo appears and Micaela hides. Escamillo announces to Jose that he is looking for a gipsy girl whom he loves madly. He says her name is Carmen, and that although she was in love with another a while ago, he understands that Carmen's amours never last more than six months. Jose challenges Escamillo, and the two start a duel with knives which is interrupted by the return of Carmen and the smugglers. Carmen grabs Jose's arm just as he is about to plunge his knife into Escamillo's breast. Dancairo, the smuggler, forbids any more fighting, for there is other work to be done. Escamillo bids them good day, and invites them all to tomorrow's bull fight in Seville. One of the smugglers finds Micaela and brings her from hiding. She tells Jose that his mother is dying, and begs him to come with her. Carmen disdainfully tells Jose to go with Micaela, that he is not fitted for a smuggler's life. Jose at first refuses to leave Carmen to a rival, but at last he agrees and goes off with Micaela, as Escamillo's voice is heard in the distance, singing the "Toreador Song."

The fourth act shows the outside of the bull ring. On his way to the bull fight, Escamillo sings a love duet with Carmen. When he has gone, Carmen's friends warn her that Don Jose is hiding in the crowd. She says she is not afraid and waits for him after the people have gone into the ring. Jose approaches her and begs her to love him again. She refuses. As Jose is pleading and Carmen is resisting, the shouts of victory come from the arena. Carmen tries to push past Jose, and Jose stabs her. Escamillo and the crowd come out of the ring. Jose shouts that he has killed Carmen, and throws himself on her body.

CAVALLERIA RUSTICANA

Pietro Mascagni

The one-act *Cavalleria Rusticana* is Pietro Mascagni's masterpiece, and, since its first production at the Teatro Costanzi in Rome, May 17, 1890, it has held its place as an indispensable feature of every house repertoire. The libretto of the opera was adapted from a play of Giovanni Verga by Giovanni Targioni-Tozzetti and G. Menasci.

The cast of characters includes:

TURIDDU (*Tenor*), a soldier
LUCIA (*Contralto*), his mother
SANTUZZA (*Soprano*), in love with Turiddu
ALFIO (*Baritone*), a teamster
LOLA (*Mezzo-soprano*), his wife

The scene is a Sicilian village, and the plot concerns the town philanderer, Turiddu. He has loved the beautiful, fickle Lola who married the teamster Alfio while he, Turiddu, was serving with the army. He is annoyed at Lola's faithlessness and consoles himself by seducing Santuzza. Lola, however, does not take her marriage to Alfio too seriously, and secretly she and Turiddu continue their former intimacy, even though Turiddu is supposed to be wooing Santuzza. As the curtain rises on an Easter morning, Turiddu is heard singing a love song to Lola. As the villagers enter the church, Santuzza starts to tell Lucia, Turiddu's mother, about her affair with her son, but is interrupted by the coming of Alfio, Lola's husband. Santuzza feels disgraced and unworthy to enter the church, so she kneels outside during the service. Lucia returns and asks Santuzza to continue the story of her relations with Turiddu. Then Alfio comes from the church, and Santuzza cannot hold back her jealousy and remorse any longer. She tells Alfio of his wife's renewed affair with Turiddu.

After the orchestra has played the beautiful Intermezzo, the villagers come out of the church. Turiddu arrives to join the merry-making. He sings a gay drinking song, but when Alfio refuses to join the festivities, Turiddu realizes that he knows of his own relations with Lola. Finally Alfio challenges Turiddu. According to Sicilian custom the two men embrace, and Turiddu shows his acceptance of the challenge by biting Alfio's ear. Turiddu bids his mother farewell, for his guilty conscience warns him of approaching death. He and Alfio go to a neighboring orchard to fight, and the villagers crowd on the stage, fearful and excited. Soon a woman is heard crying in the distance: "Neighbor Turiddu is murdered!" Santuzza falls in a faint, and the women gather around Lucia, Turiddu's mother.

§)&(§

CENDRILLON

(Cinderella)

Jules Massenet

The libretto for Jules Massenet's opera on the Cinderella story was adapted from Charles Perrault's fairy-story by Henri Cain. The opera was first produced at the Opéra Comique in Paris, May 24, 1899.

The cast includes:

CENDRILLON (*Soprano*), "Cinderella"
PANDOLPHE (*Bass*), her father
MADAME DE LA HALTIERE (*Contralto*), her step-mother
NOEMIE (*Soprano*) } her step-sisters
DOROTHEA (*Mezzo-soprano*) } her step-sisters

THE FAIRY (*Soprano*)
PRINCE CHARMING (*Tenor*)
THE KING (*Baritone*)

The first act shows the house of Madame de la Haltiere. She and her two daughters, Cendrillon's step-sisters, are busy getting ready for the ball at the king's palace. Their step-father, who is Cendrillon's own father, Pandolphe, is amused, and asks himself why he ever married such a creature as Madame de la Haltiere. When the women and her father have gone, Cendrillon enters. She sits by the fire and falls asleep. The fairy, her godmother, appears and wakes her. She tells Cendrillon that she too is to go to the ball. The fairies dress her in fine clothing and bring a carriage. The godmother warns Cendrillon to leave the ball precisely at midnight.

The second act shows the ball at the king's palace. The Prince is bored, and the King announces that the daughters of the greatest nobles in the kingdom are to pass before the Prince so that he may choose his bride. Next to the last to parade before the Prince are the two daughters of Madame de la Haltiere. Then Cendrillon appears, and the Prince is entranced with her. Madame de la Haltiere and her daughters are angry but do not recognize Cendrillon, for she is wearing magic glass slippers. Cendrillon refuses to tell the Prince her name, and as they are talking and dancing the clock strikes midnight. Cendrillon loses her slipper as she steals away.

The third act returns to the house of Madame de la Haltiere. Cendrillon comes from the ball tired and excited. She calls to the fairy godmother to forgive her for losing the slipper. Her father returns with her step-mother and step-sisters. The women are angry and quarreling about the unknown girl who charmed the Prince. Cendrillon asks what the Prince said when the unknown girl disappeared. The step-sisters lie and say that he said his eyes had deceived him, and that the unknown girl was actually ugly enough to be hanged. Cendrillon faints, and her father orders her step-mother and step-sisters to leave the room. Then he tells Cendrillon that they will all go to the country, where they will be happy once more. The scene changes to the home of the fairies, where the Prince and Cendrillon wander side by side in the meadow, separated only by a flowered hedge. Neither can see the other, but each hears the other's voice as they kneel before an oak. The Prince tells the fairy godmother of his lost happiness and Cendrillon prays her to restore it to him. The fairy waves her wand and the Prince and Cendrillon are able to see each other. They fall into a magic sleep.

The fourth act shows the terrace of Cendrillon's country home. She is sleeping and her father is bending over her. When she wakes her father tells her that she has been talking of the ball and of Prince Charming, of an enchanted oak and a lost slipper. Madame de la Haltiere rushes in to announce that the king has summoned all princesses of high rank to appear before Prince Charming. The herald of the king comes to say that the king will receive the princesses, who are to try on the glass slipper the unknown girl left behind at the ball. The scene changes to the King's court. The Prince watches the Princesses pass. Finally Cendrillon stands before him. The slipper fits her. Her father embraces her, and even her hateful step-mother greets her as "My adored daughter!" All congratulate the happy Prince and his future bride.

§)&(§

LA CENERENTOLA

(Cinderella)

Gioacchino Rossini

Gioacchino Rossini's *La Cenerentola* was his nineteenth opera, and was produced first at the Teatro Valle in Rome, January 25, 1817. The libretto by Jacopo Ferretti changes the familiar story by substituting for the fairy godmother a philosophic friend of the Prince.

The characters are:

CENERENTOLA (*Contralto*)
DON MAGNIFICO (*Bass*), her step-father
CLORINDA (*Soprano*) } her step-sisters
TISBE (*Contralto*) }
THE PRINCE (*Tenor*)
ALIDORO (*Bass*), his friend
DANDINI (*Baritone*), his valet

In the opera Cenerentola is the traditional Cinderella who is badly treated by her step-father and her step-sisters. Alidoro, the Prince's friend, comes to the house disguised as a beggar. The step-sisters drive him away but Cinderella gives him food. Alidoro tells the Prince about the beautiful and kind Cenerentola. By the terms of his father's will the Prince must marry by a certain date. The Prince would like to find a girl who loves him and not his money, so he changes clothes with his valet, Dandini, and calls at the home of Don Magnifico where he is fascinated by Cenerentola's beauty.

The second act shows a ball in the Prince's home. Cenerentola is invited and is given suitable clothes by Alidoro. Dandini, the valet, disguised as the Prince, makes love to Cenerentola, but she tells him that she loves his valet, who called at her step-father's house. During the dance she gives the supposed valet one of her bracelets. A few days later the Prince takes shelter from a storm in Don Magnifico's house. He sees that Cenerentola is wearing on her wrist a bracelet identical with the one he received at the ball. He tells of the change in costume between his valet and himself, proposes marriage and is accepted.

§)&(§

LE CID
Jules Massenet

The libretto of Jules Massenet's *Le Cid* was written by three authors: Adolphe Philippe d'Ennery, Édouard Blau and Louis Gallet, who founded it on a drama by Corneille. The opera was first performed at the Grand Opéra in Paris, November 30, 1885.

The cast includes:

COUNT DE GORMAS (*Baritone*)
XIMENE (*Soprano*), his daughter
DON DIEGO (*Bass*)
RODRIGO (*Tenor*), his son
THE KING (*Baritone*)
THE INFANTA (*Soprano*), his daughter

The action occurs in Burgos, Spain, during the twelfth century. The first act shows a salon in the house of Count de Gormas. The king is about to confer knighthood upon Rodrigo, son of Don Diego. At the same ceremony it is expected that Count de Gormas will be made guardian and preceptor of the King's daughter, the Infanta. De Gormas' daughter, Ximene, is in love with Rodrigo and he with her, and they are delighted to learn that their respective fathers approve of their marriage. The Infanta, too, is in love with Rodrigo, but because of her royal position she cannot marry him. Accordingly she restrains her feelings and promises Ximene that she will not be her rival. The scene changes to a gallery leading to the cathedral. Rodrigo is knighted by the king, who then turns to Don Diego, Rodrigo's father, and appoints him, rather than Ximene's father Count de Gormas, guardian of the Infanta. Don Diego is surprised and Count de Gormas is so enraged that he picks a quarrel with Don Diego and wounds him in a duel. Don Diego calls upon his son Rodrigo to avenge his insult.

The second act shows a street in Burgos. Rodrigo challenges the Count de Gormas and kills him in a duel. Ximene finds her father's body and demands the name of his murderer. No one will tell her, but when she sees that Rodrigo is pale she guesses that it is he who killed her father. The scene changes to a square where the people are dancing. Ximene throws herself at the feet of the king and demands that Rodrigo be punished for killing her father. Don Diego pleads for his son and tells of his provocation, but Ximene is unmoved. She demands revenge on her former lover. The king listens to advocates on each side and is still undecided when a messenger announces that the Moorish leader Boabdil is challenging Spain to Battle. Rodrigo offers himself as a leader and the king accepts him.

The third act shows Ximene's chamber. Rodrigo comes to bid farewell and to ask forgiveness. Ximene repulses him, but when he speaks gloomily of death she arouses him by describing the glory of the coming fight. Thinking that she has forgiven him, Rodrigo tells her that he will return a conqueror. The next scene is in the Spanish camp. Rodrigo summons his army to battle. Many of the soldiers refuse to fight, but a small band rallies to its leader. The third scene of the act shows Rodrigo alone in his tent. A vision of St. James promises him victory.

The fourth act shows a hall in the palace at Granada. The deserters return and announce that Rodrigo has been killed. Ximene and the Infanta are grief-stricken until the king tells them that Rodrigo is not dead, but is returning victorious. The scene changes to the palace court. Rodrigo enters and is pronounced "Le Cid," the conqueror. The king asks him to name his own reward and Rodrigo replies that he wants only Ximene's forgiveness. Ximene places her hand in Rodrigo's as the people applaud.

§)&(§

CLEOPATRA'S NIGHT

Henry K. Hadley

The libretto of Henry K. Hadley's two-act opera, *Cleopatra's Night,* was written by Alice Leal Pollock, who adapted its plot from *Une nuit de Cléopàtre,* a story by Théophile Gautier. The opera was first produced at the Metropolitan Opera House, New York, January 31, 1920.

The cast includes:

CLEOPATRA (*Soprano*), Queen of Egypt
MEÏAMOUN (*Tenor*), a young Egyptian
MARDION (*Mezzo-soprano*), maid to the Queen, in love with Meïamoun
IRIS (*Mezzo-soprano*), an Egyptian maiden

The action occurs in Egypt during the last century before Christ. The first act shows Cleopatra's summer palace, where Cleopatra's attendant, Mardion, is telling Iras of her own undying love for Meïamoun. Cleopatra comes for her bath, and as she is singing a lament about the loneliness of queens, an arrow falls beside her. Attached to it is a message of three words: "I love you." Meïamoun appears and confesses that he shot the arrow and sent the message. The guards are about to kill him, but Cleopatra stops them and asks Meïamoun if he loves her enough to die for her. He replies that he does indeed, and she offers to give herself to him tonight if he will die tomorrow. Mardion, herself in love with Meïamoun, hears the conversation and stabs herself in despair.

The second act occurs the next morning. Meïamoun is seated beside Cleopatra on the terrace of the palace. As they watch the dancing girls, a slave enters with the poisoned draught that Meïamoun must drink. Cleopatra would like to save her new lover from his promised fate, but suddenly the coming of Mark Antony is announced, and Cleopatra knows she cannot reverse her previous order. Meïamoun drinks the poison and falls dead at Cleopatra's feet. She kisses his lips as she leaves to greet Antony.

§)&(§

LE COQ D'OR

(The Golden Cockerel)

Rimsky-Korsakoff

The libretto of Rimsky-Korsakoff's *Le Coq d'Or* was adapted from a poem by Alexander Pushkin and was written by Vladimir Bielsky. The composition of this satirical opera was a defiant gesture on Rimsky's part, for it followed certain difficulties with the czarist government caused by Rimsky's arranging a revolutionary song as an orchestral piece. *Le Coq d'Or* was completed in 1907, but the government forbade its production. It was not until October 7, 1909, almost two years after Rimsky's death, that the opera was produced at Zimin's Private Theatre in Moscow. The first American production took place at the Metropolitan in New York, March 6, 1918. This presentation took the form of an "opera-pantomime" in which members of the ballet enacted the motions of the characters while singers seated in rows near the proscenium sang the vocal parts. In recent years the work has been performed at the Metropolitan as an opera, with the singers themselves acting out the various roles.

Le Coq d'Or is a satire on the stupidity of the aristocracy and the blind obedience of the common people.

The characters include:

KING DODON (*Baritone*)
PRINCE GUIDON (*Tenor*) } his sons
PRINCE AFRON (*Baritone*) } his sons
VOEVODA POLKAN (*Baritone*), the general
AMELFA (*Contralto*), the royal housekeeper
THE ASTROLOGER (*Tenor*)
THE QUEEN OF SHEMAKHAN (*Soprano*)
THE GOLDEN COCKEREL (*Soprano*)

The time and place of the action are legendary. The opera opens with a prologue in which the Astrologer tells the audience that his magical powers will bring to the stage the droll masks of an old fairy tale. The story is not true, he explains, but it has a moral.

The first act shows the palace of King Dodon, a gluttonous man who is constantly set upon by warlike neighbors.

In a council of war the head general, Polkan, disagrees with the King's two sons and the assembly becomes an uproar. The Astrologer enters and offers the King a Golden Cockerel that will foretell events and give warning of approaching danger. The King is so pleased that he promises the Astrologer anything he wishes. The Astrologer replies that power, riches and high rank create only enmity. Only love is dear to him. The bird is placed on the spire of the palace, and the King feels he is safe. He falls asleep, but is soon wakened by the crowing of the cock. He sets out with his soldiers for the enemy's territory.

The second act is laid on the battlefield. King Dodon's armies have been defeated and his two sons lie dead. As the dawn breaks, the King sees a tent which he thinks belongs to the victorious enemy commander. To his great surprise, a beautiful woman comes from the tent and sings a *Hymn to the Sun*. She is the Queen of Shemakhan. She invites Dodon to dance with her and agrees to marry him.

The third act returns to the King's palace. The people are awaiting the return of the King and his bride, who soon arrive followed by a procession of giants and dwarfs. In the midst of the merry-making the Astrologer appears and demands the Queen as payment for the Golden Cockerel. The King kills the Astrologer with a blow of his sceptre. Immediately the Cockerel swoops down from his perch and kills the King with his beak. During a clap of thunder the Queen and the Cockerel disappear, but in the Epilogue the Astrologer tells the audience not to take the story too much to heart. Only the Queen and himself are real, the others were merely a dream.

§)&(§

COSI FAN TUTTE

Wolfgang Amadeus Mozart

Mozart's *Cosi Fan Tutte* was first presented at The Burgtheater in Vienna, January 26, 1790, at a command performance before Emperor Joseph II of Austria. Its libretto is a two-act comedy by Lorenzo da Ponte. The characters are:

ISIDORA FIORDILIGI (*Soprano*)
DORABELLA (*Soprano*), her sister
FERRANDO (*Tenor*), Dorabella's suitor
GRATIANO GUGLIELMO (*Baritone*), Isidora's suitor
ALFONSO (*Bass*), a bachelor and a cynic
DESPINA (*Soprano*), maid to Isidora and Dorabella

The first act includes three scenes: a café in Naples, a garden, and a room in the house of Isidora and Dorabella. In the first scene, Alfonso, a cynical bachelor, bets the two lovers Gratiano and Ferrando, that if their sweethearts, Isidora and Dorabella, should be courted by two other lovers they will prove unfaithful. Gratiano and Ferrando are so confident of the devotion of their fiancees that they accept the wager. They pretend to leave for the army and soon return disguised as two rich Albanians. They are accordingly reintroduced to the ladies, and each proceeds to make love to the other's sweetheart—Gratiano to Dorabella and Ferrando to Isidora. The ladies resist, and it looks for a time as though Alfonso would lose his wager. He is not willing to give up so easily, and he bribes Despina, the maid, to help him. The disguised lovers seem to be heartbroken at the rebuff, and they pretend to take poison. The maid Despina comes in disguised as a physician, and revives the two men.

The two scenes of the second act show the interior and the garden of the sisters' house. The "Albanians" are still pursuing the ladies and their continued attentions are gradually melting the sisters' coldness. Dorabella gives Gratiano a locket which holds her real lover's, Ferrando's, picture. Isidora, too, begins to yield to her new suitor. the disguised Ferrando. Despina appears in another disguise, as a notary, and the "Albanians" order her to draw up a double marriage contract. Alfonso interrupts to announce that Ferrando and Gratiano are returning from the army, and will appear at any moment. The two men leave to take off their disguises and soon return in their real characters. They seize the marriage contracts and unmask Despina. As they are accusing their sweethearts of unfaithfulness, Alfonso returns. He is in excellent spirits because he has won the bet, and he manages to reconcile the couples. He insists that it is idle to scold women for flirting, for they all do it—"Cosi fan tutte!"

§)&(§

THE CRICKET ON THE HEARTH

Karl Goldmark

A. M. Willner wrote the libretto for Karl Goldmark's opera based on Charles Dickens's story, *The Cricket on the Hearth*. The work was first produced at the Staatsoper in Vienna, March 21, 1896.

The cast includes:

JOHN (*Baritone*)
DOT (*Soprano*), his wife
MAY (*Soprano*), a toymaker
EDWARD PLUMMER (*Tenor*), her former lover
TACKLETON (*Bass*), May's employer
THE CRICKET (*Soprano*)

The action occurs in an English village during the early nineteenth century. The first act shows a room in John's house, where the Cricket announces that he is the guiding spirit of the household. Dot tells the Cricket that she is soon to have a child. May, a young girl who is employed as a toymaker by Tackleton, laments the fact that she is to be married tomorrow to her employer. She is still in love with Edward Plummer, who has been gone from the village for several years. May leaves, and soon John, Dot's husband, comes home with a sailor. This sailor is actually Edward Plummer in disguise, but neither John nor the villagers recognize him.

The second act is laid in a garden. May and Tackleton are having supper together, and John makes Tackleton jealous of the mysterious stranger. The stranger, actually Edward, sees that May is marrying Tackleton only because his wealth will save her foster-father from poverty, and he tells Dot who he really is. Tackleton, in turn, sees Edward and Dot talking in low tones, and he makes John jealous of the supposed stranger's attentions to Dot. The Cricket saves the situation by lulling John to sleep, and having him dream of himself as a happy father.

The third act returns to John's house. May decides not to marry Tackleton, but to wait for Edward's return. Then she recognizes the stranger as Edward, and together they drive off in Tackleton's carriage. Dot tells John that she is to have a baby, and they, too, are reconciled.

§)&(§

CRISPINO E LA COMARE

(The Cobbler and the Fairy)

Federico and Luigi Ricci

The music of *Crispino e la comare* was composed by two brothers in collaboration, Federico and Luigi Ricci. The libretto was written by Francesco Maria Piave and the opera was first produced at the Teatro San Benedetto in Venice, February 28, 1850.

The characters include:

CRISPINO TACHETTO (*Baritone*), a cobbler
ANNETTA (*Soprano*), his wife, a ballad singer and peddler
LA COMARE (*Mezzo-soprano*), a fairy
COUNT DEL FIORE (*Tenor*)
FABRIZIO (*Bass*), a physician
MIRABOLANO (*Tenor*), an apothecary
DON ASDRUBALE (*Bass*), a miser
BARTOLO, a mason

The action occurs in seventeenth-century Venice, and the first act shows a street of the city where Annetta, the ballad singer, is unsuccessfully trying to sell her songs. Her husband, a cobbler, is trying with equal lack of success to make a living by mending shoes. They are heavily in debt, and their miserly landlord Asdrubale threatens to have them evicted unless they pay their rent. The scene changes to a lonely spot near a well. Crispino is about to commit suicide by jumping into the well when a fairy (La Comare) rises from the water and tells him that she will protect him and provide for him. She would like to revenge herself on certain doctors in Venice by making them look foolish, so she tells Crispino that he will become a famous and wealthy doctor if he will follow her advice. Whenever he attends a patient, he will know that the patient will recover if she, the Fairy, does not appear. If she is present (invisible to all but Crispino) he will know that the patient will die. After giving these instructions the fairy hands Crispino a bag of gold coins so that he may pay his debts and establish his reputation as a man of substance.

The second act returns to the street. The cobbler has put a physician's sign on his house and is ready for business. The neighbors make fun of Crispino, particularly the physician Fabrizio and Mirabolano, the apothecary, but when Crispino pays his debts with the Fairy's gold and then cures Bartolo, a mason who is severely injured by falling bricks, the crowd gathers about Crispino and hails him as a great doctor. Crispino, of course, noticed that the Fairy was not present before he attempted the "cure."

The third act shows Crispino as an illustrious and wealthy doctor, responsible for countless cures. He has become haughty and supercilious. He mistreats his wife, and is insolent even to the Fairy who made his success possible. For punishment the Fairy takes Crispino to her home below the earth. She orders him to make his will for his last hour is at hand. Crispino obeys, but begs that he be permitted to embrace his wife and children before he dies. The Fairy allows him a glimpse of his family as they are praying for his safety. Crispino then pleads for his life and promises that he will be a model husband and father. The Fairy relents and causes Crispino to fall insensible on a couch. When he awakens he finds that he is surrounded by his wife, children and neighbors. He realizes that he has been ill and that the recent interview with the Fairy was just a dream. He has, however, learned his lesson, and he remembers the promise he made to the Fairy in his dreams.

§)&(§

CYRANO DE BERGERAC

Walter Damrosch

Edmond Rostand's famous play was the basis for this opera by Walter Damrosch, and the libretto was written by W. J. Henderson, the music critic. The opera was first performed at the Metropolitan Opera House, New York, February 27, 1913. It was performed several times during that season and was then withdrawn by the composer, who felt that it needed revision. Other duties prevented him from accomplishing this purpose until 1938. In 1941 the revised opera was presented in concert form at Carnegie Hall, New York, by a group of soloists, the chorus of the Oratorio Society, and the New York Philharmonic-Symphony Orchestra.

The leading characters of the opera are:

CYRANO DE BERGERAC (*Baritone*)
ROXANE (*Soprano*)
CHRISTIAN (*Tenor*) } her suitors
DE GUICHE (*Bass*) }
MONTFLEURY (*Tenor*), an actor

The action occurs in France during the reign of Louis XIII, and the first act shows a large salon in the Hotel de Bourgoyne in Paris. A group of literary women led by Roxane are waiting for the performance of a play in which a very fat and rather ridiculous actor named Montfleury is to sing some verses by a contemporary poet. Cyrano de Bergerac, a swordsman, wit and poet, and a cousin of Roxane, has boasted that he will stop Montfleury's performance. Cyrano has an enormous nose, and is very sensitive about it. Before he arrives the conversation prepares the background for the plot, and we learn that Christian, Baron of Neuvillette, is in love with Roxane. Roxane has another suitor in the person of De Guiche, who has escorted her to the performance. Cyrano arrives and the performance begins. As soon as Montfleury starts to sing, Cyrano shouts at him, and forces him to retire. De Guiche protests and asks Cyrano if he "stops all shows by pushing into them his mighty nose." Cyrano challenges De Guiche to a duel and improvises a ballad as he wounds him. De Guiche is carried out and a hundred of his friends wait outside for Cyrano. The hero draws his sword and fights his way to safety.

The second act is laid in a pastry shop. Cyrano is secretly in love with his cousin Roxane and has come to the pastry shop to meet her. She tells him that she loves Christian, who has just become a member of the Gascony Cadets. Cyrano is a member of the cadets, and because Roxane is afraid that Christian is ill-fitted for such a rough life, she asks Cyrano to look after Christian and protect him. Cyrano hides his own love for Roxane and promises her that he will do as she asks. When she has left the Cadets enter. Cyrano manages to have a few minutes alone with Christian and he tells the young man that Roxane expects a letter from him. Christian confesses that he is a "fool in the use of words" and Cyrano offers to write his letter for him.

The third act shows the outside of Roxane's house. De Guiche tells her that he is to command the troops in the coming siege of Arras. The Gascony Cadets will be part of his army and De Guiche boasts that Cyrano will be in his power. Roxane fears for Christian's safety during the siege, so she slyly suggests to De Guiche that the worst punishment he could inflict on Cyrano would be to keep him out of action. Why does he not leave the Gascony Cadets behind when he leads the main body of troops to Arras? De Guiche thinks that this is a splendid idea, and he leaves, highly pleased with this plan of revenge. Soon Christian and Cyrano appear. Christian tries to serenade Roxane but he cannot find words for his love-making. Roxane appears on the balcony and as Christian stands under it, Cyrano imitates his voice so that Christian seems to be declaring his love in a poetic flow of impassioned words. Roxane is enchanted and Christian climbs the balcony to embrace her. A monk enters with a note from De Guiche to Roxane. This message actually tells Roxane that De Guiche is on his way to see her but Roxane tells the monk that it is a command from De Guiche to marry her to Christian. She and Christian enter the house with the monk for the ceremony, while Cyrano waits outside for De Guiche. De Guiche arrives and Cyrano detains him until the lovers appear. When De Guiche learns that he has been outwitted he announces that the Gascony Cadets will go at once to Arras.

The first scene of the third act shows the camp of the Gascony Cadets. Cyrano has promised Roxane that Christian will write her at least one letter a day, and he himself has been writing under Christian's name, not one, but two, letters every day. Roxane has been so moved by their beauty that she comes to the camp to see Christian. She tells him that his letters have been so beautiful that she would love him even if he were ugly. Christian is jealous that the words of another are needed to stir the love of his wife, and he accuses Cyrano of writing "not my love, but your own." He rushes off to the battle and is killed. Cyrano, following him into action, is wounded.

The last scene shows the garden of a Convent where the wounded Cyrano has sought shelter. Roxane comes to him and they talk of Christian. She shows Cyrano the last letter she received. Cyrano pretends to read it aloud, and Roxane notices that as he speaks, he is not looking at it. Gradually she realizes that it was he and not Christian who has been her real lover. She accuses herself of having wrecked his life, but the chivalrous Cyrano rises to his feet and denies his love for her. The exertion re-opens his wound and he bleeds to death as he whispers that he will salute God with something that enters Heaven without a stain—his soldier's snow-white plume.

§)&(§

CZAR UND ZIMMERMANN

(Czar and Carpenter)

Albert Lortzing

Albert Lortzing composed both the libretto and the music of his light opera, *Czar und Zimmermann.* It was first produced at the Stadtheater in Leipzig, December 22, 1837.

The cast includes:

PETER I (*Baritone*), Czar of Russia, working as a journeyman carpenter in the shipyards at Sardam under the name of PETER MICHAELOW

PETER IVANOW (*Tenor*), a young Russian journeyman carpenter, who has deserted from the Russian army

MARIE (*Soprano*), Peter Ivanow's sweetheart

VAN BETT (*Bass*), her uncle, Burgomaster of Sardam

GENERAL LEFORT (*Bass*), the Russian Ambassador

LORD SYNDHAM (*Bass*), the English Ambassador

MARQUIS CHATEAUNEUF (*Tenor*), the French Ambassador

The action occurs in Sardam, Holland, in the year 1690. The plot concerns the mistaken identity of the two Peters, both of them Russian and both working as carpenters in the shipyard at Sardam. The Burgomaster is seeking a Russian named Peter whom the Dutch authorities suspect of trying to entice his fellow workers into the Russian service. The Ambassadors of France and England suspect that one of the Peters is the Czar and seek an alliance with each of their respective countries. The Russian Ambassador is looking for the Czar because of revolt at home. The English Ambassador mistakes Peter Ivanow for the Czar, but the French Ambassador guesses correctly that Peter Michaelow is his man and concludes the alliance between their nations. Peter Ivanow is forgiven for his desertion and is allowed to marry his sweetheart, Marie, niece of the Burgomaster.

§)&(§

THE DAMNATION OF FAUST

Hector Berlioz

The Damnation of Faust by Hector Berlioz was first composed as a dramatic oratorio and was originally produced in concert form at Paris, December 6, 1846. Nearly a half-century later it was arranged in operatic form by Raoul Gunsbourg and presented as an opera at the Théâtre du Casino, Monte Carlo, February 18, 1893.

The libretto was adapted by Berlioz and Almire Gandonnière from Gérard de Nerval's French version of Goethe's *Faust*. Many liberties were taken with the original. In Goethe's play Faust is saved; in the Berlioz version he is taken to Hell by Mephistopheles. Berlioz set the action in eighteenth-century Hungary, for the avowed purpose of introducing the "Rákóczy March," which is the Hungarian national air.

The characters of the Berlioz opera are:

MARGUERITE *(Soprano),* a peasant girl
FAUST *(Tenor),* a philosopher
BRANDER *(Bass),* his convivial friend
MEPHISTOPHELES *(Bass)*

The first act shows Faust in his study, looking out of his window at the countryside where winter is changing to spring. He sees and hears the villagers singing and dancing and then he watches the soldiers as they march off to war to the stirring strains of the "Rákóczy March." He cannot respond to the merriment of the peasants and only for a moment is he stirred to patriotism by the military display. He sinks back into a mood of depression and melancholy.

The second act opens in Faust's workroom. He is ready to end his life. He hears an Easter hymn being sung in the church, and falls on his knees as he sings "Hosanna" with the choir. Mephistopheles appears and offers to console Faust with worldly pleasures. Unlike Faust in the Goethe story, Berlioz' Faust does not sell his soul to Mephistopheles at this time. He makes no pledge, but leaves with Mephistopheles to see what the devil has to offer.

In the next scene Mephistopheles and Faust visit a low drinking resort. Brander and a dozen of his convivial friends are seated at tables. Brander sings his "Song of a Rat" and Faust responds with the "Song of the Flea." Faust's attempt to join the spirit of the occasion is futile, and he asks Mephistopheles if he has no better pleasures than "vile speech, joy ignoble, and gesture brutal." Can he not give him back his youth? Mephistopheles tells Faust to follow him and the two disappear into a trap door.

The scene changes to a beautiful valley where Faust lies asleep on a bed of roses with Mephistopheles standing behind him. Mephistopheles conjures for Faust a dream of dancing sylphs and gnomes, and then a vision of the beautiful Marguerite. At last Faust is interested and Mephistopheles cries "The charm takes hold, he is ours." The act ends with the "Ballet of the Sylphs."

The third act shows a double setting. The left side of the stage is given over to Marguerite's chamber, with one door opening on the street and the other on a garden. The right of the stage shows a church, separated from Marguerite's house by a broad street. As the curtain rises a chorus of returning soldiers and students is singing, and as they move away Faust and Mephistopheles appear on the street. Mephistopheles shows Faust the house of Marguerite and opens the door. Faust enters the house and when Marguerite is heard approaching, Mephistopheles tells him to hide in the garden. Marguerite comes into her room, sings the ballad of the "King of Thule," and then falls asleep in a chair. Mephistopheles conjures for her a dream of Faust. When she wakes she finds the real Faust in her room. Faust makes love to her and she admits that she loves him. Mephistopheles comes to warn them that the neighbors are angry because a man has forced his way into Marguerite's room. He promises the lovers that they may meet tomorrow, and Faust escapes through the garden.

As the fourth act opens, Marguerite is in her room, remorseful for her sin and grieving that Faust does not come any more to see her. The scene changes to a forest, where Faust is longing for Marguerite. Mephistopheles tells him that Marguerite is in prison, condemned to die for the murder of her mother. To save her Faust must sign a paper which Mephistopheles has prepared. Faust agrees readily, and by signing gives his soul to Mephistopheles. Mephistopheles takes his victim to the depths of Hell. As they fall into the inferno Mephistopheles cries: "I am victorious!" The last scene shows the roofs and towers of the town. Angels descend from Heaven and reappear from the city bearing the body of Marguerite. They sing that Marguerite has been forgiven and that perhaps the Almighty will some day extend His mercy to Faust.

§)&(§

THE DAUGHTER OF THE REGIMENT

(La Fille du Régiment)

Gaetano Donizetti

The libretto of Donizetti's *La Fille du Régiment* was written by Jean François Alfred Bayard and Jules Henri Vernoy de Saint-Georges. The opera was first produced in the Opéra Comique at Paris, February 11, 1840.

The cast includes:

MARIE (*Soprano*), a vivandière of the 21st French Regiment, who has been brought up from childhood by the troops and is called the "daughter of the regiment."

THE MARQUISE DE BERKENFELD (*Soprano*), at first supposed to be Marie's aunt, but actually her mother

SULPICE (*Bass*), a sergeant of the regiment

TONIO (*Tenor*), a Swiss peasant, in love with Marie

The action takes place in the Swiss Tyrol in the year 1815, during the Napoleonic wars. The first act shows the interior of the barn belonging to an inn in the Tyrol, with the mountains in the background. The Marquise de Berkenfeld seeks protection from the French invaders who are occupying the Swiss Tyrol, and as soon as she has found shelter, Sulpice, the French sergeant, enters with Marie.

In a duet Sulpice and Marie recount the events of Marie's early life—how she was adopted by the regiment as a foundling and became its vivandière when she was grown. Her father is the entire regiment, and now she has fallen in love and must ask its permission to marry. Her suitor is a Tyrolese peasant, Tonio, who the soldiers think is a spy. When they learn that he has saved Marie from falling off a precipice, they hail him as a hero.

The second act shows the countryside of the Tyrol. First comes a scene between Tonio and Marie in which Tonio agrees to join the regiment, since the soldiers will allow Marie to marry only a member of the regiment. The Marquise appears. Sulpice learns that she is the Marquise of Berkenfeld, and the name reminds him of his former Captain, Robert. It was Robert who was the actual father of Marie, and who, just before he died, had given Sulpice a letter. The Marquise claims that Robert married her sister, and that Marie is therefore her niece. Sulpice accordingly gives Robert's letter to the Marquise, who insists that Marie live with her in her castle, where she will be properly educated.

The third act is laid in a salon of the Marquise' castle. Marie has been socially trained and is to be married to a Duke. Meanwhile Tonio has distinguished himself in battle and has become a captain in the regiment. Marie still wants to marry Tonio rather than the Duke. The Marquise confesses that she is not Marie's aunt, but her mother. It was she and not a sister who secretly married Robert. Marie feels that she must obey her mother and agrees to marry the Duke, but the Marquise finally relents and decides that her daughter shall have true happiness by marrying the man she loves—Captain Tonio.

§)&(§

THE DEVIL AND DANIEL WEBSTER

Douglas Moore

Douglas Moore used a story by Stephen Vincent Benét for this opera, which was first produced May 18, 1939, by the American Lyric Theatre Group at the Martin Beck Theatre in New York.

The characters include:

JABEZ STONE (*Bass*)
MARY STONE (*Mezzo-soprano*), his wife
DANIEL WEBSTER (*Baritone*)
MR. SCRATCH (*Tenor*)
THE FIDDLER (*Speaking part*)
JUSTICE HATHORNE (*Speaking part*)
CLERK OF THE COURT (*Baritone*)
TWELVE JURYMEN (Including Simon Girty, King Philip, Morton, and other notorious historic traitors, scoundrels and cutthroats)

Jabez Stone, a young New England farmer, has sold his soul to the devil in return for the material prosperity that has made it possible for him to marry Mary. The devil appears at the wedding in the person of Mr. Scratch, a Boston lawyer. He claims the bridegroom's soul, but Daniel Webster pleads Jabez' case before a judge and a jury which consists of the shades of famous villains summoned from Hell by the devil. Webster is so eloquent that the jury decides that the contract is not valid.

§)&(§

DINORAH

Giacomo Meyerbeer

Dinorah was originally called *Le Pardon de Poëremel,* and was the next to last opera composed by Giacomo Meyerbeer. Its libretto was written by Jules Barbier and Michel Carré, and it was first produced at the Opéra Comique in Paris, April 4, 1859. Outside of France, the opera has been entitled *Dinorah.*

The characters include:

DINORAH (*Soprano*), betrothed to Hoel
HOEL (*Bass*), a goatherd
CORENTIN (*Tenor*), a bagpiper

The action occurs in Brittany during the Middle Ages. Hoel and Dinorah were to have been married, but on the day of their wedding Dinorah's house was destroyed by a thunderstorm. Hoel has determined to rebuild Dinorah's house. He has learned from an old wizard that gold, guarded by goblins, may be found in a distant glen. If he wants this gold to help him rebuild Dinorah's house, he must stay in the glen for a year and keep absolute silence. After a year the first person who touches the gold will die, and Hoel will be able to take all he needs. Before the opera begins, Hoel has left for the glen and Dinorah thinks he has deserted her. She is half-crazed by grief and shock.

The opera opens after the year has passed. Dinorah appears in a forest wearing her bridal clothes. She is looking for her pet goat, and when she finds it she sings a lullaby. She meets a bagpiper, Corentin, who has just returned from a place inhabited by strange gnomes and elves. When he sees Dinorah in her tattered wedding dress he thinks she is a phantom who makes people dance until they die. To tease the bagpiper Dinorah makes him dance to her song until he is exhausted. Hoel appears, returned from his year in the glen. Neither he nor Dinorah recognize each other, and Dinorah runs away from the supposed stranger. Hoel is looking for somebody to touch the magic gold, and he thinks the bagpiper will be just the man for his purpose. He tells Corentin that a wizard once told him to find a white goat which will lead him to a hidden treasure. He and Corentin follow Dinorah's goat.

The second act shows the wood in the moonlight. Dinorah dances to the famous "Shadow Dance," which today is the only part of the opera generally known and played. In this dance Dinorah sees her shadow in the moonlight and thinks it is a friend. Meanwhile Hoel and Corentin reach the part of the forest where the gold is hidden. An off-stage voice warns that he who touches the gold first shall die. The bagpiper is frightened and tries to leave but Hoel detains him. Dinorah returns in pursuit of her goat. Hoel thinks she is an angel sent from Heaven to warn him against causing the death of the bagpiper, and thinks better of his plan. Dinorah starts to cross a bridge and falls into the river. Hoel jumps into the water and brings the unconscious Dinorah to the shore.

The third act shows a landscape. Hoel carries Dinorah, still unconscious. He has finally recognized her and is heartbroken. When Dinorah regains consciousness she has recovered her senses. She beholds her lover and both of them are overjoyed. Hoel gives up all thought of the treasure and goes toward the nearest church where he and Dinorah will be married.

§)&(§

DON CARLOS

Giuseppe Verdi

Don Carlos was Giuseppe Verdi's twenty-fourth opera, and was first produced at the Grand Opéra at Paris, March 11, 1867. Its libretto was written by Joseph Méry and Camille DuLocle and was founded on a drama by Schiller.

The cast includes:

PHILIP II (*Bass*), King of Spain
DON CARLOS (*Tenor*), his son, the Crown Prince
ELIZABETH DE VALOIS (*Soprano*), in love with Don Carlos, but married to his father, the king
PRINCESS EBOLI (*Soprano*), in love with Don Carlos
RODRIGO (*Baritone*), Marquis of Posa, a friend to Don Carlos
THE GRAND INQUISITOR (*Bass*)

The action occurs in sixteenth-century France and Spain. The first act shows a forest at Fontainebleau. Don Carlos of Spain is betrothed to Elizabeth de Valois, daughter of the King of France. They meet for the first time and fall deeply in love with each other, but their love-making is interrupted by a messenger who brings news that for reasons of state Elizabeth is to marry not Don Carlos, but his father, Philip II, the King of Spain.

The second act is laid at the Convent at St. Just. Elizabeth has been married to King Philip and is now the Queen of Spain, and stepmother to Don Carlos. Rodrigo advises Don Carlos to go to Flanders, where he may forget his love for Elizabeth. Don Carlos asks Elizabeth to obtain the necessary permission for him from the King. During their interview they realize that they are still in love with each other.

The third act opens in the Queen's garden. During a masked ball Don Carlos mistakes the Princess Eboli for Elizabeth and makes love to her. The Princess is herself in love with Don Carlos and she is furiously jealous when she takes off her mask and Don Carlos shows his disappointment. For revenge, she threatens to tell the King of the love affair between Don Carlos and Elizabeth, the Queen. In the second scene of the act, in a large square of Madrid, Don Carlos pleads with his father, the King, for mercy for the people of Flanders. The King refuses and Don Carlos draws his sword and offers to help these oppressed people. The King orders Don Carlos disarmed.

The fourth act opens in the King's library, where the Grand Inquisitor convinces the King that Don Carlos must be imprisoned. Princess Eboli tells the King of the love of Don Carlos for the Queen, so the King has a double reason for wanting his son punished. The scene changes to a dungeon where Don Carlos is imprisoned. Rodrigo comes to visit him, and is shot by an unknown assassin from ambush. Outside, the populace demands the release of their favorite Prince, Don Carlos, and the Grand Inquisitor yields and frees Don Carlos in order to prevent a serious outbreak. The last scene shows the Convent, where Don Carlos has come to bid a last farewell to the Queen. The King interrupts them and hands his son over to the officers of the Inquisition.

§)&(§

DON GIOVANNI

Wolfgang Amadeus Mozart

Lorenzo da Ponte supplied the libretto for Mozart's *Don Giovanni* which was composed almost immediately after the completion of *The Marriage of Figaro*. *Don Giovanni* was first produced at Prague, November 29, 1787. The hero's name is the Italian for the Spanish Don Juan, and the story tells of several of his amours and of his final downfall. Da Ponte based his libretto on the Spanish version of Bertati's *El Convivado de Peidra,* or "The Stone Guest," in which Don Juan meets his fate at the hands of the statue of a man he has killed in a duel.

The characters are:

DON GIOVANNI (*Baritone*), a Castilian nobleman
LEPORELLO (*Bass*), his servant
DON PEDRO (*Bass*), Commandant of Seville
ANNA (*Soprano*), his daughter
OTTAVIO (*Tenor*), betrothed to Anna
ELVIRA (*Soprano*), a former sweetheart of Don Giovanni
MASETTO (*Bass*), a peasant
ZERLINA (*Soprano*), betrothed to Masetto

The opening scene of the first act shows the courtyard of Don Pedro's palace in Seville. It is night and Leporello is lying on a stone bench, keeping watch while his master, Don Giovanni, is invading the bedroom of Donna Anna, Don Pedro's daughter. Suddenly Don Giovanni rushes from the palace, his hat drawn over his eyes and his sword in hand. Anna, clad in her nightgown, pursues him and tries to pull off his disguise. Don Giovanni struggles with her but by this time her screams have been heard and her father, Don Pedro, rushes to help her. Anna escapes into the palace and Don Pedro and Don Giovanni fight a duel with their swords. Don Pedro is killed and Don Giovanni and Leporello retreat hastily. Anna returns with her fiance, Don Ottavio. They find Don Pedro's body, and Ottavio swears to Anna that he will avenge her father's death.

The next scene shows a desolate spot outside the walls of Seville. It is daylight as Don Giovanni and Leporello enter. Leporello protests to his master: "The life ye lead will take ye straight to the devil." Don Giovanni silences his servant and talks of his next adventure. He sees a fair lady approaching and addresses her without realizing that she is Elvira, a former sweetheart whom he has deserted. Elvira rebukes Giovanni for his perfidy, and he, retiring in confusion, leaves his servant to explain matters. Leporello then sings one of the most famous arias of the opera: "Gentle lady, this list I would show you of the fair ones my master has courted; in Italy, six hundred and forty; in Germany, ten score and twenty; in France, double fifty; and in Spain, three thousand." Elvira swears she will have justice and that Don Giovanni will pay for his mischief.

The third scene is laid near Don Giovanni's palace in the mountains surrounding Seville. A wedding party of peasants enters with the bride and groom—Zerlina and Masetto. Don Giovanni discovers them and is fascinated by Zerlina, the bride. He invites the party to his palace and orders his servant, Leporello, to show his guests around the castle and to take particular pains in occupying the attention of Masetto, the bridegroom. He then tries to detain Zerlina. Masetto protests, but Leporello takes him away and Don Giovanni starts making love to Zerlina. He promises marriage and Zerlina is about to yield to him when Elvira appears and denounces Don Giovanni. As Don Giovanni retreats and Elvira leads Zerlina away, Donna Anna and Don Ottavio enter. Anna does not know that it is Don Giovanni who killed her father, for his face was hidden at the time, but when Elvira joins them and again denounces Don Giovanni as a perfidious rascal, Anna realizes that he is her father's murderer. She and Ottavio plan to watch him and await their chance for revenge.

The scene changes to the garden of Don Giovanni's palace, where Masetto is accusing Zerlina of unfaithfulness.

She pleads for forgiveness in the aria: "Scold me, dear Masetto," and Masetto is partially pacified, but decides to hide where he can watch Zerlina. Don Giovanni again makes love to Zerlina and Masetto comes from hiding and confronts him. Don Giovanni quiets him by taking them both into the palace where he is giving a ball for the peasants. As they disappear, Ottavio, Anna and Elvira return with masks. They too will attend the ball.

The final scene of the first act shows the ball in full progress. The guests dance the minuet and a waltz. Don Giovanni is still forcing his attentions on Zerlina. He urges Leporello to divert Masetto and then he forces Zerlina into a cabinet. Presently Zerlina screams and rushes into the ballroom. Ottavio, Anna and Elvira take off their masks and with Masetto corner Don Giovanni. He is too good a swordsman to be caught, and makes his escape.

The complications continue through the second act. Zerlina has become Elvira's maid, and in the first scene (a square outside Elvira's home) Don Giovanni is still the nobleman who would a-wooing go. He forces Leporello to change clothes with him so that in the guise of a servant he may woo Elvira's maid. Leporello, wearing Don Giovanni's clothes, makes love to Elvira and vows that from now on he will be faithful to her. Don Giovanni then serenades Zerlina in the aria "Open thy casement," but is interrupted by Masetto and a party of villagers. Don Giovanni imitates Leporello's voice and offers to help find Don Giovanni. The villagers go off in the direction Don Giovanni shows them and then Don Giovanni knocks Masetto unconscious and escapes. Zerlina finds Masetto and takes him into the house.

The second scene is laid in the courtyard of Donna Anna's house. Leporello and Elvira enter. She still thinks that he is Don Giovanni and begs him to be true to her.

Donna Anna and Ottavio come in and Leporello and Elvira hide in different corners of the courtyard. Anna and Ottavio are joined by Zerlina and Masetto and again they plan their revenge. Elvira and Leporello come from their hiding places and Leporello reveals his identity and escapes.

The next scene shows a square before the Cathedral of Seville. In the center is a marble statue of Don Pedro, Anna's father, whom Don Giovanni has killed. Don Giovanni and Leporello enter and as they are talking the statue speaks. Leporello is terrified, but Don Giovanni is defiant, and nonchalantly invites the statue to a banquet he is giving at his palace.

The final scene is laid in the banquet hall. The statue appears in the midst of the festivities, and with its marble fingers seizes Don Giovanni and leads him to a fiery pit that has opened in the middle of the floor. Demons rush out and pull Don Giovanni into the abyss. When he is gone those he has wronged come in and Leporello tells them what has happened.

§)&(§

DON PASQUALE

Gaetano Donizetti

For *Don Pasquale* Gaetano Donizetti adapted the text of an earlier opera by Stefano Pavesi, entitled *Ser Marc' Antonio,* which was produced at Milan in 1810. The libretto of the earlier opera was written by A. Anelli and was rewritten as Don Pasquale by G. Ruffino and Donizetti himself. *Don Pasquale* was performed first at the Théâtre Italien in Paris, January 3, 1843.

The cast includes:

DON PASQUALE (*Bass*), an old bachelor
ERNESTO (*Tenor*), his nephew
NORINA (*Soprano*), a young widow
DOCTOR MALATESTA (*Baritone*), a physician
A NOTARY

The action occurs at Rome in the middle of the nineteenth century. The first act shows a room in Don Pasquale's house. Don Pasquale discusses with Dr. Malatesta the stubbornness of his nephew, Ernesto, who insists on courting the young widow Norina instead of marrying a woman Don Pasquale will choose for him. Dr. Malatesta proposes that Don Pasquale himself should marry. Then he would have revenge on his nephew by cutting him off in his will and leaving his fortune to his own wife. The doctor suggests for Don Pasquale's bride a beautiful lady, who, he says, is his sister. Don Pasquale agrees to this plan, and when Ernesto appears and again refuses to give up the young widow, Don Pasquale says that he himself will marry and disinherit Ernesto. Ernesto begs his uncle to consult Dr. Malatesta, whom Ernesto considers a loyal friend. When Don Pasquale tells Ernesto that it was the doctor who suggested his marrying, and has offered his own sister as the bride, Ernesto is amazed and disgusted by his friend's perfidy. The scene changes to a room in Norina's house. Dr. Malatesta tells Norina that he has arranged a scheme that will force Don Pasquale to consent to her marriage with Ernesto. Don Pasquale has never seen Norina, so it will be easy for her to pretend that she is the doctor's sister. She will then go through a mock marriage with Don Pasquale, and will make herself so obnoxious as his wife that he will be glad to have her marry Ernesto just to be rid of her. Norina agrees to the plan.

The second act returns to Don Pasquale's apartments. Dr. Malatesta brings Norina to meet her future husband, and Norina pretends to be shy and bashful. Don Pasquale is enchanted at such modesty in a bride, and wants to be married immediately. A notary is brought in to prepare a marriage contract. Under its terms Norina receives one half of Don Pasquale's property and becomes the supreme mistress of his household. Ernesto interrupts the meeting. He sees Norina and starts to protest. The Doctor and Norina whisper to him that it is all part of a plot. Norina signs the contract and immediately throws aside her pretended bashfulness. She refuses to let Don Pasquale embrace her. When Ernesto laughs and is ordered from the house, Norina tells him to stay. She will need him as an escort. Norina summons the servants and tells them that their wages are doubled and that they are to engage many more servants. She orders horses, carriages and dinner for fifty. When Don Pasquale cries that he will not pay the bills for these extravagances, Norina reminds him that she is mistress of the establishment.

In the third act, again in Don Pasquale's apartments, Norina is giving orders to her five maids and to the milliner. Don Pasquale is groaning before a huge pile of bills. Norina starts to go to the theatre. Don Pasquale forbids her to leave but she boxes his ears and goes anyway. As she passes through the door she drops a letter. Don Pasquale picks it up and finds that it is an ardent love note arranging a rendezvous for the evening. Dr. Malatesta pretends to be sympathetic. He thinks that matters can be arranged satisfactorily and assures Don Pasquale that together they will watch over Don Pasquale's wife, his own sister. Don Pasquale agrees to leave everything to the doctor. He will follow his advice, provided his wife will leave the house at once. The scene changes to the garden. Ernesto serenades Norina. When Don Pasquale and the Doctor appear Ernesto escapes. Don Pasquale accuses Norina of having a lover. She challenges her husband to find the man. The doctor then takes charge and tells Norina that another bride will enter the house tomorrow. Norina pretends to be jealous and insulted. The doctor explains that the bride will be Ernesto's and that her name is Norina. Norina, still acting as Don Pasquale's wife, declares if Norina comes, she will leave. Don Pasquale falls into the trap. He summons Ernesto and promises him that if he will marry this Norina they are talking about, he will endow him generously. The doctor announces that Norina is present, and that a mock marriage has been performed to prevent Don Pasquale from contracting a real one. Don Pasquale is so relieved that the stormy Norina will be taken away from him that he gives the young couple his blessing.

§)&(§

LE DONNE CURIOSE

(The Inquisitive Women)

Ermanno Wolf-Ferrari

Ermanno Wolf-Ferrari's opera, *Le Donne Curiose,* uses a libretto by Luigi Sugano, which is a merry farce founded on a play by Carlo Goldoni. The opera was first produced at the Residenztheater, Munich, November 27, 1903.

The characters include:

OTTAVIO (*Bass*), a wealthy citizen of Venice
BEATRICE (*Mezzo-soprano*), his wife
ROSAURA (*Soprano*), his daughter
COLOMBINA (*Soprano*), their servant
PANTOLONE (*Baritone*)
LELIO (*Baritone*)
ELEANORA (*Soprano*), his wife
FLORINDO (*Tenor*), in love with Rosaura
ARLECCHINO (*Bass*), Pantolone's servant, in love with Colombina

The action takes place in mid-eighteenth century Venice. The first act opens in a clubhouse where the motto is "women not admitted." Two of the club members are playing checkers and they remark that although the stake is heavy, the game is not for gold, but for honor. Further conversation shows that the meetings of the club are altogether innocent and harmless, and that the members are for the most part married men who seek temporary refuge from their wives. One of the members, Florindo, is not married, but he is engaged to the daughter of an older member, Ottavio. A secret password insures against wives gaining admittance to the clubhouse and it is agreed that each member's key will be closely guarded. The members leave for their homes and plan to return later when Pantolone will be host at an elaborate stag dinner. The second scene of the first act shows a room in Ottavio's house. The women are discussing their husbands' club and are certain that wild orgies are held there. Eleanora, wife of Lelio, says that the members are alchemists looking for a *Lapis Philosophorum*, a philosopher's stone. Colombina, a servant in Ottavio's household, declares that they are searching for a hidden treasure, while Beatrice, Ottavio's wife, is certain that the men gamble for high stakes. Rosaura, daughter of Beatrice and Ottavio, and Florindo's sweetheart, fears that they entertain loose women at their meetings. When Ottavio appears, the women try unsuccessfully to gain information. Colombina tries to learn something from her sweetheart, Arlecchino, who is Pantolone's servant, and Rosaura pretends to faint so that her Florindo wili tell her the truth about the club.

In the second act, in the house of Lelio, Eleanora, Lelio's wife, finds a letter in her husband's pocket. It contains information about new keys that have been made for the clubhouse. All of the women try to get the keys by various ruses, and Rosaura finally succeeds in getting Florindo's. He is a lovesick youth and cannot resist his sweetheart's pleading.

The third act opens outside the clubhouse. The women arrive and plan to enter. In the second scene, inside the club, the men are enjoying Pantolone's banquet. The women have entered and are peeking through the keyhole of an inner door. They are amazed to find that nothing scandalous is happening and that their menfolk are merely enjoying an excellent feast. They feel that it is better to leave, but they are so curious to see the various dishes that they lean too heavily against the door and all tumble into the dining room. It is their turn to be humble and apologetic, but they are soon forgiven and everyone joins in a merry dance.

§)&(§

THE EGYPTIAN HELEN

Richard Strauss

Hugo von Hofmannsthal wrote the libretto for Richard Strauss's two-act opera, *The Egyptian Helen,* and based its plot on an episode in Homer's *Odyssey* where Telemachus finds Menelaus and Helen living together at Lacedaemon. Helen maintains peace in the family by giving Menelaus a drink of nepenthe whenever he begins to talk or think about the embarrassing events of the Trojan War. Strauss's opera was produced first in Dresden, June 6, 1928.

The cast includes:

MENELAUS (*Tenor*)
HELEN (*Soprano*), his wife
HERMIONE (*Soprano*), their daughter
AITHRA (*Soprano*), an Egyptian sorceress
ALTAIR (*Baritone*), a desert chieftain
DA-UD (*Tenor*), Altair's son

The action occurs in Egypt and Morocco in ancient times. The first act shows the home of the sorceress Aithra, in Egypt. Aithra learns that Menelaus and Helen are on an approaching ship, returning home from Troy. She hears too that Menelaus is planning to stab Helen while she is sleeping. Aithra invokes a storm which wrecks the ship and Menelaus swims to shore with Helen and comes to Aithra's house. When they arrive Menelaus continues his denunciation of his faithless wife, Helen. He enumerates the brave Greeks and Trojans who died because of Helen's beauty, and he tells Helen that he was on the point of stabbing her when they were on the ship. He raises his dagger again but Aithra uses her magic power to stop him. She gives both Helen and Menelaus a magic potion and has them carried to an island.

The second act shows an oasis in a desert. While Helen

and Menelaus are still under the spell of the magic potion, the desert chief Altair appears with his son Da-Ud. Both are conquered by Helen's beauty. Menelaus imagines that Da-Ud is Paris, and kills him with his sword. Helen persuades Menelaus to drink a second cup of the magic potion. His memory returns, he recognizes Helen as his wife, and a horse appears bearing their young child, Hermione.

§)&(§

ELEKTRA

Richard Strauss

When Richard Strauss's *Elektra* was first produced, it was considered the last word in modern music, and its ear-splitting dissonances were altogether shocking to early twentieth-century ears. Yet it was recognized that the dissonances Strauss used were wholly appropriate to the modern psychological treatment which the librettist had given the ancient Greek legend of Orestes returning to avenge the murder of his father Agamemnon. The composer was not using discords for their own sake, he was masterful in piling horror upon horror against a background of gloom and despair.

The libretto of *Elektra* was written and was adapted from the Greek tragedy of Sophocles by Hugo von Hofmannsthal. The opera was first produced at the Hofoper in Dresden, January 25, 1909.

The cast includes:

KLYTEMNESTRA (*Mezzo-soprano*), the Queen, widow of Agamemnon

AEGISTHUS (*Tenor*), her lover
ORESTES (*Baritone*), her son
ELEKTRA (*Soprano*) } her daughters
CHRYSOTHEMIS (*Soprano*) }

The opera is written in one act, and the scene is laid in a courtyard at the rear of the palace. Klytemnestra and her lover, Aegisthus, have murdered Klytemnestra's husband, King Agamemnon. Orestes, the son, was sent into exile while yet a child. For years Klytemnestra has made her daughters, Elektra and Chrysothemis, live with the servants and has forced them to perform menial tasks. Chrysothemis is of a gentle disposition and is timid, but Elektra is filled with hate and thinks of little else than avenging her father's death. As the opera opens the servants are talking of the shameful treatment Elektra has suffered. When she enters she sings of her father and of the time when he will be avenged. Chrysothemis comes to tell Elektra that the Queen and her lover are planning to throw Elektra into prison. She begs Elektra to forget her hate so that they will be allowed to leave, and she, Chrysothemis, will be free to live a woman's life, to marry and to have a child. Elektra rebukes her, and Chrysothemis flees as the Queen approaches. When Klytemnestra appears, Elektra hides her hatred for the moment and by flattery leads the Queen to talk freely. Klytemnestra asks Elektra if there is some cure for her horrible dreams. Elektra answers that Klytemnestra can be helped only by the shedding of a woman's blood. The Queen is interested, and asks what woman should be slain. Elektra refuses to be specific, but says that the rite must be performed by a man who is a stranger, yet who belongs to their household. Elektra is thinking of her brother Orestes. Finally Elektra can hide her hate and anger no longer, and she turns on her mother and tells her that it is she who will be murdered. Klytemnestra is terror-stricken. She trembles and gasps for breath. Suddenly Klytemnestra's attendant appears and whispers in her ear. When the message is repeated, and the Queen understands what has been told her, her face lights with a savage joy, and she hurries into the palace. Chrysothemis rushes in to tell Elektra that an old messenger and a youth have come to announce that Orestes, their brother, is dead. At first, Elektra will not believe it, but at last she accepts the story and tells her sister that the two of them must avenge their father. She says she has an ax ready and that when Klytemnestra and Aegisthus are dead, she will be Chrysothemis' handmaiden; she will prepare her for her lover, and she will nurse her child. Chrysothemis is afraid, and refuses to have a part in the bloody deed. Chrysothemis leaves Elektra, and the youth who has brought word of Orestes' death appears. He asks Elektra if she is one of the servants. She tells him who she is and discovers that he is Orestes. She recounts how she has waited for him to avenge the death of their father. Orestes is eager to be on with the business and Elektra cries: "Happy is he who comes to end the work!" Orestes enters the palace and soon Klytemnestra's screams are heard. Aegisthus comes and Elektra leads him to the palace where Orestes is waiting for him. There is a fierce battle inside between the servants who side with Elektra and those who take the part of Aegisthus. Orestes is victorious and Aegisthus is killed. Elektra is filled with joy and dances madly. She is so overcome by her emotions and by her exertions that she falls senseless to the ground. Chrysothemis rushes to the door of the palace crying "Orestes! Orestes!"

§)&(§

L'ELISIR D'AMORE

(The Elixir of Love)

Gaetano Donizetti

Gaetano Donizetti's *L'Elisir d'Amore,* or in English, "The Love Potion," is a tuneful opera in the conventional Italian tradition. It has for its libretto a merry two-act comedy by Felice Romani. It was produced first at the Teatro della Canobbiana in Milan, May 12, 1832, and has remained a favorite in opera houses throughout the world.

The characters include:

ADINA (*Soprano*), a rich young lady
NEMORINO (*Tenor*), a young peasant
BELCORE (*Baritone*), a sergeant
DULCAMARA (*Bass*), an itinerant quack who sells love potions

The first act shows an Italian village. Adina, surrounded by her friends, is reading a romance. Nemorino, a peasant, watches from the distance, and sings a love-sick song—*Quanto e bella.* Adina bursts out laughing, not at Nemorino, but at the story she is reading. It is the legend of Tristan and Isolde, and she tells her friends how the knight won his lady's affections with a love potion. Nemorino wishes he had some of that elixir. The sergeant Belcore appears and brings Adina a bouquet. He receives no encouragement from the lady, so Nemorino thinks he himself may have a chance. But Adina tells him that he is rather dull and that he had better go visit his sick uncle. At this Dulcamara, the quack doctor, makes an impressive entrance in a splendid carriage. He sings of the wonderful love-potion he is selling. Nemorino begs the doctor for some of his elixir, and the quack produces a bottle of wine, which he says is the love-potion. Nemorino pays for it with his last coin and as soon as the doctor has departed he drinks the entire contents of the bottle. He immediately becomes very drunk, and dances and sings. Nemorino is so sure that the potion will win Adina without any effort on his part that he pays no attention to her. Adina resents his attitude, and in her pique she agrees to marry the sergeant Belcore in three days. The tipsy Nemorino only laughs, and the angry Adina says the wedding will take place this very day. Then Nemorino sobers a little, and he begs for delay in a heartfelt plea—*Adina credimi.* Adina and her friends laugh at him and get ready for the wedding.

The second act shows the interior of Adina's farmhouse. As the wedding party retires to another room to sign the marriage contract, Nemorino is alone with the quack Dr. Dulcamara. He tells Dulcamara that the potion did not work. Dulcamara is about to give him another bottle of wine, but puts it aside when he finds that Nemorino has no more money. Belcore appears. When he learns of Nemorino's difficulty he suggests that Nemorino enlist as a soldier. By doing so he will receive twenty crowns. Nemorino agrees and is paid the money. Then he runs out in search of the doctor. Meanwhile the peasant girls have learned that Nemorino's rich uncle has died and that Nemorino has inherited his money. When Nemorino reappears the girls gather about him and make a hero of him. Adina sees him surrounded by sixteen beautiful girls and decides that he is a most acceptable suitor. She weeps, and Nemorino, convinced that the love potion is responsible for her change of heart, sings the famous aria, *Una furtiva lagrima* ("A furtive tear.") Unfortunately Nemorino has enlisted in the army, but Adina buys his soldier's contract, and they embrace just as Belcore appears. He is not seriously concerned and remarks that there are other women. The doctor returns and takes all the credit for the happy ending, and as the opera ends the peasants flock around him, eager to spend their money for his wonderful love potion.

THE EMPEROR JONES

Louis Gruenberg

Louis Gruenberg used for his two-act opera, *The Emperor Jones,* the play of the same title by Eugene O'Neill, with a libretto written by Kathleen de Jaffa. The opera was first performed January 7, 1933 at the Metropolitan Opera House in New York.

The plot concerns a powerful Negro who had been a Pullman porter until he was jailed for murdering a friend during a crap game. Then he killed a guard, escaped, and stowed away on a ship which brought him to an island in the Caribbean. There his superior intelligence enabled him to dominate the natives and to declare himself "Emperor."

Aside from the subsidiary characters, the principal members of the cast are:

BRUTUS JONES (*Baritone*), the "Emperor"
HENRY SMITHERS (*Tenor*), a Cockney trader
A NATIVE WOMAN (*Soprano*)
A WITCH DOCTOR (*Dancer*)

A brief prologue establishes the mood of the story and brings the sound of a hidden chorus chanting "De Emperor, he must die!" The first act shows the throne room of Jones's palace. A native woman enters and is seized by Smithers, the Cockney trader who has helped the "Emperor" to loot and exploit the natives. He threatens the woman with a whip and she tells him that the servants have all deserted the palace and have joined the rest of the Emperor's subjects in a revolt. Jones makes a swaggering entrance, and boasts that he has made plans for an escape, if necessary. He has hidden food along a trail which leads to the coast at a point where a French coastal boat will pick him up and take him to a faraway place where he has had his riches deposited in a foreign bank. He also tells Smithers that if he should be caught, no ordinary bullet can harm him; he can meet death only by a silver bullet which he has in his own revolver.

Jones hears the menacing, monotonous tom-tom in the distance and summons his guards and servants. None answers and he realizes that they have all deserted. Announcing with bravado that he is resigning his job of Emperor, he takes his departure, nonchalantly whistling.

In a brief interlude the angry voices of the natives are again heard calling for the death of the Emperor, and the second act shows the tropical forest through which Jones is trying to escape. Throughout the act the tom-tom of the pursuers is heard, monotonous and persistent, at first far in the distance and then always drawing closer. Jones is cocky and defiant, but gradually he loses his way. He cannot find the food he had cached nor the marks he had intended to follow. He sheds his magnificent uniform, garment by garment. In his hallucinations he imagines that he sees the victims of his former crimes at home. He shoots at them and finds that they are only shadows. His bravado deserts him and he appeals to God for forgiveness of his many sins. He sings an old spiritual he remembers from his youth—"Standin' in de Need of Prayer."

By this time his shots have revealed his location to the pursuing natives. He has used up all the cartridges in his revolver except the one that is loaded with the silver bullet. At last the witch-doctor of the tribe stands before the terror-stricken Emperor. Jones makes a final attempt at bravado by shouting "De silver bullet! You won't get me!" He turns his revolver on himself and presses the trigger. The natives dance around his body and disappear into the forest. Smithers looks at the dead Emperor and remarks that he at least died in grand style.

DIE ENTFÜHRUNG AUS DEM SERAIL

(The Abduction from the Seraglio)

Wolfgang Amadeus Mozart

In the list of Mozart's works *Die Entführung aus dem Serail* is the fourteenth of his twenty-two operas, but it is generally considered the first really German opera, since earlier works were mostly imitations and translations of foreign operas. The libretto was written by Gottlob Stephanie, who founded it on a play by Christoph Friedrich Bretzner. The opera was first produced at the command of Joseph II July 16, 1782 at the Burgtheater in Vienna.

The action occurs in the sixteenth century at the country estate of the House of Bassa, in Northern Nigeria. The characters are:

SELIM BASSA (*a speaking part*)
CONSTANZE (*Soprano*)
BLONDCHEN (*Soprano*), her servant
BELMONTE (*Tenor*), betrothed to Constanze
PEDRILLO (*Tenor*), his servant, and lover of Blondchen
OSMIN (*Bass*), overseer of the Bassa estate

In the first act Constanze and Blondchen have fallen into the hands of Selim Bassa. Belmonte is seeking Constanze, his fiancée, and is looking also for his servant, Pedrillo. He learns that Pedrillo is on the estate, and Pedrillo in turn suggests to the Selim that Belmonte be engaged as a builder. Osmin, the overseer, refuses Belmonte access to the palace, but Belmonte determines that he will abduct Constanze.

In the second act Blondchen repulses the crude love-making of Osmin, the overseer. Constanze complains to Blondchen that the Selim is forcing his love on her. When Blondchen is alone, Pedrillo approaches her. He is Blondchen's lover, and to her delight he tells her that plans are made for the rescue. Pedrillo invites Osmin to drink with him and succeeds in getting him very drunk. This gives Belmonte a chance to see Constanze.

In the third act Belmonte and Pedrillo bring their ladders to the garden. Belmonte succeeds in rescuing Constanze, but Pedrillo and Blondchen are caught by Osmin. Belmonte and Constanze are arrested by the guards at the gates of the estate and are brought before the Selim. He recognizes Belmonte as the son of an enemy, but when he is about to order his death he relents and orders all the captives freed.

§)&(§

ERNANI

Giuseppe Verdi

Ernani was Giuseppe Verdi's fifth opera, and it was first performed at the Teatro La Fenice in Venice, March 9, 1844. Its libretto was founded on a play by Victor Hugo, *Hernani,* and was written by Francesco Maria Piave.

The principal characters are:

ERNANI *(Tenor),* a bandit
DON CARLOS *(Baritone),* King of Castile
DON RUY GOMEZ DE SILVA *(Bass),* a Spanish grandee
DONNA ELVIRA *(Soprano),* de Silva's niece, whom he wishes to marry

The action takes place at Aragon, in Aix-la-Chapelle, and at Saragossa, in the year 1519. The first act opens in a mountain retreat where Ernani, the son of a Spanish duke, has taken refuge after having been outlawed by the king. He tells his followers that he is in love with Donna Elvira, who is to be married to her aged uncle, Don Gomez de Silva. He asks his fellow bandits to help him abduct her. The next scene shows a room of Elvira's apartment in de Silva's castle. The girl can find no pleasure in the wedding presents that are brought to her. Don Carlos, King of Castile, appears in disguise. He makes love to Elvira and is about to force his attentions on her when Ernani comes to her rescue. Ernani and the King recognize each other and are about to fight when de Silva enters. The King takes off his disguise and pretends to de Silva that he came to consult him about his, the King's, coming election as Emperor, and about the conspiracy against his promotion and his life. Accordingly, both the King and Ernani are allowed to leave unmolested.

The second act occurs in a hall of de Silva's palace. Ernani, disguised as a pilgrim, comes to stop Elvira's wedding to her uncle, de Silva. De Silva does not recognize him and grants him shelter from the King, who is hunting him. Elvira has been told that Ernani is dead, and is overjoyed when Ernani reveals himself to her. They embrace just as de Silva enters. De Silva cannot harm Ernani because he has promised him shelter and safekeeping. When the King arrives and demands Ernani, de Silva hides the bandit. The King refuses to withdraw his troops until Elvira is given to him as a hostage. When the invaders have gone de Silva brings Ernani from his hiding place and challenges him. Ernani proposes that they first join forces to rescue Elvira from the King. Inasmuch as Ernani owes his life to de Silva, he pledges that he will forfeit it whenever Silva blows the horn which Ernani gives him.

The third act shows the tomb of Charlemagne. De Silva

and Ernani are plotting against the King, and it is decided by ballot that Ernani shall be the one to murder him. The King has been hiding in the tomb and overhears the plot. Simultaneously, the assembly of electors has chosen the King as Emperor Charles the Fifth and as he shows himself to the conspirators in the tomb they imagine that Charlemagne has risen against them from his grave. Elvira pleads with the newly elected Emperor for her lover and Carlos, now Charles the Fifth, in a burst of magnanimity, pardons Ernani and unites him to Elvira.

The last act takes place on the terrace of Ernani's palace at Saragossa. His lands and his title as Don Juan of Aragon have been restored to him, and he has just been happily married to Elvira. Suddenly the sound of a distant horn is heard. De Silva has come to demand fulfillment of Ernani's pledge. De Silva hands Ernani a dagger and the bridegroom, true to his promise, stabs himself. Ernani faints and falls on the body of her husband.

§)&(§

EUGEN ONEGIN

Peter Ilich Tchaikowsky

Peter Ilich Tchaikowsky collaborated with K. S. Shilovsky in writing the libretto of his opera *Eugen Onegin*. The plot was based on a poem by Alexander Pushkin, written in the years between 1822 and 1831. The opera was first produced by the Imperial College of Music at the Little Theatre, Moscow, March 29, 1879. Its first public performance occurred in Moscow, January 23, 1881.

The cast includes:

MADAME LARINA *(Mezzo-soprano)*
OLGA *(Contralto)* } her daughters
TATIANA *(Soprano)* }
FILIPIEVNA *(Mezzo-soprano),* their attendant
EUGEN ONEGIN *(Baritone)*
LENSKI *(Tenor)*
PRINCE GREMIN *(Baritone)*

The action occurs in Russia, around 1815. The first act shows a garden in a Russian village on the estate of Madame Larina. Madame Larina is sitting under a tree, listening to the singing of her daughters, Tatiana and Olga. The nurse Filipievna announces the arrival of Lenski and Eugen Onegin. Lenski is courting Olga and he brings Onegin to meet the sisters. Onegin is attracted to Tatiana and the two are left alone in the garden. Tatiana falls in love with Onegin immediately, and as soon as Onegin and Lenski have left, the scene changes to Tatiana's room, where she writes a long letter to Onegin, telling him of her love for him, and begging him to call again. At daybreak she sends the unwilling Filipievna to deliver the letter in person. Onegin replies by coming at once to see Tatiana. He tells her that he is not suited to marriage, that he is fickle, and that if he should marry her he would cease to love her the day after the wedding.

The second act opens in a large room in Madame Larina's house. A merry party is in progress. While Onegin is dancing with Tatiana he overhears the old ladies gossiping about him. They say that Tatiana is foolish to have a man of such wayward habits as a suitor. Onegin is irritated and for revenge makes love to Olga. He dances with Olga, and his friend Lenski is so jealous that he challenges Onegin to a duel. The scene changes to the bank of a river where Lenski and Onegin meet at daybreak. Lenski is killed and Onegin is grief-stricken at having slain his friend.

The third act occurs several years later, in the house of Prince Gremin at Petrograd. Onegin has been away on a trip around the world and he returns to find Tatiana married to Prince Gremin. Onegin realizes that he loves Tatiana, and when he pleads with her, she admits that she still loves him but says that her fate has been decided by her marriage to Prince Gremin. In spite of Onegin's persistence she will remain true to her husband, and she sends Onegin away.

§)&(§

EURYANTHE

Carl Maria von Weber

The libretto of Carl Maria von Weber's opera *Euryanthe* was written by Helmina von Chézy, and the work was first performed at the Kärntnertor-Theater in Vienna, October 25, 1823.

The cast includes:

KING LOUIS VI *(Bass)*
ADOLAR *(Tenor)*, Count of Nevers
EURYANTHE OF SAVOY *(Soprano)*, betrothed to Adolar
LYSIART *(Baritone)*, Count of Forest
EGLANTINE VON PUISET *(Mezzo-soprano)*, captive daughter of a mutineer

The action takes place at Castle Preméry and the Burg of Nevers in the year 1110. Adolar is betrothed to Euryanthe, who lives at Castle Nevers. Eglantine, captive daughter of a mutineer, has found refuge at Castle Nevers. She too is in love with Adolar, but he is loyal to Euryanthe. Euryanthe, in turn, is loved by Lysiart, but she herself is devoted to Adolar, her betrothed.

The first act shows a hall in the King's palace. The King announces to Adolar that he wants Euryanthe to appear at court, and he asks for a song in her praise. All except Lysiart join Adolar in singing of Euryanthe's charms and beauty. Lysiart is jealous of Adolar, not only because Adolar is betrothed to Euryanthe, but also because he is a hero in battle and is the owner of a vast estate. Lysiart suggests to Adolar that Euryanthe, like all women, is not to be relied on. He boasts that he could easily win her love. Adolar resents the insinuation and wagers his life and all his lands and fortune on Euryanthe's devotion. Lysiart accepts the challenge and the wager, and promises to bring to Adolar a visible token of Euryanthe's love for himself. The King is disturbed at such talk and tries to dissuade both Adolar and Lysiart from their foolish bet. Each is determined to prove that he is right. The scene changes to the garden of the palace at Nevers. Euryanthe tells Eglantine a secret about Adolar and his former sister, Emma. Emma had been betrothed to a soldier who was killed in battle. In her grief she killed herself by drinking poison from a ring. Later she appeared in spirit to Adolar, and told him that her soul could find no rest until the tears of an innocent person in deep distress had been shed upon the ring which had caused her death and which was still upon her finger in the tomb. As soon as Euryanthe has told this secret to Eglantine, she regrets that she has broken her vow of secrecy to Adolar. The treacherous Eglantine soothes Euryanthe and assures her that the secret is safe with her. Later, when Eglantine is alone with Lysiart and learns of Lysiart's wager with Adolar, she realizes that she can use her knowledge to separate Adolar and Euryanthe.

The second act continues in the garden. Lysiart is not too sure that he can win the love of Euryanthe. Eglantine comes to him. She has been to the tomb and has taken the ring from Emma's finger. She shows it to Lysiart, who promises to marry her if she will give it to him so that he can offer it as a token of Euryanthe's love. The scene changes to the hall in the King's palace, where Adolar is being married to Euryanthe. Lysiart appears before the court, and in the presence of the King declares himself the winner of the wager. He offers Emma's ring as proof. Since Adolar believes that Euryanthe was the only person who knew the secret of his sister's ring, he concludes that Euryanthe has been unfaithful. True to the wager, he forfeits his lands and his fortunes, and goes into exile with Euryanthe, his supposedly unfaithful bride.

The third act is laid in a forest. Adolar has deserted Euryanthe and has left her to perish in the forest. The King is hunting in the forest and finds Euryanthe. She tells the King how she revealed the secret of Emma's ring to Eglantine. The King declares that the conspirators shall be punished and that Euryanthe shall be pronounced innocent. The scene changes to the garden of the castle at Nevers. Lysiart, now wealthy, is about to be married to Eglantine. Just before the wedding party arrives, Adolar learns from a group of peasants that Euryanthe is innocent, and that Lysiart plotted his downfall with Eglantine. As the bridal procession passes he challenges Lysiart. The King appears and declares Euryanthe innocent. Eglantine confesses and Lysiart stabs her. Lysiart is condemned and Adolar's estate is restored. Euryanthe and Adolar embrace, and Adolar declares that Emma's spirit may now rest in peace, for her ring has been wet by the tears of innocence.

DER EVANGELIMANN

(The Evangelist)

Wilhelm Kienzl

Wilhelm Kienzl, composer of the opera *Der Evangelimann*, wrote also its text, adapting it from a story by L. F. Meissner. The opera was first produced at the Opernhaus in Berlin, May 4, 1895.

The cast includes:

JOHANNES FREUDHOFER *(Baritone)*, a teacher at the St. Othmar Monastery
MATTHIS FREUDHOFER *(Tenor)*, his brother, clerk of the monastery
FRIEDERICH ENGEL *(Bass)*, steward of the monastery
MARTHA *(Soprano)*, Friederich's niece
MAGDALENA *(Contralto)*, a friend of Martha

The action occurs in Vienna during the latter part of the nineteenth century. The first act shows the courtyard of the Benedictine Monastery of St. Othmar. Johannes, the teacher, is jealous of his brother Matthis, the monastery clerk, because the steward's daughter, Martha, is in love with Matthis rather than with himself. Johannes tells Engel, the steward, about the love affair between Martha and Matthis, and the steward dismisses Matthis from his office as clerk. This does not satisfy Johannes, for as Matthis leaves, Johannes sees him making renewed love to Martha. Johannes sets fire to the monastery and accuses Matthis of being the incendiary. Matthis is arrested.

The second act occurs thirty years later, and the scene is laid in a courtyard of a house in Vienna. Magdalena, a former friend of Martha, meets an evangelist and recognizes him as Matthis. She is caring for Matthis' brother, Johannes, who is ill. She asks Matthis about himself, and he tells her that he served a prison sentence of twenty years and then learned that his sweetheart Martha had drowned herself from grief. For ten years he has sought comfort by being a wandering singing preacher. The scene changes to a sitting room where Johannes lies ill. In addition to a sick body he has a tortured mind. He hears outside the voice of the evangelist and he tells Magdalena to ask him in. Johannes confesses to the evangelist the crime which ruined his brother's life. Matthis tells Johannes who he is and forgives him, and Johannes feels that he may now die in peace.

§)&(§

THE FAIR AT SOROCHINTZKY

Modeste Moussorgsky

Modeste Moussorgsky did not live to complete his opera, *The Fair at Sorochintzky*. It was finished and orchestrated by M. N. Tcherepnine. The libretto was written by Moussorgsky himself, and was adapted from a tale by N. V. Gogol. The Tcherepnine version was first performed at Monte Carlo, March 17, 1923.

The characters include:

TCHEREVIK *(Bass)*, a peasant
KHIVRIA *(Mezzo-soprano)*, his wife
PARASSIA *(Soprano)*, his daughter
OKHRIM *(Bass)*, an old crony of Tcherevik's
GRITZKO *(Tenor)*, a young peasant
THE PASTOR'S SON *(Tenor)*
A GYPSY *(Bass)*

The action takes place at Sorochintzky, a village of little Russia, and the first act shows a fair. Tcherevik, an old peasant, comes with his beautiful daughter, Parassia. The young peasant Gritzko picks up an acquaintance with Parassia, and puts his arm around her waist. The father interrupts their conversation and gently reproves Gritzko, who replies that he is the son of Tcherevik's old crony, Okhrim, and that he would like to marry Parassia. This makes everything all right with Tcherevik, and he proceeds to celebrate by getting drunk with his old crony, Okhrim. On the way home he and Okhrim meet Tcherevik's wife, Khivria. When they tell her the news she is so angry that Okhrim decides he had better be off. Gritzko is disheartened, and he bribes a gypsy to help him win Parassia.

The second act shows Tcherevik's cottage. Tcherevik wakes from his drunken sleep and Khivria tells him she would have been happier if she had married the pastor's son. Then she orders him from the house. Soon the pastor's son calls on Khivria, and just as he is about to make love to her the sound of Tcherevik's voice is heard. Khivria hides the pastor's son in the attic, and Tcherevik enters with his friends and a gypsy. The ceiling groans under the weight of the pastor's son, and the gypsy frightens everyone by declaring that the place is haunted. After a number of objects have dropped through the ceiling the pastor's son climbs down. Khivria is compromised.

The third act is laid in the village square. Because of the scandal of the pastor's son, Khivria is humble. Tcherevik gives his permission for the marriage of Parassia and Gritzko. Khivria tries to object but is soon silenced. The peasants dance a hopak and rejoice at the coming wedding.

§)&(§

FALSTAFF

Giuseppe Verdi

Falstaff was Giuseppe Verdi's twenty-seventh and last opera. In his eightieth year he turned from the field of tragedy and produced a comedy which has provided operatic baritones with one of their favorite roles. The libretto of *Falstaff* was written by Arrigo Boïto, and was adapted from Shakespeare's *Merry Wives of Windsor* and from those parts of *Henry IV* which introduce Falstaff. The opera was first presented at La Scala in Milan, February 9, 1893.

The cast includes:

SIR JOHN FALSTAFF *(Baritone)*
FORD *(Baritone)*, a wealthy burgher
MISTRESS FORD *(Soprano)*, his wife
ANNE *(Soprano)*, their daughter
FENTON *(Tenor)*, Anne's suitor
DR. CAIUS *(Tenor)*, a physician, whom Ford has chosen as a husband for his daughter
MISTRESS PAGE *(Soprano)*
DAME QUICKLY *(Contralto)*
BARDOLPH *(Tenor)* } followers of Falstaff
PISTOL *(Bass)* }

The action takes place at Windsor, during the reign of Henry IV. The first act opens in the Garter Inn, where Dr. Caius complains to Falstaff that his followers, Bardolph and Pistol, have robbed him. The followers deny it and throw Caius out. Falstaff has decided to try his luck in the field of love, and has written amorous letters to two of the most respectable women in the town, Mistress Ford and Mistress Page. He orders his followers to deliver the notes. They refuse, and Falstaff gives the letters to a page. The second scene shows the garden of Ford's house. Mistress Ford and Mistress Page are talking with Dame Quickly. The two women have received Falstaff's notes. They compare the letters and find that they are precisely the same in every word. The ladies agree that they must have revenge. Anne, the Fords' daughter, meets her lover Fenton. Her father wants her to marry the wealthy Dr. Caius, but her mother promises her that she may have the young Fenton. Falstaff's followers, Bardolph and Pistol, tell Ford of Falstaff's designs on his wife, and Ford too plans revenge. He arranges that he will be introduced to Falstaff under an assumed name. The women have their own plan for vengeance, and send Dame Quickly to arrange an appointment for Falstaff to meet them the next day.

The second act begins at the Garter Inn. Bardolph and Pistol announce Dame Quickly, who brings the note from Mistress Ford and Mistress Page. Falstaff is delighted and is in an expansive mood when Ford calls on him, introducing himself as Mr. Fountain. Mr. Fountain confides that he is very much in love with Mistress Ford. He asks Falstaff to help him, so the fat knight tells him that he himself has an appointment with Mistress Ford for this very afternoon, while her husband is away. He will be glad to assist Mr. Fountain. Ford is astonished, and decides that his wife is really deceiving him. Falstaff puts on his finest clothing and he and Ford leave for the appointment with the ladies. The second scene of the act takes place in Ford's house. The women are ready for Falstaff, and have the servants bring in a huge basket filled with dirty linen. Falstaff arrives and starts making love to Mistress Ford. Dame Quickly rushes in to say that Ford is coming. Mistress Ford hides Falstaff behind a screen just before her husband enters with Dr. Caius, Bardolph and Pistol. Ford orders the men to search the house and himself looks into the linen basket. Just as he rushes out of the room, Falstaff comes from behind the screen and climbs into the basket while Mistress Ford and

Dame Quickly cover him with the soiled linen. Fenton arrives with his sweetheart, Anne Ford, and the young people decide that they can talk more quietly and privately behind the screen. Ford and the men return, still hunting for Falstaff. Ford looks at the screen and decides that Falstaff must be behind it. The men surround it, and then when they take it away, find only the two young lovers. Thwarted, they rush out again, and Falstaff, nearly suffocated, cries to the women to let him out. Mistress Ford orders her servants to carry the basket away. They take it to the window, balance it on the sill, and then drop it into the river. When Ford comes back, Mistress Ford takes him to the window and shows him what has happened to his rival.

The third act opens at the Inn. The women are not yet finished with Falstaff. They send Dame Quickly to tell him that Mistress Ford is distressed over what happened to him, and to assure him that she will have a rendezvous with him tonight in Windsor Park. Falstaff is still gullible and is much elated. This time Ford is taken into the secret, and he promises Dr. Caius that he shall have the hand of Anne, his daughter. Dame Quickly overhears the conversation and runs to tell the others. The second scene shows the park. Fenton and Anne promise to be true to each other. Mistress Ford arrives and throws a cloak around Fenton and gives him a mask. Falstaff begins making love to Mistress Ford, but is interrupted by Mistress Page, who cries that witches are coming. Falstaff is terrified, and falls on the ground, hiding his face. The others rush in, disguised as witches, and immediately fall upon Falstaff and beat him. He cries for mercy and admits his sins. Bardolph, dressed as a fairy queen comes hand-in-hand with the disguised Dr. Caius. Meanwhile Mistress Ford presents Anne disguised as a nymph, together with Fenton in his cloak and mask. Ford performs a marriage ceremony for the couple, and everybody unmasks. Ford discovers that he has married his daughter to the wrong man and Dr. Caius finds that his fairy queen is Bardolph. All are finally reconciled and have comfort in the vengeance they have taken on Falstaff.

§)&(§

FAUST

Charles-François Gounod

Charles-François Gounod's *Faust* was produced first at the Théatre Lyrique in Paris, March 19, 1859. Its libretto was written by Jules Barbier and Michel Carré, who founded it on Goethe's dramatic poem.

The plot deals with *Faust*, the mortal, who sold his soul to the Devil in return for earthly pleasures. The librettists confined themselves to a single episode of Goethe's tragedy: the affair between Faust and Gretchen, who is named Marguerite in Gounod's opera.

The cast includes:

FAUST *(Tenor)*, a Doctor of Philosophy
MEPHISTOPHELES *(Bass)*, the Devil
MARGUERITE *(Soprano)*
VALENTINE *(Baritone)*, her brother
SIEBEL *(Mezzo-soprano)*, a young man, her suitor
MARTHA *(Contralto)*, her companion

The first act shows Faust's study, where the learned Doctor of Philosophy is seated at a table covered with books and papers. He is weary of life, for he feels he has had all it can offer; each day is like the last. Death is the only remedy and he resolves to seek it through poison. Suddenly he hears a crowd of young people singing. He is envious of their youth, and he curses and cries aloud to the Devil. Suddenly Mephistopheles appears before him and asks him what he wants. Faust replies that he longs for youth and the joy of beauty's caresses. Mephistopheles promises them to him, and swears to be his servant if after death Faust will be his slave. Faust hesitates, and Mephistopheles shows him a vision of the beautiful Marguerite and asks Faust if he could love her. Faust hastens to sign the agreement, and sings, "Oh youth without measure, be mine thy delight."

The second act shows a Kermess or church fair, where the students and villagers are singing and making merry with the soldiers leaving for the battle front. Among the departing soldiers is Valentine, Marguerite's brother, who dislikes leaving his sister alone and unprotected. Siebel, a youth of the village, is in love with Marguerite, and he promises Valentine that he will protect her as though he were her brother. After this pledge of protection, a student starts to sing a song and is suddenly interrupted by the appearance of Mephistopheles in disguise, who announces that he knows a much better song. The students order him to sing it, and he responds with a satirical ballad—"The Calf of Gold Is always King." This jesting song of Mephistopheles pleases the fancy of the soldiers and students, and they offer him a glass of wine. After a ribald jest, Mephistopheles proposes a toast to Marguerite. Enraged at having his sister insulted, Valentine draws his sword. Mephistopheles draws a circle around himself, which magically breaks Valentine's sword at its first thrust. The crowd realizes that the mysterious stranger is none other than the Devil himself, and the soldiers make the sign of the cross, from which Mephistopheles shrinks. The merrymakers start again to dance and Faust sees Marguerite as she returns from church. He asks if he may escort her home, but she refuses. Faust complains to Mephistopheles that Marguerite will have nothing to do with him. Mephistopheles promises to teach Faust to woo her effectively.

The third act is laid in the garden of Marguerite's home. Faust and Mephistopheles enter and Faust sings a soliloquy to the home of the maiden. Marguerite comes from the house and seats herself at the spinning wheel. She starts to sing a ballad about the "King of Thule" but cannot remember all of it because she keeps thinking of the handsome stranger who accosted her at the Kermess. Meanwhile Mephistopheles has placed a casket of jewels where Marguerite may find them. When she sees the jewels she is dazzled. She puts them on and can hardly believe that it is she who is wearing them. She sings the famous "Jewel Song" and then Faust tells her that the jewels are hers. Mephistopheles casts a spell over the garden to keep all intruders out while Faust woos Marguerite. Together they sing a duet and as they finish Mephistopheles laughs with satiric glee.

In Act Four, Marguerite is alone in her room, spinning and enduring the tortures of remorse. From outside she hears the jeering remarks of the village girls. Siebel is the only friend who remains faithful. The scene changes to the cathedral. Marguerite seeks comfort, but while she kneels in prayer, she hears the mocking voice of Mephistopheles. She rushes from the cathedral, terror-stricken and desperate. Again the scene changes, to the square in front of the cathedral. The armies are returning, singing the soldiers' chorus. Valentine is one of the soldiers, and after the crowds have left, he learns from Siebel of Marguerite's affair with Faust. He challenges Faust to a duel, but he has no chance for life, for Mephistopheles has arranged that he be mortally wounded. As Valentine dies he curses his sister Marguerite and tells her that he is dying by her hand.

In the fifth and last act Marguerite is in prison. She has had a child by Faust and in her despair has murdered it. Faust comes to her and asks her to fly with him. When she sees that Mephistopheles is with him, she recoils in horror. Mephistopheles cries "condemned" and takes Faust to Hell. Marguerite implores the forgiveness of Heaven, and sinks lifeless to the ground. Angels come and carry her soul toward Heaven.

§)&(§

LA FAVORITA

Gaetano Donizetti

Gaetano Donizetti's *La Favorita* was first produced at the Grand Opéra in Paris, December 2, 1840. Its libretto was based on a play by Baculard-Darnand, entitled *Le Comte de Comminges,* and was written by Alphonse Royer and Gustave Vaëz.

The characters are:

ALPHONSO XI (*Baritone*), King of Castile
LEONORA DI GUSMANN *(Soprano),* his mistress
DON GASPAR *(Tenor),* the King's minister
FERDINAND *(Tenor),* a novice at the Convent of St. James of Compostella, afterwards an officer in the army of Alphonso
BALTHAZAR *(Bass),* Superior of the Convent
INEZ (*Soprano*), confidante to Leonora

The action occurs in Castile, about 1340, and the first act opens at The Convent of St. James, where the novice

Ferdinand confesses to the Superior, Balthazar, that he has fallen in love with a lady whose name he does not know. Balthazar reluctantly frees Ferdinand from his obligations, but warns him that he will return, disillusioned and heartbroken. The scene changes to the Isle de Leon, where Leonora, the King's mistress, lives in luxury. It is she whom Ferdinand loves without knowing of her relations to the King. Ferdinand comes to the island and makes love to Leonora. She returns his love and tries to prevent his learning her real station in life. She secures for him a commission in the army and sends him away. Ferdinand thinks he has won the love of a lady of high rank and hopes to become worthy of her by distinguishing himself in the army service.

The second act shows the palace of the King. Balthazar appears with an order from the Pope, commanding King Alphonso to give up his mistress Leonora and to restore his wife, the Queen, to her rightful place in his household. The King is furious but does not care to risk excommunication.

In the third act Ferdinand returns from battle. By his bravery he has saved Alphonso's army from defeat. Alphonso tells him to name his own reward, and Ferdinand asks for the hand of Leonora. The King is taken aback by this request, but faced with the Pope's command, he consents to the marriage of Leonora and Ferdinand. He announces that the wedding shall take place within an hour. Leonora loves Ferdinand too much to deceive him, and sends Inez with a message to Ferdinand telling him that she has been the King's mistress. Don Gaspar, the King's minister, intercepts the message, for he does not want such a convenient solution to the King's problems interfered with. When Leonora is married to Ferdinand, however, she thinks that he knows the truth and has forgiven her. At the wedding reception the couple is coldly received, and soon Ferdinand is told about his wife's past. Ferdinand denounces the King and Leonora.

In the fourth act Ferdinand returns to the monastery. Leonora follows him, disguised as a novice. She tells Ferdinand of the message he did not receive. He is quite willing to forgive her and to leave the monastery, but she replies that it is too late and falls dying into his arms. Ferdinand throws himself beside Leonora's dead body, where the monks find him as they return from church.

§)&(§

FEDORA

Umberto Giordano

The libretto of Umberto Giordano's *Fedora* was adapted by Arturo Colautti from a play by Victorien Sardou. It was performed first at the Teatro Lirico in Milan, November 17, 1898. The characters include:

PRINCESS FEDORA ROMANZOV *(Soprano)*
COUNT LORIS IPANOV *(Tenor),* assassin of Fedora's fiancé; later Fedora's husband
DE SIRIEX *(Baritone),* a diplomat
GRECH *(Bass),* a police officer

The first act shows the house of Count Vladimir, in St. Petersburg. The servants talk about the coming marriage of Count Vladimir to Princess Fedora. The Princess comes to meet her fiancé, and while she is waiting for him and gazing lovingly at his portrait he is brought in fatally wounded. The police suspect Count Loris Ipanov of the crime. Loris lives across the street and is supposed to be a Nihilist. After the officers have gone to find Loris, Vladimir dies, and Fedora swears that she will avenge his death.

The second act is laid in Fedora's Paris salon. She entertains Count Loris at a reception and hopes that he will reveal himself as the murderer of Vladimir. Loris falls in love with Fedora, and does indeed confess to her that he was the man who killed Vladimir. Fedora passes the word to Grech, the police officer, who plans to arrest Loris as soon as the guests have gone. After the reception Loris returns for a rendezvous with Fedora. He talks further about the death of Count Vladimir, and tells Fedora that the Count had seduced his, Loris's, wife and caused her death. On learning that the murder was justified, Fedora realizes that she loves Loris. Knowing that the trap for him is already set and that the police are waiting outside, she helps him to escape.

The third act shows Fedora's villa in Switzerland. She and Loris are married. Soon their happiness is disturbed by a spy who has discovered Loris's hiding place. He brings word that Loris's brother has been arrested, and that their mother has died from shock and grief. Loris curses the informer who brought this trouble to his family, and Fedora cringes, for she knows that it was she who told the police that Loris had killed Count Vladimir. When Loris learns the truth, he is about to kill her, even though she insists that she had informed the police before, and not after, she learned why he had committed the murder. In despair she swallows a vial of poison and dies in Loris's arms as he forgives her and begs her to live so that she may always love him.

§)&(§

FEUERSNOT

(A Famine of Fire)

Richard Strauss

This one-act opera by Richard Strauss was produced first at Dresden, November 21, 1901. Its libretto was written by Ernest von Wolzogen.

The characters include:

KUNRAD (*Baritone*), a student of magic
DIEMUT (*Soprano*), daughter of the Burgomaster

The action occurs in thirteenth-century Munich, where the citizens are following an old custom by collecting firewood for the winter. They come to the house of Kunrad, who tells them to take all the wood in his yard. When Kunrad sees in the crowd Diemut, the beautiful daughter of the Burgomaster, he is so entranced that he seizes her and kisses her. She is embarrassed at a public caress, and although she is interested in the young man, she traps him in a basket when he comes to call on her. Kunrad has studied magic, and in revenge he uses what he has learned to bring upon the town intense cold and utter darkness. The suffering people plead with Diemut to accept Kunrad's love. She was only parrying Kunrad's advances, and really loves him, so she relents, and Kunrad orders light and warmth to return to the town.

§)&(§

FIDELIO

Ludwig van Beethoven

Fidelio was Ludwig van Beethoven's only opera. Its libretto was written by Joseph Sonnleithner after Bouilly's novel,

Leonore. The opera was first produced at the Theater an der Wien in Vienna, November 20, 1805.

The plot concerns Leonore, who assumes the disguise of a boy (Fidelio) in order to rescue her husband from death in a Spanish prison.

The cast includes:

DON FLORESTAN *(Tenor)*, a prisoner
LEONORE *(Soprano)*, his wife, who disguises herself as FIDELIO
DON FERNANDO *(Baritone)*, Prime Minister of Spain
DON PIZARRO *(Baritone)*, governor of the prison at Seville
ROCCO *(Bass)*, a jailer
MARZELLINE *(Soprano)*, his daughter
JACQUINO *(Tenor)*, his assistant

The action takes place at the prison in Seville, and the first act shows its courtyard. Florestan has incurred the hatred of Pizarro, governor of the prison, and has been thrown into a dungeon. Pizarro is so sure that Florestan will soon die of starvation that he has already circulated the report of his death. Leonore, Florestan's wife, does not believe the rumor. She disguises herself as a boy, "Fidelio," and by becoming assistant to Rocco, the jailer, learns that her husband is still alive, but is to be starved to death. Marzelline, Rocco's daughter, falls in love with "Fidelio," who promises to marry her if she will keep "him" near Florestan. Don Fernando, the Prime Minister, sends word that he is coming to inspect the prison. Pizarro accordingly orders Rocco to murder Florestan so that Don Fernando will not find him there. Rocco refuses to kill Florestan, but agrees to dig a grave if Pizarro himself commits the murder. Leonore overhears the plot and sings that with God's aid she will be able to save her husband. As Fidelio, she requests that the prisoners be brought into the sunlight. She hopes that in this way she will be able to get a message to Florestan. When the prisoners come into the sunlight they sing a chorus: "O, what joy in Heaven's fresh air." Florestan is not brought out with the others.

The second act shows the dungeon of the prison. Leonore, as Fidelio, has come with Rocco to help prepare the grave. While she is digging, Rocco produces Florestan. He is so weak and emaciated that Leonore hardly recognizes him. Pizarro enters and announces: "He dies, but first he shall know his slayer." As Pizarro is about to thrust a dagger into Florestan's breast, Leonore hurls herself in front of her husband and cries, "First kill his wife." She draws a pistol and forces Pizzaro to retreat. In the midst of this episode, the Prime Minister appears on his tour of inspection. The scene changes to the courtyard. The Prime Minister orders the chains taken from Florestan and put on Pizarro. Marzelline is comforted in the loss of Fidelio by finding another sweetheart in Jacquino, Rocco's new assistant jailer.

§)&(§

THE FLYING DUTCHMAN

(Die Fliegende Holländer)

Richard Wagner

The Flying Dutchman was one of Richard Wagner's earlier operas. It was first performed at Dresden, January 2, 1843, within a few months after *Rienzi* was produced. In *The Flying Dutchman* Wagner began the development of his system of *leit-motifs,* short melodic phrases which he used to identify characters, emotions, and abstract ideas related to the plot and action.

Wagner himself wrote the libretto of *The Flying Dutchman* and its plot deals with the legend of the Dutch captain who tried to double the Cape of Good Hope in a furious storm. He swore that he would do it even if he had to keep on sailing forever. The Devil heard his oath, and condemned him to sail the seas until the Day of Judgment, aimlessly and without hope of freedom, unless he could find a woman who would love him faithfully until death. Once every seven years the Dutchman is allowed to go ashore in search of such a woman.

The principal characters of the opera are:

THE DUTCHMAN (*Baritone*)
DALAND (*Bass*), a Norwegian sea captain
SENTA (*Soprano*) his daughter
ERIC (*Tenor*), her lover
MARY (*Contralto*), Senta's nurse
DALAND'S STEERSMAN (*Tenor*)

The opera begins during one of the seven-year interruptions of the Dutchman's sentence. The first act shows a bay in Norway into which Daland, a Norwegian captain, has come for shelter from a storm. The Dutchman's ship comes to anchor beside Daland's vessel. The masts of the Dutchman's ship are black and its sails blood-red. The Dutchman meets Daland, and asks him to take him to his home, offering him a large sum for shelter. The Dutchman learns that Daland has a daughter, and he asks if he may court her. Daland is delighted at the prospect of a rich son-in-law, and he and the Dutchman set out for Daland's nearby home.

The second act shows a room in Daland's house. Senta, Daland's daughter, Mary, her nurse, and a group of Norwegian girls are spinning, and they sing the famous "Spinning Chorus" of the opera. A picture of the Flying Dutchman hangs on the wall, and Senta sings a ballad which tells the story of the legend. Eric, a huntsman who is in love with Senta, comes to tell her that her father's ship is entering the harbor. Senta starts out to meet her father but Eric detains her. He knows that Daland is anxious to find a husband for Senta, and Eric wants to be the man. He is much troubled by a dream he has had, in which Senta and her father met the man whose picture hangs in her house. Eric dreamed that Senta promised to marry the man in the picture. Senta is greatly excited, and cries that she has always been interested in the Flying Dutchman's picture and story, and that the dream must mean that he is seeking her. Eric leaves in despair, and Senta stays alone in the room, gazing at the picture. Daland asks Senta if she will marry the Dutchman and in a long duet she vows that she will share his fate and be faithful to him until death. Daland is delighted and invites the Dutchman to his own ship for a gala celebration. The Dutchman rejoices that his hour of liberation is near.

The third act shows the harbor. The Norwegian sailors on Daland's ship are dancing and singing, and maidens bring them food and refreshment. The Dutchman's ship, anchored near by, is dark, and the maidens try in vain to rouse the members of its crew and to invite them to share in the festivities. Later, while the Norwegian crew is eating and drinking, the sailors on the Dutchman's ship come to life and sing the story of their captain. While they sing, weird blue lights flicker above their ship and the waters around both ships become rough and menacing. The Norwegian sailors are frightened, and they try to drown out the voices of the Dutchmen with their own singing. Fright becomes terror, and the Norwegians run into their cabins making the sign of the cross. The Dutchmen burst into shrill laughter. They stop singing, the waters become quiet, and, as the weird lights disappear, everything becomes dark and silent. Eric appeals once more to Senta, and while he is talking to her the Dutchman sees them. Thinking that Senta is unfaithful to him he rushes off to his ship. Senta tries to follow the Dutchman and Eric cries for help. Then the Dutchman tells Daland and the Norwegian maidens who he is, boards his ship and puts to sea. Senta tries to follow but is held back. She frees herself, climbs a cliff, and shouting to the Dutchman that she is faithful unto death, throws herself into the water. The Dutchman's ship sinks, the sea rises, and against the glow of the sunset Senta and the Dutchman rise from the sea, each clasped in the other's arms.

§)&(§

LA FORZA DEL DESTINO

(The Force of Destiny)

Giuseppe Verdi

La Forza del Destino was Giuseppe Verdi's twenty-third opera. It was commissioned for performance at St. Petersburg, Russia, and was first produced there November 10, 1862. The libretto of the opera was written by Francesco Maria Piave and is a cumbersome melodrama laid in mid-eighteenth-century Spain and Italy. The principal characters are:

THE MARQUIS OF CALATRAVA (*Bass*)
LEONORA (*Soprano*) his daughter
DON CARLOS (*Baritone*), his son
DON ALVARO (*Tenor*), a native of India living in Seville
A FRANCISCAN ABBOT (*Bass*)

The first act shows a room in the house of the Marquis. Don Alvaro, a nobleman from India, is in love with the Marquis' daughter, Leonora. Alvaro is not highly regarded in Seville and the Marquis is strongly opposed to his daughter's marrying him. Leonora plans to elope with Alvaro and her father appears just as the couple are about to escape. Alvaro challenges the Marquis to take him prisoner or else to wreak vengeance on him. He throws down his pistol. The pistol discharges accidentally and fatally wounds the Marquis. The Marquis curses his daughter as he dies.

The first scene of the second act shows an inn at Hornacuelos. Don Carlos, son of the late Marquis and brother of Leonora, has sworn to avenge his father's death by killing both Leonora and Alvaro, her lover. Leonora enters, disguised as a man. When she sees her brother intent on revenge, she flees to the Convent of Hornacuelos. The second scene shows the entrance to the Convent. Leonora is kneeling in the moonlight, and in the aria, "Holy Mother Have Mercy," she prays for the Virgin's protection. She knocks at the door, and tells her story to the Abbot who shows her a hidden cave in the mountains. There she may live as a hermit, clad in the robe of a nun. The Abbot and the Franciscan monks pray that a curse may fall on anyone who comes to this spot or tries to learn who Leonora is. As Leonora enters the cave she joins the Abbot and the monks in singing another prayer, "May Angels Guard Thee."

In the third act the scene changes to Italy, to a military camp near Viletti. Alvaro has enlisted in the Spanish army. Believing that Leonora is dead he hopes to meet death himself. He sings to Leonora in Heaven to help him and to have mercy on his sufferings. He saves the life of a wounded man and does not know that it is Carlos. Nor does Carlos recognize Alvaro. They become friends, and later, when

Alvaro is wounded and thinks he is dying, the two pledge friendship in a duet, "Swear in This Hour." Alvaro hands Carlos a packet of letters. He asks that they be destroyed, and he makes Carlos promise not to read them. Instead of dying, Alvaro recovers, and in the next scene Carlos learns who he is, not by reading the letters, but by finding a picture of Leonora in the packet. Carlos challenges Alvaro, and Alvaro tries to dissuade him by protesting that he did not wrong Leonora. Carlos says that if Alvaro will not fight, he will find the still living Leonora and will kill her instead. This threat forces Alvaro to fight, and he wounds Carlos. Believing that he has killed Leonora's brother as well as her father, he is filled with remorse and decides to enter a monastery.

The fourth act returns to the Monastery at Hornacuelos. Alvaro has become Father Raphael. Carlos finds him and insists that they fight another duel. Alvaro pleads that he is a man of peace and cannot fight, but Carlos calls him a coward and so taunts him that Alvaro finally agrees that they will find a spot where they can fight it out.

In some versions of the opera the action continues at the monastery but in others the scene changes to a spot outside of Leonora's cave. Alvaro recognizes it as a place where all who come will be cursed, and he remarks that it is a fitting place for such a duel. Carlos is fatally wounded and asks Alvaro to bless him as he dies. Alvaro realizes that he is now under a curse and cannot perform the last rites for a dying man. He summons the hermit who lives in the cave to give the blessing. Leonora comes from the cave and immediately recognizes the dying man as her brother. She embraces him but he, still intent on revenge, stabs her. Alvaro flings himself from a precipice as the monks sing a *Miserere*.

§)&(§

FRA DIAVOLO

Daniel François Auber

Augustine Eugene Scribe furnished the libretto for Daniel François Auber's *Fra Diavolo*, which was first produced at the Opéra Comique, Paris, January 28, 1830.

The plot concerns a bandit, Fra Diavolo, who is disguised as the Marquis of San Marco. The principal characters are:

FRA DIAVOLO (*Tenor*), a bandit chief
LORD COCKBURN (*Bass*), an English tourist
LADY PAMELA COCKBURN (*Mezzo-soprano*), his wife
LORENZO (*Tenor*), an officer of the guard
MATTEO (*Bass*), an innkeeper
ZERLINE (*Soprano*), his daughter
FRANCESCO (*Baritone*), a miller
GIACOMO (*Bass*), a bandit
BEPPO (*Tenor*), a bandit

The action takes place during the early nineteenth century, in a Terracine village. The first act shows Matteo's tavern. An officer of the guard, Lorenzo, has come to capture the notorious bandit, Fra Diavolo. He wants to win the reward that has been offered for Fra Diavolo, and also the hand of Matteo's pretty daughter, Zerline. Lord and Lady Cockburn arrive at the inn, accompanied by another tourist, the Marquis of San Marco, whose attentions to Lady Cockburn have annoyed her husband. Lord Cockburn complains also that they have been robbed. The Marquis, actually the bandit in disguise, orders dinner and listens while Zerline tells of the exploits of Fra Diavolo. Then he resumes his attentions to Lady Cockburn and steals her locket. Lorenzo returns, boasting that he has broken up the robber band, and that he has recovered the jewelry that was stolen from the travelers. He has won the offered reward and expects to win Zerline as well.

The second act shows Zerline's bedroom. Zerline brings Lord and Lady Cockburn to their room which adjoins her own. She is delighted that she will soon be married to Lorenzo. Meanwhile, Fra Diavolo and his two followers, Giacomo and Beppo, have hidden in Zerline's room. They watch while she undresses and goes to bed, and then proceed again to rob Lord and Lady Cockburn. The victims awake and call for help. Lorenzo and the guards come to the rescue, but Fra Diavolo is still disguised as the Marquis and is able to cover the retreat of his two followers. He explains his own presence in Zerline's apartment by saying he had an appointment with Zerline. Lorenzo immediately challenges him to a duel.

The third act occurs in a forest. Fra Diavolo, stripped of his disguise, and known to all to be the bandit, is awaiting any victims who may pass. A wedding procession approaches. Zerline is unwillingly being forced to marry Francesco, the miller. Giacomo and Beppo have joined the procession and are recognized and arrested by Lorenzo. He forces them to lure Fra Diavolo into a trap and the bandit chief is shot. Before dying Fra Diavolo confesses that he had no appointment with Zerline and that she is innocent. Lord and Lady Cockburn are amazed to learn that Fra Diavolo and the philandering Marquis were the same person. Lorenzo receives the reward for capturing the bandit, and wins the hand of his beloved Zerline.

§)&(§

FRANCESCA DA RIMINI

Riccardo Zandonai

Gabriele d'Annunzio's play dealing with the thirteenth-century historical family of Rimini is the basis of Tito

Ricordi's libretto for Riccardo Zandonai's opera, *Francesca da Rimini*. The opera was first produced at the Teatro Regio in Turin, February 19, 1914.

The cast includes:

FRANCESCA (*Soprano*), daughter of Guido da Polenta
GIOVANNI, THE LAME (*Baritone*)
PAOLO, THE HANDSOME (*Tenor*)
MALATESTINO, THE ONE-EYED (*Tenor*)
} sons of Malatesta Verrucchio

The action occurs at the end of the thirteenth century in Ravenna and at Rimini in Italy. The first act shows the house of Guido da Polenta, whose daughter Francesca is to be married to Giovanni, the Lame. Giovanni is so deformed that his friends are certain Francesca will not agree to the marriage, so she is introduced to Giovanni's younger brother, Paolo, the Handsome, and is led to believe that he is her future husband. Neither speaks at the first meeting, but each falls deeply in love with the other.

In the second act, at the Malatesta Castle, Francesca has been tricked into marrying Giovanni. She reproaches Paolo for having deceived her. He says that he knew nothing of the plot, and tells Francesca that he loves her. Giovanni brings news that Paolo has been appointed captain of the commune of Florence. Paolo leaves to assume his new office.

The third act shows Francesca's apartment in the palace, where Francesca is reading the story of Lancelot and Guinevere to her attendants. Paolo pays her a secret visit. Francesca dismisses her attendants and she and Paolo continue reading the story of Lancelot. As they read of the lovers' embrace, they can restrain themselves no longer.

The two scenes of the fourth act show the hall of the castle and Francesca's apartments. The youngest brother of Giovanni and Paolo, Malatestino, the one-eyed, has learned of the affair between Francesca and Paolo. He himself has made advances to Francesca and has been repulsed. For revenge, he tells Giovanni of the lovers' secret meetings. Giovanni lies in wait outside the door of Francesca's apartment. He finds the lovers together and kills them both.

§)&(§

DER FREISCHÜTZ

Carl Maria von Weber

Carl Maria von Weber's *Der Freischütz* was first produced at the Schauspielhaus in Berlin, June 18, 1821. Its libretto was written by Johann Friedrich Kind, who based the plot on an old German legend about the "Free Marksmen" who used magic bullets. According to the legend, the free marksman is allowed seven of these charmed bullets in exchange for his soul. The first six never fail to hit the mark but if the marksman uses the seventh bullet, he himself will be killed. If he finds another marksman to use magic bullets before he has shot the seventh, his own life is spared and his supply extended.

The cast of the opera includes:

OTTOKAR (*Baritone*), Duke of Bohemia
KUNO (*Bass*), his head gamekeeper
AGNES (*Soprano*), his daughter
ANNA (*Mezzo-soprano*), her friend
MAX (*Tenor*), a ranger
CASPAR (*Bass*), a ranger
KILIAN (*Tenor*), a wealthy peasant
A HERMIT (*Bass*),
ZAMIEL, THE EVIL ONE (*speaking part*)

The scene of the opera is Bohemia in the Middle Ages, and the first act shows the Duke's target range. Kuno, the head gamekeeper, is growing old and has arranged a marksmanship contest from which he will choose a successor. The young ranger Max is eager to win the contest so that he will gain not only the post of head gamekeeper, but also the hand of Kuno's daughter, Agnes. Max loses the preliminary round to Kilian, a peasant. This is a bitter blow, for Kilian is merely an amateur. After enduring the jests and mocking of the peasants, Max is an easy prey for Caspar, a fellow ranger, who has sold his soul to Zamiel, the evil one, in exchange for magic bullets. Caspar must bring another victim to Zamiel, or he will lose his life. Caspar urges Max to try his gun. Max aims at an eagle which is flying so high that he can hardly see him, and brings it to earth with a single shot. Caspar tells Max that a magician in the Wolf's Glen will mold for him seven magic bullets that will hit any mark. When Max learns that he will have another chance to win the contest on the morrow, he agrees to meet Caspar at the Wolf's Glen.

The second act shows Agnes's room. She is worried because Max has not come to her, and also because the forest hermit has warned her of coming danger. The hermit has also promised her that her bridal wreath will protect her from harm. Max enters hurriedly. He tells her that although he lost in the preliminary contest he has shot a stag in the Wolf's Glen. He must go quickly to bring it to her. Agnes is suspicious, and begs him not to go. He refuses to listen to her pleading. The scene changes to the Wolf's Glen. Caspar tells Zamiel that Max will be the next victim. Max arrives, and although he is warned by the spirit of his dead mother, he is more impressed when Zamiel conjures a vision of Agnes drowning herself because Max has failed in the contest. With incantations accompanied by terrifying flashes of lightning, Zamiel forges the seven bullets.

The third act returns to Agnes's room. She is making preparations for her marriage to Max, which is to be held directly after the shooting contest. She prays for her lover. Her bridesmaids bring her a bridal wreath which has been blessed by the hermit. Then she opens a box of flowers and finds in it a funeral wreath. She is terror-stricken, but remembers the hermit's promise that the bridal wreath will protect her. The second scene of the third act shows Duke Ottokar's camp. The contest is being held, and the assemblage is amazed at Max's skill. He has hit the mark six times. The seventh bullet remains, and its course will be directed by Zamiel, the evil one. The Duke commands Max to shoot at a dove. Max raises his gun and fires. A woman shrieks: "I am that dove." It is Agnes, dressed in her wedding clothes. She is struck by the bullet, but the bridal wreath has saved her. Zamiel has been cheated of his latest victim and he seizes Caspar, whose day of grace has now passed. Max confesses his connection with the magic bullets and the Duke sentences him to a year of penance, after which he may have the post of head ranger and permission to marry Agnes.

§)&(§

GIANNI SCHICCHI

Giacomo Puccini

Puccini's *Gianni Schicchi* is a one-act affair which is not, like most of his works, a tragedy, but rather a sparkling, witty comedy. Its libretto was written by Giovacchino Forzano and the opera was first produced in association with Puccini's *Suor Angelica* and *Il Tabarro* at the Metropolitan Opera House, New York, December 14, 1918.

The three leading characters are:

GIANNI SCHICCHI (*Baritone*)
LAURETTA (*Soprano*), his daughter
RINUCCIO (*Tenor*), betrothed to Lauretta, and a relative of the late Buoso Donati

The other persons in the cast, like Rinuccio, are relatives of Buoso Donati, a wealthy man who has been very ill and has died just before the opera begins. Donati's relatives are gathered about his death-bed and have learned that he has left all of his fortune to a monastery. Rinuccio suggests that the relatives consult his future father-in-law, Gianni Schicchi, hoping that Schicchi may find some way of circumventing the will. Since nobody but the relatives know that the old man is dead, Schicchi suggests that he himself take Donati's place in the bed, and that he then dictate a new will to a notary. The relatives plan with Schicchi how each of Donati's minor possessions shall be apportioned, and each offers Schicchi a bribe for such items as the mule, the saw-mill, and the palace at Florence. Finally Schicchi puts on a nightgown and cap and is helped into the old man's bed. The notary is brought in and Schicchi proceeds to dictate the will. He starts by giving a few worthless trifles to various of the relatives. Then he announces that the residue of the estate shall be bequeathed to Gianni Schicchi!

The outraged relatives can do nothing. If they expose Schicchi they will be as much involved as he is. But after the notary has left they crowd about Schicchi and cry "Thief! Robber! Scoundrel!" Schicchi takes a stick and drives them from the house. The lovers, Lauretta and Rinuccio, embrace, and as Schicchi gathers up his loot he turns to the audience and points to the pair, asking if a better use for Donati's money could be imagined.

§)&(§

LA GIOCONDA

Amilcare Ponchielli

Amilcare Ponchielli's *La Gioconda,* first produced at La Scala, Milan, April 8, 1876, is most widely known today through its ballet music, "Dance of the Hours." Few who hear this work as a melodious orchestral piece realize that in the opera it accompanies a party which the villain of the opera is giving to celebrate what he believes to be the successful murder of his wife. The libretto of the opera was written by Arrigo Boïto under an anagrammatic pseudonym, Tobia Gorrio. Boïto based his plot on *Angelo,* a play by Victor Hugo.

The story is so involved and its intrigues are inspired by so many conflicting passions and love affairs, that it cannot be unraveled understandably unless these relationships are clearly set forth. The five principal characters are in love, but unfortunately each admires the wrong person. Consequently, there are five cases of unrequited affection:

BARNABA (*Baritone*), a spy of the Inquisition, is in love with
LA GIOCONDA (*Soprano*), a ballad singer, but she loves
ENZO GRIMALDO (*Tenor*), a Genoese noble, who loves
LAURA (*Mezzo-soprano*), who is married to
ALVISE (*Bass*), one of the leaders of the Inquisition

Other characters are:

LA CIECA (*Contralto*), La Gioconda's blind mother
ZUANE (*Bass*), a boatman

The action takes place in Venice, in the seventeenth century. The first act shows the court of the ducal palace. It is here that the letters for the Inquisition are received, and Barnaba, a spy, is watching a group of Venetians as they sing and dance. Barnaba is hoping to win the affections of La Gioconda, who presently appears leading her blind mother. Gioconda is looking for Enzo, whom she loves, so she repulses Barnaba's love-making. There has been a regatta on one of the canals, and Zuane, a boatman, has been defeated in the contest. Barnaba tries to avenge himself for Gioconda's rebuff by telling Zuane that he lost the regatta because Gioconda's mother, the blind La Cieca, threw a spell over him. Zuane attacks La Cieca, but the old lady is saved by the arrival of Enzo, who protects her. Enzo is in love, not with Gioconda, who loves him, but with Laura, the wife of Alvise, a leader of the Inquisition. Laura learns that Enzo is defending the old lady; she begs her husband Alvise to protect La Cieca. Cieca is so grateful that she gives Laura a rosary. Barnaba notices the loving glances that pass between Enzo and Laura, and he plots to destroy Enzo, who is his own rival for Gioconda's affections. Barnaba tells Enzo that Laura will visit him that night on Enzo's ship. Then he tells Laura's husband, Alvise, that his wife has an appointment with Enzo. Gioconda overhears Barnaba's warning to Alvise, and is jealous of Enzo's love for Laura.

The second act shows Enzo's ship. Barnaba is disguised as a fisherman and after assuring himself that everything will go as he has planned, sends for the police galleys. Enzo arrives and soon Laura joins him. They plan to elope and sail away at dawn. Gioconda interrupts them, and jealously denounces Laura. Gioconda is about to stab Laura, but Laura holds up the rosary which Gioconda's mother has given her. Gioconda is so touched that she helps Laura to escape before her husband arrives. Before leaving, Gioconda warns Enzo that Alvise and Barnaba are coming with police galleys to capture him. Enzo sets fire to his ship rather than have it taken by his enemies.

The third act is laid in Alvise's palace. Alvise has decided to kill his unfaithful wife, Laura. He orders her to drink a phial of poison. Gioconda, still eager to repay Laura for her kindness to her mother, substitutes a sleeping draught for the poison. Laura drinks it and falls asleep. Alvise finds her and thinking she is dead, invites guests to a ball where the famous "Dance of the Hours" is played. Barnaba whispers to Enzo that Laura is dead. Enzo denounces Alvise, who proudly admits that he killed his wife, and draws aside the curtains to show her supposed remains to his guests. Enzo tries to kill Alvise, but he is arrested and put in charge of Barnaba. Gioconda promises Barnaba that if he will free Enzo, she will give herself to him. Barnaba, still in love with Gioconda, consents.

The fourth act brings a happy ending to two of the lovers, but tragedy to the others. Gioconda is alone with the sleeping Laura in a ruined palace on the Adriatic. Enzo finds them, and Laura awakens. Enzo is overjoyed to learn that Laura is not dead but has been sleeping. Gioconda then helps Laura to escape with Enzo. When Gioconda is alone, she is about to end her own life with poison, but Barnaba appears to demand that she keep her promise to him. She pretends to agree, but as Barnaba is about to embrace her, she plunges a dagger into her heart and cries: "I have sworn to be thine. Take me, I am thine!" The vengeful Barnaba still tries to punish her by shouting that he has strangled her mother, but Gioconda does not hear him; she is already dead.

§)&(§

THE GIRL OF THE GOLDEN WEST

(La Fanciulla del West)

Giacomo Puccini

The Girl of the Golden West was originally a play by David Belasco based on a story by Bret Harte. It enjoyed a long run in New York in the season of 1905-06. When Giacomo Puccini composed his opera to the play, the libretto was written in Italian by C. Zangarini and G. Civinini. The opera was given its world premiere at the Metropolitan Opera House, New York, December 12, 1910.

The action takes place in a mining camp at the foot of the Cloudy Mountains in California during the days of the gold rush, 1849-50. The principal characters are:

MINNIE (*Soprano*), owner and manager of the "Polka" saloon and dance hall
JACK RANCE (*Baritone*), Sheriff
DICK JOHNSON (*Tenor*), actually "Ramerrez" an outlaw
ASHBY (*Bass*), agent of the Wells-Fargo Express Company
CASTRO (*Bass*), a member of "Ramerrez'" gang

The first act shows the barroom of the "Polka." The miners are playing cards and singing. Ashby, agent of Wells-Fargo, comes to announce that he is close on the trail of Ramerrez, an outlaw who has been leading a gang of Mexicans in a series of hold-ups and robberies. Minnie, the owner of the establishment, greets the men. All of them are in love with her, but she treats them in motherly fashion and parries their love-making. After drinking to their health, she takes her Bible and gives them a lesson in the Scriptures. Jack Rance, the sheriff, has boasted that he will marry Minnie, but when he proposes to her she asks him what he will do with his present wife. As Minnie holds Rance off with her revolver, she pleads her friendship, but says she cannot marry a man she does not love. Presently a stranger appears and announces himself as Johnson of Sacramento. He and Minnie recognize each other. They once met on the road to Monterey and he handed her a sprig of jasmine. Each has cherished the memory of that meeting. Rance is not only jealous of a stranger's attentions to Minnie, he is suspicious that this Johnson may be Ramerrez, the bandit. His suspicions are correct, but the conversation is interrupted by the appearance of Castro, a member of Ramerrez' gang, who says that he has escaped from Ramerrez, and will lead the sheriff to the spot where the outlaw is hiding. Castro's trick works, and the men follow him after leaving their gold with Minnie for safekeeping. Johnson stays with Minnie, and as they talk he falls so deeply in love with her that he puts aside his plans for a new robbery. Minnie invites him to visit her in her cabin.

The second act takes place in Minnie's cabin. Johnson comes to see Minnie, and sings to her of his love. Shots are heard outside and the posse appears, headed by Rance. Minnie hides Johnson. She does not want the miners to find her with her lover. Rance tells Minnie that Johnson is the notorious Ramerrez, and is hiding near by. Minnie protests to Rance that she does not need the protection of his men, so the posse leaves. Then Minnie turns on Johnson and rebukes him for having deceived her. He admits that he is Ramerrez but tells her that since meeting her he will be glad to give up his life of crime and will try to become worthy of her. Minnie cannot forgive him and sends him away. As soon as he has left the cabin, shots are heard outside. Minnie opens the door and brings in the wounded Johnson. She hides him in a loft over the main room of the cabin. Soon Rance appears and demands that Minnie produce the bandit. Minnie denies that he is in the house, but a drop of blood falling from the ceiling proves that she is lying. Minnie appeals to Rance's gambling instincts. She offers to play a game of poker with him. If Rance wins, he may have Minnie and Johnson. If Minnie wins, Johnson goes free. Minnie cheats and wins, and Rance leaves.

The third act shows a redwood forest. Minnie has nursed Johnson and helped him to recover, but the miners have discovered him and are about to hang him. As a last request Johnson prays that Minnie will believe that he has won his freedom, and has gone to another world where he will lead the nobler life that she has taught him. He calls her the "star of his wasted life." The miners put the noose about Johnson's neck and are about to draw the rope when Minnie appears on horseback. At first she holds the men away with her revolver. Then she pleads with them to remember how she has cared for their needs. She tells them that Johnson has reformed, that she loves him, and she begs them not to go back on her now. The men are touched by her appeal and spare Johnson's life. Johnson and Minnie bid farewell and leave to start a new life in the East.

§)&(§

GÖTTERDÄMMERUNG

See Der Ring des Nibelungen

GOYESCAS

Enrique Granados

This opera by Enrique Granados uses a libretto by Fernando Periquet which is based on characters and settings suggested by the paintings of Goya. The work was produced for the first time at the Metropolitan Opera House in New York, January 28, 1916.

The principal characters are:

ROSARIO (*Soprano*), an aristocratic lady
FERNANDO (*Tenor*), Captain of the Guard
PAQUIRO (*Baritone*), a toreador
PEPA (*Contralto*), his sweetheart

The opera is composed in three scenes or tableaux, all occurring in contemporary Madrid. The first scene shows a street on the outskirts of the city during a fiesta. Paquiro is mingling with the gay crowds and is flirting with various of the girls. Soon his sweetheart, Pépa, arrives in a dog-cart. Then the noble lady, Rosario, arrives with much ceremony to keep a rendezvous with Fernando, the captain of the guards. Paquiro complicates matters by approaching Rosario and reminding her that she once attended a candlelight ball. He invites her to attend another, and Fernando overhears the conversation and announces that he, not Paquiro, will escort Rosario to the ball. Pepa is jealous of Paquiro's conduct, and the scene ends in a heated quarrel between the four principal characters.

The second scene shows the ball. Fernando enters with Rosario, and immediately quarrels with Paquiro. A duel is arranged, and Rosario faints.

The third scene is laid in Rosario's garden. Fernando and Rosario meet for a love scene and are interrupted by a bell which announces the hour for the duel. Fernando goes to fight and Rosario follows him. Soon Rosario is heard shrieking. She enters with the mortally wounded Fernando, who dies in her arms.

§)&(§

GRISÉLIDIS

Jules Massenet

The libretto of Jules Massenet's *Grisélidis* was written by Paul Armand Silvestre and Eugène Édouard Morand. The opera was first performed at the Opéra Comique, Paris, November 20, 1901.

The characters include:

GRISÉLIDIS
ALAIN, a shepherd
THE MARQUIS
GONDEBAUD, chief of his retainers
THE PRIOR
THE DEVIL
FIAMINA, his wife

The action takes place in Provence during the fourteenth century. In the prologue Alain is in a forest, singing of his love for Grisélidis. While he is waiting for a glimpse of her,

Gondebaud and the Prior of the neighboring monastery pass by and talk about the Marquis. It seems that marriage is the only thing needed to make the Marquis' life complete. Soon the Marquis himself joins them. He has seen Grisélidis, and has fallen in love with her. When Grisélidis appears, she feels that the Marquis is sent from Heaven and agrees to marry him. The party leaves to prepare for the wedding while Alain, knowing that he has lost Grisélidis, sings: "Gates of Paradise, close upon my eyes."

The first act shows the oratory in the Chateau of Saluces. On the altar is a figure of St. Agnes holding a lamb. Grisélidis and the Marquis have been happily married for a year and are the parents of an infant son, Loys. It is time for the Marquis to join the war against the Saracens, and the Prior promises that neither Grisélidis nor the child shall leave the castle while the Marquis is away. The Marquis declares that his wife shall not be kept a prisoner, for he doubts neither her fidelity nor her obedience. When the Prior remarks that the Devil is sly, the Marquis retorts that if the Devil himself were present he would make the same statement. Immediately the Devil jumps from the altar and questions the fidelity and obedience of any woman. The Marquis reasserts his faith in his wife and as a pledge of his trust gives the Devil his wedding ring. The Devil slips the ring on his finger and goes out through the window. The Marquis takes affectionate leave of Grisélidis and leaves for the war.

The second act takes place on the terrace of the Chateau. The Devil is alone in the garden. He is joined by his wife, Fiamina, and he tells her of his plan to deceive the Marquis through Grisélidis. The Devil disguises himself as a merchant, and his wife as a Persian slave, and tells Grisélidis that the Marquis has taken a fancy to this slave-girl, has purchased her, and has sent her home to be mistress of his castle. To prove the truth of the story, the Devil shows Grisélidis the Marquis' wedding ring. The Devil then tempts the griefstricken Grisélidis with the suggestion that she take revenge on her husband by having a lover for herself. Grisélidis spurns such an idea, but as a token of obedience she hands her wedding ring to Fiamina. The Devil summons Alain, thinking that he will tempt Grisélidis. Grisélidis is deeply moved, but the approach of her child, Loys, keeps her from yielding to Alain. The Devil snatches the child and disappears.

The last act shows Grisélidis at the window of the oratory mourning the loss of her child. When she draws the curtain from the altar she finds that the statue of St. Agnes is gone. The Devil returns disguised as an old sailor. He brings news of the child, who is being held by a gallant pirate who will ransom the child for a kiss from its mother. As Grisélidis prepares to leave with the Devil, she takes the knife from his belt and sprinkles him with holy water. She leaves the Devil smarting with pain from water that is fire to him. When Grisélidis has gone, the Marquis enters. The Devil pretends that he is an old friend and tells the Marquis that his wife has been guilty of misconduct while he was away. Even now, he says, she is about to elope with a handsome sailor. Suddenly the Marquis sees his wedding ring on the Devil's finger. When Grisélidis returns, the Marquis convinces her that the Devil is responsible for the misunderstandings, including the "slave-girl" he is supposed to have purchased. The Devil reminds them of their lost child, and vanishes. The Marquis starts to take a sword from the wall, but all the weapons disappear. He and Grisélidis appeal to the cross on the altar. It is transformed into a flaming sword. The Marquis grasps it, the oratory candles burst into light, and Loys appears surrounded by a halo, and sleeping at the feet of St. Agnes.

GUNTRAM

Richard Strauss

Richard Strauss himself wrote the libretto for his first opera, *Guntram*, which was produced first at Weimar, May 10, 1894.

The cast includes:

THE OLD DUKE (*Bass*)
FREIHILD (*Soprano*), his daughter
DUKE ROBERT (*Baritone*), her husband
GUNTRAM (*Tenor*) } minstrels
FRIEDHOLD (*Bass*) } minstrels
THE DUKE'S JESTER (*Tenor*)

The action occurs in the thirteenth century in a German duchy. The Old Duke has given over his lands and the hand of his daughter Freihild to Duke Robert. Robert has proved to be a cruel tyrant. The people have revolted, but Robert has suppressed them and now their lot is even harder. The first act shows a forest by the sea to which the people have fled, and where their protectress Freihild has come fully intending to throw herself into the waters because she has been so mistreated by her husband. The kindly minstrel Guntram prevents Freihild from committing suicide. He and his companion minstrel, Friedhold, are members of the Holy Society of Peace, and they feed and comfort the fugitives. The Old Duke appears and Guntram softens his heart by telling him of the wrongs the people have endured. Guntram then accompanies the Old Duke to the palace.

The second act shows a festival at the ducal court. In the midst of a planned revolt by the vassals of Duke Robert, Guntram sings a song of peace. He advises Robert to make peace with the people, and when Robert attacks Guntram as a traitor, Guntram kills him. The Old Duke orders Guntram thrown into prison, and Freihild determines to save him. She and Guntram have fallen in love with each other.

The third act is laid in the prison. Guntram is condemned to execution, but before he dies he wants to pacify the people, who have again revolted. Freihild opens the prison gate. She tells Guntram how much she loves him and begs him to let her fly with him. At this moment news comes that the Old Duke is dead, and that Freihild is now the ruler of the people. Guntram bows to her exalted position and renounces his love for her.

§)&(§

HANS HEILING

Heinrich Marschner

Heinrich Marschner's opera, *Hans Heiling,* was produced first at the Opernhaus in Berlin, May 24, 1833. Its libretto was written by Eduard Devrient. The opera opens with an introduction, in which the principal characters are:

QUEEN OF THE SPIRITS OF THE EARTH (*Soprano*)
HER SON (*Baritone*)

The scene is the subterranean home of the spirits of the earth. The Queen's son has fallen in love with a mortal and is driven to the surface of the earth. The Queen determines that she will win her son back.

The cast of the opera which follows the introduction includes:

QUEEN OF THE SPIRITS OF THE EARTH (*Soprano*)
HANS HEILING (*Baritone*), her son in mortal form
ANNA (*Soprano*), his beloved
GERTRUD (*Contralto*), her mother
KONRAD (*Tenor*), a huntsman

The action occurs in the Hartz Mountains during the sixteenth century. Hans Heiling comes from a subterranean passage. He is the son of the Queen of the Spirits of the Earth, now in the form of a mortal. He greets Anna, his beloved. Anna asks Hans to destroy a book of magic which he carries with him, and Hans throws it into a fire. By this act he gives up all power as a spirit. His future happiness depends entirely on Anna's love. Anna persuades Hans to go with her to a country festival. At the festival Anna dances with Konrad, the hunter, and Hans is afraid he cannot keep her love.

The second act opens in a forest. Hans's fears are justified; Anna is in love with Konrad. The Queen of the Spirits of the Earth comes to Anna and tells her who Hans Heiling really is. Anna falls unconscious from fright. Konrad finds her and when she awakens she and Konrad confess their love for each other. The scene changes to the room of Gertrud, Anna's mother. Konrad and Anna ask Gertrud for her blessing on their betrothal. Hans Heiling comes with bridal jewels and Anna repulses him. She tells him that she knows who he really is. Hans stabs Konrad and escapes.

The third act opens in a rocky gorge. Hans learns from the spirits of the earth that Konrad is not dead. The spirits promise Hans that he will have vengeance if he will return to them and renounce Anna. The scene changes to a festival where Konrad and Anna are to be married. The peasants play the traditional game of blind-man's buff, and Anna, blindfolded, catches Hans Heiling, who is mingling with the throng. Konrad and the peasants come to Anna's rescue. Heiling calls on the spirits for help but the Queen of the Spirits persuades Hans to give up his desire for revenge. He sinks into the earth, vowing that no mortal shall ever see him again.

§)&(§

HÄNSEL AND GRETEL

Engelbert Humperdinck

Engelbert Humperdinck's opera for small and grown-up children is based on Grimm's fairy tale, and its libretto was written by Adelheid Wette, sister of the composer. It was first performed at Weimar, December 23, 1893.

The cast includes:

PETER (*Baritone*), a broom-maker
GERTRUD (*Mezzo-soprano*), his wife
HÄNSEL (*Mezzo-soprano*) } their children
GRETEL (*Soprano*) }
THE CRUNCH WITCH (*Mezzo-soprano*)
THE SANDMAN (*Soprano*)

The overture to the opera is in itself a concert-piece. It opens with the theme of the "Prayer" the children sing at the end of Act Two, and then presents various of the melodies from the opera. At the close of the overture the curtain rises and shows the interior of the cottage in which Peter and Gertrud live with their children, Hänsel and Gretel. Hänsel and Gretel are alone taking care of the house. They are hungry and tired and they sing and dance to keep up their spirits. Gretel sings "Susie, little Susie, what stirs in the hay?" and Hänsel answers that they have only poverty. Their mother returns and scolds them for not working harder. For punishment she sends them into the woods to pick strawberries. When they have gone, Peter, the father, returns with a basket of food. He has sold his brooms at a good profit, and is in fine spirits. He asks where the children have gone, and when Gertrud tells him that she has sent them into the forest, he is afraid that they will lose their way and fall into the clutches of the wicked Crunch Witch who lures children with her cakes and then makes them into gingerbread. Father and mother hurry out to find the children.

In the second act Hänsel and Gretel are in the woods picking strawberries. As darkness falls, the children find that they are lost. They are frightened by the faces of the wood monsters who stare at them, but soon the Sandman comes and throws sand in their eyes. As they go to sleep they sing the lovely prayer—"When I go to sleep at night, fourteen angels watch do keep." Then the fourteen angels descend from a shining ladder and surround the children to guard them while they sleep.

The third act shows the forest, with the Witch's hut concealed by the mist. The children awake and as the mist clears, they see the hut, flanked on either side by a bake oven and a cage. The hut is surrounded by gingerbread children. Hänsel and Gretel are fascinated by the house and when they touch it and find that it is made of gingerbread they start to nibble. Suddenly the Witch rushes out, grabs Hänsel and locks him in the cage. She sends Gretel into the hut for raisins and almonds to fatten Hänsel before he is made into gingerbread. When Gretel returns the Witch tells her to look into the oven. Gretel pretends to be clumsy and asks the Witch to show her how it should be done. The

Witch looks into the oven and Gretel pushes her into the fire. The gingerbread children come to life and the parents find Hänsel and Gretel after their all-night search. The Witch has been burned to gingerbread and is taken from the oven as all dance and sing a prayer of Thanksgiving.

§)&(§

HÉRODIADE

Jules Massenet

The libretto of Massenet's *Hérodiade* was written by Paul Milliet and Henry Grémont (G. Hartmann) , who founded it on a story by Flaubert, and the opera was first produced at Brussels, December 19, 1881. As in Richard Strauss's *Salome,* which used Oscar Wilde's poem for its libretto, the plot is derived from the New Testament story of the death of John the Baptist. The characterizations in the two operas are quite different, however. In *Salome* the heroine's love for the prophet is so lustful that when she is spurned, she herself demands Jokanaan's death. In *Hérodiade,* Salome's love for John the Baptist is nobler. Even though he does not return her love, she tries to save him from execution.

The characters of the Massenet opera are:

HEROD (*Bass*), the Tetrarch
HERODIAS (*Mezzo-soprano*), his wife
SALOME (*Soprano*), daughter of Herodias
JOHN THE BAPTIST (*Tenor*), a prophet
PHANUEL (*Tenor*), a Chaldean seer
VITELLIUS (*Baritone*), a Roman consul
HIGH PRIEST (*Baritone*)

The scene is laid in Palestine in the year 30 A.D., and the first act shows the courtyard of Herod's palace. Salome enters as the servants are working under the direction of Phanuel, the Chaldean seer. Salome does not know that she herself is the daughter of Herodias, for she was mysteriously separated from her mother in childhood. She is now seeking John the Baptist and in the aria *Il est doux; il est bon* ("He is good, he is kind") she tells Phanuel how the prophet saved her from the desert. Phanuel promises to help her find John. Herod comes looking for Salome, who has fascinated him by her dancing. He is joined by Herodias who complains of a prophet who has denounced her. She demands that the prophet be executed. Herod advises caution, but is interrupted by the appearance of the prophet himself, who continues his denunciations. Herod and Herodias make a hasty, confused exit, while Salome welcomes John the Baptist. She is in love with him, but he repulses her.

The second act opens in Herod's chamber. Herod, lazily reclining on his couch, is watching his dancing girls, and is disturbed because Salome is not among them. Phanuel warns Herod against his idle, luxurious ways, but Herod can think only of Salome. As he drinks a love potion he sings of the glimpses he has had of her: *Vision fugitive* ("Fleeting vision"). The second scene of the act is in a public square. Herod exorts the people to throw off the Roman yoke. Soon the sound of trumpets announces the arrival of the Romans who have been victorious under the leadership of Vitellius. Vitellius calms the people by being lenient and by restoring the temple to the Jews. When Salome and John the Baptist appear, Vitellius is impressed by the ovation John receives from the people. Herodias, hating the prophet for his denunciations, tells Vitellius that John is hungry for power. John, in turn, denounces

Vitellius, and proclaims that power comes only from God.

The first scene of the third act shows the home of Phanuel, the seer. Herodias comes to consult him about the future. She is eager to win back the love of Herod, who is fascinated by Salome. She wants also to find her long-lost daughter. Phanuel looks at the stars and sees blood, then he looks out of the window and discovers Salome. Thus Herodias learns that her rival for the love of Herod is her own daughter. The scene changes to the temple. Salome is in despair because John the Baptist has been thrown into prison. Herod makes love to her but she refuses his advances. Vitellius comes to declare the authority of Rome, and the priests demand from him the death of John the Baptist. Vitellius refers the priests to Herod, who orders the Prophet brought before him. Salome pleads for John's pardon, but Herod is so infuriated by jealousy that he sentences John the Baptist to death.

The fourth act shows first the dungeon where the Prophet awaits the execution of his sentence. Salome comforts him. He is touched by her devotion but does not return her earthly love. He urges her to escape and save herself. The High Priest offers John a pardon if he will help Herod overthrow the Roman tyranny, but John refuses to have any part in political or military affairs. The scene changes to the audience hall of the palace where Herod, Herodias and Vitellius are feasting and watching the dancing girls. Salome again begs for the pardon of John the Baptist. While she is still pleading, the executioner comes with the head of the Prophet. Salome turns upon Herodias, raises a dagger and cries: "This is your deed." Herodias cries: "I am thy mother!" Horrified, Salome answers: "Then take back the life you gave me!" and plunges the dagger into her own breast.

§)&(§

L'HEURE ESPAGNOLE

(The Spanish Hour)

Maurice Ravel

Maurice Ravel's one-act opera *L'Heure Espagnole* was first produced at the Opéra Comique in Paris, May 19, 1911. Its libretto was written by Franc-Nohain, and the principal characters are:

TORQUEMADA (*Tenor*), a clockmaker
CONCEPCION (*Soprano*), his wife
RAMIRO (*Baritone*), a muleteer
GONZALVE (*Tenor*) , Concepcion's lover
INIGO (*Bass*), a banker

The scene is laid in Torquemada's clock shop in Toledo. This is the day when Torquemada regulates the clocks of the town, and his wife Concepcion tends the shop and has time to receive lovers. Today she is expecting her current admirer, Gonzalve, but before he arrives the muleteer Ramiro comes to have his watch fixed. Ramiro announces that he will wait for Torquemada's return. While Ramiro s back is turned Gonzalve arrives and Concepcion tells him to hide in a grandfather's clock. Concepcion asks Ramiro if he can carry this clock to her bedroom, and the muleteer is not only willing but able to oblige her. Another admirer appears. This time it is Inigo, the banker, and he too is hidden in a clock which Ramiro carries off with ease. Concepcion is so impressed with Ramiro's strength that she forgets her other lovers and starts flirting with him. Soon Torquemada returns and finds Ramiro and the two men who are hidden in clocks. He is not a belligerent man, and accepts the situation by joining in a quintet with his wife and her three admirers.

§)&(§

HUGH THE DROVER

Vaughan Williams

Vaughan Williams' two-act opera, *Hugh the Drover,* was produced first at the Royal College of Music in London, July 4, 1924. Ten days later, July 14th, it was presented by the British National Opera Company at His Majesty's Theatre in London. The libretto was written by Harold Child, and the characters include:

THE CONSTABLE (*Bass*)
JANE (*Contralto*), his sister
MARY (*Soprano*), his daughter
JOHN (*Bass-baritone*), the butcher
HUGH (*Tenor*), the drover

The action occurs in a small village in the Cotswolds during the early years of the nineteenth century, about 1812. The first act shows a fair in progress on an open field near the town, at 11 in the morning on Monday, April 30th. Mary is unhappy because her father has ordered her to marry the town bully, John the Butcher. As Mary is confessing to her Aunt Jane that she does not love the butcher, Hugh the Drover overhears the conversation. He sings a song of the linnet and Mary is captivated. They start to make love to each other but are interrupted by the coming of the Constable, Mary's father, who has been warned of the proceedings by Aunt Jane. The Showman of the fair wants to arrange an exhibition fight, so Hugh offers to fight his rival, John the Butcher. After an argument about the size of the prize for the winner, Hugh the Drover demands that the prize be the hand of Mary. Hugh wins the fight and John is counted out. Hugh joins Mary but they are soon interrupted by John and the Constable. John accuses Hugh of being a paid spy of Napoleon. Hugh is arrested and put into the stocks.

The second act is laid in the market place at 4 o'clock the next morning (Tuesday). Hugh is in the stocks and Mary comes with a key she has stolen from her father. They make several attempts to escape but each time are interrupted. Finally Mary sits in the stocks with Hugh and covers herself with a cloak. Her absence from home is discovered and soon she is found sitting beside Hugh. Her father disowns her, and tells John the Butcher that she will not have one penny of dowry. John is accordingly no longer interested in Mary. The supporters of John and the friends of Hugh begin to fight when a group of soldiers arrive to take away the supposed spy of Napoleon. The sergeant recognizes Hugh as a friend and a loyal subject of the King. The sergeant says that he must have some prize for his expedition, so he claims John the Butcher and takes him away for service in the army. The Constable is now glad to give his blessing to the betrothal of Mary and Hugh the Drover.

§)&(§

THE HUGUENOTS

Giacomo Meyerbeer

Giacomo Meyerbeer's opera, *The Huguenots,* was first produced at the Grand Opéra in Paris, February 29, 1836. Its libretto was written by Auguste Eugène Scribe and Émile Deschamps.

The principal characters are:

COUNT DE ST. BRIS (*Baritone*)
VALENTINA (*Soprano*), his daughter
COUNT DE NEVERS (*Baritone*), betrothed to Valentina

RAOUL DE NANGIS (*Tenor*), a Protestant nobleman
MARCEL (*Bass*), his servant
MARGUERITE OF VALOIS (*Soprano*), betrothed to King Henry IV
URBAN (*Mezzo-soprano*), her page

The action occurs in Touraine and Paris in the yeaı 1572, during the night of St. Bartholomew when the Catholic party, led by St. Bris, plotted the massacre of the Huguenots.

The first act shows the home of Count de Nevers. The Count is anxious for peace between the Protestants and the Catholics. To further his cause he has invited his friends to meet Raoul de Nangis, a Protestant nobelman. Raoul is received in friendly fashion and when de Nevers announces that he himself is to be married, he asks Raoul whom he is in love with and offers a toast to the lady. Raoul confesses that he is in love with an unknown lady, whom he rescued from a party of wild young students who had stormed her carriage. During the drinking of toasts a veiled lady is ushered in who has asked for a word with de Nevers. The guests assume that she is de Nevers' mistress, and Raoul is shocked to see that she is the lady he rescued. He does not know that she is Valentina, de Nevers' fiancée, and that she has fallen so much in love with her unknown rescuer that she has come to ask de Nevers to release her. Nor does Raoul know that de Nevers has granted her request. Soon a page arrives and brings a note to Raoul asking him to accompany the page, blindfolded, to an unknown destination.

The second act shows the gardens of Marguerite's house. Marguerite is betrothed to King Henry IV and she, like de Nevers, is eager to bring about peace between the Catholics and Protestants. Valentina comes to tell Marguerite that de Nevers has released her from her engagement to him. Raoul is brought in blindfolded and Valentina retires.

The blindfold is removed and Raoul finds himself in the presence of Marguerite, who tells him that she has arranged a marriage for him which will reconcile the two religious parties. Catholic and Protestant nobles are brought in and both sides pledge friendship. Then Valentina enters, and Raoul recognizes her not only as the young lady he rescued from the students but also as the woman he believes to be the mistress of de Nevers. He denounces her and refuses to marry her. Valentina's father, Count de St. Bris, challenges Raoul for insulting his daughter and Marguerite orders Raoul arrested.

In the third act, showing a square in Paris, Valentina has been married to de Nevers. Her husband has given her permission to spend a day praying in the chapel, where she overhears a Catholic plot to assassinate Raoul. She finds Raoul's servant, Marcel, and tells him of his master's danger. When Marcel has gone to warn Raoul a battle starts between the Catholics and Protestants. Marguerite interrupts it and tells Raoul that Valentina is innocent, that she was de Nevers' fiancée and not his mistress. Raoul is filled with remorse and realizes that it is too late to atone for his mistake, for Valentina is now married to de Nevers.

The third act occurs in de Nevers' palace. Valentina still loves Raoul, and she welcomes him when he comes to see her. They are interrupted by the approach of de Nevers and Valentina's father, St. Bris. Valentina hides Raoul behind a tapestry where he hears St. Bris and the Catholic nobles plan to massacre the Protestants that night. He also hears de Nevers refuse to take part in the massacre, saying that he is not an assassin. The others consecrate their swords and sing a benediction. When the nobles have left Raoul comes from hiding and is about to warn his friends. Valentina detains him with loving words and the signal bell announces the beginning of the slaughter. Valentina clings to Raoul, but he shakes himself free and is shot as he leaps from the window to the street.

In the last act the wounded Raoul comes to a cemetery. Valentina follows him. They are shot by soldiers and die together.

§)&(§

THE IMMORTAL HOUR

Rutland Boughton

The Immortal Hour, by Rutland Boughton, was performed first at Glastonbury, England, August 26, 1914. Its libretto was adapted from the plays and poems of William Sharp (Fiona Macleod).

The characters include:

DALUA (*Baritone*), a shadow-god
ETAIN (*Soprano*), a lost fairy maiden
EOCHAIDH (*Baritone*), King of Ireland
MANUS (*Bass*), a peasant
MAIVE (*Contralto*), his wife
MIDIR (*Tenor*), a fairy prince

In the first act Dalua, the shadow-god who lies behind life, is mocked in the woods by ghostly voices. Etain, a fairy maiden, comes to Dalua for protection. She has lost her way and cannot remember anything but her name. She is followed by the Irish King, Eochaidh, who comes to drink at the fountain of his dreams and to find during the "immortal hour" the consummation of a love that the earth cannot appease. In the second scene of the act Dalua has arranged that Etain shall be sheltered in the cottage of the peasants, Manus and Maive. Eochaidh finds her and when he sees her he knows that his search is successful. Etain, however, cannot forget the call of the fairy-folk that lingers in her ears, even though she can remember nothing about them or about herself.

In the second act Etain and Eochaidh have been married for a year and a festival is being held in honor of the anniversary. A stranger, Midir, enters and asks a boon of King Eochaidh. The King grants the request before he learns what it is, and Midir demands that he be allowed to kiss Etain's hand. Midir is actually a fairy prince and when he kisses Etain's hand and sings to her of "the lordly ones who dwell in the hills" she falls under his spell and follows him back to the Land of Heart's Desire. Dalua, the shadow-god, touches Eochaidh, who falls to the ground.

§)&(§

IN THE PASHA'S GARDEN

John Laurence Seymour

The libretto of this one-act opera by John Laurence Seymour was written by H. C. Tracy after a story by H. G. B. Dwight. The opera was produced at the Metropolitan Opera House, New York, January 24, 1935.

The cast includes:

A PASHA (*Baritone*)
HELENE (*Soprano*), his young French wife
ETIENNE (*Tenor*), her lover
ZIMBULAGHA (*Tenor*), a eunuch
SHABAN (*Bass*), a servant

The action occurs in Constantinople in the early years of the twentieth century. The scene shows the Pasha's garden, where his wife Helene has a rendezvous with her lover Etienne. The eunuch overhears their conversation and goes to warn the Pasha. Helene hides Etienne in a large carved chest. When the Pasha comes and finds no one with his wife, he refuses to believe the eunuch's accusations. Dinner is served and the Pasha and his wife use the chest as a table. During the meal Helene pleads that she has a headache and leaves, but not before she has given the Pasha the key to the chest. The Pasha then sends for his servant Shaban and orders him to bury the chest in the garden. When this is done the Pasha throws the key into the pool.

§)&(§

IPHIGENIA IN AULIS

Christoph Willibald Gluck

The libretto of Christoph Willibald Gluck's *Iphigenia in Aulis* was adapted from Racine's *Iphigénie* by F. L. G. Lebland du Roullet. The opera was first performed at the Grand Opéra, Paris, May 19, 1774.

The cast includes:

AGAMEMNON (*Baritone*), King of the Greeks
KLYTEMNESTRA (*Mezzo-soprano*), his wife
IPHIGENIA (*Soprano*), their daughter
ACHILLES (*Tenor*), her betrothed
CALCHAS (*Bass*), the High Priest
ARTEMIS (*Diana*), (*Soprano*), the Goddess

The action takes place in Aulis after the Trojan War. The first act shows the Greek camp. Agamemnon has offended the Goddess, Artemis. She punishes Agamemnon by having unfavorable winds prevent the departure of the Greek fleet for Troy. Calchas, the High Priest, declares that the Goddess must be appeased by the sacrifice of the King's daughter, Iphigenia. Iphigenia is betrothed to the warrior Achilles, and the couple prepare happily for their wedding, not knowing of the demand for Iphigenia's sacrifice.

The second act takes place in Agamemnon's palace. Achilles is about to lead Iphigenia to the altar when Agamemnon's messenger announces that Iphigenia must die. Klytemnestra begs Achilles to save Iphigenia, and Achilles reproaches Agamemnon. Agamemnon decides that he will send Iphigenia and her mother to Mycene, where they may hide until the Goddess is appeased.

The third act shows Agamemnon's tent, where the soldiers are demanding that the King make the sacrifice the Goddess demands. Achilles urges Iphigenia to flee with him, and Klytemnestra offers to take Iphigenia's place on the altar. Iphigenia refuses and declares that she is ready for death. She offers herself to the priest, who stands ready with a dagger. Before the priest has time to stab Iphigenia, the Goddess herself appears, and announces that Iphigenia shall not die but will serve as a priestess in a foreign land.

§)&(§

IPHIGENIA IN TAURIS

Christoph Willibald Gluck

With *Iphigenia in Tauris* Christoph Willibald Gluck composed a continuation of *Iphigenia in Aulis*. The libretto was adapted from the Greek of Euripides by Nicolas François Guillard. The opera was first performed at the Grand Opéra, Paris, May 18, 1779.

In this opera Iphigenia has become the priestess of Artemis (Diana) at Tauris. In the interval between the time of the two operas, Klytemnestra has murdered her husband Agamemnon and in revenge has been slain by her son Orestes.*

The cast of *Iphigenia in Tauris* includes:

IPHIGENIA (*Soprano*), High Priestess of Diana
ORESTES (*Baritone*), her brother, a Greek
PLYADES (*Tenor*), companion of Orestes, also a Greek
THOAS (*Bass*), King of Scythia
DIANA (*Soprano*), the Goddess

The action occurs in Tauris, where the Scythians, allies of the Taurians, have incurred the wrath of the gods. The gods must be appeased by a human sacrifice and the logical victims are two strangers from Greece, Orestes and Plyades, who have been shipwrecked on the shores of Tauris. King Thoas, of the Scythians, commands Iphigenia, the priestess, to perform the sacrificial ceremony. She is loath to kill Orestes and Plyades, for she was herself a Greek and these men are countrymen even though they are strangers to her.

The first act shows the sacred wood of Diana with the temple in the background. Iphigenia is telling her fellow priestesses of a dream she has had in which her father was fatally wounded by her mother. She heard her brother Orestes call to her, and then saw him sink into the grim darkness of death. Thoas enters and tells Iphigenia that she must sacrifice the two strangers. Iphigenia prays to Diana, asking that she be allowed to die rather than be forced to take human life.

---

* These events form the plot of the opera *Elektra*, by Richard Strauss.

The second act shows the interior of the temple. Orestes and Plyades are in chains. They sing of their devotion for each other, and when they are separated, Plyades is so grief-stricken that he becomes temporarily insane. Orestes, left alone, is chided by the Furies for murdering his mother. Iphigenia comes and questions Orestes about the members of her family in Greece. He does not reveal that he is Orestes but tells Iphigenia that Agamemnon has been slain by Klytemnestra and that Orestes has killed Klytemnestra in revenge. Only the daughter Elektra remains.

In the third act, in Iphigenia's room, Orestes and Plyades are brought before Iphigenia, who declares that she will save one of them. She chooses Orestes who insists that Plyades be freed. Plyades is unwilling to let Orestes be sacrificed, but finally agrees on condition that Iphigenia will help him reclaim the statue of Diana and return it to the Greeks. Iphigenia is willing to do this, and she also plans to have Plyades deliver a letter to her sister Elektra. Thoas demands that the sacrifice be fulfilled, and while Iphigenia is summoning her courage to kill Orestes she hears him murmur in his sleep: "Iphigenia, my sweet sister." Then she knows that it is her brother she must sacrifice.

The fourth act shows the hall of sacrifice. Iphigenia tells Orestes that she is his sister. Thoas learns of Plyades' escape and demands Iphigenia's death as well as that of Orestes. Just as Thoas is about to kill Iphigenia with his own hand, Plyades returns with a band of Greeks who kill Thoas and fight the Scythians. During the battle Diana appears. She demands that her statue be returned to the Greeks, and drives off the Scythians. The priestesses remove the statue from the temple and accompany Iphigenia and Orestes to a ship waiting in the harbor.

§)&(§

IRIS

Pietro Mascagni

The libretto of Pietro Mascagni's *Iris* was written by Luigi Illica, and the opera was first produced at the Teatro Costanzi in Rome, November 22, 1898. A few months later, January 19, 1899, it was given in revised form at La Scala in Milan.

The story is laid in Japan. The principal characters are:

CIECO (*Bass*), a blind man
IRIS (*Soprano*), his daughter
OSAKA (*Tenor*), a wealthy roue
KYOTO (*Baritone*), a procurer

Iris is an innocent young girl who knows nothing of the ways of love. In the first act she is in her garden, playing with her doll. Her blind father, Cieco, hears her girlish chatter, and is pleased that she is so childlike and innocent. Osaka, worldly and rich, has seen Iris and is eager to possess her. He arranges with Kyoto, the procurer, to have her seized and taken to Kyoto's resort. To carry out their plot, the men arrange that a puppet show be given in the street near Iris's garden. The girl is delighted with the show and while she is looking at it she is quietly grabbed and taken away. To make the kidnapping legal, Kyoto leaves a small sum of money. When Iris has gone her father is told that she went to the resort of her own free will. Cieco curses his daughter and asks two peddlers to take him to Kyoto's place.

The second act shows the luxurious resort to which Iris has been taken. In her innocence she believes that she is in Heaven, everything is so beautiful. Osaka comes to her, and makes ardent love. She does not understand him, and answers his loving words and gestures by asking him to take her to her father and her garden. Osaka is disgusted and tells Kyoto that he does not want such a stupid girl. Kyoto tries to recover the small investment he has made in Iris by exhibiting her beauty to the crowds in the streets. When Osaka sees her arrayed in the gorgeous robes the geisha girls have put on her, he again wants her and tries to buy her from Kyoto. While the two men are haggling over the price, Iris's father is led in by the two peddlers. She is delighted to hear his voice, but when he curses her and throws mud at her, she jumps into a near-by sewer basin.

In the third act, ragpickers are going over the refuse thrown up by the river. They find the body of Iris clothed in the gaudy dress the geisha girls had given her. When they tear off her clothes and ornaments, she revives. As the ragpickers run away in terror, Iris, half-living and half dead, meditates on her life and her fate. She hears the voices of Kyoto, Osaka, and her father, Cieco. Each tries to justify his actions, but Iris asks, "Why? Why?" She turns toward the rising sun which she greets as the God of Day. Flowers bloom around her and her spirit is drawn into the rays of the Sun. At the end comes the chorus of the Sun: "I am I. I am Life."

§)&(§

THE ISLAND GOD

Gian-Carlo Menotti

The Island God was Gian-Carlo Menotti's third opera, and was first produced at the Metropolitan Opera House, New York, February 20, 1942. It is a one-act opera in three scenes, with a libretto by the composer, originally written in Italian and translated into English by Fleming McLeish.

Unlike Menotti's earlier operas, which are farcical comedies, *The Island God* is a tragedy. Its characters are:

ILO (*Baritone*)
TELEA (*Soprano*)
LUCA (*Tenor*)
A GREEK GOD (*Bass*)
VOICE OF A FISHERMAN (*Tenor*)

The scene is the shore of an island in the Mediterranean. On it stand the ruins of an old temple. Ilo and Telea appear through the mists from the sea. They have fled from oppressors who have seized the government of their native land. Ilo discovers the ruins of the temple and invokes its unknown god, who, when there is someone to worship him, is brought back to the living world. The god commands Ilo to rebuild the temple.

The second scene shows the temple partially restored. Luca, the fisherman, offers to bring aid to Ilo and Telea. Ilo replies that no help is needed. Telea denies this and accuses Ilo of letting his pride stand in the way of their getting much-needed assistance. Ilo consents to Luca's going for aid.

In the third scene Luca and Telea have become lovers and are afraid that they will be discovered by Ilo, who is busy restoring the temple. Luca and Telea are repairing Luca's fishnet, and fondly embrace each other when Luca proposes that they elope. Ilo approaches with his sledgehammer, but Telea throws the net over him and Luca binds him in its folds. Luca and Telea flee, and when Ilo has freed himself from the net, he cries that he has abandoned his god because his god has abandoned him. The god threatens Ilo with destruction but Ilo knows that if he himself dies the god will die too. He smashes the altar, and the god destroys him. Then the god, who lived only because of Ilo's faith, sinks back into oblivion.

§)&(§

L'ITALIANA IN ALGERI

(The Italian Girl in Algiers)

Gioacchino Rossini

L'Italiana in Algeri was the tenth of Gioacchino Rossini's thirty-eight operas, and was first produced at Teatro San Benedetto in Venice, May 22, 1813. Its libretto was written by Angelo Anelli.

The cast includes:

MUSTAFA (*Bass*), Bey of Algeria
ELVIRA (*Soprano*), his favorite wife
HALY (*Baritone*), captain of the Algerian Corsairs
LINDORO (*Tenor*), an Italian slave
ISABELLA (*Contralto*), an Italian noblewoman
TADDEO (*Baritone*), an unsuccessful suitor of Isabella

The first act opens in Mustafa's palace at Algiers. Mustafa has grown tired of his favorite wife, Elvira, and has decided that she shall marry the Italian slave, Lindoro. Lindoro is not enthusiastic because he still remembers his sweetheart in Italy. Mustafa commands the Algerian Corsair Haly to abduct for him some beautiful Italian lady to succeed Elvira. The scene changes to the seashore where Haly finds a wrecked vessel and two survivors. They are Isabella, an Italian noblewoman who is actually Lindoro's unforgotten sweetheart, and her escort Taddeo, who is wooing her unsuccessfully. When the Italians are captured and learn that they are to be taken to Mustafa's palace, they arrange that Taddeo will pose as Isabella's uncle.

The second act shows Mustafa's apartment. Mustafa is immediately delighted with Isabella, and decides that she will be a charming successor to Elvira. On Isabella's pleading Mustafa spares the life of Taddeo, who has been condemned to death because he refuses to work. Elvira enters with Lindoro, and Lindoro and Isabella recognize each other as former sweethearts. Isabella demands that Mustafa give up his plan of forcing Lindoro to marry Elvira.

The first scene of the third act shows Mustafa's palace. Although Mustafa is boasting that he will win Isabella's affections, she and Lindoro plan to escape. Mustafa rewards Isabella's supposed uncle, Taddeo, by making him "Kamaikan," whose duty it will be to bring Isabella to Mustafa whenever he sends for her. In the last scene Isabella is summoned to Mustafa's apartment. Isabella and Elvira disguise themselves and tell Mustafa that they are members of a secret society which is dedicated to sensuality. Mustafa asks to join the society and Isabella and Elvira offer to initiate him. While Mustafa is muttering incantations and following instructions for the initiation, Isabella, Lindoro and Taddeo escape. When Mustafa learns that he has been fooled he decides that there is nothing he can do but to take Elvira back as his favorite wife.

§)&(§

THE JEWELS OF THE MADONNA

Ermanno Wolf-Ferrari

Ermanno Wolf-Ferrari himself conceived the plot of his opera *The Jewels of the Madonna,* but the libretto was actually written by Carlo Zangarini and Enrico Golisciani. The opera was first performed at the Kurfürsten-Oper at Berlin in a German translation, December 23, 1911.

The cast includes:

GENNARO (*Tenor*), a blacksmith
CARMELA (*Mezzo-soprano*), his mother
MALIELLA (*Soprano*), adopted in infancy as a foundling by Carmela
RAFAELE (*Baritone*), leader of the Camorra

The action occurs in Naples, during modern times. The first act shows a square of the city, near the sea. The citizens are celebrating the festival day of the Madonna. Gennaro the blacksmith appears at the door of his house, bearing in his hand a wrought-iron candelabrum. This is an offering to the Madonna, to whom he has confided his hopeless love for Maliella. Maliella has been brought up from childhood by Gennaro's mother Carmela and she is tired of the restraint that has been placed upon her in the highly respectable atmosphere of their home. She longs for pleasure and she is excited by the merrymaking of the festival. In spite of Gennaro's warning against "stray young men," Maliella makes herself conspicuous by singing the *Canzone di Cantonella.* This attracts the attention of the Camorrists. Maliella runs from the scene when they approach. Gennaro tells his mother of his love for Maliella and Carmela explains that she adopted Maliella when Gennaro was ill as a child. She had vowed to the Madonna that if Gennaro's life was spared she would adopt a child born of sin.

Maliella returns, followed by the Camorrist leader, Rafaele and his band. Maliella at first resists Rafaele's advances and stabs him in the hand with her hatpin. Soon the procession of the Madonna passes and Rafaele jokingly asks Maliella if to win her he must steal the jewels from the Madonna and place them around Maliella's neck. Maliella shrinks from such a sacrilege, and then Gennaro approaches and tells Maliella that Rafaele is one of the worst blackguards in Naples. She retorts that it is none of Gennaro's business, that Rafaele is handsome. The procession returns and as Maliella is about to enter the house, Rafaele throws her a flower.

The second act is laid in the garden of Carmela's house. Gennaro pleads with Maliella to mend her ways, but she is bored with the quiet life she leads with Gennaro and Carmela. When Gennaro tells her that he loves her, she is shocked at love-making by one whom she regards as a brother. Maliella packs her belongings and tries to leave. When they argue about Rafaele she declares that Rafaele loves her so much he is willing to steal for her the Madonna's jewels. Gennaro locks the gate so that Maliella cannot escape, then seized by a horrible temptation he rushes out. While he is gone Rafaele and his companions serenade Maliella who embraces Rafaele through the bars of the garden gate. Rafaele and his followers are warned of Gennaro's return and escape. Gennaro reappears and unwraps a package containing the jewels of the Madonna. Maliella screams with horror, but slowly fascinated by the glitter of the jewels she puts the diadem on her head and the jewels about her neck. Gennaro is spellbound and renews his love-making. In a trance she imagines he is Rafaele and yields to him.

The third act shows the meeting place of the Camorra,

where the Camorrists are revelling with their women. When Rafaele comes he is so cold to the advances of the dancing girls that they tease him about his new-found love. He sings the praises of Maliella. Suddenly Maliella herself appears, disheveled and without the diadem in her hair. In talking with Rafaele she utters the name of Gennaro, and Rafaele jealously forces from her the admission that Gennaro has just now possessed her. She pleads that in her trance she believed it was Rafaele who was loving her, but Rafaele angrily throws her to the floor. As she falls the jewels burst from her shawl. The crowd stands back in horror. Gennaro rushes in and Maliella declares that it was he who stole the Madonna's jewels. She flings the jewels at his feet and cries: "To the sea; to the sea!" The bells of the church give notice that the theft of the jewels has been discovered, and all in the room escape, leaving Gennaro alone. He kneels before an image of the Madonna and, praying for pardon, stabs himself. As he dies a ray of sunlight falls upon the Madonna.

§)&(§

LE JONGLEUR DE NOTRE DAME

(The Juggler of Notre Dame)

Jules Massenet

The libretto of Jules Massenet's opera, *Le Jongleur de Notre Dame,* was founded by its author, Maurice Léna, on a story by Anatole France, *Etui de nacre.* The opera was first produced at the Théâtre in Monte Carlo, February 18, 1902.

The characters include:

JEAN (*Tenor*), a juggler
BONIFACE (*Baritone*), a cook
THE PRIOR OF THE MONASTERY (*Bass*)
THE MUSICIAN MONK (*Baritone*)
THE SCULPTOR MONK (*Bass*)
THE POET MONK (*Tenor*)
THE PAINTER MONK (*Baritone*)

The action occurs at Cluny, near Paris, in the sixteenth century. The first act shows the market place at Cluny. The people are celebrating May Day in front of the Convent. Jean, an old, hungry juggler, tries to amuse the crowd with his tricks. The people laugh at him and tell him the only way he can earn a penny is to sing a drinking song. Jean asks the Virgin's pardon, and sings his song. The Prior interrupts and threatens Jean with hell fire unless he reforms. The Prior asks Jean why he does not become a monk instead of remaining a vagabond. During this conversation Boniface, the Convent cook, passes by. His donkey is laden with provisions. The sight of all this food is too much for the hungry juggler. He decides to enter the Convent.

The second act is laid in the Monastery study. The several monks are engaged in their respective occupations, among them the Musician Monk who is rehearsing a new cantata for the Feast of the Virgin. Jean wishes he knew Latin so that he could praise the Virgin. He is sure that she would not understand vulgar French. The monks begin to quarrel over the comparative values of their several arts. The Sculptor and the Painter each argues for his art, and then the Poet and the Musician present their cases. The four almost come to blows but the Prior settles the argument by ordering them all to the Chapel to practice humility. Jean, the juggler, complains to the Cook, Boniface, that he cannot do anything to please the Virgin. The Cook tells Jean a story of how the humblest of flowers saved the life of Jesus when he was pursued by the King who killed children. Jean is then convinced that his humblest prayers, even though spoken in French, may reach as high as those rendered in fine language.

The third act shows the Chapel. The Painter Monk is looking with satisfaction at the picture he has painted of the Virgin and which is now hung over the high altar. Jean enters with his juggler's outfit. The Painter is shocked and goes for the Prior. Jean addresses the Virgin. He tells her that since he does not know how to do anything else, he will go through an entire performance of juggling in her honor. As he accompanies his act with his singing he occasionally interrupts himself to apologize for the words of his songs, and he assures the Virgin that he intends to be respectful. The Prior comes in time to see some of the performance. He tries to stop it but is restrained by the Cook. The other Monks join the party and are outraged at the sacrilege. They are about to put a stop to Jean's dancing when the face of the Virgin in the picture grows animated. Her arms are extended toward Jean, who is now praying fervently. The Monks cry "Miracle!" and kneel about the juggler. A light surrounds the picture of the Virgin, and Jean murmurs that at last he understands Latin. Then he dies in the arms of the Prior.

§)&(§

JONNY SPIELT AUF

Ernst Křenek

Ernst Křenek, an Austrian composer, was one of the first to compose an opera in the American jazz idiom. He wrote both the words and music of *Jonny Spielt Auf,* and encountered considerable difficulty in finding an opera house that would produce such a modern, satirical work. After *Jonny* was rejected by several leading theatres in Germany, it was finally produced at the Opernhaus in Leipzig, February 10, 1927. It scored a tremendous success and was eventually performed in more than one hundred cities and translated into eighteen languages. In 1929 (January 19th) it was produced at the Metropolitan Opera House in New York.

In the composer's own words, the opera tries to "interpret the rhythms and atmosphere of modern life in this age of technical science." The word "modern" of course, refers to the decade of the 1920's.

The principal characters are:

MAX (*Tenor*), a composer
JONNY (*Baritone*), a jazz-band violinist
DANIELLO (*Baritone*), a violin virtuoso
ANITA (*Soprano*), an opera singer
YVONNE (*Soprano*), a chambermaid

In the first scene of the first act, Max, a neurasthenic, sentimental composer, comes to a rock plateau in the Alps where he may behold and apostrophize a glacier with which he has fallen in love. Anita, the opera singer, loses her way and encounters Max in the middle of his rhapsodizing. Max explains to Anita that the glacier is the symbol of form, of nature structurally expressed, of life realized. The second scene shows a room in Anita's hotel apartment. She and Max have become lovers. He begs her to stay in the

Alps with him instead of returning to Paris where she is to create the title role in one of his operas. Anita refuses and the next scene is the corridor of the Paris hotel in which Anita is staying. Jonny, a jazz-band violinist, is telling the chambermaid Yvonne that he must get hold of the famous violin which is owned by Daniello, a virtuoso who also is a guest of the hotel. Daniello appears from his room and Jonny is furious because Daniello locks his door as he leaves. Anita comes in and sits down to write a letter. Jonny is enraptured and immediately makes love to her. She is not altogether cold to his proposals but she allows herself to be rescued by the returning Daniello, who offers Jonny a thousand-franc note to leave the lady to him, so that he may make the same proposals with more finesse and delicacy. Anita is charmed by Daniello and is perfectly willing that he go with her into her room. This time the door of Daniello's room is unlocked, and Jonny is able to enter it and steal the virtuoso's violin. In the next (fourth) scene Anita refuses to stay with Daniello. She tells him that she is off to join the composer Max but she gives him a ring that he may have as a keepsake. Daniello then discovers the loss of his violin. The chambermaid is discharged for negligence and is immediately engaged as a personal maid by Anita. Daniello is so affronted by this insult and by Anita's rejecting him, that he gives to Yvonne the ring Anita had given him, with instructions to pass it on to Max with Daniello's greetings.

The first scene of the second act shows Max waiting for Anita in a flower-filled room in the Alpine hotel. Impatiently he phones the railroad station and learns that the Paris train has already arrived. He is sure that she could not have been on it; otherwise she would have long since reached the hotel. The second scene occurs the next morning. Max has been sleeping in a chair, and at last Anita arrives. Max is overjoyed, but is soon depressed when Anita tells him that she has signed a contract to sing in America. Anita leaves the room for a moment, and Yvonne gives Max the ring that Daniello has sent, and also tells Max about the theft of Daniello's violin. Max refuses the ring and rushes out with an agonized cry. Yvonne then sees Jonny's face at the window. He has placed Daniello's violin in a banjo-case that Anita carries, and he has followed it to the Alps. He comes in through the window, takes the violin out of Anita's banjo-case and disappears. The scene changes to the rock plateau, where Max returns to consult his beloved glacier. The glacier advises Max to return to life and make the best of it. Max feels that he is forsaken, even by the glacier, and he sits dejectedly on a stone in the darkness. Gradually at the other side of the stage the hotel terrace emerges and grows lighter and more visible. The hotel guests are sitting at tables. High on the terrace is a radio loudspeaker. Anita's voice, singing, is heard from it, followed by the playing of Jonny's jazz band. Daniello joins the guests on the terrace and as he hears Jonny's band he recognizes the tone of his own violin. He rushes off to notify the police. The scene changes to a street. Jonny is running with the violin-case, for he has seen detectives watching him. He eludes three policemen and hurries to the railroad terminal. The next scene shows a platform of the station. Max enters. He has been cured of his love for the glacier and is eager to find Anita and to go with her to America. Jonny, a few steps ahead of the police, rushes in and drops the stolen violin on Max's luggage. The police find it, arrest Max, and lead him off. Anita comes looking for Max, and Daniello approaches, triumphant at the recovery of his violin and at the arrest of his rival, Max. Anita tells Daniello that Max is not the thief, and she begs him to go to the police station and to have Max released. Daniello refuses either to go himself or to let Yvonne, the maid, explain matters to the police. The Amsterdam train is heard approaching. Yvonne struggles with Daniello and Daniello falls in front of the advancing locomotive. The scene changes to another part of the station showing a gate marked "exit." Jonny enters and whispers that he must get the violin again. Yvonne begs him to save Max. Jonny is willing, provided he can get the violin. He notices a police car parked near by. He knocks the sleeping chauffeur unconscious, and takes his place in the driver's seat. Two policemen enter with Max and the violin. They get into the car and tell Jonny, disguised as the chauffeur, to "step on it." The next scene is a street on which Jonny is driving the car. He swings it around, pushes the chauffeur out and knocks the two policemen unconscious. Again the scene changes and returns to the station platform. Anita, her manager, and Yvonne are still waiting for Max, who appears at the top of the stairs. He hurries down just in time to enter a coach of the departing train with Anita, Yvonne, and the manager. As the train pulls out, Jonny is seen on a bridge-balcony, surrounded by his band, and by people dancing. Jonny sits on a clock as he leads his band, and suddenly the clock becomes an illuminated, revolving globe. Jonny stands on the North Pole and plays his violin, as the crowds of people around him dance the Charleston.

§)&(§

LA JUIVE

(The Jewess)

Jacques Halévy

Jacques Halévy wrote many operas, but *La Juive* is the only one of them which is performed today. Its leading role has long been a favorite with dramatic tenors, and in the early twentieth century it was one of Enrico Caruso's greatest parts. The opera uses a libretto by Augustin Eugène Scribe, and it was first produced at the Grand Opéra in Paris, February 23, 1835.

The action involves the persecution of the Jews in fifteenth-century Rome and Constance. Before Cardinal Brogny entered the church he was active in the persecution. When his house in Rome was burned by a mob his wife was killed and it was thought that his baby daughter also died. She, however, was saved by a Jew named Eleazar, who adopted her as his own daughter and named her Rachel.

The principal characters are:

CARDINAL BROGNY (*Bass*)
ELEAZAR (*Tenor*), a Jewish goldsmith
RACHEL (*Soprano*), his adopted daughter but actually the child of Cardinal Brogny
LEOPOLD (*Tenor*), a Prince
EUDOXIA (*Soprano*), Leopold's fiancée

The first act shows a street of Constance in front of the Cathedral. A celebration is being held in honor of the victories Prince Leopold has won against the Hussites. Eleazar, the Jew, is arrested because he will not join the celebration. Cardinal Brogny recognizes Eleazar as a Jew who once lived in Rome, and Eleazar in turn recognizes the Cardinal as the man who ordered the execution of his, Eleazar's, sons during the persecution. Eleazar curses the

Cardinal, but in spite of his malediction, the Cardinal orders him freed. Prince Leopold enters, not in military dress, but in simple clothes. He is pretending that he is a young Jew named Samuel, so that he may make love to Rachel, Eleazar's adopted daughter. During the festival Eleazar and Rachel climb the steps of the Cathedral so that they may have a better view of the crowd. Again they are arrested, and this time Leopold saves them.

The second act is laid in Eleazar's house. Eleazar, Rachel and Leopold posing as "Samuel," are celebrating the Passover. Eudoxia, fiancée of Leopold, comes to buy some jewels from Eleazar. She knows nothing of her betrothed's pursuit of Rachel, and Leopold hides so that she will not see him. Rachel realizes that something is wrong and when Eudoxia has gone she questions "Samuel," or Leopold, who tells her that he is not a Jew but a Christian, but that he is eager to elope with her. Eleazar is so angry when he hears that "Samuel" is not a Jew that he tries to kill him. He fails in his attempt, and relents. Leopold knows that the King will never consent to his marrying a Jewess, so when Eleazar insists that he wed his daughter, Leopold refuses.

The third act shows a banquet hall in the imperial palace. Eleazar and Rachel are among the crowd who are watching the festivities. They see Eudoxia bring to Leopold the jewels she bought from Eleazar, and hear her announce that she is willing to marry Leopold. For the first time Rachel and Eleazar learn that "Samuel" is the Prince. Rachel confronts Leopold and denounces him. She snatches the jewels from him and returns them to Eudoxia. Cardinal Brogny curses Leopold and also Rachel and Eleazar. He sentences them to death.

The fourth act is laid in an ante-room of the Council

Chamber. Eudoxia begs Rachel to take back her charges against Leopold. Rachel generously agrees. The Cardinal tells Eleazar that he can save himself by becoming a Christian. Eleazar refuses and informs the Cardinal that when the Cardinal's house in Rome was burned, he, Eleazar, saved the Cardinal's daughter from the flames. Brogny pleads with Eleazar to tell him where his daughter is, but the Jew says he will not do so until after his own daughter, Rachel, is executed. Even though Eleazar loves Rachel, his desire for revenge is greater than his love. In a stirring aria he tries to rationalize his scheme by singing "God directs my acts."

The fifth act shows the execution chamber. Leopold's sentence has been revoked. Eleazar and Rachel are offered their lives if they will renounce Judaism and become Christians. Both refuse and Rachel is thrown into a cauldron of boiling oil. The Cardinal turns to Eleazar and asks him to keep his promise, and now that Rachel is executed, to tell him where his daughter is. Eleazar points to the cauldron and cries: "Behold, there is your daughter!"

§)&(§

KHOVANTCHINA

Modeste Moussorgsky

Modeste Moussorgsky wrote the libretto for his last opera, *Khovantchina,* and completed most of the music before his death. It was later finished and entirely orchestrated by Rimsky-Korsakoff. The work was first performed at the Kononov Theatre in St. Petersburg, February 2, 1886.

The characters include:

PRINCE IVAN KHOVANTSKY (*Bass*), a plotter against the Czar
ANDREW (*Tenor*), his son
PRINCE VASILI GOLITZIN (*Tenor*), a reformer
DOSITHEUS (*Bass*), leader of the "Old Believers"
MARTHA (*Mezzo-soprano*), an "Old Believer"; discarded mistress of Andrew
EMMA (*Contralto*), a young German girl
TCHAKLOVITY (*Baritone*), a Boyard

The action occurs in Moscow during the reign of Peter the Great (1672-1725). The first act shows the Red Square at Moscow, where a group of radicals are gathered. Prince Ivan Khovantsky addresses the mob and urges them to oppose the Czar. The Prince's son Andrew makes love to a German girl, Emma, and as she resists him, his former mistress, Martha, scolds him for his many sins. Prince Ivan is himself charmed with Emma, and orders her taken prisoner. Dositheus, head of the "Old Believers," quiets the crowd and saves Emma.

The second act shows the apartment of Prince Golitzin, a reformer. Golitzin asks Martha to read his horoscope. Martha warns Golitzin that his wealth will not help him, and that he will be taken to Siberia. He is angry at this prophecy and quarrels with Martha. Dositheus interrupts and pacifies them. He says that Russia can be saved only by a return to religion.

In the third act, outside of Ivan's house, Tchaklovity announces that the Czar has put down the insurrection of the radicals.

The fourth act shows Ivan's country estate. Tchaklovity tells Ivan that he is summoned to a council of state, but as Ivan is changing his clothes for the journey, he is killed by assassins. The scene changes to the square in Moscow where Golitzin is being led away to exile. Dositheus mourns for the fate of Russia and Martha warns him that a trap has been set for the "Old Believers." The radicals bring in headsmen's axes for their own execution, but word comes from the Czar that they are all pardoned.

The last act shows a wood near Moscow. The "Old Believers" agree not to renounce their faith, but to sacrifice themselves on a funeral pyre. Martha applies the torch as the followers mount the pyre and the opera ends with the dying chant of the faithful.

§)&(§

THE KING'S HENCHMAN

Deems Taylor

In 1925 the Metropolitan Opera House in New York commissioned Deems Taylor to compose an opera. He in turn asked Edna St. Vincent Millay to write the libretto, and *The King's Henchman* was first performed February 17, 1927.

Because the action of the opera occurs in ninth-century England, Miss Millay wrote a dramatic poem using only words of Anglo-Saxon origin, and none of Latin derivation. The plot deals with King Eadgar who, wanting to re-marry after the death of his first wife, sends a trusted retainer, Aethelwold, to fetch for him Aelfrida, daughter of the Thane of Devon. He has heard that she is very beautiful. Like Tristan, and our own John Alden, Aethelwold himself falls in love with the lady.

The principal characters are:

EADGAR OF WESSEX (*Baritone*), King of England
AETHELWOLD, EARL OF EAST ANGLIA (*Tenor*), friend and foster-brother to Eadgar
ORDGAR (*Bass*), Thane of Devon
MACCUS (*Bass*), Master of Horse to Aethelwold
AELFRIDA (*Soprano*), Ordgar's daughter
ASE (*Mezzo-soprano*), Aelfrida's serving woman

The first act shows the hall of King Eadgar's castle at Winchester at the conclusion of a banquet. Eadgar and his nobles, some of them a bit worse for the festivities, are seated at the table. The ladies are grouped at the other end of the hall where they may hear Maccus, the harper, sing of the exploits of former heroes. Then the nobles discuss Eadgar's proposed remarriage and they learn that Aethelwold is to go to Devon for the chosen bride. Aethelwold has been selected because he is known to dislike women—"He shunneth a fair maid as she were a foul marten." Aethelwold rehearses the details of his mission. The pledge is sealed and the hero is toasted. His horse is brought to him and he takes his departure.

The second act shows a forest in Devon on the eve of All Hallow Mass. The fog is so thick that Aethelwold and his companion Maccus have become separated and enter from opposite directions. They come together only after hearing the sounds of each other's voices. Aethelwold is weary and falls into a deep sleep at the foot of a giant tree. Presently Aelfrida enters with Ase, her serving woman. Aelfrida asks Ase to leave her, for she has come to chant a spell which, she has been told, will reveal her future lover. Aelfrida sings the magic words, and as the fog clears a ray of moonlight falls on Aethelwold, asleep under the tree. Aelfrida cries: "Whatever thou art I would thou wert what thou seemest, so lord-like, so lank and young." She kisses him and he awakes. Gradually their conversation becomes impassioned. They tell each other their names, and Aethewold realizes that his new-found love is the lady he is to take to the king. He struggles between duty and love, and finally he can no longer resist. He takes Maccus aside and tells him to go back to the King and bear a message saying that Aethelwold has seen the maiden and has "found her nothing fair." Certainly she is "nothing for the King," so "whereas the Lord Aethelwold, spare the King's love, hath little else besides—the blessing of King Eadgar is sought upon the wedding of Lord Aethelwold unto the maid Aelfrida." And as Maccus departs, Aethelwold looks at Aelfrida and says: "Now I shall look no more beyond thine eyes."

The third act is laid in the hall of Ordgar's house. Aethelwold and Aelfrida are married, but are not happy. Aethelwold has a troubled conscience and his unconfessed treachery is causing him sleepless nights. Aelfrida is fretted by the cares of the household. Her father, Ordgar, is a fussy old thane, and the tempers of all three are at the breaking point. Aethelwold decides to take his bride to Ghent in Flanders. They will say farewell to Devon, and to the surroundings that cause Aethelwold remorse. As he and Aelfrida look at the sea, Maccus bursts into the room and announces that King Eadgar is at the gates, come on a friendly visit. In panic Aethelwold confesses his deception to Aelfrida. Slowly she realizes that she might have been Queen of England. Aethelwold tries desperately to save himself. He begs Aelfrida to assume a disguise; to "be foul, bent, weathered," and to keep to her bower, where none may see her but himself and the King. Aelfrida leaves and

Aethelwold thinks she will help him. The King and his party enter. The King asks to see Aelfrida, and Aethelwold starts to take him to her. Suddenly she confronts them at the head of the stairs, decked in all her jewels, proud and splendid. Eadgar's arm drops slowly from Aethelwold's shoulder, and as he realizes that his trusted friend and foster-brother has broken his pledge, he rebukes Aethelwold, not in anger, but in sorrow. With his priceless honor gone, Aethelwold can see no course open to him but to plunge his dagger into his own breast. Aelfrida cries: "God in Heaven, how he bleeds!" and the King says to her: "Have done, Aelfrida. Thou hast not tears enow in thy narrow heart to weep him worthily." The opera ends with the King intoning his lament against the chorus of retainers and woodsmen.

§)&(§

DIE KÖNIGSKINDER
(Kingly Children)
Engelbert Humperdinck

The libretto of Engelbert Humperdinck's fairy opera, *Die Königskinder,* bears the name of Ernst Rosmer, which was the pen name of Elsa Bernstein. The opera is a revision of Humperdinck's melodrama of the same name, which was performed at Munich in 1897. The revised work had its first performance at the Metropolitan Opera House, New York, December 28, 1910, with Geraldine Farrar singing the role of the Goose Girl.

The principal characters are:

THE KING'S SON (*Tenor*)
THE GOOSE GIRL (*Soprano*)
THE FIDDLER (*Baritone*)
THE WITCH (*Contralto*)
THE WOOD CUTTER (*Bass*)
THE BROOM MAKER (*Tenor*)
THE INNKEEPER (*Bass*)
THE INNKEEPER'S DAUGHTER (*Mezzo-soprano*)
TWO GATEKEEPERS (*Baritones*)

The first act shows a small sunlit glade in the Hella woods, where the Goose Girl lives in a hut with the cruel Witch. The Goose Girl lies on the grass. The Witch calls from the window, bidding the girl to be up and tending to her geese. The Witch also commands the Goose Girl to prepare a magic pastry which will poison all who eat it. Protesting, the girl enters the hut. When she comes out again she beholds a youth, shabbily dressed. A sword hangs by his side and in his hand he carries a bundle. He is the King's Son and he has left his home so that he may be free. He tells the Goose Girl of his wanderings and she asks him what a King's Son may be. Marveling at her ignorance and entranced by her beauty, he falls in love with her. He kisses her and when a gust of wind blows the girl's wreath away, he picks it up and offers in exchange his bundle, containing the royal crown. He and the Goose Girl are about to run away when she discovers that her feet are glued to the ground. The King's Son thinks that she is afraid to go with him. He tosses his crown to the grass and tells the Goose Girl that she is unworthy to be a king's wife. As he leaves her, he vows that she will never see him again until a star has fallen into a lily which is blooming near by. The Witch returns and finds the Goose Girl sighing for her lover. She scolds the girl for wasting her time on a man, and weaves a magic spell to prevent her escape. Soon the Fiddler enters, followed by the Woodcutter and the Broom Maker. They ask the Witch to help them find the King's Son. The King has died, and the people of Hellabrunn are anxious to have a king or queen to rule over them. The Witch tells the Fiddler and his two followers that the first person who enters the town gate at noon the next day should be placed on the throne. It matters not whether this person is richly dressed or in rags. The Woodcutter and the Broom Maker return to Hellabrunn, but the Fiddler stays behind hoping to see the Goose Girl. She soon appears and tells of her troubles. The Fiddler assures her that she shall wed the King's Son, but the Witch jeers and tells the Fiddler that the Goose Girl is the child of a hangman's daughter. The Goose Girl prays to her dead father and mother for help and as she kneels a shooting star falls into the lily. She runs off to the woods with her flock of geese to join her royal sweetheart.

The second act is laid near the town gate of Hellabrunn where the villagers are excitedly waiting for the coming of their new ruler. The King's Son enters, still shabbily dressed. He offers himself to the Innkeeper as an apprentice and is told that the only work available is that of a swineherd. The Councillors and Burghers arrive and invite the Woodcutter to tell of his adventures in the woods. The King's Son learns from the Woodcutter's account that a king's son, clad in princely raiment, will enter the gate on the stroke of twelve. He asks if it might not be possible that the awaited ruler would appear in rags. The crowd laughs at such a silly idea and the King's Son is called a meddler and a thief. Soon the clock strikes twelve and as the gate is opened the Goose Girl enters, surrounded by her geese. The crowd jeers and as the King's Son comes to the Goose

Girl's side to protect her, the two of them are driven from the town. The Fiddler protests in vain and rages at the villagers for their blindness.

The third act returns to the Witch's hut in winter time. The Witch has been burned at the stake for betraying the people to whom she had promised a new king or queen. The Fiddler has been tortured for defending the Goose Girl and the King's Son, and he is now living alone in the Witch's hut, tending the geese the Goose Girl left behind. The Woodcutter and the Broom Maker come with a troop of children from the village to beg the Fiddler to return to Hellabrunn. He refuses, but he agrees to help in the search for the King's Son and his bride. The Fiddler leads the children in the search and the Woodcutter and the Broom Maker go into the hut where they find the poisoned pastry the Witch had forced the Goose Girl to bake. While they are inside the King's Son and the Goose Girl appear, hungry, thirsty, and exhausted. They knock at the hut and beg the Woodcutter for food and drink. The Woodcutter refuses, and the Goose Girl, to encourage the King's Son and to hide from him the fact that she is totally exhausted, tries to sing and dance. She grows faint and falls. To save her, the King's Son offers the Woodcutter his royal crown in return for the pastry. The results of eating it are fatal, and the King's Son and the Goose Girl die, believing that they have found happiness in a land of love and flowers. The Fiddler and the children return to find the lovers dead. They place them on a bier and carry them away for burial on a high hill. As they leave they sing a lament for the Kingly Children—"Die Königskinder."

§)&(§

LAKMÉ

Léo Delibes

The libretto of this opera by Léo Delibes was written by Edmond Gondinet and Philippe Émile François Gille. The work was first performed at the Opéra Comique in Paris, April 14, 1883. The action occurs during the 1880's in and around a large city of India, which had been recently conquered and occupied by the British.

The cast includes:

NILAKANTHA (*Baritone*), a Brahman priest
LAKMÉ (*Soprano*), his daughter
GERALD (*Tenor*) }
FREDERICK (*Baritone*) } officers in the British army
ELLEN (*Soprano*) }
ROSE (*Soprano*) } daughters of the British governor

In the opening scene, Nilakantha stands before his temple and exhorts the worshippers to prepare for the day when the British invaders will be driven from the country. He talks with his daughter, Lakmé, and as he leaves he orders her attendants to guard her closely. Lakmé asks her companion to gather flowers with her, and as she goes out she lays her jewels on a table. An English sightseeing party enters—the British officers, Gerald and Frederick, and the governor's daughters, Ellen and Rose. They are charmed by the garden and they disregard Frederick's warning against violating the sacred ground of the Brahmans. After they have broken the fence surrounding the garden and have discovered the jewels that Lakmé left on the table, they decide to trespass no further. Gerald stays behind to sketch the design of the jewels so that he may have duplicates made for Ellen, his fiancée. Lakmé returns, and Gerald and the daughter of the Brahman priest are immediately fascinated by each other. Lakmé warns Gerald that the penalty for trespassing is death, and urges him to leave immediately. As soon as he has gone, Nilakantha returns. He notices the footprints of the stranger, and swears that he will find the man who has violated the sacred ground.

The second act shows the market place of the city. Nilakantha and Lakmé are disguised as beggars. Nilakantha orders Lakmé to sing, hoping that the beauty of her voice will lead the profaner of the temple grounds to reveal himself. Lakmé sings the "Bell Song" and Nilakantha's scheme is successful. Gerald recognizes Lakmé's voice, and by expressing his pleasure shows himself as the invader. Nilakantha stabs Gerald and leaves him for dead. Lakmé stays behind, finds that Gerald is still alive, and has her attendants carry him off.

The third act is laid in a forest hut, where Lakmé has nursed Gerald and brought him back to health. He and Lakmé are deeply in love and they agree to drink the waters of the sacred fountain which make love constant and lasting. While Lakmé goes to bring the water from the fountain, Gerald's fellow officer, Frederick, comes to tell him that their regiment has been ordered off to suppress a Hindu revolt. Gerald agrees to return but asks Frederick to leave him so that he may bid farewell to Lakmé. Lakmé comes with the water as Gerald hears the fife and drum of his regiment. When he refuses the draught, Lakmé realizes that she has lost her lover. In despair she secretly eats the flowers of the deadly "datura." Gerald relents and drinks the love potion. Nilakantha enters and is about to strike Gerald when Lakmé declares that they have both taken the sacred love potion. She must accordingly be the victim offered to the gods. As she utters these words, her strength fails and she dies in Gerald's arms.

THE LEGEND

Joseph Breil

Joseph Breil's one-act opera, *The Legend,* was produced at the Metropolitan Opera House, New York, March 12, 1919. Its libretto was written by Jacques Byrne.

The characters are:

COUNT STACKAREFF (*Bass*), an impoverished nobleman
CARMELITA (*Soprano*), his daughter
STEPHEN PAULOFF (*Baritone*), her lover
MARTA (*Contralto*), a servant

The action occurs in Mucovadia, a mythical country in the Balkans. Count Stackareff is a respectable nobleman by day, but at night he is a bandit, Black Lorenzo. He tells his daughter Carmelita that he has captured a rich merchant whom he is holding for ransom. Carmelita learns that her sweetheart, Stephen, is coming to see her. According to legend, this is the night of the Evil One, and when Marta the servant tells Carmelita's fortune, the ace of spades appears at every cutting. This is the symbol of death. Stephen arrives, and Carmelita learns that he has come not only to make love to her, but also to capture Black Lorenzo, dead or alive. When the Count learns of Stephen's mission he escapes through the door. Stephen realizes that he is Black Lorenzo and tries to follow but Carmelita stabs him. Two soldiers bring in the dead body of the Count, and when they see that Stephen has been killed, they shoot Carmelita.

§)&(§

A LIFE FOR THE CZAR

Mikhail Glinka

The text of Mikhail Glinka's opera, *A Life for the Czar,* was written by G. F. Rozen, and the work was first produced at St. Petersburg, December 9, 1836.

The cast includes:

IVAN SUSANNIN (*Bass*), a peasant of the village of Domnin
ANTONIDA (*Soprano*), his daughter
SOBINJIN (*Tenor*), Antonida's lover
WAUJA (*Contralto*), an orphan boy, adopted by Susannin

The action occurs in the village of Domnin, at Moscow, and in the camp of the Polish army during the year 1613. The first act shows the village, Sobinjin, Antonida's lover, brings word of the defeat of the Poles. When he makes love to Antonida, she refuses to marry him until the country has been pacified by the selection of a new Czar. News comes that the wealthy landowner, Romanov, has been selected, so there is no further barrier to the marriage.

The second act is in the camp of the Poles. When the Poles learn that their army has been defeated and that Romanov has been selected Czar, they move upon the monastery in which Romanov is living.

The third act shows the hut of Susannin, the father of Antonida. The Poles try to get Susannin to show the way to the Czar, but Susannin will not be a traitor. His adopted son, Wauja, pretends to accept a bribe to betray the Czar.

In the fourth act, which opens before the monastery, Wauja has ridden his horse to death in his attempt to save the Czar. In another scene, in a forest, Susannin is being forced to lead the Poles in a snowstorm. They already suspect that he is leading them astray, but he determines to give his life for the Czar.

The fifth act shows the Kremlin in Moscow. The Czar is safe and enters the city. Both the Czar and the people honor Antonida, Sobinjin and Wauja, and grieve for the death of Susannin, who sacrificed himself to save Romanov, the Czar.

§)&(§

LINDA DI CHAMOUNIX

Gaetano Donizetti

Linda di Chamounix was the sixty-first of Gaetano Donizetti's sixty-seven operas. Its libretto was founded on the French play, *La grâce de Dieu*, and was written by Gaetano Rossi. The opera was first produced at the Kärntnertor-Theater in Vienna, May 19, 1842.

The cast includes:

LINDA (*Soprano*)
ANTONIO (*Bass*), her father
MADALINA (*Mezzo-soprano*), her mother
MARCHIONESS DE SERVAL (*Mezzo-soprano*)
CHARLES (*Tenor*), appearing first as a young painter, but actually the Viscomte de Serval, son of the Marchioness
MARQUIS DE BOISFLEURY (*Bass*), brother of the Marchioness and uncle of Charles
PIERROTO (*Contralto*), a villager
PREFECT OF THE VILLAGE (*Bass*)

The first act is laid in the village of Chamounix, in the year 1760. Antonio and Madalina are in trouble financially and they are afraid that their landlady, the Marchioness de Serval, will evict them. Their daughter, Linda, has fallen in love with Charles, a young painter who has come to the neighborhood to sketch. Linda has another admirer in the

Marquis de Boisfleury, who hopes to seduce her. In order to gain the confidence of her parents, the Marquis assures them that they will not be dispossessed. The Prefect of the village suspects the motives of the Marquis and he suggests to Linda's parents that he take her to Paris where she may live under the protection of his aged brother. Antonio and Madalina agree to this plan and Linda starts for Paris, accompanied by Pierroto, a trusted villager.

The second act shows a Paris apartment where Linda is living in luxury. When she arrived in Paris she became separated from Pierroto and then learned that the Prefect's brother was dead. Charles, who had followed her to Paris, has revealed himself to Linda as the Marquis Viscomte de Serval, son of the Marchioness, and has proposed marriage. Meanwhile he is providing her with a sumptuous apartment. Pierroto finds Linda and brings her father, Antonio, now a beggar. Linda offers Antonio money but he hurls it back at her, thinking that she is an abandoned woman living with a lover. Meanwhile, the Marchioness has learned that her son is planning to marry a farmer's daughter, the child of her tenant, and she declares that if Charles does not marry the woman she has chosen for him, she will have Linda thrown into prison. Charles plans to thwart his mother by pretending to carry out her wishes. Linda thinks he has deserted her, and her grief drives her to madness.

The last act returns to the village. Pierroto has brought the insane Linda home. Charles follows her but she does not recognize him until he sings an old familiar love song. This brings back her memory, and then she is told that Charles's mother has given her consent to their marriage. Charles brings also the happy news that the farm has been restored to Linda's parents.

§)&(§

LOBETANZ

(Merrydance)

Ludwig Thuille

Lobetanz is an opera by Ludwig Thuille, with a libretto by Otto Julius Bierbaum. It was first produced at the Hoftheater in Karlsruhe, February 6, 1898.

The principal characters are:

LOBETANZ (*Tenor*), a wandering minstrel
THE PRINCESS (*Mezzo-soprano*)
THE KING (*Bass*)
THE HANGMAN (*Bass*)
THE JUDGE (*Bass*)

The action occurs in Germany during the Middle Ages. The first act shows a spring garden in full bloom. Lobetanz, a wandering minstrel, learns that the royal Princess has lost interest in life and is persuaded by the maidens of the court to stay and see what he can do for her. The King and the Princess enter with the royal procession. The Princess listlessly pronounces the invocation to the day of roses and the King orders his minstrels to sing a song in praise of the Princess. The minstrels sing so loudly that the Princess is frightened. The people laugh at the minstrels, and as they are mocking them, the sound of a violin is heard. The Princess listens and is delighted. Lobetanz steps forward. It is he who has played the magic strains. The King commands him to sing. Lobetanz responds with a sad song about his humble, obscure parentage and his love for a lady far above his station. The Princess is so affected that she faints. Lobetanz escapes to the woods.

The second act opens in a woodland meadow where Lobetanz is playing to the birds and singing of the Princess's beauty. The Princess appears, and she and the minstrel sing of their love for each other. They are interrupted by the arrival of the royal hunting party. Lobetanz is accused of witchcraft and is arrested. As he is led past the Princess, she falls into a deathlike coma. Lobetanz is condemned to death.

The third act opens in the prison. The Hangman comes for Lobetanz and the scene changes to the hillock on which the gallows stands. As Lobetanz is led in the people gather and bring a bier on which the seemingly dead Princess lies. The Judge pronounces the sentence and asks Lobetanz if he wishes to speak. Lobetanz asks the King to let him play once more, and promises that he will bring the Princess back to life. The King tells Lobetanz that he may marry the Princess if he succeeds. Lobetanz plays and the Princess slowly wakes, sits up, and smiles. Lobetanz takes her in his arms and carries her to the top of the hillock. The crowd is jubilant and the King invites everyone to the wedding.

§)&(§

LODOLETTA

Pietro Mascagni

Ouida's story, *Two Little Wooden Shoes,* was the basis of Pietro Mascagni's opera *Lodoletta.* The libretto was written by Giovacchino Forzano, and the opera was first produced at the Teatro Costanzi in Rome, April 30, 1917.

The cast of characters includes:

LODOLETTA (*Soprano*)
ANTONIO (*Bass*), her foster-father
GIANNOTTO (*Baritone*), in love with Lodoletta
FLAMMEN (*Tenor*), a painter

The action occurs in the year 1853, at a little Dutch village and in Paris. The first act shows the village. At the right is a cottage which is the home of Lodoletta and her foster-father, Antonio. It is Lodoletta's birthday and the villagers are decorating her cottage with flowers. Giannotto, who is very much in love with Lodoletta, brings a handsome gift. Antonio would like to give his adopted daughter a pair of little red shoes, but he has not enough money. Flammen, a painter from Paris, arrives with a party of friends. When the Parisians find that the only refreshment they can procure is milk, they move on, but Flammen is attracted by a picture of the Madonna which is set in a shrine in the wall of Lodoletta's cottage. He tries to buy the picture from Antonio, and when Antonio refuses, Flammen offers to rent it so that he may copy it. He promises to return it immediately. Antonio tells Flammen to wait until evening when Lodoletta is asleep, then he may have the picture for a short time. Flammen pays Antonio in advance, and Antonio goes to the store to buy the red shoes for Lodoletta's birthday.

Lodoletta arrives and receives the congratulations of her neighbors. Antonio returns with the shoes, and after he has given them to Lodoletta he climbs into a peach tree and showers blossoms upon the children below. While he is doing this Giannotto tries to tell Lodoletta of his love, but she puts him off. Suddenly the branch on which Antonio is sitting breaks, and the old man falls to the ground and is killed. Lodoletta is heartbroken and Giannotto tries to persuade her to come with him to his cottage where his mother will take care of her. She asks to be left alone. Flammen returns to get the picture from Antonio. He finds Lodoletta weeping, and when he learns of the tragedy he soothes her until she falls asleep with her head on his shoulder. Then he leaves her and places flowers in the shrine of the Madonna.

The second act is laid in the same setting, six months later. Flammen has taken a cottage across the way from Lodoletta's home and is painting her portrait. Their relationship has been entirely innocent and Lodoletta does not realize that she is deeply in love with Flammen. The neighbors believe that Lodoletta is Flammen's mistress, and when she starts to play with the children of the village their mothers tell them to have nothing to do with her. Giannotto reproaches Lodoletta but still offers to marry her. For the first time she learns what people are thinking and she is deeply hurt. Flammen finds her weeping and is so touched by her loveliness that he declares his love for her. When she refuses him he respects her innocence and decides to leave the village.

The third act is in Paris, in the garden of Flammen's villa. It is New Year's Eve and Flammen is host to a boisterous party. He himself has no heart for the festivities for he is still in love with Lodoletta, even though he has not seen her since he left the little Dutch village. His friends tell him that Lodoletta is probably consoling herself with another lover and they persuade him to come inside and try to enjoy the party. Lodoletta comes to the garden looking for Flammen. She believes that Flammen is a humble peasant like herself but when she looks through the windows and sees the merriment, the beautifully dressed women, and Flammen himself, she realizes that she would not fit into such a life. She starts to go away but is so exhausted that she can walk no farther. The little red shoes slip from her feet, and she sinks into the snow. She dies dreaming of her happy childhood and of Flammen's love for her. The party disbands and Flammen is left alone in the garden. He finds the shoes and Lodoletta's lifeless body.

He takes her in his arms and falls to the ground, crying that he will die with his loved one.

§)&(§

LOHENGRIN

Richard Wagner

Richard Wagner's *Lohengrin* was first produced at the Hoftheater in Weimar, August 28, 1850, a little more than five years after the initial performance of *Tannhäuser*. As in his other works, Wagner composed both the libretto and the music of *Lohengrin*.

The cast includes:

HENRY I (*Bass*), German King
ELSA OF BRABANT (*Soprano*)
FRIEDRICH TELRAMUND (*Baritone*), Count of Brabant, guardian of Elsa
ORTRUD (*Mezzo-soprano*), wife of Telramund
LOHENGRIN (*Tenor*), Knight of the Holy Grail

The action takes place during the tenth century near Antwerp in Flanders. The scene of the first act is on the banks of the Scheld. King Henry has come to Brabant to persuade its soldiers to fight against the invading Hungarians. He finds that the Duchy is filled with intrigue. Gottfried, son of the late Duke and heir to the Dukedom, has disappeared, and Friedrich Telramund, regent for Gottfried, has been persuaded by his wife Ortrud to accuse Elsa, Gottfried's sister, of having murdered her brother. Elsa appears before the King and pleads her innocence.

The King decides that the matter shall be settled by combat—a fight between Telramund and any knight who will offer to defend Elsa. Elsa declares that she will choose for her defender a knight she has seen in a dream. A herald gives a call and no one appears. Elsa falls on her knees in prayer and as the herald sounds a second call a swan appears on the river, drawing a boat in which stands a knight in armor. The knight announces that he has come to defend Elsa, and he makes Elsa promise that she will never ask him who he is or where he comes from. The knight fights with Telramund and strikes him to the ground. The knight spares Telramund's life and then turns to Elsa and asks her hand in marriage.

The second act shows the fortress at Antwerp on the night of Elsa's wedding to the strange knight. Ortrud and Telramund are in ragged garments. Telramund is in despair but Ortrud urges him to make another attempt to regain his fortunes. Elsa appears on the balcony and Ortrud, pretending that she is repentant, persuades Elsa to obtain a pardon for Telramund. Ortrud then advises Elsa to find out who this knight is that she is marrying. The herald proclaims that the King has made the strange knight Duke of Brabant. The wedding ceremony is announced and as Elsa and her attendants are about to go into the church, Ortrud steps forward and accuses the knight of being a magician. Telramund declares that the knight has beaten him unfairly, and challenges him to reveal his identity. Elsa vows her loyalty to the knight and reasserts her confidence in him.

The third act opens in the bridal chamber of the palace. First the "Wedding March" is played and then the bridal party enters, singing the "Bridal Chorus." When the guests have left, Elsa begs her husband to tell her who he is. He tries to stop her questioning but she persists. Just as he is about to answer, Telramund rushes into the room and attacks the knight. The knight kills Telramund, and then turns sorrowfully to Elsa and tells her that he will answer her questions. The scene changes to the banks of the Scheld. The King and his court are waiting for the knight, who appears with the nobles who are carrying Telramund's body. In answer to Elsa's questions, the knight explains that he is Lohengrin, one of the Knights of the Holy Grail who are pledged to aid the oppressed. When accomplishing good deeds they are allowed to be absent as long as they remain unknown. Now that Elsa has questioned him he must return. The swan reappears, and Lohengrin bids Elsa farewell. Ortrud discloses the fact that the swan is Gottfried, Elsa's brother. She, Ortrud, had changed him into a swan by sorcery. Lohengrin kneels in prayer. When a dove flies down from heaven, the swan disappears into the water, and Gottfried appears on the river bank. Lohengrin is led away by the dove as Elsa embraces her brother and weeps for the loss of her husband.

§)&(§

LOUISE

Gustave Charpentier

Gustave Charpentier composed both the libretto and the music for his opera *Louise*. When it was first produced at the Opéra Comique in Paris, February 2, 1900, it was one of the few operas that had been written dealing with contemporary life. Although the plot of *Louise* deals with the love of Louise and Julien, the city of Paris is its real hero, or heroine. The score features the street cries of the city, and the several scenes show its festivals, its myriad of lights at night, and its strange assortment of people.

Mary Garden made her debut in *Louise,* on April 13, 1900, shortly after the first production of the opera. She was studying in Paris at that time, and when the singer who was singing the title role was suddenly taken ill, Mary Garden was asked to substitute. She achieved a great success, and Louise was thereafter one of her most important roles.

The principal characters of the opera are:

LOUISE (*Soprano*)
HER FATHER (*Baritone*)
HER MOTHER (*Contralto*)
JULIEN (*Tenor*), an artist, in love with Louise
IRMA (*Contralto*)

The first act shows a garret of a Paris tenement, where Louise lives with her parents. She is employed as a sewing girl in a factory, and she has fallen in love with a young artist, Julien, who has a studio across the way from her apartment. Its balcony almost touches Louise's window, and Julien has been singing serenades to her. According to the laws of France, Louise cannot marry Julien without her parents' consent, so Julien has written a letter to the parents asking their permission. As the opera opens Louise and Julien are talking across an alleyway. Julien is waiting for an answer to his letter, and he reminds Louise that she has promised to elope with him if her father refuses permission for their marriage. Louise wavers between duty to her parents and her love for Julien. She asks Julien how he happened to fall in love with her and he replies in an aria that begins: *Depuis longtemps j'habitais cette chambre,* ("A long, long time I have lived in this room.") As Julien and Louise sing to each other of their love, Louise's mother enters and listens to their duet. They are unaware of her presence until she interrupts them. Julien disappears and the mother tells Louise that her lover is a good-for-nothing artist, a shabby, improvident Bohemian. The father returns from his day's work and the three have supper. After the father has lit his pipe, he reads Julien's letter. The mother angrily protests against even considering the proposed marriage, but the father is more judicious. He suggests that they look into Julien's character. The mother refuses even this concession, and she and Louise quarrel. The father tries to act as a peace-maker, and he reasons with Louise. She agrees to try to forget Julien.

The first scene of the second act shows a street in the Montmartre district at dawn. The revelers of the night are leaving and the morning laborers are on their way to work. Julien and some of his friends hide as Louise enters with her mother. The mother leaves Louise at the door of the dress shop, and Julien comes forward. He learns from Louise that her father has refused permission for their marriage, and he begs her to remember her promise to elope with him. Louise refuses, but promises that some day she will be his wife. She enters the shop and Julien sadly walks away. The scene changes to the inside of the sewing establishment. The girls are gathered about a table, sewing and gossiping. They tell Louise that she does not look well; they are sure she is in love. Julien's voice is heard outside, serenading Louise. At first the girls applaud Julien, but they soon grow tired of the singing and make fun of the lover. Louise says she is ill, and leaves the shop. When she is gone the girls run to the window and see Louise walking away with Julien.

The third act shows the garden of a cottage on the Hill of Montmartre. Julien and Louise are living together, unmarried. Julien tells Louise of his happiness and sings the aria *Depuis le jour.* ("Ever since the day.") Below them the lights of the city begin to shine through the darkness. Louise and Julien go into the cottage, and soon a gay Bohemian crowd comes to decorate the garden with lanterns. These friends summon the lovers and crown Louise Queen of Montmartre. In the midst of the merrymaking Louise's mother appears and the crowd leaves hurriedly. The mother does not scold Louise, but she brings news that Louise's father is very sick, and is dying from grief. If Louise will come to see him, the mother promises, she will be free to return to her lover. With this assurance, Julien allows Louise to go home with her mother.

The fourth act returns to the garret. Louise's father has recovered sufficiently to return to work, but the promise to Louise has been broken; she is being held a prisoner. She is sullen and defiant. Her father tries to reason with her, and tells her that the freedom she demands will lead only to her ruin. She seizes her shawl and tries to leave. Her father stops her, and she cries for Julien. Finally the father loses his temper and orders Louise out of the house. She screams and rushes down the stairs and into the street. The father goes to the window and calls her back. When she does not answer he rushes to the staircase calling "Louise! Louise!" Then he shakes his fist and cries: "Oh, Paris!"

§)&(§

THE LOVE FOR THREE ORANGES

Serge Prokofieff

Serge Prokofieff wrote his own libretto for his opera, *The Love for Three Oranges,* adapting it from a story by Carlo

Gozzi. It was performed first by the Chicago Opera Association at the Auditorium in that city, December 30, 1921.

The characters include:

THE KING OF CLUBS (*Bass*)
THE PRINCE (*Tenor*), his son
PRINCESS CLARISSE (*Contralto*), the King's niece
LEANDER (*Baritone*), the Prime Minister
TROUFFALDINO (*Tenor*), a comedian
FATA MORGANA (*Soprano*), a witch, protectress of Leander
FARAFARELLO (*Bass*), a devil
LINETTE (*Contralto*)
NICOLETTE (*Mezzo-soprano*)
NINETTE (*Soprano*)
} The Princesses hidden in the oranges

The place of action and the time are legendary. In the prologue the tragedians, comedians, empty-heads, and absurdities, argue as to what kind of entertainment the people want. The absurdities win, and drive the others away with shovels. In the first act, at the King's palace, the King of Clubs complains that his son is ill of a variety of ailments, all of which add up to acute hypochondria. Unless the Prince can be made to laugh he will not get well. Leander, the Prime Minister, does not want the Prince to recover, for if he dies he will put the King's niece Clarisse on the throne. The King orders the comedian Trouffaldino to organize a festival, and to produce acts which will make the Prince laugh.

The second act shows the festival. The Prince is bored until Fata Morgana, the witch and Leander's protectress, falls down clumsily. The Prince thinks this is so funny that he laughs violently. Fata Morgana puts a curse upon him. He must love the three oranges, and have no respite until he finds them and his love is returned. The Prince starts out on his journey with the comedian Trouffaldino. They are blown to their destination by the devil Farafarello.

In the third act the Prince and Trouffaldino find the three enormous oranges and pull them to the desert. Trouffaldino is thirsty and cuts open one of the oranges, hoping to drink its juice. The Princess Linette steps forth, and begs for a drink of water. The comedian cuts the second orange, and Nicolette appears. She too begs for water, and when Trouffaldino runs away, the two Princesses die of thirst. The Prince then opens the third orange, and Ninette steps out of it. The two fall in love with each other, and when she complains of thirst he finds a convenient pail of water and saves her life.

In the fifth act the Prince and Ninette return to the court. The villainy of Leander and Clarisse is revealed and they are condemned to be hanged. Fata Morgana saves them from the hangman by telling them to jump into a trap door which belches forth fire and smoke. The courtiers cry long life to the King, the Prince and the Princess.

§)&(§

LUCIA DI LAMMERMOOR

Gaetano Donizetti

Sir Walter Scott's novel, *The Bride of Lammermoor,* was the basis for the libretto which Salvatore Cammarano wrote for Gaetano Donizetti's most popular opera. The work was first performed at the San Carlo Theatre in Naples, September 26, 1835.

The action occurs in early eighteenth-century Scotland and the plot concerns a feud between the clans of Ravenswood and Lammermoor. The Lammermoors have reduced the Ravenswoods to poverty and Ravenswood castle is in ruins. Lord Henry Ashton of Lammermoor has been involved in Jacobite conspiracies against the English crown, and he hopes to offset the displeasure of the King by having his sister Lucy marry the wealthy Lord Arthur Bucklaw, who is influential at the English court.

The cast of the opera includes:

LORD HENRY ASHTON OF LAMMERMOOR (*Baritone*)
LUCY (*Soprano*), his sister
ALICE (*Soprano*), her companion
RAYMOND (*Bass*), chaplain to Henry and Lucy's tutor
EDGAR OF RAVENSWOOD (*Tenor*), Lucy's lover
LORD ARTHUR BUCKLAW (*Tenor*), whom Lucy's brother has chosen for her husband
NORMAN (*Tenor*), Lord Henry's chief retainer

The first scene of the first act shows a grove near Lord Henry's Castle of Lammermoor. Henry learns from Norman, his chief retainer, that Lucy has secretly been meeting Edgar of Ravenswood, his enemy. Henry sends his retainers to search for Edgar at his ruined castle, but they return with word that he has escaped. The scene changes to a park near the castle. Lucy is waiting for Edgar, who comes to tell her that he must leave for France. Before he goes he would like to meet her brother peacefully, and ask him for her hand. Lucy is afraid to have the two men meet, so she and Edgar pledge undying love, and Edgar leaves, assuring Lucy that she will hear from him often.

The second act opens in Lucy's apartment. In spite of Lucy's refusal to marry Lord Arthur, her brother Henry is making preparations for the wedding. He has had his retainer Norman intercept Edgar's letters from France, and he gives Lucy a forged letter from Edgar, telling her that he has found a new love in France. Henry then tells

Lucy of his own trouble with the English King, and pleads with her to marry Lord Arthur who can save him from ruin and disgrace, even from death for treason. Lucy finally consents, adding that death will soon relieve her of her sorrows. The second scene shows the hall of the castle. The guests are assembled for the wedding. Lucy greets Lord Arthur coldly and mechanically, but under the persistent urging of her brother, listlessly signs the marriage contract. Edgar suddenly appears and demands that the ceremony be stopped and that Lucy marry him, according to her promise. At this point the famous "Sextet" is sung. As it begins Edgar with drawn sword walks to the table. He asks himself why he has not already had vengeance and looking at Lucy, realizes that he still loves her. Henry sings of his fears for his own future and for the effect this excitement will have on Lucy. Lucy cries for death to save her from grief and shame, while Raymond and Alice, Lucy's companion, join with the guests in praying that Heaven will protect Lucy. All of these voices and the several conflicting emotions are blended into the harmonic pattern of the "Sextet." When it is finished Henry and Edgar rush at each other with drawn swords. Raymond keeps them apart and Henry shows Edgar the marriage contract which Lucy has signed. Edgar curses Lucy and all her family.

The third act opens in the hall of the Lammermoor Castle. The wedding guests are still there, and Lord Arthur and Lucy have retired to their bridal chamber. Raymond, the chaplain, rushes in and announces that Lucy has gone mad and has killed her husband. Then Lucy appears and in the famous "Mad Scene" sings first of joy with her lover Edgar, and then of her unhappy marriage to Lord Arthur. When she has finished, she falls dying. The scene changes to a churchyard where Edgar waits to fight a duel with

Henry. The church bell tolls and when Edgar learns that Lucy is dead, he kills himself with his dagger.

§)&(§

LUCREZIA BORGIA

Gaetano Donizetti

The libretto of Gaetano Donizetti's *Lucrezia Borgia,* written by Felice Romani, was based on Victor Hugo's play, *Lucrèce Borgia.* The opera was first produced at La Scala, Milan, December 26, 1833.

The characters include:

DON ALFONZO (*Baritone*), Duke of Ferrara
LUCREZIA BORGIA (*Soprano*), his wife
GENNARO (*Tenor*), her son
MAFFIO ORSINI (*Contralto*), a young nobleman

The action occurs in Italy, at Venice and Ferrara, during the early sixteenth century. The prologue shows the terrace of the Grimani Palace in Venice. A merry party is in progress. Maffio Orsini, a noble whose brother has been poisoned by Lucrezia Borgia, tells of his hatred for the Borgia family. His young friend, Gennaro, is not particularly interested, and lies down on a couch and falls asleep. As the noblemen leave Gennaro and go into the palace, a gondola appears at the back of the stage. From it steps Lucrezia Borgia, masked with a black domino. She approaches the sleeping Gennaro and bends over him. Gennaro does not know that he is Lucrezia's son by a former marriage and Lucrezia has concealed Gennaro's existence from her present husband, Don Alfonzo, Duke of Ferrara. The boy has been brought up by a fisherman. Lucrezia chants a prayer for Gennaro and removes her mask. He wakes and sees her. With the instinct of a cavalier, he makes love to her, but then, instinctively, he tells her that his first love has always been his mother, whom he has never seen. Lucrezia tells him always to adore his mother and to pray to heaven to spare her. The nobles come out of the palace and Orsini recognizes Lucrezia. He openly denounces her, and others accuse her of murdering their relatives. Gennaro is dumbfounded and Lucrezia, maddened by their insults, vows revenge on all but her son, who still does not know that Lucrezia is his mother.

The first act shows the entrance to Duke Alfonzo's Palace at Ferrara. Over the gate is a large escutcheon with the word BORGIA emblazoned in gilt letters. Don Alfonzo has learned that his wife Lucrezia has been paying secret visits to Gennaro, and not knowing that the youth is really her son, he is jealous. Gennaro, Orsini, and a group of their friends come out of a house at the left. They taunt Gennaro with being in love with a Borgia. He takes his sword and strikes the letter B from the escutcheon over the gate. The scene changes to a room in the palace. Lucrezia tells her husband that her family has been insulted by some unknown scoundrel who has cut the letter B from her coat of arms at the gate. Alfonzo has already heard of the deed, and has had Gennaro arrested, thinking he was taking revenge on his wife's lover. Alfonzo tells Lucrezia that the miscreant is captured and she commands that he be put to death at once. Gennaro is brought in and Lucrezia is struck with horror when she learns that he is the offender. She asks that Gennaro be pardoned, but Alfonzo will not hear of it. He accuses Lucrezia of visiting Gennaro secretly in Venice. She must choose whether Gennaro is to die by sword or by poison. Lucrezia chooses poison, and when Gennaro has drunk it and the Duke has left the room with ironic politeness, Lucrezia hastily tells Gennaro that he has drunk the poison wine of the Borgias. She draws from her waist a small phial containing an antidote. She orders him to drink it quickly and helps him to escape.

The second act shows a court by Gennaro's house. Orsini persuades Gennaro that Lucrezia's saving his life was but a trick to win his gratitude and make him her tool. The scene changes to a banquet at the Negroni Palace where Gennaro, Orsini and their friends, are drinking and singing. While the feast is at its height, a bell tolls, and a group of hooded monks enter, followed by Lucrezia Borgia. She reminds the youths of their insults in Venice and tells them that they have been making merry on the famous Borgia wine. A curtain is drawn and the party is shown five narrow coffins waiting for the victims who have already drunk the poison. Gennaro steps forward and demands a sixth coffin. Lucrezia orders her son to drink the antidote, but he refuses, as there is not enough to save his five friends. Lucrezia then tells Gennaro that she is his mother. When Gennaro dies, Lucrezia herself drinks the wine and Don Alfonzo finds her lying beside her son.

§)&(§

MADAME BUTTERFLY

Giacomo Puccini

Madame Butterfly was first a story by the American writer, John Luther Long. It was then made into a play by David

Belasco and successfully produced in New York in 1900. Puccini was so delighted with its possibilities as an opera that he commissioned his friends, Luigi Illica and Giuseppe Giacoso, to adapt a libretto. The resultant opera was produced first at La Scala, Milan, February 17, 1904.

The scene is laid in Japan during contemporary times. The principal characters are:

CHO-CHO-SAN (*Soprano*), "Madame Butterfly"
SUZUKI (*Mezzo-soprano*), her servant
PINKERTON (*Tenor*), Lieutenant, U. S. Navy
KATE PINKERTON (*Mezzo-soprano*), his American wife
SHARPLESS (*Baritone*), U. S. Consul
GORO (*Tenor*), a Japanese marriage broker
YAMADORI (*Baritone*), a Japanese nobleman
THE BONZE (*Bass*), Cho-Cho-San's uncle

The first act shows the interior of the villa which Pinkerton has rented for the period he is to be stationed in Japan. Goro is showing the place to Pinkerton. Goro is both a real estate agent and a marriage broker and has arranged for Pinkerton's "Japanese marriage" to Cho-Cho-San. According to the customary contract, the marriage is binding only as long as Pinkerton lives with his wife. After that each is free to marry again. Sharpless, the Consul, does not approve of the plan and tries to persuade Pinkerton not to trifle with a native girl's affections. Their conversation is interrupted by Cho-Cho-San herself. She is known as "Madame Butterfly" and it is soon apparent that she has fallen deeply in love with Pinkerton. She has renounced her religion and is willing to become an American wife who will always be faithful to her husband. Butterfly's relatives arrive for the ceremony. The marriage contract is signed and the guests are making merry when the Bonze, Cho-Cho-San's uncle, arrives and curses Butterfly. He has learned of her renunciation and demands that her relatives turn their backs on her and consider her an outcast. Pinkerton is annoyed and orders them all to leave his house. Alone with Butterfly, he comforts her and the two sing a duet of the happiness they will have together—*O quant' occhi fisi.*

The scene is unchanged in the second act. Three years have passed and Pinkerton has long ago returned to America. Butterfly is still waiting for him, for he promised to return when the robins nest again. Now it is Spring and Butterfly sings *Un bel di Vedremo,* ("Some day he'll come.") to the doubting Suzuki. Just as Butterfly ends her song Sharpless appears with a letter he has received from Pinkerton. In it the Lieutenant tells Sharpless that he is returning to Japan with an American wife. Butterfly is so delighted to see Pinkerton's handwriting, and to learn the first part of the message, that Sharpless does not have the heart to tell her the truth. When Goro comes to offer her a marriage contract with the wealthy Yamadori, Butterfly will have none of him, for she is married to an American, and in America married people remain faithful. As proof Butterfly shows them her fair-haired son. Butterfly prepares for Pinkerton's coming. She decorates the villa with flowers and she and Suzuki and the child watch the harbor through three little holes Butterfly has pierced in the wall of the villa. As the curtain falls Suzuki and the child have fallen asleep, but Butterfly is still watching.

The next scene occurs at dawn. Butterfly is still watching. Suzuki brings the child to her and persuades her to take a few minutes rest. Pinkerton arrives with Kate, his American wife, and Sharpless. The Americans tell Suzuki of the true situation, and Pinkerton is so affected by the flowers that he does not have the heart to stay. Mrs. Pinkerton, seeing the child, offers to adopt him. Butterfly enters as they are talking and hears enough of the conversation to understand what has happened. She tells Kate that Pinkerton may have the child if he returns in half an hour. When the Americans have gone Butterfly blindfolds the child and gives him an American flag. Then she goes behind a screen and falls upon her father's sword. Pinkerton returns and finds her dead. He kneels beside her as Sharpless takes the child and turns him away from the tragic scene.

§)&(§

MADAME SANS-GÊNE

Umberto Giordano

Umberto Giordano's *Madame Sans-Gêne* had its world premiere at the Metropolitan Opera House, New York, January 25, 1915. Its libretto was written by Renato Simoni and was founded on a play by Victorien Sardou and Émile Moreau.

The action of the opera begins during the French Revolution and continues to the time when Napoleon has become Emperor and a world conqueror. The principal characters are:

CATHERINE (*Soprano*), a laundress, known as Madame Sans-Gêne, who later becomes the wife of Lefebvre and the Duchess of Danzig

LEFEBVRE (*Tenor*), a sergeant who becomes marshal and the Duke of Danzig

FOUCHÉ (*Baritone*), a patriot in the Revolution who is later made Minister of Police

COUNT OF NEIPPERG (*Tenor*), an Austrian

NAPOLEON (*Baritone*)

QUEEN CAROLINE (*Soprano*)
PRINCESS ELISA (*Soprano*)
DE BRIGODE (*Baritone*), Court Chamberlain

The first act shows Catherine's laundry in Paris on August 10, 1792, the historic day on which the Paris mob attacked the Tuileries. Catherine has become known as Madame Sans-Gêne ("Madame Without Care") because of her fearlessness and her casual frankness. The laundry is a storm center. Fouché, a patriot, is much disturbed by the menacing crowd, but Catherine tells him to take courage. Fouché confides in Catherine that he hopes to become Minister of Police and she replies that he has as much chance of realizing that ambition as she has to become a duchess. Outside the crowd shouts that the palace has been taken. Catherine barricades her laundry. She admits a wounded Austrian officer, the Count of Neipperg, who has tried to rescue the Queen. She hides him in her own room and locks the door. Lefebvre, the police sergeant, enters with a group of soldiers. Lefebvre is Catherine's lover, whom she expects to marry. The soldiers are searching for Neipperg, and when Lefebvre enters Catherine's room he is mad with jealousy at finding Neipperg there. He does not tell the soldiers that Neipperg is in the room, but he whispers to Catherine that there is a dead man in her room. This is a trick to discover Catherine's real feelings toward the fugitive, and when Lefebvre finds that Catherine is not disturbed by the news, he knows that she is innocent. He whispers that the man is still alive and that he will arrange for his escape.

The second act occurs nineteen years later, in 1811. Catherine is the wife of Lefebvre, who has become a marshal in Napoleon's army. Now that Napoleon is at the height of his power, Lefebvre has been given the title of

Duke of Danzig, and Catherine is the Duchess. The scene is a drawing room of their magnificent château of Compiegne. Catherine is still the frank, open-hearted daughter of the people, and the lackeys who have been commissioned to teach her court manners are having a hard time. Lefebvre comes home and informs Catherine that Napoleon is so displeased with her lack of dignity that he suggests Lefebvre divorce her as quickly as possible. Catherine retorts angrily, and tells Lefebvre what he should have said to the Emperor. Lefebvre is delighted, and tells Catherine that her words are exactly the same as the ones he used. The Count of Neipperg is announced. He has come to tell Lefebvre and Catherine that though he has been dismissed by Napoleon because the Emperor is jealous of his attentions to the Empress, he must see the Empress before he leaves. Fouché, now Minister of Police, interrupts to warn Catherine that she is about to receive a visit from "their most serene and royal highnesses" and that she must be careful of her behavior. It seems that there is a conspiracy to trap Catherine into speaking indiscreetly, and thus to create a scandal. Presently Queen Caroline and Princess Elisa are ushered in. At first the call is conducted with decorum, but Catherine can stand the ill-concealed derision of the court ladies for only a short time. She loses her temper and in plain language tells them what she thinks of them. The ladies leave, promising vengeance, just as De Brigode, the court chamberlain, comes to announce that Catherine, the Duchess of Danzig, is summoned to appear before the Emperor.

The third act shows the Emperor's cabinet. Fouché reports to Napoleon that Neipperg is supposed to have gone, but perhaps is back again. The Duchess of Danzig is announced, and Catherine enters. Napoleon tells Catherine that she covers his court with ridicule, and that she should let her husband divorce her. Catherine replies that Lefebvre would not exchange her for the proudest princess. She reminds Napoleon that she helped raise the morale of his armies when they were scorned, and that as a lowly vivandière she rallied the troops and endured with them all the terrors and privations of the campaigns. Then she reminds Napoleon of the bad debts she suffered at her laundry and ends her recital by presenting the Emperor with an unpaid bill he incurred when he was a lieutenant. Napoleon is deeply touched, and as a salute he kisses a scar on Catherine's arm. Just as he is sending her away with an escort, Napoleon is warned that Neipperg is about to enter the apartment of the Empress. Neipperg is caught and although Catherine tries to intercede for him, Napoleon orders that he be shot at sunrise.

The scene is unchanged for the last act. Lefebvre has been chosen to shoot Neipperg, and Catherine pleads with him to disregard the order. When Napoleon enters, Catherine pleads with him also. The Emperor secretly doubts Neipperg's guilt, but he is eager for vengeance. He challenges Catherine to prove Neipperg's innocence. He orders her to knock at the Empress's secret door and to announce Neipperg's presence. When Catherine does as she is told the door opens slightly. A hand passes out a note, and the voice of the Empress is heard to say: "Give this to him—and my farewell." The note is addressed to the Emperor of Austria, and reads: "Since the minister of police opens my letters, I am taking recourse to the Count of Neipperg to send this by him in secret." Thus the Count is dismissed and the Empress vindicated. Napoleon relaxes and Catherine is delighted. The Emperor summons the scornful ladies of the court and extols the loyalty of his ever-faithful friend, Madame Sans-Gêne.

MADELEINE

Victor Herbert

Grant Stewart wrote the libretto for Victor Herbert's one-act opera, *Madeleine,* adapting it from a play by Adrien Decourcelles and L. Thibault, entitled *Je dine chez ma mère.* The opera was first presented at the Metropolitan Opera House, January 24, 1914.

The cast includes:

MADELEINE FLEURY (*Soprano*), an opera singer
NICHETTE (*Contralto*), her maid
CHEVALIER DE MAUPRAT (*Tenor*) } admirers of Madeleine
DUC D'ESTERRE (*Bass*) }
DIDIER (*Bass*), a painter

The action occurs in Paris on New Year's Day, about 1760. The scene is Madeleine's salon. Madeleine has received many New Year's presents but she wants most of all to have a friend to dine with her. Her admirer, Chevalier de Mauprat, declines because he has promised his mother that he will dine with her. The Duc d'Esterre, another admirer, gives the same excuse. After these refusals Madeleine invites her maid Nichette to dinner, but Nichette also says that she has promised to dine at home with her mother. Madeleine is so disappointed that she bursts into tears. Didier, a painter who was a childhood friend of Madeleine's, finds her crying, and when he learns the reason for her distress, he says that he too is dining with his mother, but would like to have Madeleine join them. Madeleine is pleased with his invitation but refuses because she has conceived another idea. When Nichette returns to say that her mother has given her permission to dine with Madeleine, Madeleine sends her back to her mother. Then Madeleine takes her mother's portrait from the wall, stands it on the table opposite to herself, and announces that she too is dining with her mother.

§)&(§

THE MAGIC FLUTE

(Die Zauberflöte)

Wolfgang Amadeus Mozart

Mozart's *The Magic Flute* has been called the first great work of music that was composed for the humbler classes of society. It was written at the suggestion of Emanuel Schikaneder, a showman who managed a theatre in Vienna. Mozart was delighted with Schikaneder's proposal. The impresario wanted the text to be in German, and Mozart was eager to compose another German opera as in the earlier *Die Entführung aus dem Serail.* Also, Mozart's finances were in bad shape and here was a chance to make money from an opera produced in a theatre.

It is not clear whether Schikaneder himself wrote the libretto of *The Magic Flute* or whether it was actually the work of a writer named Karl Giesecke, who later claimed it. At any rate, the idea for its subject was probably Schikaneder's, for both he and Mozart were Freemasons, and it is generally assumed that the work has Masonic significance.

The opera was first produced at Schikaneder's Theatre auf der Wieden, September 30, 1791. Its first reception was cold but it soon grew in popularity and became a great success. In November of 1791 Mozart became ill and was confined to his bed. Each night he held his watch in hand

and followed in his mind the progress of each performance. On the fifth of December he died.

The setting of the opera is in Egypt and the principal characters are:

SARASTRO (*Bass*), Priest of Isis
QUEEN OF NIGHT (*Soprano*), a sorceress
PAMINA (*Soprano*), her daughter
TAMINO (*Tenor*), a Prince
PAPAGENO (*Bass*), a bird catcher who becomes Tamino's attendant
PAPAGENA (*Soprano*), Papageno's sweetheart
MONOSTATOS (*Tenor*), a Moor

The overture to the opera is often heard as a concert piece, and its opening chords are said to be of Masonic significance. After an *andante* section and a lively fugue the overture comes to an end and the curtain rises on a forest, where Tamino, the Prince, has lost his way and is threatened by a huge serpent. Tamino faints from fear and fatigue, and three attendants of the Queen of Night come from their cave and kill the snake with their silver javelins. Each of the attendants falls in love with Prince Tamino and each plans to win him. They leave him in his swoon and when they are gone Papageno, the bird catcher, enters, carrying his cage on his back. He hopes to sell some of his birds to the Queen's attendants. As Papageno rests his cage on the palace steps he announces his presence with a lively tune on his panpipes. This wakes the Prince, who sees the slain serpent and believes that Papageno is the one who has saved his life. Papageno trembles at the sight of the ugly monster, but he is perfectly willing to take credit for having slain it. Meanwhile the three attendants of the Queen have returned and have overheard the conversation. They punish Papageno for lying by placing a padlock on his lips.

The attendants then tell the Prince Tamino that their mistress, the Queen of Night, is concerned about her daughter, Pamina, who, they say, has been abducted by Sarastro, the Priest of Isis. Actually, Sarastro has caused Pamina to be taken from her evil mother so that her remarkable virtues will have opportunity to develop, and she may be protected from temptation. The Queen plans to use Tamino, the Prince, as a means of recapturing her daughter, and she has her attendants show Tamino a picture of Pamina. Tamino is entranced and falls deeply in love with the image of the girl. A clap of thunder announces the approach of the Queen. The mountains open and Tamino beholds the Queen seated upon her star-covered throne. She promises Tamino that if he succeeds in rescuing Pamina, he shall have the girl's hand in marriage. Tamino gladly consents and the Queen disappears. Papageno returns and the attendants take pity on him and remove the padlock from his lips. To Tamino they give a magic flute which will protect him from all dangers, will melt the anger of men, make melancholy people happy, and change enemies to friends. Papageno is forced into the service of Tamino as attendant, and he is given a set of musical bells which have powers equal to those of Tamino's flute.

The second act shows a room in Sarastro's palace. Monostatos, the Moorish chief of Sarastro's troop of slaves, is forcing his attentions on Pamina. He threatens her with death unless she consents to be his bride. Papageno breaks into the room and frightens the Moor by his weird appearance. Papageno is equally scared and the two flee in different directions. Papageno overcomes his fear and returns to Pamina. He tells her about Tamino and persuades her to try to escape with them. A change of scene shows the entrance to the temple where Tamino is seeking entrance.

He has been turned away from two doors and tries a third. There he is met by a Priest who tells him that Sarastro is a noble man who is protecting Pamina from the witchcraft and sorceries of her evil mother, the Queen of Night. Tamino is torn by conflicting desires. He seeks true wisdom and wants to learn the real character of Sarastro, but he still has pity for the Queen of Night and he has not forgotten the picture of Pamina. He asks whether Pamina is still alive, and when he learns that she is, he puts the magic flute to his lips. He hears Papageno's panpipe answering him, and starts off to find his companion. The echoes confuse him and he goes in the wrong direction. As soon as he has left, Pamina and Papageno appear. Papageno's panpipe has aroused Monostatos and his troop of slaves. Papageno remembers the bells that the Queen's attendants have given him. When he plays them the slaves are so enchanted that they can move their limbs only to the rhythm of the music. Papageno is easily able to send them away. As soon as they are gone, and Papageno and Pamina think they can escape, Sarastro enters with his followers. Pamina throws herself at his feet, and as he lifts her gently up, Monostatos brings Tamino as a captive. Tamino and Pamina behold each other for the first time and they are so overcome with each other's charm and beauty that they rush into an embrace. Pamina explains to Sarastro that she tried to escape because of the attentions of Monostatos. Sarastro punishes the Moor, and then tells his chief Priests that Tamino and Papageno will have a chance to show their worthiness by passing through the ordeals of the temple.

In the third act the Priests are gathered in a palm grove where they debate the case of Tamino and Pamina. They also discuss Papageno and his sweetheart, Papagena. They agree that so far Tamino has proved himself worthy of admission to the final trials of courage, steadfastness, self-control, truth, and faith. Sarastro prays to Isis and Osiris that the candidates may have virtue and wisdom. The first test is of faith in Sarastro's wisdom. Tamino and Papageno are warned to beware the wiles of women and under no conditions to answer them. They are taken to a beautiful garden where Tamino is approached by the three attendants of the Queen of Night. They urge him to flee, and they tell him that he has been condemned to death by Sarastro. They remind him of his promise to the Queen of Night, and tell him that they expect him to rescue Pamina. Tamino does not answer. In another garden, Pamina has thrown herself on a bench and has fallen asleep. Monostatos finds her and is about to kiss her when a clap of thunder heralds the presence of the Queen of Night. The Queen plots revenge, knowing that she cannot take her daughter from Sarastro. She gives Pamina a dagger and tells her that unless she uses it to stab Sarastro, she will be cast from her mother's heart forever. When the Queen has vanished, Sarastro comes to Pamina and tells her gently that the probation period is almost over, and that if Tamino continues to survive the ordeals, she will have him for her own tomorrow. In the temple Tamino and Papageno are still enduring the test of silence. Papageno cannot stand the strain, but Tamino is steadfast. Pamina comes in, seeking her lover, and Tamino does not answer her words of love. Even though Pamina is deeply hurt, Tamino does not break his vow.

In the fourth act, before the Pyramids, Tamino is commanded to go into the desert. Pamina is heartbroken at her lover's coldness, and she tries to stab herself with the dagger her mother has given her. Then she hears the sound of Tamino's magic flute, and she realizes that he was merely fulfilling the terms of his ordeal. Meanwhile Papageno is given another chance. When he wishes for a wife of his own, a hag appears. Suddenly the hag changes into Papagena, his sweetheart. Papageno cannot have her yet for he has still to prove his worthiness. The scene changes to a fiery cavern where the candidates are to meet their final test. Tamino must pass through a fiery lake to join Pamina. Aided by the magic flute he passes through the flames and takes Pamina on his arm. Together they mount the broad stairs to the temple and kneel before the altar and Sarastro. In the final scene Tamino and Pamina are joined in marriage by Sarastro, and Papagena and Papageno are also united. The Queen of Night and the evil Monostatos are banished forever.

§)&(§

THE MAN WITHOUT A COUNTRY

Walter Damrosch

Walter Damrosch composed this two-act opera to a libretto by Arthur Guiterman, who based it on Edward Everett Hale's famous story of the same title. The opera was first produced at the Metropolitan Opera House, New York, May 12, 1937.

The opera, like the story, concerns the fate of Philip Nolan, a fictional character who was involved in Aaron Burr's plot to found in 1807 a new empire which would include Texas, parts of Mexico and certain territories of the United States. Guiterman added a love story and several new characters to the original story.

The characters include:

PHILIP NOLAN (*Tenor*), Lieutenant of the United States Marines
MARY RUTLEDGE (*Soprano*), his sweetheart
HARMAN BLENNERHASSETT (*Tenor*)
AARON BURR (*Baritone*)
COLONEL MORGAN (*Bass*), of the United States Marines
COMMODORE STEPHEN DECATUR (speaking part)

The opening scene of the first act shows Harman Blennerhassett's mansion on an island in the Ohio River. Blennerhassett has contributed liberally to Burr's plot, and he is giving a party for his neighbors to cover a meeting of Burr with his fellow conspirators. The host greets his guests and shows them into the house. All go in but Mary, who learns from Blennerhassett that her lover, Philip Nolan, is expected and that he is involved in Burr's conspiracy. After Mary has followed the others into the house Philip and his companions arrive. Philip stays outside and when he is alone he sings a serenade to Mary, who appears on the balcony and comes down to greet him. In a love duet Philip hints at the wealth and fame he will win from his part in the conspiracy, but Mary tells him that this means nothing to her. She wants only his love, and she warns him to have nothing to do with Aaron Burr. Mary leaves Philip, who joins the conspirators waiting for Burr's arrival. When Burr comes he sings an impassioned description of the great Southwest empire he will create. The conspirators vow allegiance and Burr orders them to separate as government agents are following him. They will meet again at Natchez. All leave but Philip Nolan, who waits for a parting word with Mary. A United States officer and a squad of soldiers land from a boat. They arrest Philip on the charge of treason against the United States. The second scene shows a courtroom in the Marine barracks at Charleston. Mary begs the sergeant for a seat in a secluded corner. Colonel Morgan and the officers enter, the doors are opened for the angry crowd, and Philip is led in by two Marines. During the examination the questions asked Philip are increasingly vehement, and the crowd grows more and more excited. Finally Philip is accused of having sought to betray the United States which he had sworn to defend. He answers hotly: "Damn these United States. I never wish to hear that cursed name again!" Colonel Morgan silences the shouting of the mob, and when the verdict of guilty is rendered he pronounces the sentence: Nolan shall have his wish and shall never again hear the name of the United States. He shall be placed aboard a man-of-war and shall sail the ocean for the rest of his life. He shall be transferred from ship to ship and shall never see his native land again. He shall be a man without a country. He shall never hear of home and none shall breathe to him his country's name. The Colonel then orders Philip's shoulder straps removed and the buttons cut from his coat. Mary faints and Philip is marched out, followed by the crowd. Mary, alone, regains consciousness and in an impassioned aria vows that she will devote her life to gaining a pardon for Philip. It is unjust, she sings, for the real culprit to go free and for Philip to suffer such a punishment.

The second act occurs several years later and opens on the deck of the U. S. Frigate *Guerriere*, anchored in the harbor of Gibraltar. Philip Nolan comes on deck but retires when he sees the midshipmen reading letters from home. A new midshipman asks about Nolan, and his companions tell him the story. They speak with affection of Philip as a kindly man who nurses them when they are ill and reads aloud to them. The mail brings a package of new books and Philip starts to read from a new poem by Walter Scott. He comes to the line:

> "Breathes there a man with soul so dead
> Who never to himself hath said,
> 'This is my own, my native land.' "

He falters, but steels himself to continue. Finally he reads: "Unwept, unhonor'd, and unsung." He lets the book drop to the deck, covers his face, and turns toward the sea, sobbing. The men tactfully retire and Philip sings of his contrition for his crime. He hopes he may be permitted to die for his country, but longs to see Mary once more. The second scene shows the deck at night. The officers are giving a party. Mary appears at the gangway and rushes into Philip's arms. She tells him that she is working for his pardon and is hopeful that it will soon come. Philip replies that he can expiate his crime only by giving his life for his country. Their scene is interrupted by the entrance of Commodore Decatur. He has come to take command of the squadron in the fight against the Berber sea robbers from Tripoli. Philip begs Decatur to let him have a part in the battle. Urged by Mary, Decatur agrees and gives Philip command of one of the deck cannon. The third scene shows the deck of the *Guerriere* during the battle off Tripoli. The Berbers climb over the decks and are hurled back by the sailors under Philip's command. Philip cuts down the Tripolitan admiral with his sword but a bullet strikes him in the breast. He is carried to the mainmast where the surgeon announces that he is dying. Philip dreams that he hears Mary's voice singing to him of his pardon and of their reunion. He dies and Decatur takes off his own sword and gently places it in Philip's arms.

§)&(§

MANON

Jules Massenet

Jules Massenet's opera *Manon* is based on the novel by Antoine Prévost, *Histoire de Manon Lescaut.* Its libretto was written by Henri Meilhac and Philippe Gille. It was first produced at the Opéra Comique in Paris, January 19, 1884.

The characters include:

COMTE DES GRIEUX (*Bass*)
CHEVALIER DES GRIEUX (*Tenor*), his son
LESCAUT (*Baritone*), a guardsman
MANON LESCAUT (*Soprano*), his cousin
GILLOT MORFONTAIN (*Bass*), Minister of Finance
DE BRETIGNY (*Baritone*), a nobleman
POUSSETTE (*Soprano*)
JAVOTTE (*Contralto*) } actresses
ROSETTE (*Soprano*)

The action occurs in France during the year 1721. The first act shows the courtyard of a tavern at Amiens. Manon is being escorted to a convent by her cousin, Lescaut. The Minister of Finance, Gillot Morfontain, is entertaining de Bretigny and the three actresses, Poussette, Javotte and Rosette. When Morfontain sees Manon he has no eyes for the other girls, and he plans to abduct her in his carriage. The Chevalier des Grieux arrives and although he is about to take holy orders, he and Manon are so fascinated by each other that they elope to Paris in Morfontain's carriage.

The second act shows des Grieux's apartment in Paris where he and Manon are living. Des Grieux is writing his father, the Count, asking for consent to his marriage with Manon. He and Manon are interrupted by the entrance of Lescaut and de Bretigny. When Lescaut demands that des Grieux state his intentions toward Manon, the Chevalier shows him the letter he has been writing. While des Grieux and Lescaut are reading the letter, de Bretigny takes Manon aside and warns her that des Grieux's father, the Count, is planning to have his son carried off that very night. Manon says she will warn des Grieux, but de Bretigny advises her against it. It will mean poverty for both Manon and the Chevalier and if she does not interfere with des Grieux's capture, she can live in luxury with him, de Bretigny. Meanwhile, Lescaut has been satisfied with des Grieux's action in writing his father. He gives the couple his blessing and leaves with de Bretigny. Des Grieux goes out to post the letter and Manon decides to let him be captured and then to join de Bretigny. She bids an affectionate farewell to her surroundings and is weeping and trembling when des Grieux returns. He tells her of a dream he has had and sings the aria, *Le Rêve,* describing the little home he plans to share with her. As he finishes there is a knock at the door. Manon has been so touched by her lover's recital of his dream that she tries to keep him from going to the door. He brushes her aside and goes to the vestibule saying that he will dismiss the person who is interrupting them. There is the noise of a scuffle, and Manon runs to the window and cries: "He has gone!"

In the third act, Manon has become the mistress of de Bretigny. She and de Bretigny mingle with the gay crowd in the streets of Paris, and meet the Count des Grieux, father of Manon's former lover. Manon hears des Grieux tell de Bretigny that his son is about to enter the priesthood at St. Sulpice. Her old love revives and she resolves to seek the Chevalier. The scene changes to the convent where the Count pleads with his son not to take the holy orders. Des Grieux insists and sings a fervent song of renunciation: *Ah! Dispar, vision.* When the father has gone Manon arrives. Affecting penitence she persuades des Grieux to flee with her.

The fourth act takes place in a gambling house in Paris. Des Grieux tries his luck at the tables, hoping to win riches for Manon. He wins consistently, mostly from Gillot Morfontain, the Minister of Finance. Finally he is falsely accused of cheating. A brawl results and des Grieux and Manon are about to be arrested when the Count arrives in time to protect his son from the police. Manon is taken prisoner as an abandoned woman.

The fifth act shows a road near Havre. Lescaut and des Grieux are waiting for the party which is taking Manon to exile. When they arrive des Grieux bribes a soldier to let him talk with Manon. He begs her to escape with him, but she is sick and weak. Begging him to forgive her unfaithfulness, she dies in his arms.

§)&(§

MANON LESCAUT

Giacomo Puccini

When Giacomo Puccini composed his setting for *Manon Lescaut,* first produced at the Teatro Regio in Turin, Italy, February 1, 1893, he adapted the same novel that the French Massenet had used for *Manon* a little less than ten years earlier. Puccini himself planned the libretto from the *Histoire de Manon Lescaut* by Antoine Prévost, but it was actually written by Domenico Oliva, M. Praga and Luigi Illica.

Puccini's opera follows the original novel more closely

than does Massenet's *Manon,* which introduced several new situations. In *Manon Lescaut* Puccini presents four relatively detached scenes, with a plot that is simpler and less involved than the five-act drama Meilhac and Gille constructed for Massenet.

The characters of the Puccini opera are:

CHEVALIER DES GRIEUX (*Tenor*)
LESCAUT (*Baritone*), sergeant of the King's guards
MANON LESCAUT (*Soprano*), his sister
GERONTE DE RAVOIR (*Bass*), Treasurer General
EDMUND (*Tenor*), a student

As in Massenet's opera, the action occurs in the early eighteenth century and the first act shows a street in front of a tavern at Amiens. Students are singing and carousing. The Chevalier des Grieux sits by himself and does not join the merrymakers. Manon and her brother Lescaut alight from a coach, and while Lescaut is in the Inn making arrangements for their accommodation, des Grieux talks to Manon. She tells him that her brother is taking her to a convent, much against her will. When he is alone, des Grieux sings of Manon's beauty in the aria *Donna non vidi mai* ("Maiden so fair.") Meanwhile Geronte de Ravoir, the dissolute treasurer-general, has seen the beautiful Manon and has determined to abduct her. He orders a swift horse and carriage. Edmund, a student friend of des Grieux, overhears this plot and warns des Grieux, who meets Manon as she comes from the Inn and persuades her to elope with him in Geronte's carriage. When Manon has gone Lescaut comforts Geronte with the suggestion that it should not be hard for a rich man to lure a woman from a poor student.

In the second act Lescaut's cynical prophecy about his

sister has come true. Manon has deserted des Grieux for the wealthy Geronte and has become the latter's mistress. She is beginning to tire of luxury and her aged lover, and even though she seems vivacious in dancing for Geronte and a group of his friends, she is ready to respond to des Grieux when he calls on her after Geronte and his friends have left. Des Grieux sings an aria which reproaches Manon for her fickleness—*Ah! Manon, mi tradisce*—and then tenderly asks her if she still loves him. Geronte returns to find Manon with her former lover. He feigns indifference, but leaves to summon the police. Manon's brother rushes in to warn Manon. Even though she has time to escape, she lingers to gather up some of her finery and is captured.

The third act shows a harbor at Havre. Manon has been convicted as an undesirable woman and is to be banished to the French province of Louisiana. Des Grieux and Lescaut bribe the guards, and are about to rescue Manon when they are interrupted by the captain of the ship. Des Grieux is so overcome with grief that the Captain agrees to smuggle him aboard the ship so that he may sail to Louisiana with Manon.

The fourth act takes place on a desolate plain in Louisiana. Manon and des Grieux wander about searching for food and shelter. Manon is so exhausted that des Grieux leaves her to find water. She thinks he has deserted her and sings that she is alone and forsaken. When he returns her strength is gone and she dies in his arms.

§)&(§

MANRU

Ignace Paderewski

Ignace Paderewski, pianist-composer-statesman composed only one opera, *Manru,* which was first performed in Dresden at the Königliches Opernhaus, May 29, 1901. The libretto of the opera was written by Alfred Nossig, who based it on a novel by J. I. Kraszewski.

The cast includes:

MANRU (*Tenor*), a gypsy
ULANA (*Soprano*), a Galician girl, recently married to Manru
HEDWIG (*Mezzo-soprano*), her mother
UROK (*Baritone*), a dwarf
OROS (*Bass*), a gypsy chief
ASA (*Soprano*), a gypsy girl, in love with Manru
JAGU (*Bass*), a gypsy fiddler

The action takes place in the Tatra Mountains of Hungary during the nineteenth century. The first act shows a mountain village. Hedwig tells the village maidens that her daughter Ulana has defied her wishes and has married Manru, a gypsy. Urok, the dwarf, is himself in love with Ulana, and he begs Hedwig to forgive her. Ulana comes and tells Urok that she feels that Manru does not love her as he did when they were first married. She refuses to leave Manru, however, and her mother drives her from the house. Urok explains to Ulana that gypsies are always unfaithful when the moon is full. Knowing that Urok is a sorcerer, Ulana asks him to brew for her a potion that will make Manru continue to love her. The gypsies come to bring Ulana back to the gypsy settlement. Hedwig curses them.

The second act occurs at Manru's hut. Ulana sings a lullaby to her baby, and Manru becomes increasingly restless. The gypsy fiddler Jagu tells Manru that he will be welcomed back to his former tribe and that he will be made its chief. Asa, the tribal queen, is particularly eager to have

Manru return, for she is in love with him. Ulana pleads with Manru not to leave her, and Jagu returns without him. After Jagu has gone Manru is more restless than ever, and the scheming Urok makes him even more discontented by reminding him of the freedom and the joys of gypsy life. Ulana gives Manru the magic potion that Urok has brewed for her. It accomplishes its purpose and Manru becomes once more the loving husband.

The third act is laid on the shore of a lake. The magic of Urok's potion has worn off and Manru again longs for gypsy life. He tries to resist the temptation to leave Ulana, and finally falls asleep, exhausted from the emotional struggle. A band of gypsies discovers the sleeping Manru. The queen, Asa, is with them and she tries to take Manru back to the camp. Oros, the gypsy chief, declares that Manru has been a traitor and is not fit to return with them. When Oros and the gypsies leave, Asa stays with Manru. She embraces him and tries to remind him of his former life. Urok reminds Manru that he has a wife and the voice of Ulana is heard from the distance. Asa's wiles have been successful; this time Manru turns to her and not to Ulana. In despair Ulana leaps into the lake. Oros returns and angrily throws Manru into the water. Urok gloats over the death of his rival.

§)&(§

MAROUF, THE COBBLER OF CAIRO

Henri Rabaud

The libretto of Henri Rabaud's *Marouf* was written by Lucien Népoty, who adapted its plot from the *Arabian*

Nights. The opera was first produced at the Opéra Comique, Paris, May 15, 1914.

The cast includes:

MAROUF (*Tenor*), a cobbler
FATIMAH (*Contralto*), the "kill-joy," his wife
THE SULTAN (*Bass*)
PRINCESS SAAMCHEDDINE (*Soprano*), his daughter
ALI (*Baritone*), a merchant
A BEDOUIN

The first act shows the cobbler's booth of the poverty-stricken Marouf, in Cairo. Marouf brings home to his shrewish wife a sugar cake. She had asked him for a honey-cake, and is so angry at being disappointed that she complains to the authorities. She cries so loudly that the officers think Marouf must have beaten her, and the cobbler is given a public whipping. Marouf is discouraged and humiliated and runs away with a group of sailors.

The second act shows a mythical city called Khaitan. Marouf's ship has been wrecked and when Marouf reaches shore, clinging to a broken mast, he is rescued by Ali, a merchant, who proves to be a boyhood friend. Ali has prospered and has become the richest man in Khaitan. He dresses Marouf in fine clothes, and introduces him as the richest man in the world. The Sultan hears about this visiting tycoon, and invites him to dinner at the palace.

The third act shows Marouf living in the Sultan's palace. The Sultan is so delighted with Marouf that he insists that he marry his daughter. Marouf is more than willing, for the Princess is beautiful and his wife in Cairo is ugly and shrewish. He becomes so enthusiastic at the prospect that he faints away. As he loses consciousness he mumbles some words that give away to the Princess his real identity and his actual poverty. But the Princess loves Marouf and wants him in spite of these drawbacks.

The fourth act is laid in the garden of the Sultan's harem. Marouf has promised that his caravans will soon arrive, bringing treasure, and when they do not come the Sultan becomes suspicious. The Princess questions Marouf and he readily admits the truth to her. She decides that they had better elope before matters come to a climax.

The fifth act shows a plain near Khaitan. A Bedouin goes in search of food for Marouf and the Princess, and while he is away the Princess tries to plow his field for him. The plow strikes a ring attached to a great flat stone. Marouf tries to lift the stone and the ring comes off in his hand. Marouf rubs the ring and the Bedouin returns in the form of a genie. He produces for Marouf all the wealth that he had boasted about, and when the Sultan arrives in pursuit of the eloping couple, he sees the caravans that Marouf has promised.

§)&(§

THE MARRIAGE OF FIGARO

Wolfgang Amadeus Mozart

The libretto of Mozart's opera was adapted by Lorenzo da Ponte from a play of the same title by Beaumarchais. *The Marriage of Figaro* is a sequel to the same author's *Barber of Seville.* In the second play Count Almaviva and Rosina are married and Rosina is disturbed by the philanderings of her husband. Other characters which appear in both plays are: Figaro, the barber, now the Count's valet; Bartolo, the physician; Basilio, the music master; and Marcellina, the housekeeper.

Mozart's *The Marriage of Figaro,* was first produced May 1, 1786, at the Burgtheater in Vienna. The cast includes:

COUNT ALMAVIVA (*Baritone*), a nobleman of Seville
COUNTESS ROSINA (*Soprano*), his wife
FIGARO (*Bass*), formerly a barber, now valet to the Count
SUSANNA (*Soprano*), betrothed to Figaro
MARCELLINA (*Contralto*), housekeeper for the Countess, formerly betrothed to Figaro
DOCTOR BARTOLO (*Basso*), a physician
BASILIO (*Tenor*), a music master
CHERUBINO (*Soprano*), a page
BARBARINA (*Soprano*), Cherubino's sweetheart

The first act shows a room in the Count's palace. The ex-barber Figaro and Susanna are making plans for their wedding. Figaro assures Susanna that now that she is to be married, the philandering Count Almaviva will stop annoying her. Their conversation is followed by a scene between Marcellina, the housekeeper, and Bartolo, the physician, which Susanna overhears by hiding in the back of the room. Marcellina tells Bartolo that Figaro had once promised to marry her. Bartolo is eager for revenge on Figaro, for it was the ex-barber who thwarted his plans to marry Rosina, now the Countess, in the earlier play, *The Barber of Seville.* Bartolo is accordingly most happy to help Marcellina in her plan for revenge. When Bartolo leaves, Susanna comes from her hiding place and she and Marcellina quarrel. They are interrupted by the page Cherubino, who is in love with Barbarina, the gardener's daughter, and he sings of his passion. After this recital the Count himself enters, and Cherubino hides behind a chair. The Count proceeds to make love to Susanna and is in turn interrupted by the appearance of Basilio, the music master. Now the Count has to hide. He drops behind the same chair that Cherubino has used, and the page has to wriggle out and slip into the chair. Susanna quickly throws a dress over him. Both the Count and Cherubino are discovered and the page is summarily dismissed.

The second act occurs in the Countess's apartment. Rosina, the Countess, decides to use Cherubino to trap her husband. With Susanna's help they dress the page as a woman, and he sings the famous aria: *Voi che sapete* ("What is this feeling?") The Count knocks on the door and before the women let him in Cherubino barely has time to jump out of the window. The Count is mystified, and becomes still more suspicious when the gardener enters and complains that the flowerbeds beneath the window are badly mussed. Figaro comes to the rescue and tries to explain matters, but Marcellina complicates the situation by pressing her breach-of-promise case against the valet. The Count postpones Figaro's marriage to Susanna.

The third act shows another apartment in the castle. The Count tells Susanna that unless she will accept his attentions he will force Figaro to marry Marcellina. Susanna pretends to yield, and promises the Count that she will meet him later in the garden. Then it develops that Marcellina is actually Figaro's mother, and one serious complication of the plot is effectively disposed of. The Countess Rosina is still determined to catch her husband in his philandering and Susanna also wants to teach her fiancé a lesson. The Countess and Susanna exchange clothes, and go into the garden, each to meet the other's lover.

The fourth act is laid in the garden. Susanna and the Countess are each disguised as the other. Cherubino comes seeking his Barbarina. He mistakes the Countess for his sweetheart and kisses her. The Count sees him and thinks that the page has kissed Susanna. The subsequent love-making becomes impossibly complicated until the Countess and Susanna explain matters and show their real identities. The Count admits that he has been fooled and punished for his infidelities. Everyone is forgiven by everyone else, and the party returns to the castle to celebrate the marriage of Figaro to Susanna and Cherubino to Barbarina.

§)&(§

MARTHA

Friedrich von Flotow

Friedrich von Flotow's *Martha* is known for its interpolation of the old Irish song, "The Last Rose of Summer," which is sung by the heroine in the second act. This, however, is merely an incident in the composer's otherwise original score.

Martha was first produced at the Kärntnertor-Theater in Vienna, November 25, 1847. Its libretto was written by W. Friedrich. The cast includes:

LADY HENRIETTA DURHAM (*Soprano*), maid of honor to the Queen
NANCY (*Contralto*), her attendant
LORD TRISTAN (*Baritone*), her cousin
PLUNKETT (*Bass*), a farmer
LIONEL (*Tenor*), his foster-brother
SHERIFF OF RICHMOND (*Baritone*)

The action takes place in England during the reign of Queen Anne. The first act shows Lady Henrietta's boudoir.

Henrietta is bored by court life and by her admirers. She craves excitement and diversion, and when she hears the servants and the villagers singing on their way to the Richmond Fair, she thinks it would be fun to go along with them, disguised as a serving girl. Nancy, her attendant, is willing, but her dignified cousin, Lord Tristan, does not approve. Lady Henrietta forces Tristan to go as their escort, dressed as a farmer.

The second act is laid at the Fair. Plunkett, the farmer, and his foster-brother Lionel, are looking for servants. Lionel knows nothing of his own parentage, except that he was adopted by Plunkett's father. He wears a ring which he was once told to present to the Queen if he should ever be in trouble. The Sheriff announces that all contracts for servants are binding for one year if money is advanced. Immediately after this announcement is made, Lady Henrietta and Nancy arrive, escorted by Lord Tristan. Plunkett and Lionel see them and immediately engage them. The girls accept the advance payment and unknowingly bind themselves as servants for a year. When they learn this sad news the girls object, but the Sheriff insists that they go with the farmers and fulfill their bargain. Tristan tries to rescue them, but the crowd holds him back.

The third act shows Plunkett's farmhouse. Lady Henrietta is Martha, and Nancy is Julia. Plunkett and Lionel are showing the girls their duties and are surprised that they know so little about housekeeping. By this time Lionel has fallen in love with "Martha." He takes from her a rose she has been wearing and refuses to return it unless she sings for him. When she has sung "The Last Rose of Summer" he tells her that he loves her. She is touched, but she refuses to take his love-making seriously, and laughs at him. Plunkett has meanwhile been trying to teach "Julia" her duties, but Nancy is so pert and saucy that he gives up trying to teach her and amuses himself by talking to her. He, too, has fallen in love. Finally the men bid their servants good night and retire. When they have gone Lord Tristan appears at the window. He has a carriage waiting and helps the girls to escape through the window.

The fourth act shows a park in Richmond and the exterior of a country tavern. As Plunkett is drinking with a group of his friends a hunting party appears. Among them is Nancy whom Plunkett recognizes as "Julia," the servant girl who escaped from his house. He demands that she return with him to fulfill her contract. She calls her friends to her aid, and Plunkett is driven away. Soon Lionel enters, and he recognizes Lady Henrietta as "Martha." He sings the air *M'appari* ("Like a Dream") and stubbornly claims "Martha." Henrietta scolds him and declares that he is a madman.

The last act opens at Plunkett's farmhouse. Lionel has given his ring to Plunkett who has taken it to the Queen. The Queen has recognized it as having belonged to a noble who was deprived of his estates for what later proved to be an unwarranted charge. To atone for this injustice to Lionel's father, the Queen has told Plunkett that Lionel is now the Earl of Derby. The news means nothing to Lionel, for his mind has become unbalanced from grief at losing "Martha." Henrietta is sent for, and she returns to the cottage as her real self, Lady Henrietta. The deranged Lionel does not recognize her, so Nancy and Plunkett, who themselves have become engaged, plan to restore Lionel's reason. They return to the Richmond Fair and arrange a re-enactment of the events that occurred when Plunkett and Lionel first met the two girls. All are dressed in the costumes they wore on that day, and when Lionel sees them he remembers what happened and his mind is cleared. He and Lady Henrietta are betrothed, and Nancy and Plunkett announce their engagement.

§)&(§

MASANIELLO
(La Muette de Portici)
Daniel François Auber

This five-act opera by Daniel François Auber was performed for the first time at the Grand Opéra in Paris, February 29, 1828. Its libretto was written by Augustin Eugène Scribe and Germain Delavigne.

The cast includes:

ALFONSO (*Tenor*), Count of Arcos and the son of the Viceroy of Naples
ELVIRA (*Soprano*), his betrothed
PIETRO (*Tenor*), a friend of Alfonso
SELVA (*Bass*), Captain of the Spanish guard
MASANIELLO (*Tenor*), a Neapolitan fisherman
FENELLA, his sister, a mute

The action occurs in seventeenth-century Naples and Portici. Alfonso has assaulted and imprisoned Masaniello's mute sister, Fenella. Fenella escapes and Masaniello leads a revolt against the tyranny of the Viceroy. Selva, Captain of the Spanish guard, tries to re-capture Fenella but Masaniello stabs him and gives his followers the order to start the revolution. Alfonso and his betrothed, Elvira, seek safety in Masaniello's hut. Masaniello does not know them and agrees to give them shelter. Later he learns who they are, but he keeps his promise. He is offered the crown of Naples, which he accepts, but he is poisoned by his former friend, Pietro, and becomes insane. Alfonso meanwhile has gathered a force to put down the rebellion. Masaniello leads the people against him and is killed in battle. When Fenella learns of her brother's death, she plunges into the sea and is drowned.

§)&(§

THE MASKED BALL
(Un Ballo in Maschera)
Giuseppe Verdi

The libretto of this opera by Giuseppe Verdi was written by Antonio Somma, who adapted it from a libretto Augustin Eugène Scribe had written for an opera by Auber —*Gustave III, Ou le Bal Masque*. The plot has an actual historical basis in the assassination of Gustavus III of Sweden during a masked ball. In the Scribe-Somma libretto the principal character, Richard, falls in love with the wife of his secretary, who assassinates him during a masquerade. Originally the scene of the opera was Italy, but during the rehearsals for the first production (at the Teatro Apollo in Rome, February 17, 1859) an Italian assassin made an attempt on the life of Napoleon III. The authorities forbade the performance of the opera, and the masses made a political issue of the ban. Verdi refused to adapt his music to a different libretto, but finally compromised by changing the scene to Colonial Boston, and making his hero "Richard" instead of "Riccardo."

In modern times the opera is often performed in its

original, and more logical form, with Riccardo the Governor, not of Boston, but of Naples.

The cast includes:

RICHARD (*Tenor*), Count of Warwick, Governor of Boston
REINHART (RENATO) (*Baritone*), his secretary
AMELIA (*Soprano*), Reinhart's wife
ULRICA (*Contralto*), a Negress astrologer
SAMUEL (*Bass*) } Conspirators, enemies of the Governor
TOM (*Bass*) }

The first scene of Act One shows the reception hall of the Governor's house in Boston. Richard inspects a list of guests for a masked ball. When he comes to the name of Amelia Reinhart, his secretary's wife, he becomes sentimental and sings the aria: "Amelia, dear sweet name!" Reinhart comes to warn Richard of a plot against his life, and the conspirators who are present, Samuel and Tom, decide that the time is not ripe for their scheme. Ulrica the Negress is brought in and is charged with being a witch. Richard laughs at the accusation and dismisses the woman. When she has gone he suggests to his courtiers that it would be something of a lark to go in disguise to Ulrica's hut and to test her powers of prophecy. Samuel and Tom decide that they too will go; they may have a chance to carry out their plot. The scene changes to Ulrica's hut, where the sorceress is brewing a magic potion. The Governor, dressed as a sailor, comes with his party, and when all have assembled they hear a knock at the door. Everyone is asked to leave except Richard, the Governor, who hides behind a curtain. Amelia enters. She tells Ulrica of her sinful love for Richard, and asks the sorceress for a cure so that she may be faithful to her husband Reinhart. Ulrica tells her of an herb that grows under the gallows of Boston. This will cure Amelia's trouble, but it must be plucked by Amelia herself. After

Amelia is gone, Richard comes from behind the curtain and Samuel and Tom return. Richard asks Ulrica to tell his fortune. She replies that he will be killed by the first man to shake his hand. Laughingly Richard holds out his hand to Samuel and Tom, but they refuse to shake it, for they are afraid that Richard will suspect them. Soon Reinhart comes, looking for Richard. The Governor offers his hand and Reinhart shakes it. Richard remarks to Ulrica that she is a poor prophetess, for Reinhart is his closest friend.

The second act shows the spot near the gallows at midnight. Amelia comes to find the magic herb and Richard follows her. She confesses to Richard that she loves him but begs him to leave her. Reinhart approaches and Amelia covers her face with a veil. The secretary has come to warn the Governor that the conspirators are waiting to kill him. Richard asks Reinhart to escort the veiled lady back to the city, and not to ask her who she is. Richard then makes his escape. The conspirators mistake Reinhart for Richard, and as they start to attack him Amelia's veil falls from her face. Reinhart learns that she is his own wife. She pleads her innocence but Reinhart denounces her and offers to join the conspirators in their plot to kill Richard.

The third act opens in Reinhart's house. Reinhart is planning to kill Amelia, but when she embraces their child, he relents and decides instead to have vengeance on Richard. He and the conspirators, Samuel and Tom, draw lots to see who shall kill Richard and Reinhart is chosen. The scene changes to the ballroom of the Governor's house where the masked ball is in progress. Richard has not heeded Amelia's warning of the plot against his life, and he has decided that he will discontinue his attentions to Amelia and send her and her husband back to England. Meanwhile Reinhart has learned how Richard will be dressed for the ball and is able to recognize him. Seeing

Richard talking with Amelia, Reinhart is filled with jealousy and stabs the Governor with his dagger. Before Richard dies, he tells Reinhart that his wife is innocent, and tells of the plan for sending them both away.

§)&(§

IL MATRIMONIO SEGRETO

(The Secret Marriage)

Domenico Cimarosa

The libretto of Domenico Cimarosa's merry two-act opera was written by Giovanni Bertati, and was founded on *The Clandestine Marriage,* a play by G. Colman and David Garrick. The opera was first produced at the Burgtheater in Vienna, February 7, 1792.

The cast of characters includes:

GERONIMO (*Bass*), a rich merchant
CAROLINA (*Soprano*) } his daughters
ELISETTA (*Soprano*) }
FIDALMA (*Mezzo-soprano*), their elderly aunt
PAOLINO (*Tenor*), a young lawyer, secretly married to Carolina
COUNT ROBINSON (*Baritone*), an English nobleman

The action occurs in Naples during the seventeenth century. Both acts take place in the house of Geronimo, whose daughter Carolina has been secretly married to Paolino. Carolina's sister Elisetta is not attractive, and Paolino tries to win the favor of his father-in-law Geronimo by arranging a marriage between Elisetta and Count Robinson, an English nobleman. When the Count arrives Paolino's plan is upset by two unforeseen factors: Elisetta is cold to the Count, and the Count himself prefers Carolina. To complicate matters further, Carolina's elderly aunt, Fidalma, takes a fancy to Paolino. Carolina refuses Count Robinson but he persists in making love to her. Elisetta discovers them and rouses the household with her jealous screams.

In the second act Count Robinson offers to take one-half of the dowry that had been promised for Elisetta if he may have Carolina instead. The miserly Geronimo agrees to this money-saving plan. Then the Count tries to get Elisetta to release him by telling her that he indulges in all the known vices. Elisetta is not deterred by this recital of sins and she and Fidalma persuade Geronimo to send Carolina to a convent. The only solution for Paolino and Carolina is an elopement. They are discovered and they finally confess that they are married. Geronimo is furious but the Count softens the father's wrath by agreeing to marry Elisetta.

§)&(§

THE MEDIUM

Gian-Carlo Menotti

This two-act opera by Gian-Carlo Menotti was produced first at the Brander Matthews Theatre of Columbia University, New York, as a feature of the University's second annual Festival of Contemporary Music, May 8, 1946. In the following February it was given three performances by the Ballet Society at the Heckscher Theatre in New York, together with the premiere performances of Menotti's most recent opera, *The Telephone*. Commencing May 1, 1947, the two operas, *The Medium* and *The Telephone,* were produced under commercial sponsorship at the Ethel Barrymore Theatre in New York, and continued at that theatre for a several months' run of nightly performances.

The libretto of *The Medium* was written by the composer, and the characters include:

MONICA (*Soprano*)
TOBY, a deaf-mute
MADAME FLORA (*Mezzo-soprano*), a medium, Monica's mother
MRS. GOBINEAU (*Soprano*)
MR. GOBINEAU (*Baritone*)
MRS. NOLAN (*Soprano*)

The scene of both acts is Madame Flora's parlor, and the action occurs in contemporary times. Madame Flora is a spiritist medium who cheats her clients with fraudulent seances. In her manifestations she uses as confederates her daughter Monica and Toby, a mute boy she has adopted. Toby is very much in love with Monica. In the midst of one of Madame Flora's seances, a cold, unearthly hand places itself about her throat. She is so terrified that she exposes her tricks to her clients. The clients refuse to be undeceived, but Madame Flora herself cannot accept a supernatural explanation of what has happened, and she believes that Toby is trying to kill her. She threatens the boy and beats him, and even though Monica begs her to spare him, she turns him out of the house. Madame Flora then becomes very drunk. While she is in a stupor, Toby returns to find Monica. In a frenzy of fear, Madame Flora takes her revolver and shoots several times through the curtain of her spirit cabinet. Toby's body falls to the floor.

§)&(§

MEFISTOFELE

Arrigo Boïto

Arrigo Boïto, the Italian composer of *Mefistofele,* was both a composer and a poet. He composed the music for several operas, but *Mefistofele* is the only one of them which is performed today. As a poet Boïto wrote the librettos for Ponchielli's *La Gioconda* and Verdi's *Otello* and *Falstaff.*

Boïto wrote the librettos of his own operas also and adapted *Mefistofele* from Goethe's *Faust.* The opera was first performed at La Scala, Milan, March 5, 1868.

The cast includes:

MEFISTOFELE (*Bass*)
FAUST (*Tenor*), a philosopher
WAGNER (*Tenor*), a student
MARGUERITE (*Soprano*)
MARTHA (*Contralto*), her mother
HELEN OF TROY (*Soprano*)

The principal action takes place in Frankfort, Germany, and in Greece, and the Prologue shows the regions of space where angels are singing the praises of God. Mefistofele, halfway between Heaven and Hell, sings a mocking song and boasts that he can tempt and seduce the great philosopher Faust.

The first act is laid in the square at Frankfort, on Easter Sunday. Faust walks through the merry crowd with his pupil Wagner. They see a friar and notice that the crowd avoids him. Faust remarks to Wagner that he must be the devil in disguise, and when the friar seems to be following Faust, the philosopher tries to elude him by going into his house. Faust does not escape, for in the study the friar reveals himself as Mefistofele, the Evil One. Mefistofele tells Faust that he can bring him the riches and delights of the world if Faust will sell him his soul. Faust agrees, and is promised youth and one hour of genuine happiness.

The second act opens in a garden, where Mefistofele offers Faust the delights of love. He introduces him to Marguerite, and while Mefistofele diverts the attention of Martha, Marguerite's mother, Faust gives the girl a sleeping potion which she in turn gives to her mother. While Martha is asleep Faust makes love to Marguerite. Later Mefistofele appears and tells Faust that it is time to leave. The next scene is laid in the Brocken where Mefistofele shows Faust the wild revelry of the demons in Hell. Flames burst from the awful depths, and Mefistofele is proclaimed master and is given a crystal ball which represents the earth. Faust sees Marguerite bound by red-hot chains.

The third act shows a prison cell. Marguerite is imprisoned after being sentenced to death for poisoning her mother and murdering the child she has had by Faust. Aided by Mefistofele, Faust offers Marguerite a chance to escape with him, but she refuses as long as Faust is associated with Mefistofele. She resists urging until dawn and finally falls dead just as the executioner enters the cell. As Faust and Mefistofele depart, an angel choir chants that Marguerite has been redeemed.

The fourth act shows the banks of a river in Greece. Mefistofele presents Faust with Helen of Troy. Faust makes ardent love to her, and takes her in his arms as Mefistofele returns to Brocken.

In the Epilogue Faust has again become an old man. Sitting in his study he is remorseful for all he has done. While he is reading his Bible Mefistofele appears and tries again to tempt him by evoking sirens who surround him. Faust reads in his Bible that the lowest of sinners may repent and be saved. He prays for forgiveness. Mefistofele sinks into the earth and Faust falls dead. A shower of roses falls upon his body, and the angel chorus sings that he has been triumphant in death.

§)&(§

DIE MEISTERSINGER VON NUREMBERG

(The Mastersingers of Nuremberg)

Richard Wagner

Richard Wagner's *Die Meistersinger,* was first produced at the Hoftheater in Munich, June 21, 1868. In the list of the composer's works it followed the composition of *Tristan und Isolde* (1857–59) and preceded *Götterdämmerung* (1869–74). Wagner himself wrote the libretto of *Die Meistersinger,* and founded his story on the customs and traditions of the German Mastersingers of the fourteenth, fifteenth and sixteenth centuries. These Mastersingers joined together in societies which were similar to the guilds of handworkers. A member's musical merits were judged according to elaborate sets of rules, and his advancement in the society depended on his passing a series of tests. The various grades of membership ranged from apprentice to master. The Hans Sachs of Wagner's music-drama was an actual person who was born and died in Nuremberg (1494–1576). He was a shoemaker by trade, and his poems and master-songs were gathered together and published in 1906.*

The principal characters of *Die Meistersinger* are:

HANS SACHS (*Bass*), a cobbler
POGNER (*Bass*), a goldsmith

* In G. Müner's edition of *Das Singebuch des Adam Puschmann.*

EVA (*Soprano*), his daughter
MAGDALENA (*Contralto*), Eva's nurse
DAVID (*Tenor*), apprentice to Hans Sachs, in love with Magdalena
BECKMESSER (*Bass*), the town clerk
WALTHER VON STOLZING (*Tenor*), a Franconian knight
A NIGHT WATCHMAN (*Basso*)

The action occurs in Nuremberg during the sixteenth century. The first act shows the interior of St. Catharine's Church. During the service Walther sees Eva, the daughter of Pogner, the goldsmith. She and Walther fall in love with each other at first sight, but Walther learns that Pogner has announced that Eva will marry the winner of the forthcoming song contest. Beckmesser, the town clerk, is in love with Eva, and he has made up his mind that he will win the contest and Eva's hand. Walther decides to enter the contest and is given a preliminary trial before the Mastersingers. First he is given a few instructions in regard to the strict, arbitrary rules by David the apprentice, and then he sings for the judges. Beckmesser is the "marker," and he gives Walther so many bad marks that the Mastersingers decide that the knight is a poor singer.

The second act shows a street. On one side is the house and cobbler's shop of Hans Sachs, and on the other the home of Pogner and his daughter, Eva. Sachs realizes that Walther has a most beautiful voice, even though his singing was contrary to the rules of the Mastersingers. Eva meets Walther and tells him that though he has failed in the preliminary test, she will elope with him no matter who wins the final contest. The approach of Beckmesser forces the lovers to hide. Beckmesser serenades Eva with the song he is planning to sing in the contest but he is interrupted by the singing of Hans Sachs, sitting outside his cobbler's shop. The two argue, and Sachs finally says he will let Beckmesser sing without interruption if he, Sachs, is allowed to beat his hammer on a shoe every time Beckmesser makes a mistake. Beckmesser starts his song again and Sachs pounds his hammer so often that Beckmesser becomes hopelessly mixed up. The neighbors gather, and finally Magdalena, Eva's nurse, calls to Beckmesser from a window and tells him to stop singing. David, the apprentice, sees Magdalena in the window and he thinks Beckmesser has been serenading her. David is in love with Magdalena and he takes a club and starts to beat Beckmesser. During the riot that follows Eva and Walther try to escape, but Sachs prevents them. He drags Walther into his shop and sends Eva to her home across the street. The street quiets down and the night watchman calls the hour and announces that all is well.

The third act opens inside Sachs's shop. Walther tells Sachs about a wonderful melody he has heard in a dream. He writes down the first two verses of his song, and then goes where he will be alone to improvise a third verse. He leaves the manuscript on a table where it is discovered by Beckmesser. Beckmesser decides that he will sing this song at the contest and he puts the manuscript in his pocket. Sachs sees Beckmesser take the song, but he does not stop him, for he has a plan for making the Mastersingers hear Walther in the contest. Eva comes with a shoe to be fixed. Sachs tells her about Walther's song, and then calls David and Magdalena to hear it. The scene closes with a quintet, in which Walther, Sachs, Eva, David and Magdalena sing Walther's master-song. The scene changes to a field on the shores of the Pegnitz River, where the song contest is to take place. The people are all assembled and they first watch the entrance of the apprentices, who dance merrily.

Then comes the dignified, somewhat pompous entrance of the Mastersingers. As the contest begins, Beckmesser sings the melody he stole from Walther. He confuses it with another song, and his whole performance is a failure. Sachs then tells who is the real author of the song and demands that Walther be heard. Walther sings his prize song, and both the melody and its performance amaze the people and force the Mastersingers to recognize the young man's genius. He is awarded the prize and wins the hand of Eva.

§)&(§

MERRY MOUNT

Howard Hanson

The libretto of Howard Hanson's *Merry Mount* was written by Richard L. Stokes, who based its plot on the New England legend of Merry Mount and the Cavaliers who settled there under the leadership of Thomas Morton. These Cavaliers are supposed to have caused much consternation among the Puritans by their love of wordly pleasures. The opera was first produced at the Metropolitan Opera House, New York, February 10, 1934.

The cast includes:

WRESTLING BRADFORD (*Baritone*), a Puritan clergyman
PRAISE-GOD TEWKE (*Baritone*), elder of the congregation
PLENTIFUL TEWKE (*Mezzo-soprano*), his daughter
MYLES BRODRIB (*Baritone*), Captain of the ship, *Trainband*
PEREGRINE BRODRIB (*Soprano*), his son
SAMOSET (*Bass*), an Indian chief

Members of the Merry Mount Colony:

THOMAS MORTON (*Baritone*), their leader
LADY MARIGOLD SANDYS (*Soprano*), his niece
SIR GOWER LACKLAND (*Tenor*), her fiancé
JACK PRENCE (*Tenor*), a clown

The action occurs in the year 1625 and the first act shows the Puritan village. As the worshippers come from the church on a Sunday morning they are exhorted by the preacher, Wrestling Bradford, to shun the plots of Satan. When the villagers have gone to their homes, Bradford confesses to Praise-God Tewke, the elder, the torments he suffers in his dreams. Demons torture him to sign the Devil's Book, and courtesans lure him with fleshly temptations. Among the courtesans is Astoreth, pagan goddess of the moon. Tewke recommends matrimony as the cure for Bradford's troubles, and he offers him his daughter, Plentiful Tewke. Plentiful is more than willing, and she and Bradford are betrothed. When Bradford kisses her he exclaims: "Away! Thou hast no medicine to cure my wound!", and she replies: "Alas, I only know I love thee!" A group of children enter, led by Peregrine Brodrib. The preacher admonishes them, and after he has left, Peregrine subjects them to a catechism. The catechism is interrupted by Jack Prence, a clown, who teaches the children to play the English game of "barley-break." Peregrine's father, Myles Brodrib, finds them playing and learns that Prence belongs to a party of Cavaliers which has recently landed in New England and is setting up a colony where "they would fain rear up an Empire of Jollity, with song and pastime, revel and Maypole dance." Tewke and Bradford are summoned, and Prence is tied to a whipping-post and flogged. His cries bring Lady Marigold Sandys, another member of the Cavalier Colony. When Bradford sees Marigold he is amazed to find that she resembles the Astoreth of his dreams. Marigold calls for help and Thomas Morton and Sir Gower Lackland come in answer. The Puritans and other Cavaliers gather about, and when Bradford learns that Marigold and Lackland are to be married that afternoon, he demands that the Puritans attack the Cavaliers' camp at once.

The second act shows the Cavaliers' camp a few hours later. The Cavaliers have erected a Maypole and are dancing around it. Samoset and the Indians are welcomed, and the marriage of Marigold and Lackland is about to be performed when Bradford enters, denounces the Maypole and summons the Puritans. The Cavaliers are defeated and taken back to their ship, and the Puritans hack down the Maypole.

The third act opens in a forest. Bradford has followed Marigold. He sends away her guards and makes love to her. She repulses him and just as he is forcing her to kiss him, Lackland comes to her rescue. He and Bradford fight and Tewke and the Puritans join the battle. Lackland is killed and Marigold promises vengeance. Tewke orders Marigold held as a prisoner, and rebukes Bradford for his faithlessness to Plentiful. Bradford prays to God for forgiveness, sinks exhausted on the ground and falls into a restless sleep. The scene changes, and Bradford, in his dream, finds himself in the Valley of Tophet, where the monsters of Hell appear in the guise of Cavaliers and Puritans. Lackland, as Satan, summons Bradford. He tempts the preacher with offers of a kingdom and with concubines. Bradford refuses until Marigold appears. She is now Astoreth, and when Bradford beholds her he declares that if he may possess her he will sign the Devil's Book. He curses New England and is branded on the forehead.

The fourth act returns to the village. Samoset and the

Indians are raiding the settlement. Samoset is killed and the Indians are driven away. Bradford enters with Plentiful. When he is asked to pray for his congregation he refuses, remembering the curse he uttered in his dream. He confesses his dream, and when Marigold appears, he denounces her as the source of his sin. When she utters the name of Lackland, he jealously declares that he will go to Hell with Marigold, and openly repudiates God. He shows the Puritans a brand on his forehead. Then he conjures up a flaming pyre, takes the fainting Marigold in his arms, and leaps into the fire.

§)&(§

THE MERRY WIVES OF WINDSOR

Otto Nicolai

Shakespeare's comedy was the basis for Otto Nicolai's comic opera, *The Merry Wives of Windsor,* which was first performed at the Opernhaus in Berlin March 9, 1849. The libretto was written by Solomon Hermann Mosenthal.

The plot follows Shakespeare closely, but confines itself to the adventures of Falstaff and the two ladies, Mrs. Ford and Mrs. Page. The love of Fenton and Anna is incidental, and Falstaff's boisterous followers, Bardolph, Pistol and Nym, are omitted.

The characters of Nicolai's opera include:

SIR JOHN FALSTAFF (*Bass*)
MR. FORD (FLUTE), (*Baritone*)
MRS. FORD (FLUTE), (*Soprano*)
MR. PAGE (*Baritone*)

MRS. PAGE (*Mezzo-soprano*)
ANNA PAGE (*Soprano*), their daughter
FENTON (*Tenor*), her chosen lover
SLENDER (*Tenor*), a suitor of Anna, favored by Mr. Page
DR. CAIUS (*Bass*), a physician, favored by Mrs. Page as a suitor for Anna

The action occurs in and around Windsor, England, in the seventeenth century. The first act shows a courtyard between the houses of Mr. Ford and Mr. Page, whose wives are comparing the identical love letters they have received from Falstaff. They plan revenge, and Mrs. Ford invites Falstaff to her house. The other characters are then introduced: Slender, a rich foolish young man, whom Mr. Page has selected as a husband for his daughter, Anna; Dr. Caius, the physician, whom Mrs. Page favors as Anna's suitor; and Fenton, whom Anna herself has chosen and who sings a tender love duet with her. The scene changes to a room in Ford's house, where Mrs. Ford prepares to receive Falstaff. Mrs. Page hides when Falstaff appears. When Falstaff starts to make love to Mrs. Ford, Mrs. Page interrupts to warn of Mr. Ford's approach. The women put Falstaff in a large clothes basket, and tell the servants to throw it into the Thames.

The second act opens at the Inn of the Garter. Ford introduces himself to Falstaff under the name of Brook, and asks Falstaff to make love to Mrs. Ford for him. Falstaff agrees, and tells Ford that he has already received an invitation from the lady. The second scene shows the garden of Mr. Page's home. Fenton drives away his rivals, Slender and Dr. Caius, and sings another love duet with Anna. In the third scene, in Mr. Ford's house, Mrs. Ford again receives Falstaff. Ford appears and Mrs. Page hides Falstaff in an adjoining room, where she dresses him in the clothes of a woman fortune-teller who was a former enemy of Mr.

Ford. Meanwhile Ford denounces his wife for harboring a lover. She denies it, and says that only the fortune-teller is in the house. When Ford sees the woman he thinks is his old enemy, he beats her with a cudgel. Thus Falstaff comes to grief a second time.

In the third act, which opens in a room at the Pages' house, the wives tell their husbands of their pranks, and the four of them decide to make Falstaff the butt of their jokes at a masquerade party in Windsor Park. Mr. Page plans to have Anna married to Slender during the festivities, while Mrs. Page schemes to have her married to Dr. Caius. Mr. Page tells Slender that Anna will be wearing a green dress; Mrs. Page tells Dr. Caius that Anna will be dressed in red. Fenton makes sure that she is actually dressed in neither color, and while Slender and Dr. Caius find that the maidens they have wedded are actually pages in women's clothes, Fenton and Anna are really married. Meanwhile the merry scene in the park turns out to be a nightmare for Falstaff. He is teased and pommelled by elves and spirits and his flirtatious designs are publicly exposed.

§)&(§

MIGNON

Ambroise Thomas

Like *The Bohemian Girl* of Balfe, Ambroise Thomas's opera *Mignon* tells the story of a maiden who was kidnapped in childhood and who grows up without knowing who she really is. The libretto of *Mignon* was written by Michel Carré and Jules Barbier and was founded on

Goethe's novel *Wilhelm Meister*. The opera was first produced at the Opéra Comique in Paris, November 17, 1866.

The characters include:

MIGNON (*Mezzo-soprano*), a girl adopted by the gypsies
LOTHARIO (*Basso*), an aged, wandering minstrel
GIARNO (*Basso*), the gypsy leader
WILHELM MEISTER (*Tenor*), a German student
LAERTES (*Baritone*), a strolling actor
PHILINA (*Soprano*), an actress
BARON FRIEDRICH (*Tenor*)

The first act is in eighteenth-century Germany, in the courtyard of an inn. The villagers are talking about the appearance of Lothario, a wandering minstrel who has gone mad from seeking his daughter, lost in childhood. A band of gypsies arrive, among them Giarno, the leader, and Mignon, a young girl dressed as a boy. The strolling players, Philina and Laertes, hear the confusion from their rooms in the inn and come to the balcony in time to see Giarno command the footsore and weary Mignon to dance. When Mignon refuses Giarno starts to beat her. Old Lothario tries to protect her but is no match for Giarno. Wilhelm Meister, a young German student, draws his pistol in time to save Lothario. Wilhelm thinks Mignon is a boy and when she tells him the little she remembers of her childhood in the aria *Connais-tu le pays?* ("Knowest thou the land?"), he buys her from the gypsy and takes her with him as a page. Meanwhile, Wilhelm has become infatuated with Philina, the actress. Baron Friedrich, another of Philina's admirers, has invited the players to his uncle's castle, and is not pleased when Wilhelm and Mignon accompany them.

The second act opens in a boudoir in the castle. Philina is making herself beautiful for the role of Titania in *A*

Midsummer Night's Dream. Wilhelm enters with Mignon, who has already fallen in love with him and is secretly jealous when he makes love to Philina. Left alone in the room, Mignon uses Philina's make-up and puts on one of the actress's gowns. Wilhelm returns and discovers that his page is a girl. He tells her that they had better part. Philina finds Mignon in her clothes and is highly amused. Mignon is so stung by Philina's sarcasm that she tears off the gown, puts on her gypsy clothes, and leaves in humiliation. The second scene shows the park of the castle. The performance of *A Midsummer Night's Dream* is being given in the conservatory. Mignon is despondent and is about to drown herself in the lake. Lothario comes in time to stop her. Mignon looks at the conservatory and says that she wishes it would be destroyed by fire. The people come from the conservatory and praise Philina for her performance. She responds by singing the famous polonaise: *Io son Titania!* ("I am Titania!") Philina finds that she has dropped the flowers Wilhelm had sent her, and sends Mignon to the conservatory for them. While Mignon is gone, the building bursts into flames. Lothario has interpreted Mignon's wish literally. Wilhelm rushes into the conservatory and brings back in his arms the unconscious Mignon, clasping in her hands the shriveled bouquet.

In the last act, Wilhelm, Mignon and Lothario are at a castle in Italy to which they have come to bring about Mignon's recovery. Wilhelm has discovered that he is in love with Mignon. Lothario finds himself in familiar surroundings. His mind clears, and he realizes that this is his real home; that he is the Marquis of Cypriani, and that Mignon is his long-lost daughter. He is delighted to bestow her hand on the gallant Wilhelm Meister.

§)&(§

MIREILLE

Charles-François Gounod

Gounod's *Mireille* was first produced at the Théâtre Lyrique in Paris, March 19, 1864. Its libretto was written by Michel Carré, who founded the story on *Mireïo*, a poem by Frédéric Mistral.

The cast includes:

RAMON (*Bass*), a wealthy farmer
MIREILLE (*Soprano*), his daughter
VINCENT (*Tenor*), Mireille's suitor
VINCENETTE (*Mezzo-soprano*), his sister
AMBROISE (*Bass*), father of Vincent and Vincenette
TAVEN (*Contralto*), a fortune-teller
OURRIAS (*Bass*), a rival suitor for Mireille's hand, favored by her father Ramon

The action occurs in the province of Millaine, in legendary times. The first act shows a mulberry plantation where Mireille is being teased about her love for the poor but handsome basketmaker Vincent. Mireille admits that she loves Vincent, but Taven, the fortune-teller, warns her that her father will be opposed to such a match. Vincent himself comes and he and Mireille sing a love duet.

In the second act, at the arena of Arles, the herdsman, Ourrias, makes love to Mireille, and tells her that he has her father's consent to their marriage. Mireille refuses him. Ambroise, the father of Vincent, asks Ramon, Mireille's father, to consent to the marriage of Vincent and Mireille. Ramon refuses insultingly and Mireille declares that she will marry no one but Vincent.

In the third act, on Ramon's farm, Ourrias wounds Vincent with an iron trident. Vincent's sister, Vincenette, tells Mireille that Vincent is badly wounded, and Mireille starts on a pilgrimage in his behalf to the Church of St. Marie.

The fourth act shows the church. Mireille enters with a band of pilgrims. Vincent appears but Mireille does not recognize him. She falls unconscious in his arms and as the pilgrims chant she awakes and recognizes him. She points upward and declares that they will forever be united. Ramon is repentant, and blesses their union.

§)&(§

MONA

Horatio Parker

Horatio Parker's *Mona* was awarded a prize of $10,000 in a contest conducted in 1911 by the Metropolitan Opera Association in New York, and was first produced at the Metropolitan March 14, 1912. The libretto was written by Brian Hooker, and its story tells of Mona, princess of Britain in the days of the Roman invasion, who is torn between her love for the son of the Roman governor and her hatred of the Roman invaders.

The characters include:

MONA (*Mezzo-soprano*), Princess of Britain
ENYA (*Soprano*), her foster-mother
ARTH (*Bass*), a British tribesman, husband of Enya
GLOOM (*Baritone*), their son, a Druid
NIAL (*Tenor*), a half-wit
CARADOC (*Baritone*), chief Bard of Britain
THE ROMAN GOVERNOR (*Baritone*)
QUINTUS (*Tenor*), his son, known to the Britons as GWYNN

The action occurs in Southwest Britain at the end of the first century, A.D. The first act shows the interior of Arth's hut. Above the door appears the Druid sign of the Unspeakable Name. While Enya is busy about the house and Nial is lying by the fire, Gwynn is pleading with Mona to marry him. Although he is actually the son of the Roman governor, his mother was a Briton, and all his life he has mingled with the Britons, who do not know that he is Roman. His chief concern has been to maintain peace between the two peoples. Mona tells Gwynn that although she loves him, she cannot marry him, for she has seen in her dreams a vision of the Roman oppressors being pushed back into the sea, and of herself leading her people. She shows a birthmark on her breast, the sign of the Unspeakable Name. Arth, Enya's husband, brings a sword which he has taken from a Roman soldier. Mona recognizes it as the sword of her dream, and is now certain that she is destined to lead her people against the Romans. Gwynn tries in vain to talk of peace. When Caradoc, the Bard, and Gloom, the Druid, come to swear allegiance to the Druid sign, Gwynn is driven away and banished.

The second act occurs a month later, at the Druid temple in the forest. Gwynn has been trying to save Mona, who has been stirring the Britons to revolt. Several times he has held back the Roman garrisons and has caused Mona's life and the spirit of the rebellion to be spared. Gwynn's father, the governor, reproaches him for his actions. Gwynn replies that he hopes to keep the tribes from making war, and the governor promises that if the Britons will not make war they will be spared. If, however, they attack they will be crushed without mercy. Gwynn meets Mona. For the moment her love for him makes her forget her warlike plans, but when he talks of peace she turns against him and calls to the Britons for help. They fall upon Gwynn but Mona cannot see him killed. She lies to save him, and he is mad prisoner as the Britons rush out to battle against the Roman garrison.

The third act shows a plateau on the edge of the forest. The battle has gone against the Britons. Arth has been killed and Gloom mortally wounded. Gwynn has escaped, and he tries to prevent further bloodshed. He reveals his Roman parentage to Mona and she stabs him for being a traitor, not realizing that he has been trying to bring about a true peace. When the governor comes with his soldiers Mona is taken prisoner. She learns that Gwynn had spoken the truth, and that if she had followed her womanly instincts and her love for Gwynn, she might have accomplished her aims without bloodshed.

§)&(§

MONNA VANNA

Henri Février

Maurice Maeterlinck's drama, *Monna Vanna,* is the libretto for Henri Février's opera of the same name. The work was first produced at the Grand Opéra in Paris, January 13, 1909.

The principal characters are:

PRINZIVALLE (*Tenor*), Commander of the Florentine army
GUIDO (*Bass*), Commander of the army of Pisa
MONNA VANNA (*Soprano*), Guido's wife
MARCO VANNA (*Bass*), Mona's father

The action occurs in Pisa during the Middle Ages. The first act shows Guido's palace. Pisa is under siege by the

Florentine army and its citizens are starving. Guido, the commander, sends his wife's father, Marco, to beg mercy from Prinzivalle, the enemy general. Marco returns with word that Prinzivalle will be glad to lift the siege and supply the people of Pisa with provisions if Guido's wife, Monna Vanna, will come to his tent at night clad only in her mantle. Guido will not hear of her going, but Monna Vanna is willing to sacrifice herself to save her people from starvation. Encouraged by her father, Monna Vanna disregards Guido's jealous refusal and leaves for Prinzivalle's tent, wearing only her mantle.

The second act shows Prinzivalle's tent. When Monna Vanna arrives she is surprised to find that the general is not a barbarian but a man of learning and refinement. She recognizes him as a childhood friend in Florence. When she tells him that she loves her husband, he respects her fidelity and makes no advances. True to his word, he orders a supply-train of wagons sent to Pisa. His own army believes him to be a traitor, and messengers bring word that his troops are marching on his tent. Monna Vanna persuades Prinzivalle to come with her to Pisa.

The third act is laid in a room in Guido's palace. Monna Vanna arrives with Prinzivalle. She explains to Guido that she has been treated with courtesy and respect but Guido is too jealous to believe her. He orders Prinzivalle cast into a dungeon and Monna Vanna is so outraged that her love for her husband turns to hatred.

The fourth act shows the dungeon. Monna Vanna now loves Prinzivalle. She brings a key and unlocks the door. She and Prinzivalle escape and leave Guido to the loneliness that his jealousy and distrust have created.

§)&(§

NATOMA

Victor Herbert

Natoma is one of the two grand operas that Victor Herbert composed. Its libretto was written by Joseph Deighn Redding and it was produced first at the Metropolitan Opera House in Philadelphia, February 25, 1911.

The cast includes:

DON FRANCISCO (*Bass*), a Spanish nobleman
BARBARA (*Soprano*), his daughter
NATOMA (*Soprano*), an Indian girl
PAUL MERRILL (*Tenor*), an American lieutenant
JUAN BAUTISTA ALVARADO (*Baritone*), a young Spaniard
JOSE CASTRO (*Baritone*), a half-breed
FATHER PERALTA (*Bass*), Padre of the Mission

The action occurs on the coast of California in the year 1820. The first act is laid at the hacienda of Don Francisco on the island of Santa Cruz. Don Francisco is expecting his daughter Barbara to return from the convent school. He welcomes a visiting party of huntsmen, led by Alvarado and Castro. Natoma, an Indian maid, enters with Lieutenant Merrill, who has landed from an American ship lying in the harbor. Merrill asks Natoma to tell him about herself and her people. She explains that she is the last princess of her tribe, and she shows Merrill an abalone which she wears on her neck. It is a symbol of aid and prosperity from the Great Spirit. By this time Natoma has fallen in love with Lieutenant Merrill, but she hides her feelings as she greets Barbara, who arrives with her companions from school. When all the others have gone into the house, Alvarado, the Spaniard, serenades Barbara. She, however, like Natoma, has fallen in love with Lieutenant Merrill, and it soon develops that the Lieutenant has fallen in love with her. When they are alone the Lieutenant and Barbara sing a love duet. Alvarado is determined to have Barbara for himself, and Natoma overhears him plotting with his friends to kidnap Barbara during a festival which will be held on the mainland the following day.

The second act shows the front of the Mission Church. Natoma is sad and depressed, for she knows that the Lieutenant loves Barbara. She is loyal to her friend, however, and she joins in the cordial greetings that Barbara receives from her father and the others. The Lieutenant arrives and sings a patriotic song. When the dancing begins Alvarado persuades Barbara to be his partner. He makes love to her and she repulses him. Castro, the half-breed, challenges anyone to dance with him the Indian "Dagger Dance." Natoma accepts, and when the dance is finished, she raises her dagger and stabs Alvarado, knowing that he is about to kidnap Barbara. During the tumult that follows Father Peralta appears at the door of the Mission. Natoma drops her dagger, and falls in penitence at the Padre's feet.

The third act shows the interior of the Mission. The penitent Natoma sings the aria, "Beware of the Hawk." The Padre tells her that she has committed a great sin but he assures her that she may find forgiveness from the Madonna. Natoma decides to atone for her sin by becoming a nun. People come to the church for the service, and Barbara is with the Lieutenant. Natoma approaches them, takes the abalone from her neck and places it over Barbara's head. The doors of the church open. Barbara passes into the garden, and the doors close behind her.

§)&(§

LA NAVARRAISE

Jules Massenet

Jules Massenet's opera, *La Navarraise,* was produced first at Covent Garden in London, June 20, 1894. Its libretto was written by Jules Claretie and Henri Cain.

The cast includes:

GARRIDO (*Bass*), General of the Royalist troops
REMIGIO (*Bass*), a farmer
ARAQUIL (*Tenor*), his son, a sergeant in the regiment
ANITA (*Soprano*), a girl of Navarre

The action takes place in Spain, during the Carlist war. The first act shows a square in a Basque village. Anita is looking for her lover Araquil, a sergeant in the Royalist army. She finds him and as they greet each other, they are interrupted by Araquil's father, Remigio. Remigio is not pleased with his son's engagement to Anita. He wants a rich daughter-in-law, and he prohibits the marriage unless Anita can produce a dowry of two thousand douros. Anita is an orphan and has no way of getting so large a sum. Later she overhears General Garrido offer a fortune to anyone who will capture the Carlist leader, Zuccaraga, dead or alive. She approaches Garrido and says that she will capture Zuccaraga if he will promise to keep what she has done a secret. When Anita has gone on her mission Araquil hears from a lieutenant that Anita has been seen approaching Zuccaraga's headquarters. The Carlist chief is known to have a weakness for women and Araquil jumps at conclusions.

The second act shows the same scene. Anita returns, pale and dazed. She asks Garrido for the money he promised, for she has shot Zuccaraga in his tent. Garrido satisfies himself that she is telling the truth and gives her a bag of gold. Soon Araquil is brought in, wounded. Anita shows him the gold and tells him that now she is rich enough to marry him. Araquil thinks that she obtained the money by selling herself to Zuccaraga. He denounces Anita, and as he dies he hears the tolling of the bell which announces Zuccaraga's death. Anita tries to kill herself, and curses the Virgin for not letting her die. As the bell continues to toll she shows that she is mad by asking if this is her wedding day.

§)&(§

NORMA

Vincenzo Bellini

Norma was the eighth of Vincenzo Bellini's eleven operas, and was first produced at La Scala in Milan, December 26, 1831. Its libretto was written by Felice Romani, and was founded on a play by Alexandre Soumet.

The scenes of the opera are laid in Gaul during the Roman occupation, about 50 B.C., and the cast includes the following characters:

OROVESO (*Bass*), Chief of the Druids
NORMA (*Soprano*), his daughter, the High Priestess
ADALGISA (*Contralto*), a priestess
POLLIONE (*Tenor*), the Roman proconsul

The first act is laid in the forest of the Druids. Oroveso announces to the Druids that his daughter, Norma, the High Priestess, will come to cut the sacred mistletoe. By this act she will declare war against the invading Romans, for she alone has the power to declare war or peace. Norma does not cut the mistletoe. Instead, she rebukes the Druids for wanting to war against the Romans, and she invokes peace from the moon singing the famous aria, *Casta Diva* ("Queen of Heaven"). Norma has a reason for not declaring war: she has secretly married Pollione the Roman proconsul, and has thus broken her vows of chastity. She is the mother of two children by Pollione. Pollione is not faithful to Norma. He has transferred his affections to another virgin of the temple, the priestess Adalgisa. Pollione meets Adalgisa secretly and begs her to renounce her religion and elope with him to Rome. Adalgisa consents at first, but her conscience is troubled and she confesses her sin to Norma, asking pardon and absolution. Norma is inclined to sympathize with Adalgisa, for she herself has secretly broken her vows, but when Pollione enters, and Norma learns that he is the one who has tempted Adalgisa, she denounces him bitterly.

The second act shows Norma's apartments. Her two children lie asleep on the couch. Norma has made up her mind to kill them, but she cannot overcome her maternal instincts. When Adalgisa enters, Norma offers her the children. If Adalgisa will take care of them, Norma will consent to her going away with Pollione. She herself will atone for her sins on the funeral pyre. Adalgisa will not hear of Norma's making such a sacrifice. Instead, she will go to Pollione and urge him to return to Norma.

The second scene of the second act (sometimes performed as a third act of the opera) is laid in the temple. Pollione has not only refused to return to Norma, he tries to abduct Adalgisa by force while she is conducting the sacred rites at the temple. Norma discovers him during this attempt, and angrily strikes her shield, summoning the warriors. She declares that this is the time for war, and the warriors seize Pollione and bring him before Norma for judgment. Norma offers Pollione his freedom if he will return to Rome and leave Adalgisa. Pollione refuses. Norma is about to sentence him when her love overcomes her. She takes the wreath from her brow and publicly confesses her own guilt. The Druids prepare the funeral pyre, and Norma mounts it. Pollione is so moved by her sacrifice that his love for her returns, and he too ascends the pyre and perishes with Norma.

§)&(§

OBERON

Carl Maria von Weber

The libretto of Carl Maria von Weber's fairy opera, *Oberon,* was written by James R. Planché and was founded on Villeneuve's story, *Huon de Bordeaux,* and Sotheby's translation of C. M. Wieland's German poem, *Oberon.* The first performance of the opera was given at Covent Garden, London, April 12, 1826.

The characters include:

OBERON (*Tenor*), King of the Fairies
TITANIA (*Speaking part*), his Queen
PUCK (*Alto*), his attendant
HARUN-AL-RASHID (*Bass*), Caliph of Bagdad
REZIA (*Soprano*), his daughter
FATIMA (*Mezzo-soprano*), her attendant
SIR HUON DE BORDEAUX (*Tenor*)
SHERASMIN (*Baritone*), his esquire
BABEKAN (*Baritone*), a Persian prince
ALMANZOR (*Baritone*), Emir of Tunis
CHARLEMAGNE (*Bass*)

The action occurs in Fairyland, in Bagdad and in Tunis in the year 806 A.D. The first act opens in Oberon's palace. Oberon has quarreled with his wife, Titania, who vows that she will not return to him until he has found two lovers who will remain true to each other through all trials and temptations. Puck tells Oberon about a gallant knight named Sir Huon who has killed the son of Charlemagne. For this deed Sir Huon has been commanded to go to the Caliph's palace at Bagdad, to slay whoever sits at the Caliph's right hand, and to claim the Caliph's daughter Rezia as his bride. Oberon sees in Sir Huon a possible candidate for the constant lover who will cure his own troubles. He shows Huon a vision of the Caliph's daughter, Rezia, and causes a vision of Sir Huon to be shown to Rezia. The two fall in love with each other before they even meet. Then Oberon gives Huon a magic horn which will summon Oberon whenever Huon needs him. The scene changes to the harem at Bagdad. Rezia tells her maid Fatima that she would rather die than wed Prince Babekan, to whom she is betrothed, particularly after seeing the vision of Sir Huon. Sir Huon appears and announces that he will rescue her and slay her unwelcome fiancé.

The second act opens in the palace of the Caliph where Prince Babekan is seated by the Caliph. Rezia and the Prince are to be married but as Rezia is brought in, Sir Huon enters, and Rezia rushes into his arms. The Prince challenges Huon and Huon kills him. Then Huon sounds the magic horn and the members of the court stand as though frozen. Huon and Rezia are taken to a vessel bound for Greece. As they set sail, Rezia sings the famous aria: "Ocean! Thou Mighty Monster." In the next scene the ship is wrecked. Huon loses the magic horn and Rezia is carried off by pirates.

The third act shows the garden of Almanzor, the Emir

of Tunis. The pirates are planning to sell Rezia to the Emir. Oberon brings Sir Huon to Tunis and the knight forces his way into the garden just as the Emir is trying to force his attentions on Rezia. Huon attacks the Emir and is captured by the guards just as his friend Sherasmin brings him the magic horn. Huon blows the horn and his enemies are petrified. Oberon comes to rescue the lovers. Huon is pardoned by Charlemagne, and Titania is reconciled to Oberon because he has found lovers who are faithful under all conditions.

§)&(§

THE OLD MAID AND THE THIEF

Gian-Carlo Menotti

This is an opera written for radio. It was commissioned from Gian-Carlo Menotti by the National Broadcasting Company and was first presented over its network April 22, 1939. It was given its first stage performance by the Philadelphia Opera Company, February 11, 1941.

The libretto was written by the composer and its cast includes:

MISS TODD (*Contralto*), an old maid
LAETITIA (*Soprano*), a servant
MISS PINKERTON (*Soprano*), a gossip
BOB (*Baritone*), a tramp

The farcical plot concerns Miss Todd and her pretty young servant Laetitia. Both are lonely because neither has a man. Bob, a young tramp, asks for a night's lodging and the ladies take him in for a week. Miss Todd tells her neighbors that he is a cousin from Australia. Miss Pinkerton, the gossip, tells Miss Todd that there is an escaped convict hiding in their neighborhood, so Miss Todd and Laetitia assume that their lodger is the fugitive. Laetitia feels that it is better to be strangled by a man than to live without one.

Bob is treated handsomely. The women bring him his breakfast in bed, and Miss Todd begins stealing from the local merchants and from the neighbors to give him everything he asks for. When he tells her that what he wants most is a drink, she raids a liquor store at night, even though she is a leader in the local temperance society. The neighbors credit these thefts to the escaped convict and the police order a house to house search. Miss Todd and Laetitia warn Bob that the police are coming for him, and he assures them that he is only a harmless tramp. When he learns that Miss Todd has been stealing for him, he tells her that she should be locked up for her thieving. She is so angry at this ingratitude, that she goes for the police. While she is away Bob and Laetitia loot the house and elope. Bob has decided that if he is to be regarded as a criminal he may as well be an efficient one.

The opera is subtitled: "How a virtuous woman made a thief of an honest man."

§)&(§

L'ORACOLO
(The Oracle)

Franco Leoni

The libretto of this one-act opera by Franco Leoni was adapted by Camillo Zanoni from a story by Chester Bailey

Fernald, entitled *The Cat and the Cherub*. The opera was first produced at Covent Garden, London, June 28, 1905.

The cast includes:

CHIM-FEN (*Baritone*), proprietor of an opium den
WIN-SHEE (*Basso*), a learned doctor
WIN-SAN-LUY (*Tenor*), his son
HOO-TSIN (*Bass*), a wealthy merchant
HOO-CHEE (*Contralto*), his little son
AH-YOE (*Soprano*), Hoo-Tsin's niece
HUA-QUEE (*Soprano*), Hoo-Chee's nurse

The action occurs in the Chinese quarter of San Francisco during modern times, on the fifth hour of the Chinese New Year's day. At dawn the revelers and opium addicts are making their way homeward, while the religious members of the community are entering the temple for prayer. Chim-Fen, proprietor of an opium den, pretends to make love to Hua-Quee, nurse to Hoo-Chee, the little son of the wealthy merchant, Hoo-Tsin. This love-making is only to persuade the nurse to steal a fan from her employer's house. Win-San-Luy, son of the learned doctor Win-Shee, is in love with Ah-Yoe, Hoo-Tsin's niece, and as day breaks, he and Ah-Yoe sing a love duet as the sound of a hymn comes from the church. Hoo-Tsin asks the doctor, Win-Shee, to predict the future of his little son Hoo-Chee. Win-Shee consults the book of stars and finds that tragic events are in store for him. Chim-Fen overhears the conversation and determines to have a part in shaping these events. He kidnaps Hoo-Chee and hides him in his opium den. Then he offers to find the child if his father will reward him with the hand of his niece, Ah-Yoe, in marriage. Hoo-Tsin, the father, agrees, but San-Luy, the niece's lover, declares that he will recover the child. He asks for a similar reward. Win-San-Luy suspects that Chim-Fen has stolen the child and he fights his way past Chim-Fen into the opium den where he finds Hoo-Chee. Chim-Fen seizes an ax and kills Win-San-Luy. Then he pushes the child through a trap door into the cellar. Ah-Yoe discovers the body of her lover and becomes insane, and Win-Shee, overwhelmed by the death of his son, vows to discover the murderer.

The second scene occurs two nights later. Win-Shee begs the gods to aid him, and hears the cries of Hoo-Chee coming from under the trap door. He finds the boy and takes him to Hoo-Tsin, his father. Win-Shee suspects Chim-Fen and waits for him. Chim-Fen comes by, befuddled with drink, and Win-Shee, tragically calm, motions to him to sit beside him on a bench. Then Win-Shee grabs Chim-Fen by the throat and strangles him. Win-Shee hears a policeman approaching. He props up the body of Chim-Fen and pretends to be talking to him as the policeman passes. When the officer has gone, the body falls to the ground.

§)&(§

ORFEO ED EURIDICE
(Orpheus and Eurydice)
Christoph Willibald Gluck

The libretto of Christoph Willibald Gluck's *Orfeo* was written by Ranieri de' Calzabigi, and the opera was first performed at the Burgtheater in Vienna, October 5, 1762.

The cast includes:

ORPHEUS (*Contralto*), the singer
EURYDICE (*Soprano*), his bride
AMOR (*Soprano*), God of Love
A HAPPY SHADE (*Soprano*)

The action takes place in Greece and in the lower world, and the first act shows the tomb of Eurydice, where Orpheus and his friends are mourning the death of his bride. Orpheus prays to the gods for her return. He is ready to make any sacrifice, even to descend into Hades to save her. Amor, the God of Love, tells Orpheus that Zeus has heard his prayer, and that he may enter Hades and by his singing try to persuade Pluto to release Eurydice. If Orpheus is successful, he must under no circumstances look back on Eurydice until he has passed the River Styx. If he disobeys this order, Eurydice will die immediately. Orpheus departs joyfully, with Amor's blessing.

The second act is laid at the entrance to Hades. When Orpheus appears he is threatened by the Furies who revile him for trying to enter. Orpheus sings of his love for Eurydice and the Furies are so delighted with the sweetness of his voice and the beauty of his song that they stand aside and let him pass the gate to the lower regions.

The third act shows the Valley of the Blessed where the pure in heart dwell in peace and contentment. The spirits dance to the songs of the birds and the murmur of the brooks. Orpheus is greeted by the chorus of happy shades. They bring Eurydice to him. He turns his face from her, takes her by the hand and gently leads her away. Eurydice does not know about Amor's command and cannot understand why Orpheus will not look at her.

The fourth act shows a forest. Orpheus has led Eurydice through a cave, and hurrying ahead calls to her to follow. She is mystified and hurt, and she begs him to look back at her. She will die, she says, unless she knows that he loves her. Orpheus can resist no longer and he takes Eurydice lovingly in his arms. Eurydice sinks to the ground, dead. Orpheus is grief-stricken and sings one of the most beautiful laments in the literature of music—"I have lost my Eurydice." The god Amor is so touched by the devotion Orpheus has shown that he forgives Orpheus for disobeying his command and restores Eurydice to life.

§)&(§

OTELLO

Giuseppe Verdi

When Giuseppe Verdi produced *Aïda* in 1871 he was fifty-eight years old. For sixteen years afterwards that opera was considered the crowning achievement of his career. Then in 1887, on February 5th, the seventy-four-year-old Verdi astounded the musical world by producing *Otello,* the greatest and finest opera he had yet written. Shakespeare's tragedy was made into an opera libretto by Arrigo Boïto, without material alterations of plot or characterization. The first performance was given at La Scala in Milan.

The cast includes:

OTELLO (*Tenor*), a Moor in the service of Cyprus, now governor of Venice
DESDEMONA (*Soprano*), his wife
IAGO (*Baritone*) } lieutenants to Otello
CASSIO (*Tenor*) }
EMILIA (*Contralto*), wife of Iago
RODERIGO (*Tenor*), a gentleman of Venice
MONTANO (*Bass*), former governor of Cyprus
LODOVICO (*Bass*), Ambassador of Venice

The action of the opera occurs in Cyprus during the fifteenth century. The first act shows an open square at

Cyprus where Otello is welcomed by the people after winning a victory over the Turks. He has appointed Cassio as his first lieutenant and this appointment enrages his other lieutenant, Iago. Iago schemes for revenge by poisoning the mind of Otello against his wife, Desdemona, and involving Cassio as her supposed lover. As his first move in the plot, Iago gets Cassio drunk. Cassio, encouraged by Iago, picks a quarrel with Montano, the former governor of Cyprus. As swords are drawn Otello enters and rebukes his aides for fighting among themselves. Cassio is deprived of his command. When the crowd has dispersed Otello is alone with Desdemona, his wife. They sing a love duet.

The second act is laid in a room in the castle. Iago starts in earnest to arouse Otello's jealousy. He first sympathizes with Cassio, and urges him to enlist the aid of Desdemona in regaining Otello's favor. As Cassio goes to find Desdemona, Iago sings his *Credo,* saying that he believes in a cruel God who has made man in his own vile image, fashioned only for evil. Soon Cassio returns with Desdemona. Iago hurries to fetch Otello, and then calls the Moor's attention to his wife, who is talking with Cassio. Soon Desdemona comes to Otello and urges him to reinstate Cassio. Otello pleads that he has a headache, and wiping his brow with Desdemona's handkerchief, angrily throws it aside. Emilia, Desdemona's attendant and Iago's wife, picks up the handkerchief and Iago slyly forces her to give it to him. Soon Otello and Iago are left alone. Iago tells Otello that he has seen Desdemona's handkerchief in Cassio's room and offers to help Otello punish the guilty ones.

The third act shows the great hall of the castle. Otello asks Desdemona to lend him her handkerchief. When she hands it to him he declares it is not the one he wants and insists on a particular handkerchief which he gave her as a present. She says she will find it in her room, and Otello denounces her in a burst of uncontrollable rage. She is mystified at his strange anger, and when she is gone Otello sings a soliloquy saying that no blow could have been so terrible as this. Soon Iago joins him. He tells Otello that he has heard Cassio utter Desdemona's name in his sleep and he persuades Otello to hide as he himself talks with Cassio. Iago then engages Cassio in a conversation which Otello cannot hear. He can only see their gestures. Cassio laughingly hands Iago Desdemona's handkerchief. He found it in his room and he wonders who put it there. Otello sees the laughter and the handkerchief, and as Cassio leaves he comes from hiding, insane with jealousy and rage. He asks Iago to bring him some poison with which he may kill Desdemona. Iago advises Otello to strangle Desdemona in the bed she has dishonored. He himself will take care of Cassio. As Otello agrees to this plan, the Venetian Ambassador, Lodovico, comes to announce that Otello has been recalled to Venice and that Cassio has been appointed governor of Cyprus. Otello is disturbed by this announcement and Desdemona weeps in sympathy for him. Otello believes that she is weeping because she is to be separated from Cassio. He cannot control his anger, and he throws Desdemona to the ground. He himself falls in a faint and as the crowd outside hail their hero, "Otello, the Lion of Venice," Iago looks at the prostrate Moor and sneers: "Behold your Lion of Venice!"

The fourth act takes place in Desdemona's bedroom. Desdemona says good night to Emilia and sings an *Ave Maria,* asking for the protection of the Virgin. She falls asleep and Otello enters. He broods over the couch and stoops to kiss Desdemona. She wakes and Otello asks if she has prayed, for he would not kill her soul. Deaf to her denials of guilt, Otello hurls accusations at her and strangles her. Emilia returns and shrieks when she sees what has happened. The household rushes in, including Iago. Emilia denounces her husband Iago, and declares that Desdemona was innocent. She tells how Desdemona's handkerchief was taken from her by Iago. Otello draws his dagger and stabs himself. As he dies he looks upon Desdemona's lifeless form and cries: "I kissed thee ere I kill'd thee."

§)&(§

PAGLIACCI

Ruggiero Leoncavallo

Ruggiero Leoncavallo wrote both the libretto and the music of his two-act masterpiece, first produced at the Teatro dal Vèrme in Milan, May 21, 1892. Its tragic plot deals with a play within a play. The characters in the inner play act parts similar to those they play in the outer drama, which represents their supposedly real lives.

The characters are:

CANIO (*Tenor*), leader of a rural theatrical troupe who appears as the
PUNCHINELLO, the clown in the inner play
NEDDA (*Soprano*), Canio's wife, who plays COLUMBINE
TONIO (*Baritone*), who has the role of TADDEO
BEPPO (*Tenor*), who plays HARLEQUIN
SILVIO (*Baritone*), a villager

For a Prologue, Tonio comes before the curtain and announces that the story the audience will see enacted is taken from real life; that the actors are men and women with human hearts. The curtain then rises on the first act, showing a village in Calabria. A traveling theatrical troupe is just arriving, and Canio and his wife, Nedda, announce to the crowd that an exciting play will be performed at seven o'clock. Canio leaves for the village inn, and Tonio makes love to Nedda. She cuts Tonio across the face with her whip and he slinks away, vowing revenge. Presently Silvio enters. He is a villager who is in love with Nedda. He begs Nedda to elope with him. She admits that she loves him and finally promises to elope with him after tonight's performance. Meanwhile Tonio has overheard their love-making and has gone to the inn to fetch Canio. Tonio and Canio arrive in time to hear Nedda and Silvio bidding each other a fond farewell, but Canio is too late to discover who his wife's lover is. He tries to catch him, but Silvio escapes. When Canio returns he tries to stab Nedda, but Beppo snatches the dagger from him, and persuades Nedda to dress for the evening's performance. Canio then sings the famous aria *Vesti la Giubba* ("On with the Play") and the curtain falls as he finishes its last line: "Laugh for the pain that now is breaking your heart."

The second act shows the performance. The villagers enter and take their seats in front of the stage. Nedda warns Silvio to look out for Canio. The play begins and the members of the troupe enact situations almost identical with those they had played in real life before the performance. Nedda as Columbine takes advantage of the absence of her husband Punchinello (played by Canio), to receive Harlequin (played by Beppo). Taddeo (played by Tonio) enters. He makes love to Columbine (Nedda) and is repulsed. Harlequin arrives and he and Columbine are having supper together when Taddeo warns them that Punchinello, the husband, is returning. Harlequin escapes, and Punchinello demands that Columbine tell him the name of her lover. Canio suddenly forgets that he is Punchinello, and the similarity between his make-believe situation and his actual jealousy is so close that he demands again and again that Nedda tell him who her lover is. Even the audience comes to realize that this is not play-acting. Canio becomes so frenzied that he picks a knife from the table and stabs Nedda. Dying, she calls to Silvio for help. Silvio rushes to the stage, and Canio stabs him also, crying: "No clown am I, but a man!" The villagers rush to the stage and disarm Canio. He stands in a stupor and murmurs: "The comedy is ended."

§)&(§

PALESTRINA
Hans Pfitzner

Hans Pfitzner composed both the text and the music of his opera *Palestrina,* which was first produced at Munich, June 12, 1917. The plot concerns the historic episode of the composer Palestrina saving church music from total condemnation at the Council of Trent. There are no female characters in the opera.

In the first act Palestrina is grieving over the death of his wife. Cardinal Borromeo tells him that the Council of Trent is so disgusted with the insincere, florid style of the church music then in vogue that it is about to ban all music but plain-song from the services. The Cardinal begs Palestrina to compose a Mass that will be so inspiring that the Council will be convinced that dignity and sincerity are possible in the contrapuntal style of composition. Palestrina refuses the Cardinal's request, but when his caller has gone he is visited by the spirits of nine composers of the past, who persuade him to accept the challenge of the Council. Angels appear to Palestrina, singing passages from an actual Mass of Palestrina, now known as the Mass of Pope Marcello. Palestrina writes the notes of the Mass, as though from the angels' dictation.

The second act shows the Council in session. In a satire on the materialism that guided such councils, the prelates are quarreling and unable to understand anything about the significance of the work that has been submitted to them. One of the Bishops cannot even pronounce Palestrina's name, and the Council is adjourned for refreshment.

The third act returns to Palestrina's house in Rome. The new Mass has been shown to the Pope, who comes to give his blessing to the composer and his glorious Mass. The opera ends as Palestrina plays the small organ in his house, and the crowd outside hails him as the savior of church music.

§)&(§

PARSIFAL

Richard Wagner

Parsifal was the last of Richard Wagner's music-dramas. It was composed in the years 1877–82 and was first produced at the Festspielhaus in Bayreuth, July 26, 1882.

Wagner composed both libretto and music for *Parsifal,* He based the work on the medieval legend of the Holy Grail, using the version found in the poems of the German Minnesinger, Wolfram von Eschenbach. The Holy Grail was the sacred chalice from which Christ drank during the Last Supper, and in which were caught the last drops of His blood as He hung on the cross. In Wagner's version of the legend the Grail and the Sacred Spear with which Longius pierced the side of Christ were brought down from Heaven by a band of angels who placed them in the care of Titurel. Titurel built for them a temple in the mountains of northern Spain which was called Montsalvat. Here an order of knights was founded to protect the sacred relics. Only the pure in heart could gain access to the temple, and none but the noble and brave could remain in its service.

When Titurel became old he was succeeded by his son Amfortas. Amfortas fell victim to the wiles of an enchantress named Kundry, who was in the service of the magician Klingsor. Klingsor became vengeful because he was not made a knight. In the original legend Kundry was the prototype of the Wandering Jew who mocked at Christ on the cross and was condemned to perpetual laughter. In *Parsifal* Wagner depicts Kundry as a woman who seeks atonement in service to the Grail, but who is condemned to periodical lapses into a magic sleep during which she becomes a slave to the powers of evil. Amfortas was wounded by the magician Klingsor when Klingsor wrested from him the Sacred Spear, and he sustained a wound that will not heal until a pure and unsophisticated youth shall come to Montsalvat, and after resisting temptation, shall regain the Spear and touch Amfortas' wound with it. The action of *Parsifal* begins with the coming of this simple youth.

In *Parsifal* Wagner's theories of composition reach their highest development. There are no arias or set pieces. The musical structure is built on a system of *leit-motifs* (leading motives, or themes) each characterizing, and associated with, the persons and spiritual or ethical ideas of the drama. There are motifs for the Last Supper, for the Grail, for Faith, for the Sacred Spear, for Parsifal himself, for Kling sor, Kundry, and the other characters, as well as the Good Friday motif and the Good Friday Spell.

The principal characters are:

AMFORTAS (*Baritone*), keeper of the Holy Grail
TITUREL (*Bass*), his father
GURNEMANZ (*Bass*), keeper of the gate
PARSIFAL (*Tenor*), the simple youth, known as the "Guileless Fool"
KLINGSOR (*Baritone*), a magician
KUNDRY (*Mezzo soprano*), an enchantress

The action occurs during the Middle Ages at Montsalvat in the mountains of Spain. The first act shows a wood near the Grail Mountain. Gurnemanz and a group of young squires are conducting their morning devotions. Gurnemanz declares that the wound of Amfortas can be healed by one man alone. Kundry rushes in bringing balsam from Arabia which she hopes may heal the wound. Amfortas is borne in on a litter. He is not hopeful that Kundry's ointment will help him but he takes it and is carried to the lake for his bath. Gurnemanz continues his explanation to the squires of how Amfortas received his wound, and is interrupted by a wild swan falling to the ground. Parsifal enters carrying a bow. It is he who shot the swan. Gurnemanz questions Parsifal, and finds that he is completely unaware of the wrong he has committed and totally ignorant about himself and the world. Kundry knows about him, however, and explains that he is an orphan. Gurnemanz realizes that this youth may be the "pure, guileless fool" whose coming was promised, and he leads Parsifal toward the Temple of the Grail. Kundry crawls into a thicket and falls into a deep sleep.

The scene changes to the interior of a great hall where the knights are gathered for the Communion service. Amfortas is borne in on a litter and in spite of his pain, uncovers the Grail, which becomes illumined as the knights partake of the Lord's Supper. Parsifal watches and understands nothing of what is taking place. Gurnemanz is disgusted with him, and thinking that he is only a stupid fool, warns him against shooting any more swans and pushes him out of the hall.

The second act shows Klingsor's castle. Klingsor uses his magic arts to rouse Kundry from her deep sleep and then orders her to seduce Parsifal. Kundry protests, but Klingsor mocks her for her remorse and insists that she overcome the power of this youth whom he recognizes as the "Guileless Fool" who may break his power. The castle sinks in the darkness and the scene changes to a luxuriant garden. Parsifal enters and is surrounded by enticing flower girls. Kundry appears as a woman of bewitching beauty. She puts her arms around Parsifal and kisses his lips. For the first time Parsifal knows passion, but he also feels what seems to be the pain of Amfortas' wound. He realizes how Amfortas was tempted to sin in these same gardens. Pushing Kundry aside he denounces her. He tells her that if he succumbs to her charms he will be damned too. Kundry calls to Klingsor. The magician hurls the Sacred Spear at Parsifal. Instead of hitting Parsifal, the Spear hangs in midair over his head. Parsifal grasps it and makes the sign of the Cross. Kundry falls unconscious and the castle sinks in ruins.

The third act occurs at Montsalvat, many years later. Parsifal has spent the time in wandering, always keeping the Sacred Spear. The first scene shows a meadow near the Grail Mountain, on Good Friday. Gurnemanz finds Kundry asleep in a thicket. He rouses her and sets her to menial tasks. Parsifal comes, heavily armored and carrying the Sacred Spear. Gurnemanz is filled with joy. He removes

Parsifal's armor and sprinkles his head with water. Kundry anoints Parsifal's feet and dries them with her hair. Parsifal baptizes Kundry, and bids her trust in God. Bells summon the knights to prayer, and Parsifal is dressed in a robe of the Grail Knights. The scene changes to the interior of the Grail Temple. The knights bring Amfortas on a litter. He is suffering intense pain and begs the knights to slay him and relieve him of the agony of once more looking at the Holy Grail. Parsifal enters and touches Amfortas' wound with the Sacred Spear. It is healed instantly. Kundry dies forgiven for her sins, the Grail glows with light, and a white dove hovers over Parsifal's head as he kneels before the Grail.

§)&(§

THE PEARL FISHERS
(Les Pêcheurs de Perles)
Georges Bizet

The libretto of Georges Bizet's *The Pearl Fishers* was written by Michel Carré and Eugène Cormon (pen name of Pierre Etienne Piestre). The opera was first produced at the Théâtre Lyrique, Paris, September 30, 1863.

The characters are:

LEILA (*Soprano*), a priestess
NADIR (*Tenor*), a pearl fisher
ZURGA (*Baritone*), a chieftain
NOURABAD (*Bass*), high priest

The action of the opera takes place on the coast of Ceylon during the barbaric period. The first act shows a Ceylonese village where the pearl fishermen are gathered for a ceremonial dance and festival at which a new tribal chieftain is to be selected. Zurga is chosen and as he accepts the honor he discovers a long-lost friend of his youth—Nadir. The two friends greet each other affectionately and recount the events of their youth. They had once quarreled over a beautiful maiden, whom they had known as Leila. They believe that the intervening years have cured them both of their infatuation, and they swear eternal friendship. A mysterious, veiled priestess comes to pray for the success of the fishermen. Zurga urges her to pray for his people night and day, and promises her that if she will keep her vow of chastity she will receive a pearl of great price. If she breaks her vow, she will meet death. As the priestess is about to take her vows, she sees Nadir and hesitates. Nourabad, the high priest, tells her that there is yet time to renounce her pledge, but she refuses, and enters the temple. Nadir realizes that the priestess is Leila, the maiden who caused his quarrel with Zurga. He also finds that he still loves her. Leila, from the distance, sings her song of prayer for the fishermen, and Nadir calls to her softly. Leila answers and Nadir goes to join her.

The second act shows a ruined temple on the shore. Nadir begs Leila to defy the priests, renounce her vows, and fly with him. Leila falls into his arms. Nourabad, the high priest, discovers them and announces to the people that Leila has proved faithless. When the priest tears the veil from Leila's face, Zurga recognizes her and learns that his friend, Nadir, has betrayed him. He orders them both executed. Nadir is taken away in chains and Leila is led off by the priests.

The third act opens in Zurga's tent. Leila pleads for Nadir's life. Zurga replies by openly making love to her, and when she scorns him, he flies into a rage. Nourabad enters and announces the execution. The scene changes to a wild part of the jungle, where a funeral pyre has been erected. A red glow is seen in the distance and Zurga tells the natives that it is not the dawn they see, but the light from their burning homes. They rush off to save their children and their household possessions, and Zurga, left alone with the lovers, tells them that he has forgiven them, and that he kindled the fire in order to save them both. With an ax, he severs their chains and bids them flee. The natives return, and learning that Zurga had caused the destruction of their homes, force him to mount the funeral pyre. As the flames roar about Zurga, the forest catches fire and the entire community perishes with the lovers, Nadir and Leila.

§)&(§

PELLÉAS ET MÉLISANDE

Claude Debussy

Claude Debussy's opera, composed to Maurice Maeterlinck's drama, was first performed at the Opéra Comique, Paris, April 30, 1902.

The cast includes:

ARKEL (*Bass*), King of Allemonde
GENEVIEVE (*Soprano*), his daughter-in-law
GOLAUD (*Baritone*), Genevieve's older son, grandson of King Arkel
PELLÉAS (*Tenor*), the younger son
MÉLISANDE (*Soprano*)
YNIOLD (*Soprano*), Golaud's son.

The action takes place in Allemonde, in ancient times. The first act opens in a forest, where Mélisande, a young maiden with long, yellow hair, sits brooding over a fountain. Golaud, the king's grandson, discovers her. He is fascinated with her and leads her away. The scene changes to a hall in Arkel's castle. Genevieve reads a letter from her son, Golaud, which tells that he has married a strange maiden named Mélisande. If Golaud sees a light in the castle he will know that he will be received at home with his wife. Pelléas, Golaud's younger brother, hurries to prepare the light. The next scene shows the gardens of the castle. Mélisande is impressed by the gloominess of the castle, and also by the handsome features of her brother-in-law, Pelléas. She is sorry to learn that he is going away to-morrow.

The second act begins at a pool in the park. Pelléas and Mélisande are together. She playfully drops her wedding ring into the pool. Pelléas tells Mélisande that it cannot be recovered, and when Mélisande asks what she shall tell Golaud, Pelléas advises her to tell him the truth. In the next scene Golaud is lying wounded in the castle. He was thrown from his horse at the same moment that Mélisande lost her ring in the pool. As Mélisande nurses Golaud he notices that her ring is not on her finger. When he asks her about it, she tells him that she lost it in a cave where she had gone to escape the tide. Golaud is angry, and orders her to go find the ring even though it is night. He sends Pelléas with her. When Pelléas and Mélisande reach the cave, the light of the moon shows three beggars crouching inside. Mélisande is frightened and Pelléas leads her away.

At the beginning of the third act Mélisande is standing on the balcony of her apartment. As she combs her long hair it falls about Pelléas. Golaud appears. He is angry and jealous, and he takes Pelléas into the castle and shows him the deep, dark pits below the vaults. As they come out to the terrace, Golaud warns Pelléas to be less affectionate toward Mélisande for she is about to have a child. Then Golaud questions his small son, Yniold, and what he learns from the boy makes him more jealous. He holds Yniold up to the window and the child tells him that he sees Pelléas and Mélisande looking at each other disconsolately.

In the fourth act Pelléas and Mélisande talk in the castle and agree to meet once more at the fountain. Old King Arkel is worried about Mélisande. He is afraid that she will not live long, and is convinced that she is innocent. The jealous Golaud does not believe him and handles Mélisande so violently that Arkel interferes. Pelléas and Mélisande meet at the fountain and Mélisande finally confesses that she loves him. As they embrace Golaud comes from a hiding place and kills Pelléas with his sword.

The fifth act shows Mélisande's bed-chamber. She has given birth to her child and her strength is failing. Golaud, aware at last that Mélisande was innocent of wrongdoing with Pelléas, begs for forgiveness. She grants his wish with her last breath and dies. The old king takes the child in his arms and says: "A life is ended, a life begins."

§)&(§

THE PERFECT FOOL

Gustav Holst

Gustav Holst himself wrote the libretto for his one-act opera, *The Perfect Fool,* which was produced first at Covent Garden, London, May 14, 1923.

The cast includes:

THE FOOL (*speaking part*)
HIS MOTHER (*Contralto*)
THE WIZARD (*Baritone*)
THE PRINCESS (*Soprano*)
THE TROUBADOUR (*Tenor*)
THE TRAVELER (*Bass*)

As the opera opens the Wizard is performing a magic rite. The ancient prophecy has said that the Princess will wed a man who will perform "the deed no other man can do," and the Wizard wants to be that man. Accordingly, he has the Spirits of the Earth prepare him a drink for working magic. The Spirits of Water add to it the essence of love distilled from ether, and the Spirits of Fire are commanded to dwell within the cup that holds the magic brew. When the concoction is finished the Wizard is tired and lies down to sleep. At this point the Mother enters, dragging with her the Fool, her son. She thinks that he may win the Princess, for it was prophesied at his birth that some day he "would win a bride with a glance of his eye, kill a foe with a look, and achieve what others failed to achieve with a single word." Much to his Mother's disgust the Fool falls asleep as soon as they have entered. She tries to wake him, but he merely yawns and goes back to sleep. The mother wakes the Wizard and begs him to help her. The Wizard curses her for disturbing him but is pacified by her statement that she is a woman and the curse is uncalled for. The Wizard thinks this is a compliment, and tells her of the magic potion which will enable him to win the Princess when she comes to choose a husband. The Wizard tells the Mother to wake him when the Princess arrives, and then goes back to sleep. While he is asleep the Mother conceives the idea of pouring the magic potion down her son's throat, and of filling the Wizard's cup with plain water. As soon as she has changed things around the Princess enters, ready to hear the addresses of her suitors. The Wizard tries first. He drinks from his cup and remains unchanged. The Princess is annoyed and dismisses him. The Wizard leaves in a rage, vowing that he will have revenge. Then the Troubadour and the Traveler each have a turn at wooing the Princess, but the Troubadour fails in the cadenza of his song, and the Traveler makes no impression in a Wagnerian recital of his travels and exploits. Then the Princess sees the Fool. The prophecy that he will win a bride with a glance of his eye is fulfilled, for the Princess falls in love with him immediately. A messenger comes with the news that the Wizard has filled the countryside with demons who are setting everything on fire. The Wizard himself returns, urging his imps to further destruction. The Mother raises the Fool's head and holds it in such a position that the Wizard has to look at it. When the Wizard sees the Fool he disappears in flames amidst a clap of thunder, and the second prophecy is fulfilled—that the Fool shall kill a foe with one look. It remains only for the Fool to conquer with a single word. The Princess approaches him and asks: "Do you love me?", and the Fool answers "No." The people are at first enraged, but then they decide that since it is customary for one to love and the other to be loved, it will be entirely proper to have the Princess and the Fool marry without the Fool's consent. The Fool again falls asleep as the Priest is about to place a crown upon his head.

§)&(§

PETER GRIMES

Benjamin Britten

Benjamin Britten, an English composer, composed *Peter Grimes* on commission from the Koussevitzky Music Foundation. The opera was first performed at Sadler's Wells Theatre in London, June 7, 1945, and was first presented in America at the Berkshire Music Center, August 6, 1946. It was later produced at the Metropolitan Opera House in New York, February 12, 1948.

The libretto, written by Montagu Slater, was derived from The Borough, a poem by George Crabbe which depicts various characters in a Suffolk fishing village. Among them is Peter Grimes, a harsh and solitary man who three times takes a boy from a neighboring orphanage as apprentice because he cannot handle his nets without a helper. Each boy dies, and the neighbors think it is because Grimes has treated each one cruelly. Grimes is tried and acquitted for lack of evidence, but he is still suspected, and is driven to insanity by the hostility of his fellow-townsmen.

The librettist and composer built their plot around this episode, and included, among others, the following characters:

PETER GRIMES (*Tenor*), a fisherman
BOY (JOHN), (*Mute part*), his apprentice
ELLEN ORFORD (*Soprano*), a widow, schoolmistress of the Borough
NED KEENE, an apothecary
MRS. SEDLEY (*Contralto*), a gossip and scandalmonger
SWALLOW, a lawyer
CAPTAIN BALSTRODE (*Baritone*), a retired merchant skipper
REV. HORACE ADAMS, the rector
HOBSON, a carrier

The time of the opera is around 1830 and the Prologue shows the interior of the Moot Hall of the Borough, which is a small fishing town on the East Coast of England. Peter Grimes is under cross-examination at the inquest Swallow is conducting into the death of Peter's apprentice. In spite of the general fear and mistrust of Grimes, there is not evidence enough to hold him, and Swallow dismisses him with a warning.

The opening scene of the first act shows the beach and the exterior of several buildings of the Borough. Peter is faced with the impossibility of working his boat without help, but Ned Keene, the apothecary, has found him a new apprentice at the workhouse. Ellen Orford, the schoolteacher, offers to accompany the carrier to the market town, and to bring the boy home to Peter. The scene changes to the inside of the tavern. A storm is howling outside and the fisherfolk are seeking shelter. Peter comes into the tavern to wait for Ellen and the boy. News comes that a landslide has swept away part of the cliff by Peter's hut, but the carrier's cart reaches the Borough in spite of the storm and the floods. Peter takes the boy to his desolate hut while the fishermen mutter threateningly.

Act Two occurs later in the summer, and the first scene shows the beach and the Borough street, as in the first act. Ellen walks in with Peter's apprentice boy. She is shocked to learn from his torn clothing and the bruises on his neck that Peter has begun to mistreat him. When Peter arrives Ellen questions him, and after a quarrel Peter angrily sends the boy off to look for a shoal he has observed out at sea. Meanwhile, Mrs. Sedley has overheard the conversation between Ellen and Peter and has spread the news that Peter is again abusing his apprentice. The Rector and Swallow set out for Peter's hut, followed by the indignant townsfolk. The second scene is in Peter's hut. Peter arrives with the boy and orders him to get ready for fishing. The boy is so frightened that Peter relents and tries to soothe him, but his language becomes wild and it is apparent that he will eventually become mad. The voices of the approaching villagers are heard and Peter, in confusion, chases the boy out of the cliff-side door of the hut. The boy slips and falls, and Peter climbs down after him as the townspeople arrive. The Rector and Swallow find only an empty hut and it occurs only to Balstrode to look out of the closed cliff-side door. He is one of the few who feel kindly toward Peter, and he says nothing about what he may have seen.

Act Three occurs a few nights later. The first scene shows the village street. There is a dance at Moot Hall and the town is gay and festive. Mrs. Sedley talks with Ned Keene and tells him that she has her own idea of what happened to Peter and the boy, both of whom have been missing for three days. Then she hears Ellen telling Balstrode about a jersey that was found washed up on the beach. She urges the fishermen to hunt for Grimes. A brief intermission marks the passage of a few hours. A thick fog has come in and the only sounds are the fog-horn and the voices of the men. Peter staggers in, exhausted and demented. He shrieks in answer to the distant voices. Ellen discovers him and vainly tries to soothe him. Balstrode comes to her aid and tells Peter to get his boat, to row out of sight of land, and then to sink it. Peter obeys, and Balstrode takes Ellen away from the scene. After another pause the dawn is breaking as the men return from their man hunt. As the villagers start their regular tasks, word comes from the coast-guard station of a boat sinking far out at sea.

§)&(§

PETER IBBETSON

Deems Taylor

Peter Ibbetson was Deems Taylor's second opera and was first produced at the Metropolitan Opera House, New York, February 7, 1931. Its libretto was written by the composer and Constance Collier, and was adapted from a novel by George du Maurier.

The cast includes:

PETER IBBETSON (*Tenor*)
COLONEL IBBETSON (*Baritone*), his uncle
MARY, DUCHESS OF TOWERS (*Soprano*)
MRS. DEANE (*Mezzo-soprano*)
ACHILLE GREGOUX (*Tenor*), an innkeeper
MAJOR DUQUESNOIS (*Bass*), a veteran

The people of the Dream:

PASQUIER DE LA MARIERE (*Baritone*), Peter's father
MARIE PASQUIER (*Soprano*), Peter's mother
MADAME SERASKIER (*Soprano*), Mimsey's mother

The first act shows a ball given by Mrs. Deane at her country home. Colonel Ibbetson, an obnoxious, elderly roue, sings to the assembly a song which he claims is his own composition, but his nephew, Peter, arriving late, inadvertently exposes the old man as a plagiarist. The Colonel is furious, and tells Mrs. Deane that Peter is really his son, rather than his nephew. Peter has an opportunity to talk with Mrs. Deane and he tells her of his childhood in France. He describes a sweetheart named Mimsey, whom, he says, he will never forget. Peter tells Mrs. Deane how Mimsey taught him to "dream true." Though they were apart, by "dreaming true" at the same time they could meet each other whenever they both wished it. At this point Mary, Duchess of Towers, arrives. She and Peter look at each other with interest. Each feels that they have met before.

The second act opens in an inn near Paris. Peter has been to his old home but has found no one he remembers. At the inn he meets Major Duquesnois, a veteran. The Major was a friend of Peter's childhood but he does not recognize Peter. Looking out of the window Peter sees the Duchess of Towers riding by in her carriage. Again he wonders where he has seen her before and as he rests on a couch in the room he falls asleep and begins to dream. The scene changes to a garden at Passy and the audience sees and hears what takes place in Peter's dream. He is a boy of twelve, known to his friends as Gogo. He is playing with Mimsey. Peter's father and mother are there, too, as well as Mimsey's mother. The quiet of the scene is shattered by the entrance of Peter's uncle who insults Peter's mother. Peter rushes to his mother. Then he wakes and the scene returns to the inn. The Duchess of Towers enters, seeking protection from a storm. She and Peter recall their meeting at Mrs. Deane's ball, and as they look at each other they finally realize that he is Gogo and she is Mimsey. They embrace and Peter tells her of the dream he has just had. She has been having an identical dream and realizes that they have been "dreaming true." She tells Peter she is married and that they must never meet again, not even in their dreams.

The third act is laid in London and opens in Colonel Ibbetson's rooms. Mrs. Deane and her mother call on the Colonel and try to regain some compromising letters. They meet Peter and show him a letter in which the Colonel stated that Peter's mother was his mistress. The Colonel arrives and when Peter is alone with him he asks his uncle whether or not he is his father. The Colonel insultingly answers that he has no way of knowing. In an altercation the Colonel attacks Peter. Peter strikes him in self-defense and kills him. In the second scene Peter is in Newgate Prison. He has been sentenced to death for murdering his uncle. He refuses to tell why he killed the Colonel and is about to be led to the scaffold when Mrs. Deane hurries in with word that the sentence has been commuted to life imprisonment. Peter begs for death, for he has nothing to live for. Mrs. Deane consoles him and brings him a message from Mary, telling him to sleep and "dream true." Peter knows the significance of these words and seats himself in the chaplain's chair. He is soon asleep and the scene changes for his dream. Peter returns to a little lake near Paris where he and Mimsey used to play. Mary greets him tenderly and tells him that she will be with him as long as she lives. Their dream life is the only thing that is real now. The final scene occurs in the prison, thirty years later. Peter lies dying on the couch. Mrs. Deane is beside him and tells him that Mary has just died. Peter knows it already for this is the first time in all the years in prison that she has not come to him in his dreams. As Peter grows weaker the walls of the prison vanish. Peter rises from his couch, again young, and finds Mary waiting for him.

§)&(§

PHILÉMON ET BAUCIS

Charles Gounod

Jules Barbier and Michel Carré wrote the libretto for Charles Gounod's opera, *Philémon et Baucis,* and the work was first produced at the Théâtre Lyrique in Paris, February 18, 1860.

The characters are:

PHILÉMON (*Tenor*), an old peasant
BAUCIS (*Soprano*), his wife
JUPITER (*Baritone*)
VULCAN (*Bass*)

The action occurs in Phrygia during mythical times. Philémon and Baucis, a devoted old couple, are sitting contentedly in front of their cottage. During a storm that follows, Jupiter and Vulcan appear, disguised as wayfarers. Their real purpose in coming is to punish the offending people of Phrygia. Philémon and Baucis welcome the strangers and Philémon lights a fire to dry their clothing. Baucis brings food, and the gods are so pleased by their cordial reception that Jupiter changes the water into a pitcher of wine. Baucis realizes that her guest is Jupiter. The god quiets her fears and offers to grant any wish she may have. Baucis wishes that she and her husband may be young again. Jupiter promises not only to fulfill this wish but also to spare Philémon and Baucis the punishment he and Vulcan are about to inflict on their countrymen. Philémon and Baucis fall asleep as Jupiter casts a spell over them.

The second act follows an intermezzo, during which the Phrygians are punished by a terrific storm. Baucis wakes from her sleep and finds a handsome youth beside her. Philémon then awakes, and does not at first recognize the young woman he sees. Looking around, the two see a magnificent palace instead of a cottage. Jupiter returns and himself falls in love with the youthful Baucis. He makes love to her and she escapes into the woods. Jupiter follows her and kneels before her. Baucis remains faithful to Philémon, but is nevertheless flattered by the attentions of a god. Philémon become jealous and quarrels with Baucis. Vulcan scolds the couple for quarreling, and when Baucis realizes that she has hurt her husband's feelings she begs Jupiter to make them both old again. Philémon realizes that Baucis still loves him, and he seconds her request. Jupiter is astonished at such devotion and tells them to remain young. He promises never again to disturb their happiness.

§)&(§

THE PIPE OF DESIRE

Frederick S. Converse

Even though this one-act opera by Frederick S. Converse has not been performed for many years, it is most important historically. It was the first opera by an American to be produced at New York's Metropolitan Opera House, March 18, 1910. Previous to that, on January 31, 1906, the opera had been performed at the New England Conservatory of Music in Boston. The libretto of *The Pipe of Desire* was written by George Edward Burton, with the following characters:

IOLAN (*Tenor*), a peasant
NAOIA (*Soprano*), his betrothed
THE OLD ONE (*Bass*)

The elves are at work in a forest, commanded by the Old One, their king. Iolan, a peasant, comes to claim his bride, Naoia. The elves salute Iolan, and declare a holiday even though the Old One wants them to keep on working. Iolan invites the elves to a wedding feast. The Old One is silent and Iolan mocks him. The elves tell Iolan that the Old One possesses the Pipe of Desire, through which he can rule the world. To prove its power to the doubting Iolan, the Old One plays a tune which makes the elves dance. Iolan declares that the elves danced merely because they wanted to stop working. The elves are angry at Iolan's unbelief and they urge the Old One to play the Pipe for Iolan alone. Iolan finds himself forced to dance, and in a fit of temper he grabs the Pipe and declares that he will make the Old One dance. At first he can produce only discords but when he starts to play a love song for Naoia he conjures up the scene of a cottage. Then the Pipe refuses to play any more and the Old One tells Iolan he has made selfish use of it. He himself takes the Pipe and, as he plays on it, Naoia comes from the cottage, dangerously ill. In delirium she goes barefoot into the forest and falls dead at Iolan's feet. Iolan, desperate, throws his money into the bushes and curses the Old One. The Old One tells him that it is his own folly that has caused the tragedy. Iolan becomes repentant and the elves persuade the Old One to play again. First the Old One plays the song of Autumn, and then the song of Winter. Iolan loses his self-confidence and his youthful energy. He feels himself growing old and senses the approach of death. He looks upward and sees Naoia on the rocks above him. He goes up the path to meet her, and they depart together.

§)&(§

PIQUE-DAME
(The Queen of Spades)

Peter Ilitch Tchaikowsky

Modeste Tchaikowsky, brother of the composer, wrote the libretto for Tchaikowsky's opera, *Pique-Dame*. The plot was adapted from a story by Alexander Pushkin, and the opera was first produced at the Maryinsky Theatre, St. Petersburg, December 19, 1890.

The cast includes:

HERMANN (*Tenor*), an army officer
PRINCE JELETSKY (*Baritone*)
THE COUNTESS (*Mezzo-soprano*)
LISA (*Soprano*), her granddaughter

The action takes place in St. Petersburg at the end of the nineteenth century. The first act opens in a public summer garden of the city. Hermann is talking to a number of his friends about the card-playing of last night. He would like to play for large stakes, but he cannot afford it. He confesses to his companions that he is hopelessly in love with an unnamed lady, but that he is too poor even to think of marrying a woman of high station. Prince Jeletsky enters with the old Countess and her granddaughter, Lisa. He introduces Lisa as his fiancée and as his friends congratulate him, Hermann recognizes Lisa as the lady he secretly loves. The Countess and Lisa in turn recognize Hermann as a mysterious man who has attracted them by his gloomy and sad appearance. When the Prince and the ladies have gone, Hermann hears his friends tell the story of the Countess. As a young woman she was an inveterate gambler. At one time she lost all her money in Paris. A certain count gave her in return for her favor the secret of a certain card combination which would never fail to win. She was told that when she revealed this secret to three persons she would die. By this time she has already told it twice—to her husband and to a lover. Meanwhile she has been so successful at cards that she has been nicknamed "Pique-Dame" or the "Queen of Spades." When Hermann hears this story he realizes that if he obtains the secret he will become rich and will be able to win the love of Lisa. The second scene shows Lisa's room. Lisa cannot forget Hermann's face and appearance. Suddenly he appears on the balcony and threatens to shoot himself if Lisa will not return his love. They are interrupted by the Countess, and Hermann hides behind a screen. He repeats to himself what he has heard from his friends, that death will come to the Countess when she has told the secret three times. When the Countess has gone Hermann comes from his hiding place and tells Lisa that he goes now to his death, because she will not love him. She bids him to stay and live and they embrace each other.

The second act shows first a masked ball, where the Prince is mystified by Lisa's coldness. Hermann comes in response to a note Lisa has sent him, and she gives him the key to the house in which she and the Countess live. The scene changes to the Countess's apartment. Hermann begs the Countess to tell him the secret of the three cards. When the Countess refuses he threatens her with a pistol and she dies of fright. Lisa finds Hermann in her grandmother's apartment, and when the confused Hermann confesses that he was seeking the secret of the cards and not a rendezvous with herself, she denounces him as a murderer.

The third act first shows Hermann in his barracks, where he has received a letter from Lisa asking him to meet her at midnight along the Winter Canal so that he may convince her that he did not intentionally kill the Countess. The funeral procession of the Countess passes and her spirit comes to Hermann. The spirit commands him to marry Lisa and to place his fortunes on three cards—three, seven and ace. Insanely Hermann repeats these names and goes to meet Lisa. In the second scene of the act Lisa and Hermann meet at midnight on the banks of the canal. They are reconciled and plan to elope. But Hermann insists that they first visit the gambling rooms. His talk begins to ramble insanely, and finally in madness he throws her from him, not knowing any more who she is. Lisa is frightened and heartbroken. Knowing that her lover is insane she throws herself into the canal. The last scene is laid in the gambling house. Hermann invites Prince Jeletsky to play with him. Staking large sums of money on each hand, Hermann wins first with the three, and again with the seven. At the last hand Hermann draws not the expected ace, but the Queen of Spades. The ghost of the Countess appears before him. Imagining that she has come for his life, Hermann draws his dagger and stabs himself.

§)&(§

PORGY AND BESS

George Gershwin

For his most ambitious stage work, and his only so-called "serious" opera, George Gershwin chose as his subject a play called *Porgy*, by Du Bose Heyward, which had already been successfully produced by the Theater Guild in New York. The play was adapted as a libretto by Du Bose and Dorothy Heyward in collaboration with George Gershwin's brother, Ira Gershwin. The result was a true example of folk-opera. It was first produced by the Theater Guild in Boston, September 30, 1935. It subsequently enjoyed a long run in New York, and, starting September 13, 1943, it was revived for an even longer run at the Majestic Theatre, New York, and for an extended road tour.

The cast includes:

PORGY (*Baritone*), a cripple
CROWN (*Baritone*)
ROBBINS (*Tenor*)
SERENA (*Soprano*), Robbins' wife
CLARA (*Soprano*)
SPORTIN' LIFE (*Tenor*)
BESS (*Soprano*)
JAKE (*Baritone*)
FRAZIER (*Baritone*), a lawyer

The first act opens in Catfish Row, in the Negro section of Charleston, South Carolina. In former years this row of houses had been occupied by the aristocracy but now it is a tenement. As the curtain rises a crap game is in progress on a summer evening, and above the voices of the players Clara is heard singing a lullaby ("Summertime") to her baby. During the game Crown and Robbins quarrel. Crown stabs Robbins and kills him. Crown escapes, and now that he is a fugitive, Sportin' Life, the dope peddler, tries to induce Bess, Crown's mistress, to go to New York with him. Bess refuses him and seeks refuge from the police in the room of Porgy, the cripple who goes about in a little cart pulled by a goat. The next scene shows the room of Robbins' widow on the following night. The neighbors are gathered to accomplish a saucer burial. Friends of the deceased throw coins into a saucer until there is enough money to bury his remains. Detectives come to find where Crown is.

The second act opens in Catfish Row. Porgy and Bess are living together happily. Bess has reformed and is proving a worthy mate for the gentle, kind Porgy. Lawyer Frazier persuades Bess to buy from him a proper divorce from Crown. When the lawyer learns that Crown and Bess were not married, he announces that the price for a divorce when a couple is not married is $1.50, rather than the customary $1.00 to separate married couples. Porgy shows his contentment by singing "I got plenty of nuthin'," and he and Bess sing of their love in the duet: "Bess, you is my woman now." The second scene shows the Kittawah Island, where the Negroes are having an all-day picnic. Sportin' Life makes fun of the religious Negroes by singing "It ain't necessarily so." Just as it is time to go home, Crown appears before Bess. He has been hiding on the island, and he persuades Bess to stay with him. The next scene returns to Catfish Row, a few days later. Bess comes back to Porgy, and Porgy is glad to forgive her. A hurricane sweeps down on them, and word comes that Jake's boat is wrecked. The Negroes shout and pray and suddenly Crown appears. He ridicules them for being afraid and rushes off for a boat in which to rescue Jake.

The third act shows Catfish Row at night. Sportin' Life tells Bess that Crown is still alive. Crown appears and crawls toward Porgy's room hoping to find Bess. Porgy leans out of his window and stabs Crown to death. The police are called, but no one in Catfish Row will tell them anything about the murder. The police insist that Porgy identify the body. Porgy refuses to look at Crown and is taken to jail. In the next scene, still in Catfish Row, Sportin' Life again tries to persuade Bess to run away with him, this time telling her that Porgy is still in jail. To tempt her he leaves a package of dope on her doorstep. When he has gone Bess comes from her room and takes the package. The last scene occurs a week later. Porgy returns, released from jail. He looks for Bess. At first the neighbors are silent, but finally they tell him that she has gone to New York with Sportin' Life. Porgy asks how far it is to New York. When he learns that it is a thousand miles away, he mounts his goat cart and starts out to find Bess.

§)&(§

THE POSTILLION OF LONGJUMEAU

Adolphe Adam

The libretto of this opera by Adolphe Adam was written by Adolphe de Leuven and Leon Brunswick (pseudonym of Leon Levy). The work was first produced at the Opéra Comique in Paris, October 13, 1836.

The principal characters are:

CHAPELOU (*Tenor*), a postillion who becomes SAINT PHAR, a famous singer
MADELAINE (*Soprano*), a hostess, who becomes known as MADAME DE LATOUR
BIJOU (*Bass*), a wheelwright
MARQUIS DE CORCY (*Bass*)

The time of the opera is 1766, and the first act shows the village of Longjumeau. Chapelou, the postillion, is celebrating his marriage to Madelaine, the hostess. Bijou, the wheelwright, is jealous of Chapelou, and he is hurriedly repairing the wheel of the Marquis de Corcy's carriage, for he knows that as soon as it is fixed, Chapelou will have to drive the Marquis de Corcy. De Corcy is an impresario in search of a new tenor. He hears Chapelou sing, and he is so impressed that he makes Chapelou a brilliant offer. Chapelou is likewise impressed, and he leaves his bride and goes off with de Corcy.

The second act shows the garden of Madelaine's country house. She has been living with a rich aunt and has returned as an heiress under the name of Madame de Latour. Meanwhile Chapelou has become a famous singer and has taken the name of Saint Phar. Bijou, the wheelwright, has also become a singer and is a member of the chorus at the opera house. Saint Phar and Madame de Latour proceed to fall in love in their new characters, each ignorant of the other's former identity. St. Phar proposes marriage, but knowing that his former marriage to Madelaine would stand in his way, he persuades a fellow opera singer, Bourdon, to disguise himself as a priest and to perform a mock marriage ceremony. The Marquis de Corcy complicates matters by himself wooing Madame de Latour, the former Madelaine.

In the third act, laid in an apartment of Madelaine's house, the plot reaches its climax when the Marquis de Corcy reveals that Saint Phar is actually Chapelou, the former postillion. Madame de Latour then confesses that she is Madelaine, and everyone except the Marquis is happy.

§)&(§

PRINCE IGOR

Alexander Borodin

Alexander Borodin composed both the libretto and music for as much of his opera *Prince Igor* as he lived to finish.

After his death the work was completed by Rimsky-Korsakoff and Alexander Glazounov. The opera had its first performance at the Imperial Opera House in St. Petersburg, November 4, 1890.

The cast includes:

PRINCE IGOR (*Baritone*)
YAROSLAVNA (*Soprano*), his wife
PRINCE GALITSKY (*Bass*), her brother, Prince Igor's brother-in-law
VLADIMIR (*Tenor*), son of Prince Igor and Yaroslavna
SCOULA (*Bass*)
KHAN KONTCHAK (*Bass*), of the Polovtsky
KONTCHAKOVNA (*Contralto*), his daughter
OVLOUR, a Polovtskian guard
EROCHKA (*Tenor*)
KHAN GZAK

The action occurs at Poultivle in Russia and in the camp of the Polovtsky. The prologue shows the market-place of Poultivle. Prince Igor is about to start on a campaign against the Polovtsky. While the people are singing a rousing farewell, the sun is momentarily eclipsed. Igor's wife, Yaroslavna, and the people, interpret this eclipse as an evil omen, but Igor is not afraid. He turns over the government to his brother-in-law, Prince Galitsky. As Igor departs with his son Vladimir, two rascals, Scoula and Erochka, decide to desert the army and to enter the service of the pleasure-loving Prince Galitsky.

The first act opens in the courtyard of Prince Galitsky's house. Galitsky is making the most of his temporary power and would like to make it permanent. He promises the people anything they want in the way of pleasure, and proposes to dip into Igor's treasury to provide wine and feasting for everybody. Scoula and Erochka are enthusiastic over such ideas and sing their praise and allegiance to Galitsky. A group of maidens enters and announces to Galitsky that one of their number has been abducted. The girls beg Galitsky to find and release their companion. Galitsky mocks the maidens and boasts that he himself is the abductor. When the girls have been frightened away, Galitsky again promises license and revelry. The people shout that they will make him permanent ruler in place of Igor. The scene changes to a room in Prince Igor's palace, where Yaroslavna is lamenting the absence of her husband. The maidens who appeared before Galitsky come to her, and beg for protection. Yaroslavna denounces her brother Galitsky for his wanton conduct. She overcomes his defiance by tell him that she is legally the ruler in her husband's absence. Galitsky grudgingly agrees to free the girl he has abducted. Messengers arrive with word that Prince Igor and Vladimir have been defeated and captured. A division of the enemy is at that moment attacking the city and the suburbs are already in flames.

The second act is laid in the enemy camp of the Polovtsky. Vladimir and Igor are prisoners, and Vladimir has fallen in love with Kontchakovna, daughter of the enemy leader, Khan Kontchak. Vladimir serenades Kontchakovna, and tells her that her father favors their marriage, but that his own father disapproves. Igor appears and sings a lament for his condition of servitude. Ovlour, a captive guard, offers Igor a horse on which he may escape, but Igor feels that it would be dishonorable to flee. Khan Kontchak approaches Igor and assures him that he is not a captive but an honored guest. The Khan offers Igor his freedom if he will agree to drop the war and never again to fight the Polovtsky. Igor refuses, and says that if he were free he would enlist a larger army. The Khan admires such frankness and orders his slaves and dancers to entertain Igor with the Polovtskian dances.

The third act shows another part of the Polovtsky camp. Igor sees the victorious Polovtskian soldiers returning from Poultivle. They bring with them spoils and captives and Igor is filled with horror at the misfortunes of his wife and his people at home. He finally overcomes his prejudice against escaping and accepts Ovlour's offer of aid. Ovlour manages to get the soldiers drunk as they are dividing their loot. Kontchakovna learns of the plot to escape and she begs Vladimir not to leave her. Igor reminds Vladimir of his duty and insists that he go too. Kontchakovna balks Igor by sounding the alarm the moment that he himself escapes. She clings to Vladimir and delays him. The soldiers rush in and are about to kill Vladimir for his father's escape when they are interrupted by the Khan. He forbids them either to follow Prince Igor or to kill Vladimir. He admires Igor's courage, and if they cannot have the father they can secure the son by giving him a mate. Vladimir and Kontchakovna are delighted.

At the beginning of the fourth act Yaroslavna is standing on the terrace of her ruined palace. Her lamentation is soon turned to joy by the return of her escaped husband Igor. The rascally Scoula and Erochka change the song they have been singing in ridicule of Prince Igor to one in his praise. In their great hurry to seem loyal to the man who is now in power, they ring the town bell to summon the people for the return of their prince. All welcome Igor with great rejoicing.

§)&(§

LE PROPHETE

Giacomo Meyerbeer

Giacomo Meyerbeer's *Le Prophete* was first produced at the Grand Opéra in Paris April 16, 1849. Its libretto was written by Augustin Eugène Scribe, who based its plot on the uprising of the Anabaptists in Holland in the sixteenth century and on the career of their leader, John of Leyden.

The cast includes:

JOHN OF LEYDEN (*Tenor*)
FIDES (*Mezzo-soprano*), his mother
BERTHA (*Soprano*), his sweetheart
COUNT OBERTHAL (*Baritone*)
JONAS (*Tenor*)
MATTHISEN (*Bass*)
ZACHARIAS (*Bass*)
} Anabaptists

The first act shows the countryside near Dortrecht, with the castle of Count Oberthal at the right. Bertha, an orphan, has become betrothed to John of Leyden, but she must have the permission of the Count to marry him. Accordingly she comes to the castle with John's mother, Fides. Before Bertha and Fides have audience with the Count, three Anabaptists, Jonas, Matthisen and Zacharias, attack the castle and are repulsed. The Count then turns his attention to Bertha and is so pleased with her appearance that he refuses her request to marry John, and makes her a prisoner.

The second act shows an inn at Dortrecht where John and his mother are tavern-keepers. The three Anabaptists come to talk with John. They are impressed with his resemblance to David, and they ask him to be their leader. John tells of a dream he has had, and sings the aria: "Under the vast dome of a splendid temple." The Anabaptists declare that this dream means that John is destined to be their king. John refuses, thinking of his coming marriage to Bertha. As soon as the Anabaptists have gone, Bertha rushes in, crying that the Count abducted her and that she has escaped. John hides Bertha just as the Count arrives. The Count warns John that he has seized his mother, Fides, and that she will be killed unless John gives up Bertha. John decides to save his mother and the Count takes Bertha away. When the Anabaptists return John agrees to lead them and thus have revenge on Count Oberthal. John leaves a bloody garment behind so that his mother will think he has been killed.

The third act is laid in the Anabaptist camp. A party of noblemen have been taken prisoners. Count Oberthal is present in disguise, and overhears a plan to storm the town of Münster. He is recognized and the Anabaptists are about to kill him when he tells John that Bertha has escaped. John spares his life, and prepares to lead his followers against Münster.

The fourth act shows a square before the Cathedral in Münster. John's mother, Fides, is begging for food. She and Bertha think that John is dead and they swear to be revenged on the Anabaptists, who, they think, killed him. By this time John has led the Anabaptists to victory. They have captured the city and enter with John, their prophet, at their head. As they pass into the cathedral where John is to be crowned king, they march to the music of the famous "Coronation March." Fides recognizes John as her son, but he knows that it would be fatal for him to acknowledge her, so he denounces her publicly. Fides realizes the situation and declares that she must have been mistaken. She is thereupon declared insane.

The fifth act opens in the vaults under the palace at Münster. Fides is a prisoner and when John comes to her she denounces him for representing himself as a prophet and for his part in the Anabaptist uprising. He begs her forgiveness. Bertha joins them and is overjoyed to learn that her lover is still alive. Soon she realizes that he and the Prophet are the same person, and shrinking from the thought of his bloody deeds she stabs herself with a dagger. The scene changes to the great hall of the palace where a banquet is to be held. John has learned that Bertha, before her death, had lighted a fuse leading to a powder magazine beneath the castle. He knows too that the Anabaptists have hatched a counter-plot against him, and he makes no effort to escape when the Count and the Anabaptists take him prisoner. He joins the party at the banquet and tells them that they are all his prisoners. Flames rise from the floor and Fides rushes to John's side and forgives him just before the final catastrophe.

§)&(§

I PURITANI
(The Puritans)

Vincenzo Bellini

Vincenzo Bellini's *I Puritani* was produced first at the Theatre Italien in Paris, January 25, 1835. The libretto was written by Carlo Pepoli, who founded its plot on a play by F. Ancelot and X. B. Saintine—*Têtes Rondes et Cavaliers.*

The cast includes:

LORD GAUTIER WALTON (*Bass*), the Puritan governor-general
ELVIRA (*Soprano*), his daughter
SIR GEORGE WALTON (*Bass*), Elvira's uncle

LORD ARTHUR TALBOT (*Tenor*), a Cavalier, who loves Elvira and is in turn loved by her
SIR RICHARD FORTH (*Baritone*), a Puritan, in love with Elvira
QUEEN HENRIETTA (*Soprano*), widow of Charles I

The action takes place near Plymouth, England, in 1635, shortly after the execution of Charles I. The first act is laid outside the fortress at Plymouth. Civil war is raging between the Puritans under Cromwell and the Stuart royalists. Lord Walton, the Puritan governor-general, is favorably inclined toward the marriage of his daughter Elvira to the Puritan Sir Richard Forth. Elvira, however, loves the Cavalier Arthur Talbot. The scene changes to Elvira's apartments where Elvira's uncle, Sir George, persuades Lord Walton not to force Elvira to marry Richard, but to let her wed the Puritan Arthur. Arthur arrives with an armful of presents which includes a beautiful wedding veil. When Arthur is in the castle he discovers that one of the prisoners is actually Queen Henrietta, the widow of the late king. She has been summoned to court and is probably destined for execution. Arthur determines to save her. He puts the wedding veil over her head and as he and the Queen leave the castle the guards think they are the bride and groom, and allow them to pass. When Elvira hears of the escape she thinks that Arthur has eloped with Henrietta. She becomes insane and the Puritans swear that they will avenge Arthur's supposed infidelity.

The second act shows the Puritan camp. Parliament has condemned Arthur to die for helping Queen Henrietta to escape. Elvira is still demented and she sings an aria: "It was here in sweetest accents he would call me." Sir George pleads with Sir Richard to pardon Lord Arthur. Richard agrees on condition that Arthur comes to the castle unarmed. If he is still an enemy of the Puritans he must die.

The third act shows a garden near Elvira's home. Lord Arthur, fleeing from his enemies, comes for a last word with Elvira. When she sees Arthur, her reason returns and she learns that her lover was not unfaithful to her, but was merely helping his Queen to escape. Drums are heard announcing the coming battle between the Puritans and the royalists. Arthur is found and arrested. Since he is still a royalist sympathizer, he is condemned to die. Elvira again loses her sanity, but a message arrives from Cromwell announcing the complete defeat of the royalists and extending pardon to all prisoners. Elvira is made sane by this joyful news and she and Arthur are happily united.

§)&(§

THE QUEEN OF SHEBA

Karl Goldmark

Karl Goldmark's *The Queen of Sheba* was first performed at the Opernhaus in Vienna, March 10, 1875. Its libretto was adapted from the Old Testament and was written by Solomon Hermann Mosenthal. The cast includes:

KING SOLOMON (*Baritone*)
HIGH PRIEST (*Bass*)
SULAMITH (*Soprano*), daughter of the High Priest
ASSAD (*Tenor*), betrothed to Salumith
QUEEN OF SHEBA (*Mezzo-soprano*)

The action occurs in Jerusalem and the Syrian desert during the reign of King Solomon. In the first act King Solomon is in his palace waiting for a visit from the Queen of Sheba. Meanwhile preparations are being made for the wedding of the High Priest's daughter, Sulamith, to Assad, the King's favorite. Assad returns from escorting the Queen and tells Solomon that he does not love Sulamith. He has been entranced by an eastern woman whom he surprised by accident as she was bathing in a stream in Lebanon. Solomon pleads with Assad to be faithful to Sulamith and Assad promises to do so. His promises are soon forgotten when the Queen of Sheba arrives, lifts her veil, and Assad discovers that she is the lady of the bath. He starts toward her impulsively but she refuses to recognize him.

The first scene of the second act is laid in the moonlit garden of the palace. Assad and the Queen meet. They confess their love for each other, and when the Queen learns that Solomon has commanded Assad to marry Sulamith on the following day, she jealously urges Assad to fly with her to Arabia. The next scene is in the temple, where Assad is to be married to Sulamith in the presence of King Solomon and the Queen of Sheba. Assad beholds the Queen and throwing aside the wedding ring casts himself at her feet. The Queen declares that she does not know Assad and has never seen him. Assad is condemned by the priests. The King stays the execution and the Queen softly whispers Assad's name. He hears her and starts praying to her as a goddess. Again the priests condemn him, this time for blasphemy.

The third act shows the festival chamber of the palace. A reception is being held in honor of the Queen of Sheba. The Queen pleads with Solomon for the release of Assad, and tries to charm him with her wiles. When he refuses and spurns her advances, she angrily leaves Jerusalem. Sulamith approaches the King. She too pleads for Assad and declares that she will retire from the world and devote the rest of her life to the worship of God.

The fourth act takes place in the desert. Assad's life has been spared and he is now a wandering exile. Repentant, he longs to see Salumith, and when the Queen of Sheba finds him is unaffected by her seductive pleading. Finally Salumith comes, accompanied by her handmaidens, and on her way to the seclusion of a cloister. Assad, exhausted from his wanderings, dies in her arms as she forgives him.

§)&(§

RAMUNTCHO
Deems Taylor

Deems Taylor was himself the librettist for his third opera, *Ramuntcho,* which he based on a novel by Pierre Loti. The opera was completed in 1937 and was first performed by the Philadelphia Opera Company at the Academy of Music in that city February 10, 1942.

The scenes of the opera are laid in the Basque village of Etchezar. The principal characters are:

RAMUNTCHO (*Tenor*)
GRACIEUSE (*Soprano*), his sweetheart
DOLORES (*Contralto*), mother of Gracieuse
MARCELIN (*Baritone*), a postman

The first act opens in a deserted house on the Spanish border, where Ramuntcho and his companions are carrying on the risky business of smuggling. They have almost been captured by the customs officers, but have managed to escape. The scene changes to a public square in Etchezar. Ramuntcho is leading a game of pelota. His sweetheart

Gracieuse tells him that although her mother, Dolores, is opposed to her marrying him, she will do so if he will give up smuggling. Ramuntcho is due to serve three years in the army and he and Gracieuse promise each other that they will write each other every day while he is away in the military service.

The first and second scenes of the second act are devoted to the lovers' farewell scenes, and the third scene occurs two years later. Gracieuse is distressed because she has had no word from Ramuntcho. The postman passes and tells her that as usual there is no letter for her. As Gracieuse leaves her mother comes in and talks to the postman. He silently takes a packet of letters from his pouch and hands it to her. It develops that he has also been giving to Dolores the letters Gracieuse has written to Ramuntcho. Dolores burns the letters in the fireplace. Gracieuse thinks that Ramuntcho has forgotten her, and enters a convent as a nun, to "find peace in the arms of God."

The third act takes place a year later. Ramuntcho has finished his three years of military service and returns to Etchezar. The postman confesses his treachery and Ramuntcho plans to take Gracieuse from the convent by force. Gracieuse still loves Ramuntcho but she respects her vows. She tells Ramuntcho that she belongs to God forever.

§)&(§

DAS RHEINGOLD

See Der Ring des Nibelungen

§)&(§

RIENZI

Richard Wagner

Although an earlier opera by Richard Wagner, *Das Liebesverbot,* was produced at Magdeburg in 1836, it was withdrawn after a second performance; therefore *Rienzi* is Wagner's first successful opera. The libretto, written by Wagner himself, was derived from Bulwer-Lytton's novel, *Rienzi: The Last of the Tribunes.* The opera was first produced at the Hoftheater in Dresden, October 20, 1842.

The characters include:

COLA RIENZI (*Tenor*), last of the Roman Tribunes
IRENE (*Soprano*), his sister
STEFANO COLONNA (*Bass*), head of the House of Colonna
ADRIANO (*Mezzo-soprano*), his son
PAOLO ORSINI (*Bass*), head of the House of Orsini
RAIMONDO (*Bass*), Papal legate
BARONCELLO (*Tenor*) } citizens of Rome
CECCO (*Bass*) } citizens of Rome
A MESSENGER OF PEACE (*Soprano*)

The action occurs in Rome during the fourteenth century. The plot deals with Rienzi's ambition to re-establish the glories of Rome and to deliver it from the oppression of the rival houses of nobles, the Orsini and the Colonni. In the first act, laid in a Roman street in front of the Church of St. John Lateran, the young nobles of the Orsini faction are trying to abduct Irene, a sister of Cola Rienzi. The Orsini are interrupted by their enemies, the Colonni, and young Adriano Colonna rescues Irene, who is his sweetheart. The Orsini and the Colonni fight each other until Rienzi appears and appeals to them. He compares the ancient glories of Rome with the present degradation that has been caused by the lawlessness and despotism of the nobles. The nobles agree to finish their quarrel outside the city gates the next morning. Rienzi plans that this shall be a battle between the people and both houses of nobles, and that the nobles shall return to Rome as prisoners of the forces of the Republic. He obtains the support of the church and arranges for an armed uprising of the people, who hail him as a liberator and Tribune.

The second act shows a reception room of the Capitol. Rienzi has been successful, the nobles are defeated, and messengers of peace bring news that peace prevails over all Roman lands from the mountains to the sea. Rienzi has been invested by the people with supreme power. A banquet is held at which Paolo Orsini tries to stab Rienzi. Rienzi has been warned of the plot by Adriano Colonna, and he wears an inner coat of armor which resists the dagger. The nobles, both Orsini and Colonni, admit the conspiracy, and are condemned to death. Both Adriano Colonna and Rienzi's sister, Irene, plead for forgiveness of the nobles, and Rienzi relents, much to the disgust of the citizens Baroncello and Cecco.

In the third act, at a public square, the people are again at war with the nobles. The Orsini and Colonni have risen again, and once more Rienzi must lead the people against them. Adriano is torn between two emotions—loyalty to his family and his love for Rienzi's sister. He tries to block Rienzi's way as the Tribune leads his forces to battle.

The fourth act returns to the square of St. John Lateran. The nobles have now secured the support of the church, and the Pope has made an alliance with the Emperor of Germany. Adriano incites the people to revolt against Rienzi and tries unsuccessfully to persuade Irene to renounce her brother. Rienzi appears in all his power, but as he mounts the steps of the church, the Papal legate Raimondo appears at the door and pronounces upon him the ban of excommunication.

The fifth act opens in a hall of the Capitol. Adriano again urges Irene to leave Rienzi, but she says she will cast her lot with her brother. The scene changes to the outside of the Capitol. Rienzi kneels in prayer, and Irene insists on staying beside him. The people rush in and throw torches into the Capitol. Rienzi and Irene appear on the balcony. Adriano rushes into the burning building, trying to save Irene. The building collapses and all three die in the ruins.

§)&(§

RIGOLETTO

Giuseppe Verdi

Giuseppe Verdi's *Rigoletto* was first produced March 11, 1851, at the Teatro La Fenice in Venice. Its libretto was written by Francesco Maria Piave and was adapted from *The King Amuses Himself* by Victor Hugo.

The cast includes:

DUKE OF MANTUA (*Tenor*)
RIGOLETTO (*Baritone*), a hunchback, the Duke's jester
GILDA (*Soprano*), Rigoletto's daughter
COUNT CEPRANO (*Bass*)
COUNTESS CEPRANO (*Soprano*), his wife
COUNT MONTERONE (*Baritone*)
SPARAFUCILE (*Bass*), an assassin
MADDALENA (*Contralto*), his sister

The action occurs in Mantua, Italy, during the sixteenth century. Rigoletto is a hunchback jester at the court of the Duke of Mantua. Members of the court hate him for the mocking insults he hurls at them. Rigoletto pays regular visits to a secluded spot on the outskirts of the town, and it is supposed that he goes to see a sweetheart. Actually, he visits his daughter, Gilda, whom he is sheltering from the too-gay life of the court.

The first act shows the Ducal Palace. During a gay party the cynical and profligate Duke confides to a courtier that he is pursuing a lovely, unknown maiden whom he has seen in church. He knows that she lives in a remote part of the city, where a mysterious stranger visits her every night. The Duke sets forth his standards of conduct in the aria *Questa o quella* ("In my heart all are equally cherished") . He further shows his moral ethics by immediately making love to the Countess Ceprano, and by discussing with Rigoletto how he may get rid of her husband. One of Rigoletto's duties is to aid the Duke in the carrying out of his love affairs. When Monterone, father of another of the Duke's victims, appears, Rigoletto mocks him. Monterone lays a father's curse on Rigoletto. The scene changes to a deserted street. Rigoletto, wrapped in a cloak, comes to visit his daughter, Gilda. Rigoletto is brooding over the curse of Monterone and when the assassin Sparafucile offers his professional services in ridding him of any of his enemies or friends, Rigoletto tells the assassin that he may need him later. Rigoletto soliloquizes on the distastefulness of his own profession of mocking and helping to keep the Duke supplied with sweethearts. As he enters the courtyard of the house where Gilda lives, his mood changes. He sings a duet wth his lovely daughter, who does not even know her father's name. She begs him to tell her who they both are, but he asks her not to stir his memories. When Rigoletto has gone the Duke calls on Gilda. He is disguised as a poor student, and he tells her that his name is Walter Malde. After he has left Gilda sings the famous *Caro Nome* ("Dearest Name") . As she finishes her song, a crowd of courtiers enters, armed and masked. They still think that Gilda is Rigoletto's sweetheart and they seek revenge for his numerous insults by stealing his supposed mistress. Rigoletto sees them and remembers Monterone's curse.

The second act shows an apartment in the palace. Rigoletto finds Gilda. She confesses her affair with the unknown stranger, and Rigoletto, guessing that the disguised student is the Duke, vows that he will have vengeance. Gilda still loves the Duke and pleads with her father to forgive him.

The third act shows a rustic inn which is the home of Sparafucile, the assassin, and his sister Maddalena. The Duke is inside, making love to Maddalena. Rigoletto passes by with Gilda, who is disguised in man's clothing. He shows his daughter how fickle her lover is, and they listen while he sings the song *La donna e mobile* ("Woman Is Fickle"). This is followed by the famous quartet, in which Rigoletto and Gilda stand on one side of a wall, Rigoletto planning revenge and Gilda singing of the perfidy of her lover, while the Duke makes love to Maddalena on the other side. After the quartet, the Duke retires to his room at the inn. Outside Rigoletto tells Gilda to go to Verona, where he will join her later. Then Rigoletto meets Sparafucile and hires him to murder the Duke. As Rigoletto leaves, Gilda returns. She hears Maddalena beg Sparafucile to spare the Duke's life. Sparafucile agrees that if any one else enters the inn, he shall be killed as a substitute victim. Then he can put that person's body in the sack he is to deliver to Rigoletto. Gilda determines to sacrifice herself for her lover. She enters the inn and Sparafucile stabs her. Sparafucile puts her body in the sack and gives it to Rigoletto who is waiting outside. When Rigoletto is about to throw the sack into the river, he hears the sound of the Duke's voice singing *La donna e mobile.* He opens the sack and finds the body of his own daughter.

DER RING DES NIBELUNGEN
(The Ring of the Nibelungs)
Richard Wagner

Richard Wagner worked for twenty-six years on the writing and composition of the *Ring of the Nibelungs.* He became interested in Scandinavian, German and Icelandic sagas, and selected from them the legends which he altered to fit his own purpose. The first attempt at using this material took the form of a poem called *Siegfried's Death,* which Wagner wrote in November, 1848. He soon realized that the material was too great for a single opera, and in 1851 he wrote another dramatic poem called *Young Siegfried,* to preface *Siegfried's Death.* Later *Young Siegfried* was named merely *Siegfried,* and *Siegfried's Death* became *Die Götterdämmerung* or "The Twilight of the Gods." In 1852 Wagner wrote still another drama, *Die Walküre* ("The Valkyries"), which he placed in front of *Siegfried,* and then *Das Rheingold,* which he described as a "fore-evening" to the entire cycle. A few copies of the entire poem were printed for private circulation in 1853.

Although the librettos of the four music-dramas were written in reverse order, the music was composed in proper sequence. *Das Rheingold* was composed in 1853-54, and *Die Walküre* between the summer of 1854 and the spring of 1856. Between the autumn of 1856 and July, 1857, Wagner composed the first act and part of the second act of *Siegfried.* Work on the *Ring* was put aside from the summer of 1857 until July, 1865, for a period of eight years. During this time Wagner composed two single operas which he thought would be more practicable for production in the ordinary German opera houses—*Tristan und Isolde* and *Die Meistersinger.* For the production of the *Ring,* Wagner wanted a theatre of his own which would have adequate facilities for the elaborate scenic effects he had planned. In May of 1864 King Ludwig of Bavaria promised Wagner the necessary backing, but the King was so impatient to hear Wagner's new works that he would not wait for the completion of a special theatre. Accordingly *Das Rheingold* and *Die Walküre* were performed separately in Munich in 1869 and 1870, respectively. Meanwhile *Siegfried* was finished in the autumn of 1869, and *Die Götterdämmerung* in November, 1874. These two numbers of the *Ring* were first performed when the entire cycle was presented at the Festspielhaus in Bayreuth in August of 1876.

The underlying theme of the *Ring* is the god Wotan's lust for power. He has had built by giants a great castle, Walhalla, which is the home of the gods. When the time comes for paying the giants, Wotan has to use the gold which was stolen from the Rhine-maidens by the Nibelung dwarf, Alberich. Alberich has fashioned from the gold a ring which gives its owner power over the world. When Wotan takes the ring from Alberich, the dwarf lays a curse upon it. Thus the *Ring,* with its curse and its power, passes into the hands of the giant Fafner. Wotan's problem is to make sure that this power will not pass to one who will use it for the destruction of the gods.

The music of the entire *Ring* cycle is constructed from *leit-motifs* (leading motives or themes) which exemplify and identify the characters, the emotions, and the situations of the drama.

§)&(§

DAS RHEINGOLD

(The Rhinegold)

Das Rheingold is the prelude to the *Ring* cycle, and was first performed as a single music-drama at the Hoftheater in Munich, September 22, 1869. It introduces a number of characters who appear throughout the cycle.

WOTAN (*Baritone*), head of the gods
FRICKA (*Contralto*), his wife
DONNER (*Bass*), god of thunder
FROH (*Tenor*), god of rain
LOGE (*Tenor*), god of fire
FREIA (*Soprano*), goddess of youth
ERDA (*Contralto*), spirit of the earth
ALBERICH (*Baritone*)
MIME (*Tenor*) } Nibelung dwarfs
WOGLINDE (*Soprano*)
WELLGUNDE (*Soprano*)
FLOSSHILDE (*Contralto*) } Rhine-maidens
FAFNER (*Bass*)
FASOLT (*Bass*) } giants

The first act shows the bottom of the Rhine River. In the upper part of the setting the river seems to be flowing steadily, while at the bottom the waters become misty. Craggy rocks rise from the river bed. The three Rhine-maidens swim about sportively and fail to give close attention to the Rhinegold they are supposed to guard. Alberich, the Nibelung dwarf, climbs on a rock and watches the Rhine-maidens. When he calls to them in uncouth language they are repelled by his ugliness. After a while they begin to tease the dwarf and pretend to flirt with him. Whenever he tries to embrace one of them she slips away, and he is no match for such expert swimmers. Finally Alberich loses his temper and shakes his fist at the Rhine-maidens. A light begins to glow in the water and soon the central rock shines radiantly. This is the gold waking from its sleep. Alberich questions the Rhine-maidens and learns that the world's wealth may be won by the person who can fashion a magic ring from the gold. This person, however, must be one who has forsworn love. Alberich decides that since the Rhine-maidens have spurned him, he will forswear love and win the mastery of the world. He climbs to the central rock, grasps the gold, and cries: "Love now I curse forever!" He tears the gold from the rock and plunges into the depths of the river. Darkness falls on the river and Alberich's mocking laughter comes from its bottom.

The rocks disappear in the darkness and the setting is filled with black waves which seem continually to sink. Gradually the waves are replaced by clouds which turn to a fine mist, showing an open space on a mountain top. Dawn lights the scene and a castle appears on a cliff at the back of the stage. Between it and the foreground is a deep valley through which the Rhine flows.

This second scene shows the supreme god Wotan and his wife Fricka asleep on a flowery bank. They awaken and find that the giants Fafner and Fasolt have finished building the castle, Walhalla. Wotan is much pleased but Fricka reminds him of the bargain he has made with the giants, to give them her sister Freia, goddess of youth. Wotan laughs and says he made the bargain in jest. The giants come for their reward and Wotan hopes that Freia's brothers, Donner and Froh, will be able to save her. They are powerless and the giants start to take Freia away. The flowers wither and the gods begin to age. Loge, the god of fire, conceives a plan to win Freia from the giants. He and Wotan will get the Rhine-gold from Alberich, and give it to the giants in exchange for Freia. The giants agree, but insist that if the gold is not obtained quickly, the gods will lose Freia forever.

The third scene shows Alberich's cave. The dwarf has forged the gold into the magic Ring, and has thus gained power over all the Nibelungs. He has made slaves of them and forces them to dig still more treasure from the earth. He has made his brother Mime forge for him the Tarnhelm, a helmet which changes its wearer into any form he wishes, or makes him invisible. Wotan and Loge come into the cave. Alberich is immediately suspicious of them, but Loge is crafty. He pretends to be skeptical about the magic helmet, and challenges Alberich to show its powers. First Alberich changes himself into a dragon, and when Loge asks him if he can make himself into something very small, he becomes a toad. Wotan steps on the toad, and Loge seizes the helmet. When Alberich resumes his natural appearance Wotan and Loge bind him and take him away.

The last scene returns to the mountain slope near Walhalla. Wotan and Loge enter, dragging Alberich with them. They force Alberich to order the Nibelungs to bring the treasure. Alberich is willing to part with the treasure and the Tarnhelm because he knows the Ring will give him the power to gain more gold. The gods demand the Ring also, and as Alberich hands it over in a rage, he curses the Ring and declares that it will bring ruin and misfortune to anyone who possesses it. Fasolt and Fafner return with Freia, and demand that the gold they are to receive make a pile high enough to hide Freia. When the gold is piled all the crevices must be filled, one of them with the Tarnhelm, and finally, the last with the Ring. Wotan refuses to give up the Ring, and the giants start to take Freia away again when Erda, the spirit of the earth, warns Wotan that the Ring has been cursed. Wotan accordingly hands the Ring to the giants. The curse has its effect immediately. The giants quarrel over the Ring, and Fafner kills Fasolt, his brother. Fafner takes the gold and his brother's body, and departs. Wotan then leads the gods to the castle of Walhalla, over a rainbow constructed by Donner, the god of thunder. From the Rhine comes the song of the Rhinemaidens, lamenting the loss of their gold.

DIE WALKÜRE
(The Valkyries)

Die Walküre was first performed at the Hoftheater in Munich, June 26, 1870.

In the interval between *Das Rheingold* and *Die Walküre*, Wotan has learned from Erda, the earth goddess, that the gods will perish if the Nibelung dwarf Alberich regains the Ring from the giant Fafner. Fafner has used the magic helmet, the Tarnhelm, to change himself into a dragon and thus guards his treasure. Wotan's problem has been to find a hero who will save the gods. Because of the gods' moral code, Wotan may not regain the Ring by craft or by violence. It must be won by someone without any direct aid from himself. Through a union with Erda, Wotan has had nine daughters, the Valkyries, (*Die Walküre*) whose duty it is to bring to Walhalla the bodies of slain heroes. At Walhalla the heroes are brought to life again and become guards for the threatened gods. Brunnhilde is the chief of the Valkyries.

In roaming the earth Wotan has contracted also a union with a mortal woman who has borne him two children, Siegmund and his sister Sieglinde, the Wälsungs. Wotan hopes that Siegmund may grow to be the hero who will some day save the gods, but his plans have been thwarted by the hunter, Hunding, who raided the home of the Wälsungs, killed the mother, and carried Sieglinde off to be his wife. Siegmund has been left alone and unprotected, at the mercy of all men and of every creature.

The characters of *Die Walküre* are:

WOTAN (*Baritone*), the supreme god
FRICKA (*Contralto*), his wife
BRÜNNHILDE (*Soprano*), chief of the Valkyries, Wotan's daughters by Erda, the earth goddess
SIEGMUND (*Tenor*) } the Wälsungs, Wotan's children by
SIEGLINDE (*Soprano*) } a mortal woman
HUNDING (*Bass*), Sieglinde's husband

The first act shows the interior of Hunding's hut. Siegmund enters, exhausted and fainting. He falls on the floor and is found there by Sieglinde, who gives him food and drink. Sieglinde does not know that Siegmund is her brother, and he does not recognize her. Gradually they fall in love with each other. Hunding returns and recognizes Siegmund as an enemy. He tells Siegmund that the laws of hospitality demand that he be safe for the night, but that in the morning he must die. Sieglinde prepares Hunding's evening drink and puts into it a sleeping potion. Then she shows Siegmund a sword that her father ("Wolfe," actually Wotan) had thrust into the trunk of a tree that rises in the center of the hut. This sword will protect any one who is strong enough to draw it out of the tree. Siegmund makes a mighty effort and pulls the sword from the tree trunk. Siegmund and Sieglinde at last recognize each other and Siegmund declares that he has been guided to the hut to free his sister and his bride. Sieglinde falls into Siegmund's arms.

The second act shows a rocky pass in the mountains. Wotan commands Brunnhilde, chief of the Valkyries, to ride to the defense of Siegmund, who with his sister-bride

Sieglinde is being pursued by Hunding. Brunnhilde calls to the other Valkyries, but before they have a chance to ride away, Fricka, Wotan's wife, appears. She rebukes Wotan for wanting to help Siegmund, and insists that Siegmund be punished for his incestuous union with his own sister, Sieglinde. Wotan is much disturbed at the thought of losing the god's protector, Siegmund, but he finally yields to Fricka's insistence. He tells Brunnhilde to protect Hunding rather than Siegmund. In the battle between Siegmund and Hunding, Brunnhilde disobeys her father and helps Siegmund, but Wotan shatters the sword he had left for Siegmund, and Siegmund is killed. Brunnhilde gathers the pieces of the shattered sword, takes Sieglinde in her arms and rides away. Wotan then kills Hunding.

The third act is at the summit of the rock of the Valkyries. To the music of the "Ride of the Valkyries," the Valkyries come home through the clouds. Brunnhilde knows that Wotan is pursuing her and is afraid of his anger. Her sisters will not help her against their father. Brunnhilde sends Sieglinde into the forest. Sieglinde is to have a child, and Brunnhilde prophesies that he will be Siegfried, the hero who will later save the gods from destruction. She gives Sieglinde the pieces of the shattered sword, and tells her that some day it will be re-forged and will again become a magic weapon. Wotan overtakes Brunnhilde. She must be punished for her disobedience, and Wotan announces that she will be put into a deep sleep and will belong to the first man who finds her and awakens her. Brunnhilde pleads with her father against such an indignity, and her father relents and promises her that only a hero brave enough to break through the fire he will build around her will be able to win her. Looking at her tenderly he places her gently on the rocks. As the orchestra plays the

"Magic Fire" music, the flames break out around Brunnhilde sleeping on the summit of the rocks.

SIEGFRIED

Siegfried was first performed August 16, 1876, when the entire *Ring* had its first complete production at the Festspielhaus in Bayreuth, August 13, 14, 16, 17, 1876.

In the interval between *Die Walküre* and *Siegfried* Sieglinde has given birth to Siegfried. Sieglinde died in childbirth, and left Siegfried in the care of Mime, the Nibelungen dwarf, brother of Alberich. Sieglinde also bequeathed to Siegfried and Mime the broken pieces of Siegmund's sword. Mime plans that these pieces will be reforged into a sword with which Siegfried will slay the giant Fafner, who has used the Tarnhelm, or magic helmet, to change himself into a terrible dragon. In this form Fafner guards the treasure. If Mime can get possession of the Ring, he will be able to rule the world.

The characters of *Siegfried* are:

SIEGFRIED (*Tenor*)
MIME (*Tenor*) } Nibelungen dwarfs
ALBERICH (*Baritone*) }
WOTAN (*Baritone*), the supreme god
FAFNER (*Bass*), the giant who has changed himself into a dragon
BRUNNHILDE (*Soprano*), a Valkyrie, daughter of Wotan and the earth goddess, Erda
ERDA (*Contralto*), the earth goddess
THE WOODLAND BIRD (*Soprano*)

The first act shows Mime's forge in the forest. Mime is trying to forge a sword for Siegfried, and he laments the fact that the youth breaks every sword he makes for him. The metal of the pieces that Sieglinde left for Siegfried are too hard for an ordinary smith to handle. Siegfried enters leading a bear. He teases Mime and frightens him by setting the bear on him. Siegfried takes the sword Mime has just forged and easily smashes it. Then he tells Mime how much he despises him, and asks him who his real mother and father were. Mime explains that Siegfried is the son of Sieglinde and Siegmund, who was killed by a hunter. He also tells him about the pieces of the sword which Sieglinde left for him. Siegfried commands Mime to re-forge the pieces and returns to the forest. While he is away Wotan appears in the guise of the Wanderer. Wotan has a long talk with Mime, and tells him that only a person who does not know fear can forge the sword. Its name is Nothung, and he who can forge it will also take Mime's head. Mime is terrified, and has hardly recovered his composure after Wotan's departure when Siegfried returns from the forest. Mime tests Siegfried and finds that he knows nothing about fear. In fact, he would like to learn about it. Mime continues with a terrifying description of the dragon, Fafner, and Siegfried is eager to see him and fight him. When he learns that Mime cannot forge the sword from the pieces, Siegfried pushes him aside and forges it himself. Meanwhile Mime has planned that when Siegfried has conquered the dragon and secured the treasure, he will then give Siegfried a sleeping potion. While Siegfried is asleep, Mime will kill him.

The second act shows the entrance to the dragon's cave. Alberich, Mime's brother, lies in wait for the hero who will slay the dragon. Alberich will then kill the slayer of the dragon and regain the Ring. Once he has obtained possession of the Ring he will use it to destroy the gods. Wotan appears and tells Alberich that the hero is coming.

He also explains to Alberich that this hero is ignorant of the gods and of the significance of the Ring, and that he, Wotan, will give him no help. The youth will win or lose by his own strength. Alberich then tries to make a bargain with Fafner. If Fafner will give Alberich the Ring, he will tell him how to save his life. He can keep the rest of the treasure for himself. Fafner refuses. He wants to keep everything he has. Siegfried comes with the sword, and lies down and listens to the sounds of the forest and the songs of the birds. While he listens the orchestra plays the famous "Forest Murmurs." Finally Siegfried blows his horn and wakes the dragon. In the fight that follows Siegfried plunges the sword (Nothung) into the dragon's heart. As the dragon dies a few drops of his blood fall on Siegfried. These enable Siegfried to understand what the bird says to him. The bird tells Siegfried of the dragon's treasure, and Siegfried goes into the cave to find it. While he is inside Alberich and Mime quarrel. Mime tries to bargain. He shall have the Ring and Mime the Tarnhelm. Alberich cries that Mime shall have not even a nail. Mime shouts that he will call Siegfried to avenge him with the sword. Siegfried returns from the cave and the dwarfs notice that he has brought with him only the Ring and the Tarnhelm. They know also that he has chosen these not because he knows their value, but because the bird has advised him to take them. Alberich goes into the forest and Mime approaches Siegfried. The dragon's blood has enabled Siegfried to understand Mime also, so he hears not what the dwarf is actually saying, but what he is thinking. When Mime offers Siegfried a draught of the cordial he has brewed, Siegfried knows that it is a sleeping potion, and that Mime will kill him while he is asleep. Siegfried kills Mime, and then learns from the bird that a beautiful maiden, Brunnhilde, is sleeping on a rock surrounded by fire which only a great hero can penetrate. He follows the bird in search of Brunnhilde.

The third act is laid in a wild spot in the mountains. Wotan talks with Erda, the earth goddess and mother of Brunnhilde. He tells Erda that he no longer fears the downfall of the gods. He welcomes their destruction, and will leave the rule of the world to Siegfried, who now possesses the Ring, and to Brunnhilde. Wotan blocks Siegfried in his search for Brunnhilde and tests his courage. Siegfried angrily breaks Wotan's spear. He finds the fiery mountain and rushes through the flames to Brunnhilde. He kisses Brunnhilde and awakens her. She recognizes Siegfried as the hero who has freed her, and as Siegfried continues to make love to her, she realizes that she is a woman and yields to his embrace.

DIE GÖTTERDÄMMERUNG
(The Twilight of the Gods)

Like *Siegfried, Die Götterdämmerung* was first performed during the initial performance of the entire *Ring* cycle at Bayreuth. *Die Götterdämmerung* was presented August 17, 1876.

The characters of *Die Götterdämmerung* are:

SIEGFRIED (*Tenor*)
BRÜNNHILDE (*Soprano*)
GUNTHER (*Baritone*), king of the Gibichungs
GUTRUNE (*Soprano*), his sister
HAGEN (*Bass*), half-brother of Gunther and Gutrune. His father is Alberich
ALBERICH (*Baritone*), the Nibelungen dwarf
WALTRAUTE (*Mezzo-soprano*), a Valkyrie

WOGLINDE (*Soprano*)
WELLGUNDE (*Soprano*) } The Rhine-maidens
FLOSSHILDE (*Contralto*)
THE NORNS (*Mezzo-sopranos*), spinners of fate

Die Götterdämmerung opens with a Prelude which shows Brunnhilde's rock. The Norns are spinning the fate of men and gods. The thread breaks and the Norns know that destruction is near. Siegfried, who has been wed to Brunnhilde, decides to search for new adventures. As he bids farewell to Brunnhilde he leaves with her the Ring, and takes with him the Tarnhelm, or magic helmet, and Nothung, his sword. Brunnhilde gives him her horse, Grane.

The first act opens in the hall of King Gunther's castle. Gunther lives with his sister, Gutrune, and their half-brother, Hagen, who is the son of the Nibelungen dwarf, Alberich. Hagen has learned from Alberich the history of the magic Ring, and he is eager to get it back for him. Siegfried visits Gunther's court, and Hagen recognizes him. He gives Siegfried a magic potion which makes him forget Brunnhilde and fall in love with Gutrune. Gunther promises Siegfried that he may have Gutrune, if he, Gunther, can marry Brunnhilde. Since Siegfried alone can pass through the fire which surrounds Brunnhilde, he uses the Tarnhelm to change his appearance to that of Gunther, and leaves to fetch Brunnhilde. The scene changes to Brunnhilde's rock. Siegfried comes in the guise of Gunther, and Brunnhilde cannot understand how a stranger could pass through the fire. She tries to use the Ring for protection, but Siegfried takes it from her and forces her to accompany him to Gunther's castle.

The second act shows a river bank before the hall of the Gibichung king Gunther. Hagen plots with his father Alberich to regain the Ring. Siegfried appears in his own form. He tells Hagen that he has brought with him Brunnhilde and that she may now become Gunther's wife. Gutrune welcomes Siegfried and they prepare a feast in honor of Gunther and Brunnhilde. When Brunnhilde comes she is shocked to find Siegfried and Gutrune together, apparently much in love with each other. Brunnhilde sees the Ring on Siegfried's finger and demands to know how it came there. Because of the magic drink Siegfried still does not remember his past relations with Brunnhilde, and cannot give her an explanation. Brunnhilde denounces Siegfried, and Siegfried thinks she has lost her mind. Gunther, Brunnhilde and Hagen plan to kill Siegfried. Brunnhilde tells the others that Siegfried's vulnerable point is his back. That is not protected because he has never retreated and turned his back to an enemy.

The third act is laid on the banks of the Rhine. As Siegfried rests after hunting, the Rhine-maidens come to the surface of the water and beg him to give them the Ring which was originally fashioned from their gold. Siegfried refuses, and they prophesy that he will die this very day. Gunther and Hagen join Siegfried and Hagen gives Siegfried another drink which restores his memory so that he remembers Brunnhilde. As Siegfried tells of his search for Brunnhilde, Hagen slips around and plunges a spear into his back. The scene changes to the hall in Gunther's castle. Siegfried's body is carried in on a litter. Hagen demands the Ring from the dead hero's finger, but Gunther refuses to give it up. Hagen and Gunther fight, and Gunther is killed. Hagen tries to take the Ring from Siegfried's finger and Siegfried's arm rises threateningly. Brunnhilde orders a funeral pyre for Siegfried and she summons two ravens to notify Loge, the god of fire, to set fire also to Walhalla, the home of the gods. To the music of "Siegfried's

Funeral March," Siegfried's body is placed on the pyre. Brunnhilde calls for her horse Grane, mounts him, and herself rides into the flames. The waters of the Rhine rise and the Rhine-maidens come to the surface and snatch the Ring from the ashes. The distant Walhalla is seen in flames.

§)&(§

RIP VAN WINKLE

Reginald de Koven

Reginald de Koven was one of several composers who have used Washington Irving's *Rip Van Winkle* as the subject for an opera. De Koven chose for a libretto an adaptation of the legend by Percy MacKaye. MacKaye made a number of changes in the plot. Instead of being a drunkard, Rip is the victim of a sleeping potion, and rather than being married to a nagging wife, he is engaged to Nicholas Vedder's daughter, Katrina. The opera was first performed by the Chicago Opera Company, in Chicago, January 2, 1920.

The principal characters are:

RIP VAN WINKLE (*Baritone*)
NICHOLAS VEDDER (*Bass*)
KATRINA VEDDER (*Soprano*) } his daughters
PETERKEE VEDDER (*Soprano*) } his daughters
HENDRICK HUDSON (*Baritone*)
A GOOSE GIRL (*Mezzo-soprano*)

The action takes place in the Catskill Mountains during the eighteenth century. The first act shows a village green.

Rip is engaged to Vedder's daughter, Katrina, a young lady of shrewish disposition. At the moment he has been on a fishing expedition with Peterkee, Katrina's younger sister, and both of them have stayed overtime and have forgotten that Rip is soon to be married. Following a thunder clap, the shade of Hendrick Hudson appears. Every twenty years he and the crew of the *Half Moon* visit the Catskills for a bowling game, and the noise of their bowling has sounded like thunder. Hudson invites Rip and Peterkee to visit him in the mountains where he will give Rip a magic flask. Katrina tells Rip that if he fails to return the next night she will marry the schoolmaster's son.

The three scenes of the second act are laid in the Catskills. In the first scene Rip and Peterkee are on their way to Hendrick Hudson's retreat. In the second scene Rip helps one of the ghostly crew carry two kegs of liquor, and in the third scene Hudson greets Rip and Peterkee at the summit of the mountains. Hudson wants Rip to marry Peterkee instead of Katrina, and he plots with his followers to keep Rip in the mountains until the time of their next bowling game, twenty years hence. Peterkee is allowed to win the magic flask, and is taken safely home, while Rip is given a sleeping potion.

The third act shows the mountain top twenty years later. Rip wakens, and is now old and white-bearded. The second scene shows Peterkee's house. She finds the magic flask in a chimney niche. Rip enters, but Peterkee does not recognize him. In the third scene a wedding party welcomes Peterkee on the village green, where she is to be married to the schoolmaster's younger son. Rip in his tattered clothes comes to claim Katrina. He does not yet realize that twenty years have passed since he was in the village, and that Katrina has long since been married to the schoolmaster's older son. Peterkee takes pity on the old man, and lets him drink from the magic flask. Instantly Rip becomes young again. Hudson appears with his crew, and Peterkee is married to Rip, rather than to the schoolmaster's younger son.

§)&(§

ROBERT THE DEVIL

Giacomo Meyerbeer

The libretto of Giacomo Meyerbeer's *Robert the Devil* was written by Augustin Eugène Scribe and Germain Delavigne, and the opera was produced first at the Grand Opéra in Paris, November 21, 1831.

The cast of characters includes:

ROBERT (*Tenor*), Duke of Normandy
BERTRAM (*Bass*), the Evil One in disguise, actually Robert's father
RAMBALDO (*Tenor*), a minstrel
ISABELLA (*Soprano*), Princess of Sicily
ALICE (*Soprano*), Robert's foster sister
KING OF SICILY (*Bass*)

The action occurs in Palermo, Sicily, during the thirteenth century. The plot concerns Robert of Normandy who is the son of an illicit union between the Duchess of Normandy and the Devil in the guise of Bertram, who seduced her. Robert has become notorious for his recklessness and evil deeds, and has become known as Robert the Devil. He has been banished from Normandy, and as the opera opens, he is wandering in Sicily where he has fallen in love with the Princess Isabella.

The first act shows a camp near Palermo, where Robert and his mysterious companion Bertram are feasting with the knights. Rambaldo, a minstrel from Normandy, sings a ballad about the notorious exploits of Robert the Devil, and tells how he was born of a union between the Duchess and the Devil. Robert is outraged and orders the minstrel's arrest. Alice comes to Robert and pleads for Rambaldo. She proves to be Robert's foster sister, and he is so affected at seeing her that he agrees not only to release Rambaldo but to allow Alice to marry him. Alice tells Robert that his mother has died. She hands him a document containing her will, which he is not to read until he has proved himself worthy. Robert gives the will back to Alice and tells her to keep it until he has earned the right to read it. Robert confides in Alice that he is in love with Isabella. Alice offers to carry a message to the Princess, and Robert is about to take part in the tournament of the knights where he can win the hand of the Princess. Bertram interrupts their conversation and Alice is horrified to find in Bertram a resemblance to Satan. Bertram manages to make Robert forget the tournament by tempting him to gamble. Robert loses everything, even his horse and armor.

The second act shows a chamber in the palace where Alice brings to Isabella a letter from Robert. Isabella sends Robert money for new weapons and armor so that he may appear for her in the tournament. Bertram agains lures Robert away.

The third act opens in the entrance to Satan's cave. Bertram meets the demons and tells them he is planning to capture Robert's soul. He is told that he has until midnight of tomorrow to accomplish the deed. Rambaldo comes to meet Alice but Bertram makes him forget Alice by giving him a bag of gold. When Alice comes, Bertram threatens her and sends her away in horror. Robert appears and Bertram promises that all his possessions will be restored if he will take a twig from the grave of St. Rosalie. The scene changes to the graveyard of the condemned nuns. The spirits of the nuns arise in the form of lovely maidens who beguile and allure Robert and finally persuade him to steal the magic branch from St. Rosalie's grave.

The third act returns to the palace. Robert comes with the magic branch and through its powers is able to make himself invisible. With the branch he puts the knights and ladies to sleep. He plans to abduct Isabella, but when she pleads with him, he breaks the magic branch in two. The spell is broken, the knights come to life and attack Robert, who is again taken away by Bertram.

The last act is laid at the entrance to the Cathedral of Palermo. Robert enters with Bertram, who is uneasy on such sacred ground. Bertram tries to get Robert to leave, but when the sound of music comes from the Cathedral, Robert denounces Bertram. Bertram then tells Robert that he is his father, and Robert, through a sense of filial duty, is about to follow him. Alice tells Robert that Isabella is waiting in the Cathedral ready to marry him. Robert still feels a duty to Bertram and is about to sign a compact to forfeit his soul when Alice hands him his mother's will. Robert reads it and finds that it is a warning against his father. As Robert is still hesitating the clock strikes midnight. Bertram's time for capturing Robert's soul has expired and he sinks into the earth. The doors of the Cathedral open. Robert is married to Isabella and Rambaldo is married to Alice.

§)&(§

LE ROI D'YS
(The King of Ys)
Edouard Lalo

Subtitled "A Legend of Brittany," this opera by Edouard Lalo uses a libretto written by Edouard Blau. It was first performed at Paris in the Opéra Comique, May 7, 1888.

The cast of characters includes:

THE KING (*Bass*)
MARGARED (*Mezzo-soprano*) } his daughters
ROZENN (*Soprano*) }
MYLIO (*Tenor*)
KARNAC (*Baritone*), the enemy chieftain
SAINT CORENTIN (*Bass*)

The action takes place in the land of Ys, of which Saint Corentin is the patron and protector. The first act is laid on the terrace of the King's palace. A truce has been declared in the war between the forces of the King and Prince Karnac, and the price of peace is that Margared, the King's daughter, is to be married to Karnac. After the people have rejoiced in the coming wedding and the resultant peace, Margared confides in her sister, Rozenn, that she really loves Mylio, a prince of their own people who has sailed to distant lands and has been reported dead. Rozenn is troubled by Margared's confession, for she too loves Mylio. When Margared has gone to meet Karnac at the altar, Mylio appears. The rumor of his death was false. He loves Rozenn as she loves him, and they greet each other joyfully. Rozenn tells Margared of Mylio's return and of her betrothal to him. Margared is outraged and publicly refuses to marry Karnac. The enemy prince throws his gauntlet at the feet of the king and declares that the war will continue. Mylio refuses the gauntlet and accepts Karnac's challenge.

The second act shows a hall in the palace. When the King sends Mylio to battle with his blessing, Margared hears Rozenn bid farewell to Mylio as her "husband." In spite of her sister's pleading she plots revenge. The scene changes to a spot on the plain near the ancient chapel of Saint Corentin. Mylio has been victorious and the defeated Karnac takes refuge in the chapel. Margared meets him there and plots with him to open the sluice gates which will flood the city. As they leave to carry out their plan, the statue of Saint Corentin comes to life and warns against the crime. Margared falls on her knees.

The third act opens on a gallery of the King's palace. Mylio and Rozenn are about to be married. Margared watches the procession and Karnac urges her to continue with their plan. She reminds him of the Saint's warning, but he arouses her jealousy by describing the wedded happiness of Rozenn and Mylio. Margared goes with Karnac to open the gates. Mylio and Rozenn return from their wedding. Margared comes back in time to observe their happiness. Her heart is touched and she begins to regret the deed she has already committed. Soon an uproar brings word that water is rising in the city. Mylio announces that he has caught Karnac and killed him. All flee to a hillock where the people have taken refuge. While they are standing on the hill a voice from above declares that when it has received its prey, the vengeful flood will ebb away. Margared cries that it was she who helped Karnac open the gates. She climbs to the highest cliff and leaps into the water. Saint Corentin appears on the cliff and the sky brightens.

§)&(§

ROMEO AND JULIET

Charles-François Gounod

The libretto of Charles-François Gounod's opera, *Romeo and Juliet,* was written by Jules Barbier and Michel Carré, who followed Shakespeare's tragedy closely, both in structure and dialogue. Except for the introduction of a minor character, Stephano, the cast is the same as that of the original. The opera was first produced at the Théâtre Lyrique in Paris, April 27, 1867.

The characters include:

ROMEO (*Tenor*), of the house of Montague
MERCUTIO (*Baritone*), his friend
STEPHANO (*Soprano*), his page
CAPULET (*Bass*), a noble
JULIET (*Soprano*), his daughter
TYBALT (*Tenor*), cousin to Juliet
PARIS (*Baritone*), a young nobleman
FRIAR LAWRENCE (*Bass*)

The action occurs in Verona during the fourteenth century, and has for its background a feud between the houses of Montague and Capulet. The first act shows the ballroom of the Capulets where Juliet is making her entrance into society. After her father has introduced her to the guests Juliet sings of her happiness in the famous waltz song. Romeo enters with a party of his friends. Because he is a member of the rival house of Montague, his coming is an impertinence which might well cost him his life. Romeo and Juliet see each other and immediately fall in love. When the guests have gone to the banquet hall the lovers are left alone to sing a love-duet. As it ends, Tybalt, a hot-headed Capulet, returns and recognizes Romeo. He denounces him as a Montague, and Romeo draws his sword. An open quarrel is averted by Capulet, who does not want a fight to disturb his brilliant party. Romeo is allowed to leave quietly.

The second act is devoted to the balcony scene, almost literally transcribed from Shakespeare. In effect it is an extended love-duet between Romeo and Juliet.

The third act opens in the cell of Friar Lawrence, where Romeo and Juliet have come asking to be secretly married. The Friar is glad to perform this service, for he feels that such a union may heal the breach between the Montagues and Capulets. The scene changes to a square in front of the Capulet palace. Stephano, Romeo's page, sings an impudent song about the Capulets. This provokes a fight which Romeo tries to stop. He is unsuccessful, for Tybalt, the Capulet, kills Mercutio, Romeo's friend, and Romeo in revenge kills Tybalt. He is sentenced to banishment.

In the fourth act Romeo visits Juliet in her room for a last farewell. When he has gone Capulet comes to tell Juliet that she is to marry Count Paris. He does not know of her marriage to Romeo. Juliet asks Friar Lawrence to help her. The Friar gives her a potion which will put her into a death-like trance for forty-eight hours, and thus help her to escape. She drinks the potion and falls into her father's arms as he arrives with Paris.

In the fifth act Juliet is lying in the Capulet burial vault. The Friar has sent word to Romeo telling him that the drug Juliet has taken is harmless, but Romeo has not received the message. He returns believing Juliet is dead. He enters the tomb and when he sees her prostrate form he swallows a deadly poison. Juliet revives and when she learns that Romeo has poisoned himself, she stabs herself with a dagger and dies in his arms.

§)&(§

LA RONDINE

(The Swallow)

Giacomo Puccini

La Rondine was Giacomo Puccini's eighth opera. Its text was translated by Giuseppe Adami from a German libretto by A. M. Willner and H. Reichert. *La Rondine* was first produced at Monte Carlo, March 27, 1917. The cast includes:

MAGDA (*Soprano*), of the demi-monde
RAMBALDO (*Baritone*), a banker who supports Magda
RUGGERO (*Tenor*), a student who falls in love with her
PRUNIER (*Baritone*), a poet

The action occurs in Nice and Paris at the time of the second French empire. The first act is laid in Magda's Paris house, where she lives in luxury with all of her expenses paid by the rich banker, Rambaldo. A customary levee is being held, attended by writers, artists, businessmen, and Magda's fellow demi-mondaines. Prunier, the poet, reads to the assemblage a newspaper article which claims that sentimental love is now fashionable in Paris. Most of the company laugh derisively but Magda's memory is stirred, and she tells her friends about her only real romance. As a young girl she escaped from the home of her aunt to visit the Bal Bullier, a Paris night resort. There she met a young student, danced with him, and fell in love. When Magda finishes her story, Prunier offers to tell her fortune. From her palm he prophesies that she will be like the swallow; she will leave her home, but like the swallow, she will return to it. Presently a young man arrives. He is Ruggero, whose father is a friend of Rambaldo's. Ruggero is received cordially and when he says that he would like to see the night life of Paris, he is advised to visit the Bal Bullier. Ruggero follows the suggestion, and soon the guests leave. Magda, left alone, finds an advertisement of the Bal Bullier. Her memories are awakened. She decides to disguise herself as a grisette and re-visit the scene of her early love-affair.

The second act shows the Bal Bullier. Magda meets the young Ruggero. She tells him of her early love affair. At first they joke about it, but soon their talk of love becomes earnest, and presently they realize that they have fallen in love with each other. Meanwhile Rambaldo has been watching them from the balcony, and approaches Magda, offering to take her home. She refuses and declares that she loves Ruggero. She renounces her life of luxury, and leaves with Ruggero.

The third act occurs in a cottage at Nice, where Magda is living happily with Ruggero. He knows nothing of her past life, and has written to his mother, asking for permission to marry Magda. Magda is fearful, and grows tense when the answer arrives. Ruggero asks Magda to read the letter from his mother and Magda learns that the old lady sends her blessing to the innocent young girl who is to marry her son, and welcomes her to the family. Magda is conscience-stricken. She reveals her past to Ruggero and declares that she will leave him forever rather than ruin his young life. True to the prophecy of Prunier, the poet, she returns like the swallow to what had been her home, the gay life of Paris.

§)&(§

DER ROSENKAVALIER

Richard Strauss

Der Rosenkavalier was first produced in Dresden, January 26, 1911. In contrast to the horrors of his earlier *Salome* and *Elektra,* Strauss chose this time for his libretto a merry comedy by Hugo von Hofmannsthal.

The characters include:

PRINCESS VON WERDENBERG (*Soprano*)
BARON OCHS OF LERCHENAU (*Bass*)
OCTAVIAN (*Mezzo-soprano*), a young gentleman of noble family
HERR VON FANINAL (*High Baritone*), a rich merchant, recently ennobled
SOPHIA (*High Soprano*), his daughter

The action takes place in Vienna during the reign of Maria Theresa in the eighteenth century. The first act shows the boudoir of the Princess. Octavian is making love to her, and is interrupted by Baron Ochs, a broken-down roué. Octavian has no time to escape, so he puts on the clothes of the Princess' maid and becomes "Mariandel." The Baron has come to ask the Princess to name a suitable gentleman to carry for him to Sophia the customary silver rose. This is a love-token which implies a proposal of marriage. Sophia's father, Faninal, is very rich, and although the Baron considers that he will be marrying beneath his own station, it is necessary that he repair his broken fortunes by such a marriage. When the Baron sees Octavian disguised as a maid he is diverted from his errand. He leers at "Mariandel" and asks her to have supper with him. The Princess dismisses the Baron by promising him that she will find a suitable rose-bearer, and when the Baron has gone she appoints Octavian to the office.

The second act shows Faninal's house. Octavian brings the silver rose and he and Sophia immediately fall in love with each other. They are interrupted by Faninal who brings the Baron for the formal signing of the wedding contract. The Baron's coarseness is highly offensive to Sophia and Octavian resents his remarks so much that he challenges the old rake to a duel. In the fight Octavian wounds the Baron in the hand. Sophia declares that she will not marry the Baron and her father says that if she does not she must become a nun. Thereupon she and Octavian scheme to compromise the Baron. Presently a letter is brought to him—a note from "Mariandel," reminding him of his date with her. It is at this point that the famous "Letter Scene" of the opera occurs.

The third act is laid in a private room at an inn. Octavian is again dressed as "Mariandel." Before the Baron arrives various accomplices to the plot are hidden about the room. The Baron arrives and is disturbed by "Mariandel's" resemblance to his enemy, Octavian. Then he is completely unnerved by the tricks that are played on him. Faces appear in panels; a widow comes to claim him as her husband; children call him "papa"; and as a climax a police officer arrests him for leading young girls astray. The Baron makes such a muddle of his explanations that even Faninal denounces him. A happy ending follows, and the young lovers are united.

§)&(§

ROSSIGNOL
(The Nightingale)

Igor Stravinsky

Igor Stravinsky's *Rossignol* is an opera-ballet which was first performed by the Ballet Russe at the Grand Opéra in Paris, May 26, 1914. The libretto was written by Stravinsky and S. Mitousoff, and was derived from a fairy-tale by Hans Christian Andersen.

The characters include:

THE NIGHTINGALE (*Soprano*)
THE KITCHEN-MAID (*Soprano*)
THE FISHERMAN (*Tenor*)
THE EMPEROR OF CHINA (*Bass*)
THE CHAMBERLAIN (*Bass*)
THE COOK
THREE AMBASSADORS FROM JAPAN
THE BONZE
DEATH

The action occurs in China in a legendary period. The first act shows a landscape on the shore of the sea. The Fisherman in his barque tells of the Nightingale and his beautiful voice. The Nightingale sings of the stars and the dewdrops. Presently the Emperor's Chamberlain and staff appear. They have come in search of the Nightingale, for the Emperor has heard about its beautiful singing. After the searchers have mistaken the baa-ing of the Fisherman's lamb and the croaking of the frogs for the Nightingale's voice, the Cook finds the real Nightingale. The members of the staff promise the bird that if he will come to the court and sing for the Emperor, he will be made the Chief Cook at the Court. The Nightingale accepts the offer.

The second act follows an entr'acte, *The Currents of Air,* and shows the porcelain palace of the Chinese Emperor. The Emperor makes an impressive entrance and the Nightingale sings for him. The song is so lovely that it brings tears to the Emperor's eyes. When the Emperor offers the Nightingale the Order of the Golden Slipper, the bird replies that the Emperor's tears are all the reward he wants. The conversation at the court is interrupted by the arrival of three ambassadors from Japan, who bring the Chinese Emperor a gift from their Emperor. It is a mechanical nightingale, made of silver and gold and set with rubies, diamonds and sapphires. It is made to sing, and when it has finished the Chinese Emperor asks to hear the live Nightingale again. He then learns that the real bird has flown away unnoticed. The Emperor angrily orders the live Nightingale banished to the far frontiers of his realm. The mechanical bird is given a place of honor at the side of the Emperor's bed.

The third act is laid in the Emperor's bed-chamber. The Emperor is ill and Death has already placed an imperial crown on the Emperor's head and is about to take his sword and banner. The Emperor cries for musicians to drive Death away. The Nightingale appears in answer. He sings tenderly of the rest and quiet of the churchyard, of the pale moonlight, and the dew on the roses around the mossy tombstones. This makes Death so homesick that he takes the imperial crown from the Emperor and gives him back his sword and banner. Giving up all his claim on the Emperor, Death hurries away. The Emperor offers the Nightingale any reward he desires, but the Nightingale wants nothing. He promises to come and sing for the Emperor every night from twilight to dawn. The courtiers come to pay their last respects to the dead Emperor. The bed-curtains are drawn back, the room is flooded with sunshine, and the Emperor himself greets his courtiers with a cheery good morning.

§)&(§

RUSSLAN AND LUDMILLA

Mikhail Glinka

Russlan and Ludmilla was Mikhail Glinka's second opera, and it was first produced at the Imperial Opera in St. Petersburg, December 9, 1842. Its libretto was written by V. F. Shirkov and K. A. Bakhturin, who founded its plot on a poem by Alexander Pushkin.

The cast includes the following characters:

PRINCE SVETOZAR
LUDMILLA, his daughter
RUSSLAN, a nobleman } suitors of Ludmilla
RATMIR, a Tartar Prince } suitors of Ludmilla
FARLAF, a Varangian chief
FINN, a wizard
CHERNOMOR, a dwarf
NAINA, an evil fairy

In the first act Prince Svetozar is entertaining two suitors for the hand of his daughter, Ludmilla. Ludmilla favors Russlan. During the reception the lights go out and when they are relighted Ludmilla has disappeared. Her father promises that the suitor who brings her back unharmed shall marry her.

The second act shows the cavern of Finn, the wizard. Finn tells Russlan that Ludmilla is the prisoner of a villainous dwarf named Chernomor. Finn warns Russlan that the evil fairy Naina will try to prevent him from rescuing Ludmilla. The scene changes to a battlefield, where Russlan looks for magic weapons which will help him.

The third act occurs in Naina's palace. Naina has promised Farlaf, the Varangian prince, that she will help him find Ludmilla. She accordingly tries to divert the other suitors from the search. She imprisons the Tartar Prince Ratmir, and exposes him to the siren song of three Persian girls, and to a visit from a former sweetheart who begs him to return to her. Naina tries to get Russlan also to listen to the song of the sirens, but the wizard Finn protects him from temptation.

The fourth act shows the home of Chernomor, the dwarf. Ludmilla is his prisoner, and refuses to be diverted by a ballet which is danced for her amusement. Russlan enters with a magic sword. He conquers the dwarf and rescues Ludmilla, but the dwarf has put Ludmilla into a deep sleep, and Russlan cannot rouse her. He carries her lifeless body away with him.

In the fifth act Russlan places a magic ring upon the sleeping Ludmilla's finger. She wakens, and her father, Prince Svetozar, keeps his promise by giving her hand to Russlan, who has rescued her.

§)&(§

SADKO

Rimsky-Korsakoff

Rimsky-Korsakoff composed both libretto and music for *Sadko,* which was first performed at Moscow, January 7, 1898.

To many music lovers *Sadko* is important chiefly because its score contains the universally played and sung "Song of India." The plot of the opera concerns the legendary Sadko, a gousla player. Through his travels he finds the Princess of the Sea who transforms herself into the Volkhova River, thus opening a water route from Novgorod to the sea.

The cast includes:

SADKO (*Tenor*), a gousla player, or minstrel
LIOUBAVA (*Mezzo-soprano*), Sadko's wife
THE KING OF THE SEAS (*Bass*)
VOLKHOVA (*Soprano*), the King's youngest daughter, Princess of the Seas
A VIKING MERCHANT (*Bass*)
A HINDU MERCHANT (*Tenor*)
A VENETIAN MERCHANT (*Baritone*)

The action of the opera occurs in Novgorod, on the sea and in its depths, in a semi-mythical and semi-historic period. The first act opens in the hall of the Merchant's Guild at Novgorod. The merchants are giving a banquet for several traders from distant lands, and they call upon Sadko, the minstrel, to sing about the ancient glories of the city of Novgorod. Sadko sings, but not about past glories. Instead he sings a new ballad of his own, which declares that if he had the riches of the merchants of Novgorod he would buy up the whole city, charter a fleet of ships, and sail away in search of new markets. Inasmuch as Sadko himself is a shabby fellow, the merchants jeer at him and the sheriffs throw him out of the hall. In the second scene Sadko wanders on the shores of Lake Ilmen, where he sings and plays on his gousla. Volkhova, Princess of the Seas, rises from a ripple in the silvery moonlight and, followed by her sisters and her attendants, she comes to Sadko and tells him that his song has touched her heart. Sadko again sings, and he and the Princess fall in love with each other. She must return to her father, the King of the Seas, but before she leaves she tells Sadko that if he casts his net into the lake he will catch three little fishes with golden scales. These will be his talismans, signifying wealth and happiness.

In the opening scene of the second act, Sadko's wife,

Lioubova, is leaning out of the window looking for her husband. Sadko returns, acting as though he were in a trance. He brushes his wife aside; he must hurry to the harbor to tell the people of Novgorod about the three fishes he will catch in his net. The next scene shows the port of Novgorod on the banks of Lake Ilmen. Ships crowd the harbor and merchants from distant lands are showing their wares to the people of Novgorod. A band of pilgrims chants a warning against the evils of wealth. Sadko arrives and tells the leading citizens and merchants of the city about the three little fishes. He stakes his head against the merchants' riches that he can catch the fishes in his net. The wager is accepted and Sadko is given a canoe. He paddles to the middle of the lake, casts his net and brings up three fishes with glittering gold scales. When he comes back to shore the admiring crowds gather around him, while the fish become gold bullion. After Sadko is hailed a hero, the merchants realize that by the wager they have lost all their wealth to Sadko, but Sadko is generous, the bullion is his and he can afford to return to them the riches they have bartered. The ships, however, are Sadko's and he immediately plans his voyage. He asks three foreign merchants to tell him of their lands, and each responds with a song describing his native country: the Viking merchant with the "Song of the Viking Guest," the Hindu merchant with the "Song of India," and the Venetian merchant with the "Song of the Venetian Guest."

The third act takes place twelve years later, and opens aboard Sadko's ship, *The Hawk.* Sadko has become fabulously wealthy, but now he is becalmed and is told that he has failed to share his fortune with the King of the Seas. He and his companions empty barrels of treasure into the water, but without result. Sadko decides that he must go to the depths of the ocean to address the King and pay tribute to him. He advises his companions to return to their homes, and playing on his gousla he floats away on a raft. As he sinks into the waters he hears Volkhova's voice calling him. The next scene is laid in the ocean depths and in the palace of the Sea King. The King and the Queen, Pale Wave, are seated on their thrones, and the Princess Volkhova is spinning seaweed. When Sadko comes the King rebukes him for failing to pay tribute, but the Princess pleads for Sadko, and tells him to play and sing. Sadko's music is so beautiful that the King is touched and gives Sadko the hand of the Princess in marriage. As the wedding procession is formed the King asks Sadko to play for dancing. Sadko starts softly, then louder and faster until the dance is wild and mad. The King and Queen dance with their subjects. Suddenly the King stops. He orders hurricanes and mountain torrents which will swell and cause rivers to overflow. He commands the waves of the sea to spare neither ship nor human being. Suddenly an old pilgrim appears. He strikes Sadko's gousla from his hands, and orders the King to descend to the lowest depths of the sea, deposed of his kingdom. He commands the Princess to change herself into the River Volkhova, and he rebukes Sadko for wasting his time playing to the people of the sea. He bids Sadko return to Novgorod and to use his music for celebrating the greatness of his native city. Sadko and the Princess start for Novgorod on a conch-shell drawn by seagulls. The last scene shows Lake Ilmen. Sadko and the Princess arrive on the shore. Realizing that Sadko must return to his wife, the Princess kisses him gently and dissolves into the mist. Lioubova finds Sadko and greets him joyfully. As they embrace they see a newly formed river sweeping over the green meadows, heading toward the sea. Ships glide into the harbor, led by *The Hawk.* Sadko welcomes his companions, while the people of Novgorod hail their hero, Sadko. He starts to play on his gousla and sings a song which is echoed by his neighbors—a hymn of praise to the River Volkhova.

§)&(§

SALOME

Richard Strauss

Oscar Wilde's dramatic poem, *Salome,* is the libretto for Richard Strauss's opera, which uses a German translation prepared by Hedwig Lachmann. *Salome* was first peformed in Dresden, December 9, 1905.

The cast includes:

HEROD (*Tenor*), Tetrarch of Galilee
HERODIAS (*Contralto*), wife of Herod, formerly the wife of Herod's brother
SALOME (*Soprano*), daughter of Herodias by her former marriage
JOKANAAN ("John the Baptist") (*Baritone*), the prophet
NARRABOTH (*Tenor*), a young Syrian captain

The opera is written in one act which occurs in Tiberias in Galilee in the year 30 A.D. The scene is the sumptuous terrace of Herod's palace. At the back is a cistern in which Jokanaan has been imprisoned because of his teachings and because of his denunciation of Herod and Herodias. As the opera opens a banquet is being held inside the palace, and a group of soldiers is guarding the cistern. Narraboth, the captain, remarks on Salome's beauty, while the voice of Jokanaan is heard from the cistern proclaiming the coming of the Messiah. Salome comes from the palace to escape the amorous eyes of Herod. She hears the voice of the prophet. She is fascinated and orders Narraboth to bring Jokanaan before her. The prophet again denounces Herodias and advises Salome to avoid her mother's sinful ways. Salome is overcome by her desire for Jokanaan and sings "I long to kiss thy mouth, Jokanaan." Narraboth is so horrified by Salome's unholy desires that he slays himself with his sword. Even though he dies at her feet, Salome does not notice him. Jokanaan again denounces Salome and goes back toward the cistern. Salome seizes him and lets herself be dragged along the ground as he walks. Herod and Herodias, followed by the banqueters, come from the palace. Herod leers at Salome and once more the warning voice of Jokanaan is heard. Herodias demands that he be killed, but Herod is afraid of the consequences. The denunciations and prophecies continue insistently, until the nervous, fidgety Herod turns to Salome for diversion. He orders her to dance for him. To overcome her refusal he offers her as a reward anything up to the half of his kingdom. Salome then starts the dance of the seven veils, discarding one veil at a time, and finishing almost nude. When she has finished she demands her reward, which on the urging of her mother, is nothing less than the head of Jokanaan. Herod is horrified and tries to dissuade her. Salome insists and at last Herod orders the executioner to do away with Jokanaan. The headsman descends into the cistern. A thud is heard and the headsman returns with a platter bearing the bloody head of the prophet. Salome demands the head, and begins another dance as she holds it, singing, "I am athirst for thy body, and neither wine nor fruit can appease my desire." Herod, aghast, orders the lights extinguished. Salome continues to dance in the semi-darkness. Herod can stand the unholy sight no longer; he orders the soldiers to kill Salome.

§)&(§

SAMSON AND DELILAH

Camille Saint-Saëns

Ferdinand Lemaire wrote the libretto of this opera by Camille Saint-Saëns, adapting his plot from the Old Testament, Book of Judges. The opera was first performed at Weimar, December 2, 1877. The first performance in France was given at Rouen, March 3, 1890, and the first Parisian performance, at the Grand Opéra, November 23, 1892.

The cast includes:

SAMSON (*Tenor*)
HIGH PRIEST OF DAGON (*Baritone*)
DELILAH (*Soprano*), daughter of the High Priest
ABIMELECH (*Bass*), Satrap of Gaza
AN OLD HEBREW (*Bass*)

The action takes place at Gaza in Palestine about 1140 B. C. The first act shows a public square in Gaza where a group of Hebrews is mourning in bondage before the gates of the heathen temple of the Philistines. Samson bids the Hebrews to find new courage, but they are without arms, without a leader, helpless and despondent. Abimelech, a satrap of the Philistines, comes with his warriors to mock the captive Israelites. Samson attacks Abimelech, and with a strength sent from Heaven seizes Abimelech's sword and runs it through him, warding off the warriors as they press against him. Samson and the Israelites leave the body of Abimelech in the square, where it is found by the High Priest. The High Priest orders the guards to avenge Abimelech, but their blood turns to water in their veins and they are powerless. A messenger rushes in with the news that the Israelites have overrun and conquered the Philistines. The priest and his guards are forced to flee with the body of Abimelech. Samson returns at the head of his victorious band of Hebrews, singing a song of praise and thanksgiving. The door of the temple opens and from it comes the beautiful, treacherous Delilah, bearing garlands of flowers for the victors. Delilah goes directly to Samson and sings: "I come with a song for the splendor of my love who has won in the fray." The priestesses dance as Delilah sings, and Samson is fascinated, even though he prays for divine help in resisting her charms. An old Hebrew warns Samson against the power of Delilah's wiles but as the curtain falls Samson hesitates and shows that his determination to resist has wavered.

The second act occurs at Delilah's home in a valley. Delilah is waiting for the coming of her lover, Samson. The High Priest urges her to conquer Samson completely and she promises to do her best. As the High Priest leaves, Samson returns. Delilah is not sure of him yet, so she sings the famous aria: "My Heart at Thy Sweet Voice." As she finishes, a storm gathers. As the storm increases Delilah pleads with Samson to tell her the secret of his strength. Samson tries to resist, and summons the last of his moral power and denounces Delilah. She coaxes him and when the storm bursts, she leads him into her house. There she learns that his strength lies in his hair. She calls to the Philistines for help. The soldiers rush in and cut Samson's locks and overpower him.

The first scene of the third act shows Samson in prison, loaded with chains, blinded, and with his locks shorn, slowly turning a heavy mill, grinding corn for the Philistines. Near at hand is a group of Hebrew captives. Samson prays God to have pity on him, and to forgive him for having listened to Delilah. The Philistines take Samson to the magnificent hall where the High Priest and the Philistines are feasting and rejoicing over the downfall of the Hebrews. Delilah taunts Samson. He cannot reply to her, but with bowed head he prays for one minute's strength. He whispers to a boy to lead him to the great pillars which support the temple. Straining at the columns, he pushes them aside so that the temple crashes and destroys all who are in it.

§)&(§

SAPHO

Jules Massenet

The libretto of Jules Massenet's opera *Sapho* was based on a novel by Alphonse Daudet, and was written by Henri Cain and Arthur Bernède. It was first performed at the Opéra Comique in Paris, November 27, 1897.

The cast includes:

CAOUDAL, a sculptor
FANNY, a model
JEAN GAUSSIN, a countryman
CESAIRE, his father
DIVONNE, his mother
IRENE, his cousin and childhood companion

The action occurs in Paris, and at Avignon.

The first act shows the reception room of Caoudal's studio. Caoudal is host to a fancy-dress ball. Jean Gaussin comes from the studio and is about to leave. He is from the provinces and cannot enjoy the free and easy ways of the artists' world. He meets Fanny, one of the models who is attending the party, and falls in love with her at first sight. Fanny is delighted to find an unsophisticated youth who is not an artist. She does not want him to learn about her past, so when supper is announced she slips away with him unnoticed.

The second act shows Jean's lodgings in the rue d'Amsterdam. Jean's father and mother, Cesaire and Divonne, have helped their son settle his apartment and are now leaving and taking with them Irene, Jean's cousin and childhood companion. Jean and Irene sing an affectionate duet recalling their childhood. When they have gone Fanny calls on Jean. As she admires his new home she sees a statuette of Sapho which was wrought by Caoudal with herself as a model. She is almost trapped into revealing her past but she checks herself and uses her charms to arouse Jean to ardent love-making.

The third act is laid outside a cottage at Ville d'Avray where Jean and Fanny have been living together. Jean is deeply in love and Fanny has put her former life behind her, now that she has found real love for the first time. After Jean and Fanny have sung a love-duet, Caoudal comes with a party of his artist-friends to visit the inn near Jean's cottage. Jean returns in time to meet Caoudal, who asks him casually if he is still living with "Sapho." Jean does not at first understand, but soon he learns that Fanny is called "Sapho" because she was the model for Caoudal's statue. For the moment Jean denies his relations with Fanny, and

Caoudal remarks that it is just as well, for she had many lovers and is the mother of a child who is living with her father. At this revelation Jean becomes furious and admits his affair with Fanny. He denounces her wildly. Fanny returns and learns that she has been exposed. She cries out against the cruelty which has deprived her of the one pure love of her life.

In the fourth act Jean is at the home of his parents in Avignon. His mother and Irene try to comfort him. Fanny comes to beg Jean to return to her. He is aroused by her appeals, but his father and mother persuade him not to surrender to Fanny's wiles.

The last act returns to the cottage at Ville d'Avray. Jean comes to Fanny and tells her that after days and nights of emotional struggle he has given up his home and parents to be with her. After he talks with Fanny, Jean falls asleep. Fanny realizes that they can never be happy together and slips quietly away.

§)&(§

THE SCARLET LETTER

Walter Damrosch

The libretto of Walter Damrosch's opera, *The Scarlet Letter,* was adapted from Nathaniel Hawthorne's novel by George Parsons Lathrop. The opera was produced first at the Boston Theatre in Boston, Massachusetts, February 10, 1896.

The librettist took a number of liberties with Hawthorne's story. He eliminated the character of Hester's child, Little Pearl, by having her die in infancy before the beginning of the action. Other incidents are changed, remodeled and transposed, and new episodes and situations introduced.

The cast includes:

HESTER PRYNNE (*Soprano*)
REV. ARTHUR DIMMESDALE (*Tenor*)
ROGER CHILLINGWORTH (*Baritone*), a hunchback, actually Roger Prynne, Hester's husband
REV. JOHN WILSON (*Bass*)
GOVERNOR BELLINGHAM (*Bass*)

The action occurs in seventeenth-century Boston. The first act shows the market place, where a crowd is gathered outside of the jail demanding death for Hester Prynne, the adulteress. She came to Boston several years ago without her husband and has since borne a child to an unknown father. The Governor quiets the people, and demands that Hester reveal the name of her lover. She refuses, and the Governor asks the young minister, Arthur Dimmesdale, to plead with her. Dimmesdale grows pale, but tries to persuade Hester to tell her lover's name. When Hester continues to refuse, the Governor announces that he will not condemn her to death, but that she must always wear the scarlet letter "A" on her breast. She will be an exile from the community, speaking to no one. Meanwhile a man who calls himself Roger Chillingworth arrives on the scene, recently landed from a sailing vessel. He is actually Roger Prynne, Hester's husband. He recognizes Hester as his wife, and resolves to keep his identity secret. He will discover the guilty man and when he knows his secret he will torture him with his knowledge. When the people have gone into the church, Chillingworth approaches Hester. She recognizes him with horror, and he tells her that he has come as Roger Chillingworth and not under his real name, Roger Prynne. If Hester tells who he is, he will destroy the man who has been her lover. The people come from the church. Several of them are carrying Arthur, who has fainted. Hester instinctively rushes to Arthur and kneels beside him. As the people shove her aside, Chillingworth mutters to himself: " 'Tis he. O wonder of darkness—I have found the man!"

The second act is laid in a forest, with Hester's hut at one side. She is an outcast and everyone shrinks from her. Meanwhile Chillingworth has established himself as a physician and the Governor asks him to do what he can for Arthur, the young minister, who is in failing health. Chillingworth advises Arthur to tell him whatever dark secrets may be troubling him. Arthur shudders, and then Chillingworth suggests that he call on Hester, to "appease her conscience" with his sympathy. Chillingworth pretends to leave while Hester and Arthur talk. Hester tells Arthur that Chillingworth was her husband. Arthur suggests that they both take poison, but Hester refuses, and plans instead that she and Arthur flee to England on a vessel that is soon to sail.

The third act returns to the market place. Hester learns from the ship-master that Chillingworth has booked passage on the vessel. She is desperate and tries to warn Arthur. Arthur, pale and trembling, takes Hester by the hand and leads her to the scaffold. He addresses the people and confesses that he is the father of Hester's child. He tears away the ministerial band from his breast and shows the letter "A" branded in scarlet on his skin. Chillingworth realizes that he has lost his victim. Arthur dies on the scaffold and Hester drinks from the phial of poison. As she dies the people sing:

Thou, Hester, over us triumph hast won;
Towards mercy turning our sullen hate.
Thou, Arthur, though repenting late,
May God thee pardon!

§)&(§

SCHWANDA
DER DUDELSACKPFEIFER
(The Bagpiper)

Jaromir Weinberger

The story of *Schwanda,* written by Milos Kareš, is a modern version of the Pied Piper legend in which the hero is able to charm even the Devil with his bagpipes. In composing the music for this folk-opera, Jaromir Weinberger became the natural successor to his Czech countryman, Smetana. Just as Smetana composed *The Bartered Bride* as an expression of Czech nationalism when his country had become free of the tyranny of the Austrian Habsburgs, so did Weinberger compose *Schwanda,* picturing the life of the Bohemian peasants, at a time when Czecho-Slovakia had again become an independent nation. *Schwanda* is a folk-opera, not because it uses actual folk-songs in its score, but because its rustic spirit is so thoroughly representative of the Czech tradition. *Schwanda* was first performed at the Czech Theatre in Prague, April 27, 1927.

The cast includes:

SCHWANDA (*Tenor*), a farmer, the bagpiper
DOROTA (*Soprano*), his wife

BABINSKY (*Baritone*), a robber
QUEEN ICE-HEART (*Mezzo-soprano*)
SORCERER
THE DEVIL (*Bass*)

The scenes of the opera occur near a Czech village and in Hell, and the first act shows Schwanda's farm, where a party of soldiers is hunting for Babinsky, the robber. Dorota, Schwanda's wife, sends the soldiers away, telling them that no stranger has been there. As soon as they have gone Babinsky comes from a tree in which he has been hiding. He is much impressed by Dorota's beauty and he plans to win her from her husband. In order to get Schwanda away from the farm, Babinsky tells him that if he will play his pipes at the court of Queen Ice-Heart he will gain riches and almost anything he wants. Schwanda is interested and goes away with Babinsky. When Dorota finds that they are gone she decides to follow and see what her husband is up to. The scene changes to the Court of Queen Ice-Heart. The Queen has sold her heart to a Sorcerer and is in his power. Schwanda plays such merry music on his bagpipes that the atmosphere of gloom and despair is transformed to happiness and laughter. The enraged and defeated Sorcerer leaves, and the Queen kisses Schwanda and offers to marry him and give him half of her kingdom. At this moment Dorota appears. She objects to the new arrangement and when the Queen learns that Schwanda already has a wife she orders him tried and executed. The third scene of the first act shows a public square outside the city gate. A headsman is ready to chop off the Bagpiper's head. Schwanda is granted a last request: he may play his bagpipes before he dies. But the Sorcerer has hidden the pipes and the execution proceeds. The headsman raises the ax and brings it down on Schwanda's neck. Instead of Schwanda's head rolling off, it looks up, delighted to find that Babinsky has substituted a broom handle for the ax. Babinsky hands Schwanda his bagpipes and Schwanda plays a merry tune which starts everyone dancing back into the city—the Queen, the Sorcerer, and all the crowd. Dorota, and Babinsky and Schwanda are left alone, and Babinsky encourages Dorota to scold her husband for his unfaithfulness. Schwanda declares that if he ever kissed the Queen he hopes that the Devil may take him immediately to Hell. Lightning flashes and thunder crashes as the bagpiper sinks into the earth. Babinsky immediately renews his love-making, but Dorota resists him and is so unhappy that he promises to go to Hell to rescue Schwanda.

The second act opens in Hell where Schwanda is about to be tortured for refusing to play his bagpipes for the Devil. Babinsky appears and offers to play cards with the Devil. If the Devil wins he gets the souls of Schwanda and Babinsky. If Babinsky wins he gets half the Devil's kingdom. The Devil wins but Babinsky proves that he cheated. Babinsky is generous and gives back the half of the Devil's kingdom. Schwanda then plays his pipes and the devils and imps start dancing. Babinsky and Schwanda are released and leave for the upper world. The second scene returns to Schwanda's farmyard. The bagpiper and Babinsky return from Hell, and Babinsky again tries to get Dorota from Schwanda. He tells Schwanda that Dorota is much changed; that the twenty minutes Schwanda spent in Hell were actually twenty years, so that Dorota has meanwhile grown bald, deaf and lame. He urges Schwanda not to try even to see his wife. Schwanda is unimpressed and calls aloud for Dorota, who rushes in to embrace him, more beautiful than ever. Babinsky admits defeat and leaves with the thanks of the grateful Schwanda and Dorota. The neighbors come to congratulate the pair on the happy ending of their troubles.

THE SECRET OF SUZANNE

Ermanno Wolf-Ferrari

Ermanno Wolf-Ferrari's *The Secret of Suzanne* is designated as an "Italian Interlude in One Act." Its libretto was written by Enrico Golisciani and it was performed first at the Hofoper in Munich, December 4, 1909.

There are only three characters in the opera:

COUNT GIL (*Baritone*)
SUZANNE, COUNTESS GIL (*Soprano*), his wife
SANTE, a speechless servant

The action occurs in Piedmont, Italy, in modern times. The scene is the drawing room of the Count's home. The Count comes in from the street, distressed because he has seen a woman on the street who resembles his wife. She is not in the habit of going out alone. Now that he is in the house he has an added reason for being disturbed: he smells tobacco smoke. He himself does not smoke, nor does his servant, Sante. There must be a strange man about. The Countess welcomes the Count and for the moment he forgets his suspicions. He and his wife have chocolate together and sing a love duet. The Count embraces his wife, and notices the odor of tobacco on her clothes and in her hair. He declares that he has discovered her secret, and the Countess, thinking that he means her secret habit of cigarette smoking, answers in a way that makes him more suspicious than ever. The Count rages about the room looking for the supposed lover's hiding place. He throws the furniture and bric-a-brac about. The Countess leaves and the Count is in despair. Sante, the servant, restores the room to a semblance of order while the orchestra plays the famous interlude of the opera. The Countess returns and the Count announces that he is going away. The Countess tries to relieve his suspicions, and then hands him his hat and gloves. When he is gone, the Countess needs relaxation and asks Sante for a cigarette. She has barely lighted it when the Count returns. The Countess tosses the cigarette in the fire, but the smoke stays in the room and the Count smells it. He becomes furious again, and searches the house for the culprit. The Countess asks him what he is looking for and he answers savagely, "My umbrella." The Countess hands him his umbrella, and the enraged Count breaks it over his knees and rushes out again, hoping to catch the lover outside. The Countess is so upset that she needs another cigarette. As she is slowly puffing it the Count appears at a window. Again smelling smoke he is sure that he can now catch the man and he leaps through the window. The Countess holds the cigarette behind her and as the Count grabs her he burns his hand. In this way he learns the horrible secret—his wife smokes. The Count is so happy to learn that no lover is involved that he forgets his prejudice against smoking. He even goes so far as to take a few puffs from his wife's cigarette, and as they smoke together they sing a duet: "All life ends in smoke."

§)&(§

SEMIRAMIDE

Gioacchino Rossini

Semiramide was the thirty-third of Gioacchino Rossini's thirty-eight operas and was first produced at the Teatro la Fenice in Venice, February 3, 1823. Its libretto, by Gaetano Rossi, was based on Voltaire's tragedy, *Semiramis*.

The cast includes:

SEMIRAMIDE (*Soprano*), Queen of Babylon, widow of King Ninus
ARSACES (*Contralto*), Commander of the army, actually Ninius, son of King Ninus and Semiramide
GHOST OF NINUS (*Basso*)
OROE (*Bass*), Chief of the Magi
ASSUR (*Baritone*), a Prince of the royal blood
AZEMA (*Soprano*), a Princess

The action occurs in ancient Babylon. The characters have their counterparts in Greek tragedy. Semiramide is akin to Klytemnestra. With her lover Assur (Aegisthus) she has murdered her husband Ninus (Agamemnon), who is in turn avenged by their son Arsaces (Orestes).

The first act of *Semiramide* shows the temple of the god Belus. Ninus has been murdered and a festival is in progress during which Semiramide, his widow, will name his successor. Assur expects to be chosen, for he has been the Queen's lover, and it was he who helped her murder her husband. Semiramide is planning to have a new lover, the handsome Arsaces who has led her armies to victory. It is he whom she will name as king. During the religious rites strange omens appear. The people regard them as warnings of evil and they await the return of Arsaces from his visit to the Oracle. Arsaces comes with a scroll from the Oracle which tells that the king was murdered and that punishment will fall on the guilty ones. Arsaces is planning to marry the Princess Azema, but Assur tells him that he himself wants Azema and that he, Assur, is to be appointed to the king's throne. The scene changes to a garden where Semiramide tells Arsaces that if he will be patient, Assur's plans will be thwarted. The next scene is laid in a hall in the palace. Semiramide announces to the court that Arsaces is to be successor to the throne and also her husband. Arsaces replies that he does not want the throne; all he desires is the Princess Azema. Suddenly the tomb of Ninus opens. The dead king's ghost appears and commands Arsaces to come with him into the tomb.

The second act opens in an ante-room of the palace. Semiramide meets Assur, and each accuses the other of murdering Ninus. The scene changes to the interior of the sanctuary. Arsaces returns from his interview with the Ghost of Ninus. The Ghost has told him that Ninus's son Ninius is still alive. Then Arsaces learns from Oroe, chief of the Magi, that he, Arsaces, is the long lost Ninius, that he is the son of Semiramide and Ninus, and that Ninus was murdered by Semiramide and Assur. The Magi commands Arsaces to avenge his father's death. Oroe shows Semiramide a paper signed by Ninus just before his death, telling of the murder. When Semiramide learns that Arsaces is her son, she urges him to kill her. This he will not do, for she is his mother. He pursues Assur to the tomb and is about to stab him when Semiramide comes between them and herself receives the thrust of the weapon. Arsaces starts to stab himself when he falls fainting in the arms of the Magi chief and the guards arrest Assur.

§)&(§

LA SERVA PADRONA

(The Maid Mistress)

Giovanni Pergolesi

La Serva Padrona, by Giovanni Battista Pergolesi, is an early eighteenth-century work, and the oldest opera in the present-day repertory. It was first produced at the Teatro San Bartolomeo in Naples, August 28, 1733. Its libretto was written by G. A. Federico, and not by J. A. Nelli, to whom it is commonly attributed. Federico provided a merry one-act farce, with two singing characters, and a third who does not sing nor speak:

UBERTO (*Bass*), a bachelor
SERPINA (*Soprano*), his maid
VESPONE, Uberto's valet

The action is laid in Naples during the early eighteenth century. The scene is a room in Uberto's house where Uberto is waiting for his maid Serpina to bring him his chocolate. When she does not come Uberto sends his valet Vespone to fetch her. Serpina complains that she is mistreated, that Uberto imposes on her, and that she wants to be mistress of the house. Uberto is outraged at such effrontery and starts to go out for a walk. Serpina will not let him go. Uberto decides that he must have a wife to control Serpina so he sends Vespone out to find one for him. Serpina, however, has made up her mind that she will be Uberto's wife. Accordingly, she plots with Vespone. He is to disguise himself as a soldier and pretend that he is to marry her. Then she tells Uberto about this Captain Tempest, whom she is to marry. His name describes his temper, she says. When Uberto hears this, he feels a slight twinge of jealousy and something akin to love for Serpina. Has she not been his maid since she was a mere child? Captain Tempest is introduced, and he is indeed a terrible-looking person. He does not speak, so Serpina interprets his gestures and his whisperings. The Captain wants Serpina's dowry in advance immediately, 4,000 crowns. Uberto objects to paying any such sum, and the Captain starts to draw his sword. The frightened Uberto asks if nothing can be done to placate the man and make him withdraw his suit. Serpina replies that the Captain will give her up only if Uberto himself will marry her. Uberto agrees, Vespone takes off his disguise, and all three are happy at the solution of their problems.

§)&(§

SHANEWIS

Charles Wakefield Cadman

Shanewis, or *The Robin Woman,* music by Charles Wakefield Cadman, was produced first at the Metropolitan Opera House, New York, March 23, 1918. Its libretto was written by Nelle Richmond Eberhart.

SHANEWIS (*Mezzo-soprano*), an Indian girl, "The Robin Woman."
MRS. EVERTON (*Contralto*)
AMY EVERTON (*Soprano*), her daughter
LIONEL RHODES (*Tenor*), Amy's fiancé
PHILIP HARJO (*Baritone*) foster-brother of Shanewis

The action occurs in the Western United States during contemporary times, and the plot is derived from a story told to the librettist by a member of the Creek tribe of Indians. Shanewis, or the Robin Woman, is an Indian maiden whose lovely voice has attracted the attention of Mrs. Everton, a wealthy Californian. She has sent Shanewis to New York for musical training and later invites her to spend the summer at her California home. Here Shanewis meets Lionel Rhodes, the fiancé of Mrs. Everton's daughter Amy. Lionel falls in love with Shanewis, and she with him, but she insists that before deciding on their engagement, Lionel must visit her home on the reservation. Then he will see if his love endures.

Shanewis makes an excuse for leaving Mrs. Everton's home, and returns to the home of her tribe. Lionel secretly follows her and is fascinated rather than repelled by the customs and manners of the Indians. Mrs. Everton and Amy have learned that Lionel has gone to the reservation and they follow him. They urge him not to marry an Indian girl. When Shanewis discovers that Lionel has been engaged to Amy, she will have none of him. She is grief-stricken, and when her foster-brother Philip Harjo finds her crying, he thinks that Lionel has betrayed her. He shoots Lionel through the heart with an arrow, and Amy and Shanewis kneel beside him as he dies.

§)&(§

SIEGFRIED

See Der Ring des Nibelungen

§)&(§

SIMON BOCCANEGRA

Giuseppe Verdi

Simon Boccanegra was Giuseppe Verdi's twentieth opera. It was first produced at the Teatro La Fenice in Venice, March 12, 1857. A quarter of a century later, March 24,

1881, it was performed at Milan with its libretto revised by Arrigo Boïto. Fifty-one years after the first production of the revised opera, *Simon Boccanegra* had its initial performance in the United States, at the Metropolitan in New York, January 28, 1932.

The libretto of the opera was written by Francesco Maria Piave and was founded on a Spanish drama by A. Garcia Guttiérez. The action takes place in fourteenth-century Italy, when Genoa was a republic and the Guelph and Ghibelline quarrels were still being waged in the Northern provinces. The cast includes:

SIMON BOCCANEGRA (*Baritone*), a pirate who becomes First Doge of Genoa
PAOLO ALBIANI (*Bass*), a goldsmith who helps to elect Boccanegra and becomes his favorite courtier
PIETRO (*Baritone*), a Genoese commoner
JACOPO FIESCO (*Bass*), a nobleman of Genoa
MARIA BOCCANEGRA (*Soprano*), daughter of Simon Boccanegra. Her mother was the daughter of Fiesco. As AMELIA GRIMALDI she is brought up by Fiesco, her grandfather, who does not know her true identity
GABRIELE ADORNO (*Tenor*), a Genoese nobleman, in love with Maria

A Prologue precedes the three acts of the opera. Paolo Albiani, the goldsmith, and Pietro, are conspiring to elect a fellow commoner to the Doge's throne. They decide upon Simon Boccanegra, who as a pirate has helped to extend the dominion of Genoa, but has not been able to win the recognition of the wealthy nobleman, Fiesco. Boccanegra was once secretly in love with Fiesco's daughter, Maria, who bore him a child and was subsequently held prisoner by her father. Boccanegra realizes that if he becomes Doge, Fiesco cannot keep Maria away from him, and for this reason he consents to be elected. As Boccanegra approaches the door of Fiesco's palace, he is confronted by Fiesco. Fiesco tells Simon that Maria is dead, and that he will never forgive him unless he yields to him the child that his daughter bore him. Simon cannot do this, for the child wandered away after the death of her nurse. As Simon and Fiesco part the crowds enter hailing Boccanegra as Doge.

The first act occurs twenty-five years later. With the aid of Paolo Albiani, Simon Boccanegra has become a tyrant. Fiesco, for political safety, has changed his name to Andrea, and he has living with him an orphan whom he has brought up as an heiress under the name of Amelia Grimaldi. He does not know that she is actually his own granddaughter, Maria Boccanegra, daughter of Simon. Fiesco has organized a revolt against the rule of Simon Boccanegra and as the act opens Amelia is in the gardens of Fiesco's palace, talking to her lover, Gabriele Adorno, who is one of Fiesco's conspirators. Simon, the Doge, appears and claims Amelia's hand for his favorite courtier, the former goldsmith Paolo Albiani. Amelia confesses to Simon that her true name is not Grimaldi, and by a locket she has worn since childhood, she and Simon discover that she is Simon's daughter. As they embrace, Amelia tells Simon that she is in love with Adorno. The scene changes to the Council chamber. Simon tells the goldsmith Paolo that Amelia cannot be his bride. Paolo is furious and secretly arranges to have Amelia abducted. Soon Adorno rushes in. He believes that Simon has ordered the kidnapping of Amelia and he is about to stab him when Amelia comes to plead for the Doge's life. Simon demands that Amelia tell him the name of her abductor. She replies that the man is in the council chamber. Simon then orders everyone present to pronounce a curse upon the kidnapper, and Paolo is thus forced to curse himself.

The second act shows Simon's private chambers. Paolo drops a vial of poison in the Doge's drinking bowl. To make sure of the tyrant's death he persuades Adorno to murder Simon, by telling Adorno that Simon has designs upon Amelia. When Adorno is alone with Amelia he accuses her of being in love with Simon. She admits the truth of what he says, but claims that it is a pure love. Simon is heard approaching and Amelia hides Adorno in an alcove. Amelia pleads with her father to spare the life of his enemy, Adorno. Simon agrees and asks to be left alone. When Amelia is gone he drinks from the poisoned drinking bowl. As he becomes drowsy Adorno comes from his hiding place. He is about to stab Simon when Amelia halts him. He learns that Simon is Amelia's father, and declares that he will fight with Simon against Fiesco and the conspirators.

The third act is laid in the court of the palace. The revolt has been crushed. Paolo has turned traitor and is condemned to death. As he passes Fiesco he tells him that Simon will be the first to die because he himself has poisoned him. Fiesco then learns that Amelia is Simon's daughter, and therefore his own granddaughter. He realizes that the condition he made for forgiveness of Simon has long since been fulfilled, the child that his daughter bore to Simon was given to him many years ago. The feud is accordingly at an end, and before Simon dies he gives his blessing to the marriage of Amelia and Adorno, and bequeaths the Doge's crown to Adorno.

§)&(§

SNEGUROTCHKA

(The Snow Maiden)

Rimsky-Korsakoff

Rimsky-Korsakoff's *Snegurotchka* is sub-titled "A Legend of Springtime." The composer adapted its libretto from a play by Alexander Nicholevich Ostrovsky which was based on an old Russian folk-tale. The opera was first performed at St. Petersburg, February 10, 1882.

The cast includes:

SNEGUROTCHKA (*Soprano*), the Snow Maiden
KING WINTER (*Bass*) } her parents
FAIRY SPRING (*Contralto*) } her parents
LEL (*Tenor*), a shepherd
KOUPAVA (*Mezzo-soprano*), a maid of the village
MIZGUIR (*Tenor*), a Tartar merchant
BOBYL (*Baritone*), a villager
BOBYLCKA (*Contralto*), his wife
THE CZAR

The action occurs in the land of the Berendeys in prehistoric times. The Prologue takes place on the Red Mountain, near the castle of Berendey, capital of the Czar. Snegurotchka, the Snow Maiden, has been reared in the chilly forests by her parents, King Winter and Fairy Spring. When the first ray of sunlight and love touches her she must die, but while she is innocent of love she is safe from the fatal caress of the sun god. Snegurotchka has heard the songs of the shepherd Lel and has seen him making merry with the village girls. She would like to exchange her secluded existence for the active life of a mortal. Her parents reluctantly grant her wish and entrust her to the care of the villagers, Bobyl and Bobylcka. In parting, Fairy Spring tells her daughter that if she is ever in trouble to come to the valley of the god Yarilo, where anything she wishes will be granted.

The first act shows a suburb of Berendey, with Bobyl's hut at the right. Snegurotchka has found that the life of a mortal is sad and disillusioning. Lel, the shepherd, is cold and indifferent, and Snegurotchka cannot make herself love the Tartar merchant Mizguir, even though Mizguir is madly in love with her and for her sake has deserted his fiancée, the village maiden Koupava.

In the second act the jilted Koupava comes to the palace of the Czar to demand justice. Mizguir is brought before the Czar and offers as his defence the fact that Snegurotchka is so beautiful that none could resist her. Snegurotchka appears. The Czar finds it hard to believe that she is incapable of loving, and he promises a generous dowry to any suitor who can arouse her dormant love before sunrise. Mizguir is freed so that he may have a chance in the contest.

The third act shows a clearing in the sacred forest where the Berendey peasants are celebrating an Arcadian festival. Lel, the shepherd, makes love to Koupava, who consoles herself for Mizguir's desertion by responding. Mizguir makes love to Snegurotchka, and when he presses her too closely a woodland spirit sends him off to chase a vision of Snegurotchka through the thickets. Snegurotchka tries to separate Lel and Koupava, and when she fails, remembers her mother's promise. She hurries off to find Fairy Spring in the valley of Yarilo.

The fourth act takes place in the valley. Snegurotchka stands on the shore of a lake and calls for her mother. Fairy Spring appears and is so moved by her daughter's pleading that she grants her the power to love as a mortal. She warns Snegurotchka to avoid the sun's rays. When Snegurotchka again meets Mizguir she falls in love with him and Mizguir leads her to the Czar, where she confesses her love for

Mizguir. While she is speaking a ray of sunlight falls upon her. She melts in an exaltation of love and disappears. Mizguir curses the cruelty of the gods and throws himself into the lake, while the people sing a hymn to the midsummer sun.

§)&(§

LA SONNAMBULA

(The Sleepwalker)

Vincenzo Bellini

La Sonnambula was Vincenzo Bellini's seventh opera. Composed to a libretto by Félice Romani, it was first produced at the Teatro Carcano, Milan, March 6, 1831. Following its first presentation in America (November 13, 1835, in English at the Park Theatre, New York), it became well known in this country. Once when it was performed at the Park Theatre by a company of Italian, German and English singers (October 22, 1847) it was sung in three languages simultaneously. The opera was frequently parodied in New York. In 1839 it was the subject of a burlesque entitled "The Roof Scrambler," and in 1845 an "Ethiopian Burlesque" called "Lo! som am de Beauties" was offered at Palmo's Opera House.

The cast of *La Sonnambula* includes:

TERESA (*Mezzo-soprano*), a miller
AMINA (*Soprano*), her adopted daughter
ELVINO (*Tenor*), Amina's fiancé
LISA (*Soprano*), an innkeeper, in love with Elvino
ALESSIO (*Bass*), a peasant, in love with Lisa
COUNT RODOLFO (*Bass*)

The action occurs in a Swiss village during the early nineteenth century. The first act shows the village square, where the townsfolk are rejoicing at the forthcoming wedding of Amina and Elvino. Lisa, the innkeeper, does not join the merrymaking, for she, too, is in love with Elvino. The bride and bridegroom come to sign the marriage contract and no sooner has Elvino placed the ring on Amina's finger than a stranger gallops in on horseback. He is actually Count Rodolfo, traveling incognito, on his way to his castle. He is tired and asks lodging at the inn. He is much interested in the festivities and is so attentive to Amina that Elvino becomes jealous. The peasants tell the Count of a ghost that haunts the countryside, but he laughs at their warning and asks Lisa to show him to his room. When he has gone Elvino scolds Amina for showing an interest in the stranger.

The second act takes place in the Count's room at the inn. Lisa comes to ask him if he is comfortable. As she leaves she drops her handkerchief. Presently Amina appears. She is walking in her sleep, and the Count soon discovers that she is not conscious of what she is doing. Lisa is not so charitable, and when she learns that Amina is in the Count's room, she hurries to tell Elvino. The Count is chivalrous and leaves the room by way of a window. Amina lies on the bed, and Elvino and the villagers find her sleeping there. She wakes in astonishment, and is unable to explain matters to Elvino. He throws her aside scornfully.

The third act opens in a valley near the Count's castle. Amina and her foster-mother are on their way to the castle where they will ask the Count to explain the real facts to Elvino. They meet Elvino, who once more denounces Amina and takes her wedding ring from her. The scene changes to the exterior of Teresa's mill. Elvino has proposed marriage to Lisa and is taking her to the church. The Count appears and declares that Amina is innocent, but Elvino will not listen. Teresa then shows Elvino Lisa's handkerchief which was found in the Count's room. Elvino believes that Lisa, too, is faithless. Suddenly Amina appears at the window of the mill, again walking in her sleep. She climbs down over the mill-wheel. As she reaches the ground safely she sings of her love for Elvino, who is now convinced of her innocence. He wakes her with an embrace and joyfully restores the ring to her finger. Everyone is happy except Lisa, who is left only the shame of having had her handkerchief found in the Count's room.

§)&(§

STRADELLA

See Alessandro Stradella

§)&(§

THE SUNKEN BELL

(La Campana Sommersa)

Ottorino Respighi

The libretto of Ottorino Respighi's opera *La Campana Sommersa* was written by Claudio Guastalla, and was adapted from the drama of Gerhart Hauptmann. The opera was first produced at the Stadt-theater, Hamburg, November 18, 1927.

The principal characters are:

HEINRICH (*Tenor*), the Bellcaster
MAGDA (*Soprano*), his wife
RAUTENDELEIN (*Soprano*)
THE WITCH (*Mezzo-soprano*), her grandmother
NICKELMANN (*Baritone*), the old man of the well
THE FAUN (*Tenor*)
THE PASTOR (*Bass*)
THE SCHOOLMASTER (*Baritone*)
THE BARBER (*Tenor*)

The time and the place of the story are legendary. The first act shows a mountain meadow surrounded by pine trees. Rautendelein is sitting on the raised curb of an old well. She is an elf-like creature who is hardly more than a child, and she is talking to Nickelmann, the old man of the well, and to the Faun. The Faun boasts that it was he who wrecked the cart which was carrying the bell to the new church on the top of the mountain. Soon the Bellcaster, Heinrich, appears. He is griefstricken at the loss of his masterpiece which has sunk to the bottom of the lake. Exhausted, Heinrich sinks to the ground. Rautendelein takes pity on him. She longs for the life and pleasures of a mortal, and she falls in love with Heinrich and draws a magic circle about him which will keep others away. Her grandmother, the Witch, cautions her that Heinrich is a mortal and must die, but Rautendelein does not heed the warning. Soon the Pastor, the Schoolmaster, and the Barber come from the village to find Heinrich, but as they approach his sleeping, seemingly dead form, they cannot penetrate the magic circle. The Witch breaks the spell and allows the three villagers to carry Heinrich away. When they have gone Rautendelein can take no pleasure in the games of the elves, and in spite of the warning of the old man of the well, who himself loves her, she goes to the village where mortals live.

The second act shows the living room of Heinrich's home. Magda, his wife, is waiting to hear the first stroke of the new bell from the mountain church. Soon Heinrich is brought home, dying, and he tells Magda of the loss of the bell. Unless he can draw new life from magic sources, he says, he will be unable to create new works. The Pastor brings a strange girl to the house and tells Magda that she will help her take care of the Bellcaster. The girl is Rautendelein and with her love she revives Heinrich and gives him the strength of youth.

The third act shows a hut in the mountains. Heinrich has abandoned his family and is living with Rautendelein. With the help of gnomes, and of Nickelmann and the Faun, he is creating finer and greater works than he has ever made before. The Pastor urges him to return to his family, but Heinrich declares that he is going to build a temple for a new cult which will bring happiness to all. "If I ever deviate from my purpose," he declares, "may the sunken bell toll again!" When the Pastor has gone, Heinrich takes Rautendelein into his arms and kisses her. They are interrupted by the threatening murmur of the villagers who have come to destroy Heinrich, Rautendelein, and the new temple. Heinrich defeats them singlehanded and returns to Rautendelein's embraces. Again they are interrupted, this time by the wraiths of Heinrich's children who carry an urn containing the tears their mother wept as she leapt into the lake, grieving over her husband's unfaithfulness. As the children stand before Heinrich the bell is heard tolling from the bottom of the lake. Heinrich is recalled to his mortal life. He casts Rautendelein aside and rushes out into the darkness.

The last act returns to the scene of the first act, the meadow. Rautendelein has married her first lover, Nickelmann, the old man of the well. Heinrich returns; he must see Rautendelein before he dies. The Witch grants permission, and Rautendelein appears. At first she does not want to recognize Heinrich. Then she reproaches him for having driven her into the well, but as Heinrich dies, she relents and kisses him tenderly.

§)&(§

SUOR ANGELICA
(Sister Angelica)

Giacomo Puccini

This one-act opera by Giacomo Puccini was first performed together with *Il Tabarro* and *Gianni Schicchi,* at the Metropolitan Opera House, New York, December 14, 1918. Its libretto was written by Giovacchino Forzano.

The action takes place at a convent near Florence, Italy, in the seventeenth century. The principal characters are:

SISTER ANGELICA
THE PRINCESS, her aunt
THE ABBESS
THE MISTRESS OF NOVICES
THE SISTER MONITOR

Seven years before the time of the opera, Angelica became involved in a love affair and gave birth to a child. Her family compelled her to enter the convent and she has not heard from any of her relations until now, when the Abbess tells her that her aunt, the Princess, is coming to call on her. The Princess tells Sister Angelica that she has come to have her sign a document which will permit Angelica's younger sister to marry. When Angelica asks about her own child, the aunt replies heartlessly that he died two years ago. Angelica is heartbroken. She drinks poison and then prays to the Virgin not to let her die in mortal sin. A miracle follows. The Virgin appears on the steps of the little church and gently puts the child into Angelica's arms. Angelica dies as the choir of nuns and angels chant "Thou art saved."

§)&(§

IL TABARRO
(The Cloak)

Giacomo Puccini

The libretto of this one-act opera by Giacomo Puccini was adapted by Giuseppe Adami from Didier Gold's play, *La Houppelande*. The opera was first performed at the Metropolitan Opera House, New York, December 14, 1918, in company with *Suor Angelica* and *Gianni Schicchi*.

The scene is laid in present-day Paris and the principal characters are:

MICHELE (*Bass*), a barge-owner
GIORGETTA (*Soprano*), his wife
LUIGI (*Tenor*), a longshoreman

The entire action occurs on Michele's barge. Michele suspects his wife of being in love with Luigi. He hears her arranging with Luigi that she will light a match as a signal when it is safe for him to come to the barge. Later Michele himself lights a match. When Luigi climbs up the side of the barge, Michele strangles him and covers his body with a cloak. Giorgetta comes on deck. She asks Michele if she may rest by him under his cloak. Michele triumphantly throws open the cloak, and Giorgetta shrieks as her lover's body rolls at her feet.

§)&(§

THE TALES OF HOFFMANN

Jacques Offenbach

Jacques Offenbach was famous chiefly for light operas, but his last work, *The Tales of Hoffmann,* is generally accepted as a grand opera. It is known most widely through its *Barcarolle,* but it is still often performed in its entirety in opera houses. The first performance of the opera was given February 10, 1881, shortly after the composer's death, at the Opéra Comique in Paris.

The libretto, by Jules Barbier and Michel Carré, was based on three fantastic stories by the German romance-writer, composer, theatrical manager and lawyer, Ernst Theodor Wilhelm Hoffmann, who lived from 1776 to 1822.

Numerous versions of the Offenbach opera are in existence, and they all differ in detail. The essentials of the plot are common to all of the versions. Hoffmann, the poet, is the central character, and the three acts of the opera show him as the hero in the three different episodes, each based on a story actually written by the real Hoffmann.

In the Prologue Hoffmann is seen at an inn. His friends joke about his being in love with Stella, the leading singer at the opera house. Hoffmann denies it, and tells about three of his former love affairs. Each of these provides the plot for each of the three acts, respectively.

The characters of the first episode are:

HOFFMANN (*Tenor*), the poet
NICLAUS (*Soprano*), his friend
OLYMPIA (*Soprano*), a mechanical doll
SPALANZANI (*Tenor*), an apothecary, who has constructed Olympia
COPPELIUS (*Baritone*), the Devil in the guise of a magician

Spalanzani has constructed Olympia with the aid of Coppelius. She is so lifelike that Spalanzani is exhibiting her to the public as his daughter. When she sings she is so beautiful that Hoffmann falls in love with her. Niclaus tries to dissuade Hoffmann from his mad infatuation but Hoffmann will not listen. Olympia then dances, and something in her mechanism goes wrong. Coppelius becomes angry and smashes Olympia and tells Hoffmann that she is only an automaton.

In the second act the characters again include Hoffmann and Niclaus. The Devil also re-appears, this time in the guise of Dapertutto. The others are:

GIULIETTA (*Soprano*), a courtesan
SCHLEMIL (*Bass*), her lover

The scene is a canal in Venice. Giulietta, the courtesan, is entertaining her friends, and she and Dapertutto sing the famous *Barcarolle*—"Oh, Night of Love." Hoffmann appears and immediately falls in love with Giulietta, disregarding the advice of his friend, Niclaus. Giulietta has a lover, Schlemil, who has sold his soul to Dapertutto. Dapertutto is eager to possess Hoffmann's soul, so he has Giulietta persuade Hoffmann to exchange it for her love. Giulietta tells Hoffmann that he may have the key to her bedroom if he can get it away from her present lover, Schlemil. Hoffmann challenges Schlemil and kills him in a duel. Then he sees the faithless Giulietta sail down the canal in the arms of Dapertutto.

In the third act Hoffmann meets the devil for a third time, now in the person of Dr. Miracle. He also meets:

ANTONIA (*Soprano*), and CRESPEL (*Bass*), her father

Antonia's mother was a singer. Antonia, herself, would like to sing, but she is a consumptive and her father, Crespel has forbidden it, for he is afraid that the exertion will be too much for her lungs. Hoffmann is very much in love with Antonia, and being fond of music, he waits to hear her voice. Dr. Miracle conjures up a vision of Antonia's mother, who begs the girl to sing. Antonia obeys, and overtaxing her strength, dies in Hoffmann's arms. Whereas Hoffmann had been astonished by the outcome of his first love affair and disillusioned by the second, this time he is truly heartbroken.

The Epilogue of the opera returns to the tavern, where Hoffmann has finished telling his companions of his three loves, where first he worshipped beauty, then was overcome with lust, and finally met pure love. Each time he was thwarted by the Devil. Now he has had enough. He is very drunk by this time, and falls asleep with his bottle, dreaming of the Muse who never is unfaithful and who from now on will be his only love.

§)&(§

TANNHÄUSER
Richard Wagner

Richard Wagner's *Tannhäuser* was first produced at the Hoftheater in Dresden, October 19, 1845, a little less than three years after the first production of *The Flying Dutchman.* Wagner wrote the libretto for *Tannhäuser,* basing his plot on Scandinavian legends.

The principal characters are:

TANNHÄUSER (*Tenor*), a knight and minstrel
WOLFRAM VON ESCHENBACH (*Baritone*), his friend
HERMANN (*Bass*), Landgrave of Thuringia
ELIZABETH (*Soprano*), his niece
VENUS (*Soprano*)

The action occurs at Thuringia and the Wartburg in the thirteenth century. Tannhäuser, a minstrel knight, has sought refuge from the cares of the world in the Hill of Venus, at Thuringia. It is there that the Goddess of Love holds court in the midst of eternal revelry, and destroys the souls of men who fall victim to her charms. As the first act opens at the Hill of Venus, Tannhäuser has dwelt with Venus for a whole year, and has become satiated with the monotonous joys of love. He longs to return to his earthly life with its mingled pain and joy. He begs Venus to release him, and although she offers him still new diversion, he pleads eloquently for his freedom. Venus finally relents, but warns Tannhäuser that he will return to her. The scene changes to a valley between the Wartburg and the Horselburg. Tannhäuser watches a party of Pilgrims, singing the "Pilgrims' Chorus," as they make their way to Rome. He falls on his knees in prayer, and is discovered by a party of minstrel knights led by the Landgrave. They recognize Tannhäuser as their long-lost member who had left them because he had been unsuccessful in a song contest. Wolfram tells Tannhäuser that even though he may not have won the contest, his singing has won the heart of the Landgrave's niece Elizabeth, whom Wolfram himself loved unsuccessfully. Tannhäuser agrees to join the knights in a song contest that is to be held at the Wartburg.

The second act shows a hall in the Wartburg. Elizabeth has heard that Tannhäuser has returned, and she sings joyfully: *Dich theure Halle, gruss ich wieder.* ("Oh! Hall of Song, I greet thee again.") Wolfram brings Tannhäuser to her. Presently the knights assemble for the song contest. Wolfram sings first—a song in praise of pure and ethereal love. Tannhäuser replies to Wolfram's song by singing of the sensuous, carnal love he has enjoyed with Venus. The knights are shocked and uphold Wolfram's conception of love. Tannhäuser continues with a song in praise of Venus herself, and the knights are so enraged that they rush at Tannhäuser with drawn swords. Elizabeth saves Tannhäuser from the knights. The chorus of the Pilgrims is heard in the distance. Tannhäuser becomes penitent once more, and decides to join the Pilgrims in their journey to Rome where he will ask for forgiveness.

The third act shows the valley of the Wartburg. Elizabeth is kneeling before a shrine. The Pilgrims are returning from Rome. Elizabeth questions them but can learn nothing about Tannhäuser. She sings a prayer to the Virgin. Wolfram joins her and asks to accompany her in the pilgrimage she is making to dedicate herself to the Virgin. Elizabeth is grateful but tells Wolfram she will go alone. Wolfram sadly sings his "Song of the Evening Star," and when he has finished he encounters Tannhäuser, haggard and in rags. As Venus had prophesied, Tannhäuser is planning to return to the Venusberg. He tells Wolfram of his reception by the Pope, of how he has not been pardoned, but has been told that it would be as impossible for him to be absolved as it would be for his Pilgrim's staff to put forth fresh leaves. Venus appears in a vision and beckons to Tannhäuser. Wolfram pleads with Tannhäuser and reminds him of Elizabeth. Tannhäuser finally resists Venus, and a band of mourners comes with a bier holding the body of Elizabeth. Tannhäuser kneels beside the bier, and as he himself dies a second band of Pilgrims returning from Rome brings news of a miracle. The Pilgrim's staff which Tannhäuser left in Rome has brought forth fresh leaves.

§)&(§

THE TELEPHONE

Gian-Carlo Menotti

Gian-Carlo Menotti composed both the libretto and music for the one-act opera, *The Telephone*. It was first performed as a curtain raiser for Menotti's *The Medium*, when that work was presented by the Ballet Society at the Heckscher Theatre in New York, February 18, 1947. Starting May 1, 1947, the two operas were given a Broadway production at the Ethel Barrymore Theatre in New York, and enjoyed a continuous run of nightly performances.

There are only two characters in *The Telephone*, LUCY (*Soprano*) and BEN (*Baritone*). Lucy is a lady who is so addicted to the use of the telephone that the only way Ben can talk with her long enough to propose marriage is to leave her house and go to the nearest phone booth and call her on the telephone. She accepts him and he writes down her number so that he can call her every day while he is away on a business trip.

§)&(§

THE TEMPLE DANCER

John Adam Hugo

The Temple Dancer, music by John Adam Hugo, was first presented at the Metropolitan Opera House, New York, March 12, 1919. In 1922 it was performed in Chicago and in 1925 at Honolulu. The libretto by Jutta Bell-Ranske, tells of a dancer in the temple of the God Mahadeo. She loves a man of different religion who is in dire need. To help him the dancer plans to steal from the temple the jewels which are purchased through the prostitution of the temple dancers.

The two principal characters are:

THE TEMPLE DANCER (*Soprano*)
THE TEMPLE GUARD (*Tenor*)

The opera is written in one act. As the curtain rises, a service is being held in the temple. When it is over the Dancer enters in disguise. As she is taking the jewels the Guard discovers her. To protect herself she winds the holy snake about her body and performs a seductive dance. The Guard is aroused by her beauty and offers protection if she will yield to him. As the Dancer loosens her outer robe the Guard discovers a letter from the Dancer's lover, which tells of the plan to steal the jewels. The Guard curses the Dancer. She pretends to faint, and begs for a drink of water.

After she has sipped the water, the Dancer secretly drops poison into the cup, and begs the Guard to drink to her courage in meeting death. The Guard drains the cup laughingly and dies. The Dancer seizes the jewels and is struck dead by lightning at the feet of the Guard.

§)&(§

THAÏS

Jules Massenet

A novel by Anatole France was the basis for Jules Massenet's opera, *Thaïs,* and the libretto was written by Louis Gallet. The opera was first performed at the Grand Opéra in Paris, March 16, 1894.

The plot concerns Athanael, a member of the Cenobites, which was a group of monks who lived together in the desert of Thebes during the early Christian era. In his attempt to reform a courtesan this Cenobite monk falls deeply in love with her. The cast includes:

ATHANAEL (*Baritone*), a Cenobite monk
NICIAS (*Tenor*), a young voluptuary
THAÏS (*Soprano*), a courtesan
PALEMON (*Bass*), head monk of the Cenobites

The first act begins at the Cenobite huts on the banks of the Nile. Athanael returns from Alexandria, where he has gone to protest against the sinful ways of the city. He is weary and discouraged, for he has made little headway against the ruling spirit of the town, a beautiful courtesan named Thaïs. Athanael plans to return to Alexandria and to convert Thaïs. When he falls asleep he sees her in his dreams, posing half-naked before a crowd in the Alexandria theatre. Athanael wakens and, gathering his fellow-monks, tells them that he going back to Alexandria immediately. His companions warn him against such an errand, but he will not listen.

The scene changes to the house of Nicias in Alexandria. Nicias welcomes his former friend, Athanael, even though Athanael is dressed humbly and shabbily. The monk tells Nicias of his errand. Nicias is scornful. He tells Athanael that he himself is paying extravagantly for the privilege of being the accepted lover of Thaïs. Nevertheless, he will help his old friend. He is giving a dinner that very evening for Thaïs. Athanael shall attend it, and in order that he may be suitably robed to meet Thaïs in luxurious surroundings, Nicias' slaves will clothe him in purple and fine linen. Thaïs arrives and when Athanael tells her bluntly that he has come to bring her to the only true God, she tries to allure him with her smiles. She poses in the manner in which she appeared in Athanael's dream. The monk is horrified, but Thaïs tells him that if he will come to her house she will listen to him.

The second act opens in Thaïs's house. Thaïs returns from the banquet, weary of fugitive love. She prays to Venus for eternal beauty. Then she awaits Athanael, who she hopes will be her next lover. Athanael pauses at the door, spellbound at her beauty. Then he comes into the room and tells Thaïs that the love he offers is from God. At first she answers him flippantly, but as he continues and tells her that the joys of eternal life are infinitely greater than the sordid pleasures of the world, she is impressed by his earnestness. Yet she is frightened, and when the voice of Nicias is heard outside she becomes defiant. Athanael is patient, and tells Thaïs that he will pass the night on her doorstep. As the scene changes to the outside of Thaïs's house the orchestra plays the beautiful "Meditation" which is the symbol of Thaïs's conversion. In the next scene Athanael is asleep on the doorstep. Sounds of revelry come from the house, but soon Thaïs appears at the door. She is ready to follow Athanael, who offers to take her to a monastery. He insists that she destroy everything connected with her former life, and when she asks if she may not take with her a small statue of Eros, he smashes it to the ground and orders her to go inside and set fire to all her earthly possessions. Nicias and his companions come from a house across the street. Nicias has won a fortune at the gambling table, and he leads his friends in singing and dancing. Soon flames burst from Thaïs's house, and she appears, dressed in humble clothing. As she joins Athanael, the crowd threatens the monk and tries to take Thaïs from him. Nicias comes to rescue by throwing handfuls of gold coins to the crowd. Athanael and Thaïs escape while the people are scrambling and fighting for the gold.

The third act shows an oasis in the desert. Thaïs is exhausted from the long journey, and Athanael tenderly bathes her bleeding feet and brings her water to drink. The nuns come singing the *Pater Noster* and Athanael gives Thaïs into their care. She and Athanael bid each other farewell, Thaïs spiritually exalted and Athanael filled with earthly love. The scene changes to the Cenobite colony, where the returning Athanael is congratulated on the success of his mission. He is deeply troubled, and he confesses to Palemon, the chief monk, that in spite of his prayers, he is deeply in love with Thaïs. Palemon leaves Athanael to his prayers, and then Athanael sees a vision of Thaïs, first as a courtesan and then dying at the monastery. He rushes to the desert with a cry of grief.

The fourth act (sometimes performed as the third scene

of Act Three) shows the gardens of the monastery where Thaïs lies dying, surrounded by the nuns. Worn with penance she has come to be looked upon as a saint. Athanael comes to her and tries to revive her so that she will return to earthly love. She repeats to the monk the phrases that he used in converting her, then she looks toward Heaven and dies as she calls to God. Athanael falls to the ground with a despairing cry.

§)&(§

TIEFLAND
(Lowland)

Eugene d'Albert

The celebrated pianist-composer Eugene d'Albert wrote sixteen operas, of which *Tiefland* was the sixth. It was first produced at the German Theatre, Prague, November 15, 1903, and its libretto was adapted by Rudolph Lothar from Angel Guimerá's Spanish play, *Terra baixa*.

The principal characters are:

SEBASTIANO (*Baritone*), a rich landowner
TOMMASO (*Bass*), a village patriarch
PEDRO (*Tenor*), a shepherd
MARTHA (*Mezzo-soprano*), a village girl
NURI (*Soprano*), a village girl

The plot concerns the shepherd Pedro, who has lived for as long as he can remember in the rocky fastness of the Pyrenees. Every night he has prayed to the Holy Mother to send him a wife. Sebastiano, the landowner, has a mistress, Martha, for whom he is anxious to find a husband so that he himself may marry a wealthy heiress. Pedro seems to be the answer to his problem, so in the Prologue of the opera, Sebastiano takes Martha to Pedro in the mountains, and tells him that he may have her for his wife if he will come to live in the lowlands. Pedro is delighted at the fufillment of his prayers and readily consents. Martha is less eager for marriage, and she refuses even to look at Pedro.

The first act shows the interior of a mill. Sebastiano's retainers are gossiping about their master's discarding his mistress and passing her on to Pedro. For Pedro, happily unaware of the truth, they have nothing but scorn. The marriage ceremony is performed and the villainous Sebastiano plans to pay his usual nightly visit to Martha's apartment, even though it is Pedro's and Martha's wedding night. Martha tries to avoid Sebastiano by not entering her room. She also repulses Pedro, even though his kindly, gentle ways are beginning to make her love him. Pedro is merely confused.

The second act shows the same scene, early the next morning. Nuri, a village girl, tells Pedro that she is knitting him a fine jersey. Martha becomes jealous of Nuri and drives her away. Pedro follows Nuri, and Martha, distraught, confesses the situation to old Tommaso, the village patriarch. Tommaso advises Martha to explain everything to Pedro, for the wise old man knows that Pedro really loves her. Pedro tells Martha that he is returning to his solitude in the mountains. Martha begs Pedro to take her with him. After a mental struggle in which he tries to kill Martha, Pedro relents, and he and Martha prepare to flee to the mountains together. Sebastiano arrives, boisterously congratulating the couple on their marriage. Then he sarcastically commands Martha to dance to the strumming of his guitar. Pedro, enraged, rushes at Sebastiano, but is held back by the villagers.

In the third act, still in the same scene, word of Sebastiano's conduct has reached the ears of his wealthy fiancee, and she has rejected him. This makes Sebastiano even more desirous of Martha, but Martha has come really to love Pedro. She repulses Sebastiano and calls for Pedro, who bursts savagely into the room. Pedro and Sebastiano fight with bare hands, and Pedro finally throws Sebastiano dead to the ground. Pedro calls for the villagers and asks them why they do not still laugh. Then he takes Martha in his arms and carries her off to the mountains.

§)&(§

TOSCA

Giacomo Puccini

Tosca was Giacomo Puccini's fifth opera. Its libretto was founded on a play by Victorien Sardou, and was written by Luigi Illica and Giuseppe Giacosa. The opera was first produced in the Teatro Costanzi at Rome, January 14, 1900.

The characters include:

FLORIA TOSCA (*Soprano*), a famous singer
MARIO CAVARADOSSI (*Tenor*), a painter
BARON SCARPIA (*Baritone*), Chief of Police
CESARE ANGELOTTI (*Bass*), a revolutionary, escaped from prison
SPOLETTA (*Tenor*), a police agent
A SACRISTAN (*Baritone*)

The action takes place at Rome in the month of June, 1800, and the first act shows the interior of the Church of Sant'Andrea alla Valle. As the curtain rises Angelotti appears in convict's clothes. He has escaped from prison and has been directed to the foot of the Madonna by his sister, the Attavanti. He takes refuge in the Attavanti chapel at the right of the stage. Mario, the painter, comes to resume work on a picture he is painting of the Madonna. He has used as a model for the face of the Virgin an unknown lady who has come regularly to the church to pray. He compares her likeness to a miniature he carries of his sweetheart, Tosca, and is impressed by their similarity. He sings the aria, *Recondita armonia* ("Sweet Harmony"), and muses on the strange way their separate features blend into an harmonious whole. Angelotti comes from hiding and appeals to Mario for help in escaping and for food. They are old friends, and Mario gives him the contents of his own lunch basket. It then develops that the unknown model is Angelotti's sister, the Attavanti. Angelotti dresses in the women's clothes his sister had left for him in the chapel, and hides hurriedly, carelessly dropping a fan belonging to his sister. Tosca comes to see her lover, Mario, and is jealously disturbed when she recognizes the likeness of the Attavanti in the picture Mario is painting. Mario quiets her and promises to meet her at her cottage. When Tosca has gone he goes to help Angelotti escape. Scarpia, the chief of police, appears. Angelotti has been tracked to the church. Scarpia finds the fan which Angelotti dropped and when Tosca returns, he shows it to her. Through her jealous outburst, Scarpia learns that Mario has been there too, and that he must be an accomplice in Angelotti's escape. When Tosca leaves, Scarpia orders his agents to follow her, and as the choir chants a *Te Deum* he kneels in mock prayer, muttering that through the destruction of Mario he will himself gain possession of Tosca.

The second act shows the apartments of Scarpia. He is waiting for news of Mario and Angelotti. He hears Tosca singing for a party the Queen is holding on the terrace below, and he sends her a message that he has word of Mario. Spoletta, Scarpia's agent, comes to say that Angelotti cannot be found, but that Mario has been captured. Mario is brought in and refuses to tell where Angelotti is hiding. Scarpia orders him to the torture chamber. Tosca appears and Scarpia greets her effusively. He tells her that her lover is being tortured in the next room. He opens the door so that she may hear Mario's cries. Mario shouts to Tosca to tell nothing, but she cannot endure the sound and sight of Mario's agony. Finally, she tells where Angelotti is hidden. Mario, exhausted, is again brought in. The scene is interrupted by a messenger bearing news that Napoleon has defeated the Italian troops. Mario revives sufficiently to hear the news and is so rejoiced that the Italian tyrants may be overthrown that he gives a shout of victory. For this treason Scarpia condemns Mario to death. When Mario has been led away, Scarpia makes love to Tosca. She weeps as she refuses him and sings the aria *Vissi d'arte* ("Love and Music") in which she pleads that she has given her life to art and love, that she has been devout and charitable, and does not deserve such cruelty. Tosca continues to resist Scarpia. She sees a dagger lying on his desk. She tells Scarpia that she will yield to him if he will cancel the order for Mario's execution and will give to Mario and herself a passport to leave the country. Scarpia says he cannot cancel the execution, but he will instruct Spoletta to arrange a mock shooting, in which Mario can pretend to drop dead and later escape. He whispers secret instructions to Spoletta and then draws up the passport. While he is writing Tosca takes the dagger from his desk. When he takes her in his arms she forces the knife into his body, crying, "Thus will Tosca yield her kisses!" She places candles at the head of the dead Scarpia and crosses herself as she quietly leaves the room.

The third act shows the terrace of San Angelo castle. Mario is brought from his cell, and is told that he has only an hour to live. He sings the aria *E lucevan le stelle* ("Stars were shining"), as a farewell to his beloved and to his art. Tosca tells him that she has killed Scarpia, and that she persuaded him to order a mock execution. Laughingly they plan that Mario will pretend to fall and when he is left for dead they will use the passport for escape. The execution is staged and Mario falls. When the firing squad has gone, Tosca rushes to Mario and tells him all is safe. He does not answer, and Tosca discovers that he has really been shot. She throws herself on his body just before Spoletta approaches with soldiers. Scarpia's body has been found and they are coming for her as the murderess. Before they can capture her, Tosca climbs to a parapet of the castle and leaps to her death.

§)&(§

DIE TOTE STADT
(The Dead City)
Erich Korngold

Die Tote Stadt, music by Erich Korngold, was first produced at Hamburg, Germany, December 4, 1920. Less than a year later, November 19, 1921, it was presented at the Metropolitan Opera House, New York, with Maria Jeritza in the leading soprano role.

The libretto of the opera was written by Paul Schott, who founded it on a play by Georges Rodenbach, entitled *Bruges-la-mort*. The plot concerns a bereaved husband who lives chiefly in the past, and who cherishes above all else the memory of his dead wife. Appropriately the action is set against a background of the Belgian city, Bruges, which at the time of the opera, the late eighteenth century, has not yet regained the dominant position it lost after the sixteenth century. In effect, it is a dead city.

The cast includes:

PAUL (*Tenor*), a widower
FRANK (*Baritone*), his friend
BRIGITTA (*Contralto*), his servant
MARIETTA (*Soprano*), a dancer

The three acts of the opera are called "pictures," for they are mostly dream sequences which occur within the single setting of Paul's living room in his house at Bruges. At the beginning Paul's servant, Brigitta, admits Paul's friend, Frank. While Frank waits for Paul, Brigitta tells him of the morbid life Paul leads, thinking only of his wife and the past, and cherishing above everything else her pictures, long locks of her hair, and various of her possessions. Paul greets Frank enthusiastically, and tells him that Marie, his wife, still lives. He has seen a woman in Bruges who is like her in every feature. He does not know who she is, but he will soon find out, for he has asked her to visit him. Frank warns Paul against worshipping a phantom, and leaves, advising his friend to let the dead sleep in peace. Marietta arrives. She is a dancer belonging to a traveling opera company and is a living image of Marie. Paul is fascinated as Marietta drapes Marie's scarf about her and plays on Marie's lute. They are interrupted by the voices of Marietta's companions outside, and Marietta realizes that it is time for her rehearsal, where she is to dance the part of Helen in *Robert the Devil*. When she has gone Paul falls asleep in an armchair facing Marie's portrait. Soon Marie steps from the frame and warns him that Marietta is another woman, but Paul in his dream cannot distinguish between them, and, as Marie disappears, he sees Marietta dancing a seductive dance in the theatre.

In the second picture Paul is still dreaming in the armchair. He watches himself walking near the house where Marietta is staying. He sees his friend Frank as an imaginary rival and quarrels with him. In a succession of episodes he watches a party serenade Marietta, and sees her dance wantonly. When Marietta impersonates a nun in a profane manner, Paul can stand by no longer and tries to tear from her the winding cloth she is wearing. Marietta of the dream knows that it is Marie, and not herself, whom Paul is worshipping, and she determines to triumph over the dead woman and to make Paul love her for herself. She persuades Paul to take her to his home.

The third picture shows the dreaming Paul watching himself at home with Marietta. She is determined that she will make Paul love her, and challenges him by winding Marie's hair about her and dancing madly about the room. Paul can stand such a desecration no longer and in a frenzied rage he strangles Marietta. At this point the real Paul awakes from his dream in the armchair and realizes that he has been living through a horrible nightmare. Marietta returns, as though she had just gone away. She has come to get the flowers she had left. Paul hands the flowers to her without comment, and she leaves shrugging her shoulders. Frank returns, and again urges Paul to leave Bruges and start life anew. This time Paul agrees.

LA TRAVIATA

Giuseppe Verdi

The libretto of Giuseppe Verdi's opera, *La Traviata,* was adapted by Francesco Maria Piave from the famous play by Alexandre Dumas, *fils, La Dame aux Camélias,* known in English as *Camille.* The opera was first performed in Venice at the Teatro La Fenice, March 6, 1853.

The principal characters are:

VIOLETTA VALERY (*Soprano*), a courtesan
ALFREDO GERMONT (*Tenor*), her lover
GIORGIO GERMONT (*Baritone*), Alfredo's father
FLORA BELOIX (*Soprano*), a friend of Violetta's
BARON DOUPHAL (*Baritone*), a former lover of Violetta's
DR. GRENVILLE (*Bass*)

The action occurs in Paris and its suburbs about 1700. The first act shows the salon of the notorious courtesan, Violetta. In the midst of a gay party Alfredo is presented to Violetta as one of her admirers. At her request he sings her a jolly drinking song. Alfredo dances with Violetta, and presently she becomes faint, showing symptoms of the consumption that is later to cause her death. She tells the guests to go on with the dancing, and as they pass into another room, she talks alone with Alfredo. His solicitude for her health is so sincere that she realizes he is really in love with her. They sing a love duet: *Un di felice* ("O Rapturous Moment!"). When Alfredo and the other guests have gone, Violetta thinks about this new emotion that has come over her. For the first time in her life she is the object of true love. She sings the aria *Ah fors'è lui* ("The one of whom I dreamed"). Then she remembers that she is only a courtesan and realizes that such an affair can lead only to tragedy. As she sings *Semper libera* ("Ever free shall I still wander") she determines to shut true love out of her life, and to wander madly from pleasure to pleasure.

The first scene of the second act shows the interior of a villa near Paris. Violetta has abandoned her life of pleasure and is living quietly with Alfredo. Alfredo learns by chance that Violetta is selling her house in Paris to pay the expenses of the villa. He cannot tolerate such a state of affairs and he leaves for Paris, hoping to raise some funds of his own. While he is away Giorgio Germont, Alfredo's father, calls on Violetta. He tells her that his son's affair with a woman of her reputation will ruin the young man. Violetta greets Germont with such a calm dignity that the father is disarmed. He drops his arrogant manner and pleads with her. He tells her that Alfredo's sister is about to marry a noble. If Alfredo's affair with Violetta becomes known, the noble will refuse to marry Alfredo's sister. Violetta is touched by Germont's appeal. She writes Alfredo a note and asks her maid to give it to him when he returns. When Alfredo returns he finds Violetta gone. Germont tries to console his son, but Alfredo believes that Violetta has willfully deceived him, and he rushes out to follow her to Paris. The scene changes to a salon in the house of Flora, one of Violetta's friends. A masked ball is in progress. Alfredo is gambling and winning large stakes. Violetta has again become the mistress of a former lover, Baron Douphal, and when she enters on the Baron's arm, Alfredo denounces her. He flings at her feet the money he has won and calls upon the assembly to witness that he has paid back the money Violetta spent on him when they were living together. Alfredo's father reproves him for such heartless conduct. Alfredo realizes that Violetta really loves him, and he is filled with remorse for insulting her.

The third act is laid in Violetta's bedroom. Violetta is very ill. The doctor tells Annina, the maid, that her mistress is in the last stages of consumption and has only a few hours to live. Meanwhile Germont has told Alfredo that Violetta's return to her former life was a sacrifice on her part, made voluntarily so that she would not ruin Alfredo's life and his sister's marriage. Alfredo comes to Violetta in her illness and she clasps him in her arms. Together they sing the duet *Parigi, O Caro* ("Beloved Paris") and they resolve that they will never part again. The exertion is too much for Violetta. She gives Alfredo her portrait and as she tells him to remember her by it, she dies in his arms.

§)&(§

TRISTAN UND ISOLDE

Richard Wagner

Richard Wagner's *Tristan und Isolde* was first performed at the Hoftheater in Munich, June 10, 1865. Its libretto was written by Wagner himself. The story is based on an old legend which has been treated by many poets, by the German Gottfried von Strassburg, by Matthew Arnold, Swinburne, Tennyson, and others. In Wagner's opera the principal characters are:

KING MARK OF CORNWALL (*Bass*)
TRISTAN (*Tenor*), his nephew
ISOLDE (*Soprano*), Princess of Ireland
BRANGÄNE (*Mezzo-soprano*), her friend and attendant
KURWENAL (*Baritone*), Tristan's servant
MELOT (*Tenor*), a courtier

The action occurs in ancient times in Cornwall, Brittany, and at sea.

Before the opera begins certain events have taken place which form the background of the plot. Tristan, fighting for Cornwall against the Irish, has slain Sir Morold who was betrothed to the Irish Princess Isolde. Tristan himself was wounded, and learning that the Princess was skilled in the use of balms for healing, he disguised himself and went to her for aid. She was glad to help him, until she learned that he was the man who had killed her lover. Then as she was about to strike him their eyes met, and she became powerless against him. She kept the secret of his identity, completed his cure, and helped him escape. Later Tristan returned to Ireland, this time under his true name, and with a mission from his uncle, King Mark of Cornwall. The King had chosen Isolde for his wife and had sent Tristan to bring her from Ireland. Isolde's parents were eager for the match, for they knew it would bring peace between Ireland and Cornwall. Although she secretly loved Tristan, Isolde felt that she must accompany him to Cornwall and marry the King.

The opera opens on the deck of the ship on which Tristan and Isolde are returning to Cornwall. Isolde is torn between her secret love for Tristan and her hatred for him as the slayer of her lover, Morold. She decides that both she and Tristan shall die by poison. She orders her attendant Brangäne to prepare a draught. Brangäne mixes instead a love potion. Tristan and Isolde drink it and behold each other first in amazement and then in ecstasy. They embrace as the ship approaches the shores of Cornwall.

The second act is laid in the garden of King Mark's palace. Isolde and the King have been married, and the King is away on a hunting expedition. Brangäne tells Isolde that the King is suspicious of her love for Tristan, and that the hunting trip is a ruse. Melot, the courier, is watching Tristan and Isolde and hopes to trap them while the King is supposedly absent. Isolde refuses to heed the warning. She signals to Tristan and when he comes he and Isolde are oblivious to everything but each other. Kurwenal, Tristan's servant, warns that the King is approaching. He is too late, for King Mark and Melot surprise Tristan and Isolde and find them together. The King reproaches Tristan, but despises Melot's trickery still more than Tristan's faithlessness. Tristan challenges Melot and is fatally wounded in the fight that follows.

The third act shows Tristan's castle in Brittany. Kurwenal has brought the wounded Tristan home. He has sent for Isolde, hoping that she may use successfully her art of healing. When Isolde arrives, the delirious Tristan rises and tears the bandages from his wounds. As Isolde approaches him he falls into her arms and dies. King Mark and Melot arrive soon after Isolde. Their real mission is to forgive and unite the lovers, but Kurwenal does not know this and kills Melot. Melot's soldiers kill Kurwenal, and King Mark finds Isolde dying of grief beside her dead lover. Isolde sings the beautiful *Liebestod* ("Love death"), and dies as King Mark prays over her body.

§)&(§

IL TROVATORE
(The Troubadour)
Giuseppe Verdi

Il Trovatore was first produced at the Teatro Apollo in Rome, January 19, 1853. A little more than two years later,

May 2, 1855, it was given its first American performance at the Academy of Music, New York. The libretto of the opera was written by Salvatore Cammarano, and was based on a Spanish play by A. García Gutiérrez.

The plot is founded on a situation similar to the basic idea of *The Bohemian Girl*: a child of noble parents is reared by gypsies and grows up without knowing his real origin.

The cast includes the following characters:

COUNT DI LUNA (*Baritone*)
COUNTESS LEONORA (*Soprano*), in love with MANRICO, and also courted by COUNT DI LUNA
AZUCENA (*Contralto*), a gypsy
MANRICO (*Tenor*), actually GARZIA, the twin brother of COUNT DI LUNA, but supposedly a gypsy who has become a wandering troubadour
FERRANDO (*Bass*), a servant to COUNT DI LUNA

In the opening scene of the first act Ferrando tells his fellow servants the story of their master's younger brother, Garzia. When Garzia was a small child, his nurse awoke one night to find a gypsy hag singing by his bed. The nurse summoned the servants of the household and the gypsy was thrown out. Soon Garzia's health began to fail and it was assumed that the hag had cast a spell over him. She was captured and condemned to be burned at the stake. Meanwhile Garzia disappeared, and when the gypsy was burned the charred remains of a young infant were found around the stake. The father of the two boys refused to believe that it was Garzia who was burned. He had a presentiment that his younger son was still living, and on his deathbed he made his older son, the present Count di Luna, promise that he would keep on searching for Garzia. The second scene shows the garden of the Count's palace. Leonora is with Inez, her attendant, and is waiting for the handsome troubadour, Manrico, who has been serenading her. Inez warns Leonora against falling in love with the troubadour, for she knows that the Count di Luna is in love with Leonora, and she fears trouble. Leonora replies that she would rather die than give up Manrico. She and Inez retire to Leonora's apartments and the Count enters. He is about to call Leonora when he hears the troubadour playing on his lute. Manrico enters and sings a *Romanza* in which he begs Leonora to love him. Meanwhile the Count has stepped aside and has covered himself with his cloak. Leonora comes from the palace, and mistaking the cloaked figure of the Count for Manrico, goes to him, crying "My beloved!" Manrico shouts "deceiver" and Leonora, realizing her mistake, confesses her love for Manrico. The Count challenges Manrico and they retire to fight a duel.

The second act shows the gypsy camp. The gypsies are at work and as they strike their hammers on the anvils they sing the "Anvil Chorus." Azucena is seated near the fire, and Manrico, wrapped in a cloak, is lying on a mattress. Azucena is supposedly Manrico's mother, but she confesses to him that she is only his foster-mother. It was her own mother who was executed for casting a spell over Count di Luna's brother, and she tells Manrico that instead of throwing into the flames the noble child, she had by mistake sent her own son to destruction. Manrico asks, "Then who am I?", but Azucena has told enough; she reminds him that she has been a tender and true mother to him. Then he and Azucena talk of recent events. Manrico has been the victor in the duel with Count di Luna, but has spared the Count's life. Manrico escaped and joined an army that was opposing the forces of Count di Luna. He was severely wounded in battle and left for dead. Azucena found him, brought him back to the gypsy camp and has now nursed him back to life. Azucena commands Manrico to avenge her for the loss of her real son. A messenger appears, bringing news that Leonora, believing Manrico to be dead, is about to take the veil at a convent. Although Manrico is not yet fully recovered from his wounds, he puts on his armor and hurries off. The second scene shows the convent. Count di Luna waits outside with his troops, planning to kidnap Leonora before she takes her vows. He sings an aria about the happiness he will soon have *Il balen del suo* ("Of her smile"). Inside, the nuns are heard singing and outside the Count's followers shout simultaneously of their own plans to capture Leonora. As the nuns come from the convent with Leonora, she stops to say farewell to her attendant, Inez, and just as she turns to enter the chapel, the Count and his men rush at her. At the same time Manrico appears with his soldiers. They overcome the Count and his men and rescue Leonora.

The third act opens in the Count's military camp. He is besieging Castellor, the stronghold to which Manrico has taken Leonora. Azucena tries to get through the enemy lines to reach Manrico, but she is captured and taken before the Count. Ferrando, the old servant, recognizes her. In her confusion she calls for Manrico, and the Count believes that she is Manrico's mother. Ferrando accuses her of having caused the death of the Count's brother, and the Count orders that she be burned at once. The scene changes to a hall adjoining the chapel at Castellor. Even though the Count is likely to attack the stronghold at any moment, Manrico and Leonora are about to be married. After Manrico has sung an aria declaring his devotion, the music of the chapel organ announces the beginning of the marriage service. Manrico takes his bride's hand and starts toward the altar when a messenger interrupts with the news that Azucena has been captured and is at that moment being led to the stake. Manrico seizes his sword, summons his soldiers, and shouts his rage and horror in the great aria, *Di quella pira* ("Of that dark scaffold").

The fourth act shows first the outside of a prison tower at the Count's castle. Manrico has been captured in the battle to save Azucena and has been sentenced to death. Leonora listens to the *Miserere,* first chanted by a chorus and then by Manrico, bidding farewell to Leonora. She pleads with the Count to spare Manrico, and offers to give herself to the Count if he will only let Manrico live. The Count accepts her offer, but Leonora thwarts him by secretly drinking a vial of poison. The scene changes to the interior of the prison. Azucena lies asleep on a couch and Manrico watches over her. Leonora staggers into the room and warns Manrico to save himself. She falls dead and when the Count comes he finds that he has been cheated of his prize. He orders Manrico executed immediately. Manrico is taken away and the Count drags Azucena to the window where she must watch her son's death. As the headsman's ax falls, Azucena tells the Count that Manrico was his own brother. Then she cries "Thou art avenged, O mother!"

§)&(§

THE TRUMPETER OF SÄKKINGEN

Viktor Nessler

The libretto of Viktor Nessler's *The Trumpeter of Säkkingen* was written by Rudolf Bunge, who founded it upon a poem by Joseph Victor von Scheffel. The opera was first produced at the Stadttheater in Leipzig, May 4, 1884.

The characters include:

WERNER KIRCHHOF (*Baritone*), a student
CONRADIN (*Baritone*), a trooper
THE MAJOR-DOMO (*Tenor*)
THE RECTOR MAGNIFICUS (*Bass*), of Heidelberg University
THE BARON OF SCHÖNAU (*Bass*)
MARGARETHA (*Soprano*), his daughter
THE COUNT OF WILDENSTEIN (*Bass*)
THE COUNTESS (*Mezzo-soprano*), the Count's divorced wife, cousin of the Baron
DAMIAN (*Tenor*), the Count's son by a second marriage

The action takes place in Heidelberg and Säkkingen toward the end of, and after, the Thirty Year's War. The Prologue shows the courtyard of the Castle at Heidelberg. At one side students are drinking and at the other side soldiers are making merry. The Major-domo demands quiet but neither soldiers nor students pay any attention to him. Werner, a student, climbs upon a table and borrowing a trumpet from the trooper Conradin plays a love song. The soldiers are delighted with the performance and try to get Werner to join them. Finally the roistering becomes so noisy that the Rector of the University tries to quiet the students. They make fun of him and are expelled. Werner and his fellow-students decide to join the army.

The first act shows a square in Säkkingen. It is now the year 1650 and the war is over. Conradin has entered the service of the city. He welcomes Werner, who has become an army trumpeter. During festivities a crowd of rebellious peasants insults the Countess Wildenstein and her cousin, Margaretha, who is the daughter of the Baron of Schönau. Werner protects the titled ladies from the mob. The scene changes to a room in the Baron's castle. Count von Wildenstein calls upon the Baron and proposes that his son Damian marry the Baron's daughter, Margaretha. The Baron is delighted. The Countess brings Margaretha home and the Baron is enraged when he hears of the attack of the peasants upon the ladies. As a reward for protecting the Countess and the Baron's daughter, Werner is appointed trumpeter of the Castle. Margaretha is delighted, for she has already fallen in love with Werner.

The second act is laid on the terrace of the castle. Werner tells Conradin that he is in love with Margaretha. Werner and Margaretha meet and their love scene is interrupted by the Countess. The Baron arrives and orders Margaretha to marry the Count's son, Damian. Werner is commanded to leave.

The third act shows the courtyard of the Castle which the peasants are besieging. Damian proves to be a coward, and Werner takes charge and drives the peasants away. He is wounded in the fight, and, as his wounds are bound, a mark is discovered on his body which proves that he is the son of the Count and Countess Wildenstein. He had been stolen in childhood by gypsies. The Baron is delighted to have a noble son-in-law.

§)&(§

TURANDOT

Giacomo Puccini

The libretto of Giacomo Puccini's last opera was written by Giuseppe Adami and Renato Simoni. The composer did not live to finish the work, and its last duet and finale were completed by Franco Alfano. The opera was first performed at La Scala, Milan, April 25, 1926.

The characters include:

PRINCESS TURANDOT (*Soprano*)
EMPEROR ALTUIM (*Tenor*)
TIMUR (*Bass*), the dethroned Tartar King
CALAF (*Tenor*), his son, the unknown Prince
LIU (*Soprano*), a young slave girl
PING (*Baritone*), the Grand Chancellor
PANG (*Tenor*), the General Purveyor
PONG (*Tenor*), the Chief Cook
THE PRINCE OF PERSIA (*Baritone*)
THE EXECUTIONER (*Baritone*)
A MANDARIN (*Baritone*)

The action occurs in Peking during legendary times. The first act shows the walls of the Imperial Palace where the people are standing in the square listening to a mandarin as he reads a death decree. The Princess Turandot will marry any man of noble blood who will solve three riddles she has set. If a man fails to solve the riddles he must die. Accordingly, the young Prince of Persia is condemned to die, for he is the latest to fail the test. The crowd grows unruly and shouts its disapproval. During the excitement an old man falls to the ground. He is Timur, the dethroned King of the Tartars. He is helped by Liu, a slave girl, and by his son Calaf, the unknown prince. Liu secretly loves Calaf. The Prince of Persia is brought in. The crowd calls for mercy, and the unknown prince denounces Turandot, just as she herself appears on the scene. The crowd falls to the ground in homage. The unknown prince alone remains standing. Turandot makes a gesture which signifies death and the executioner bows in assent. The prince is now a victim to Turandot's charms, and in spite of the pleadings of his father and Liu, he sounds the gong as a signal that he has accepted the challenge.

The second act opens in a pavilion of the Imperial Palace. Ping, Pang and Pong are enumerating the thirteen candidates for Turandot's hand who have lost their heads. They pray that Turandot will soon relent, and will cease to despise and defy love. They are interrupted by a blare of trumpets which announces that another victim is ready to take the test. The scene changes to the square outside the palace. Before a vast assemblage Turandot reminds her people that she has taken the oath to avenge on her own lovers the abduction of a princess, centuries ago, by a foreign invader. She warns the unknown prince of the fate that awaits him but he is not afraid. Then, one by one, he gives the correct answers to the puzzles: first "Hope," second, "Blood," and third, "Turandot." Turandot's father, the Emperor, tells her that she must now fulfill her promise. She pleads with the unknown prince to give up his claim. The Prince replies that if she can discover his name before dawn, he will free her from her oath and consent to die.

The first scene of the third act shows the palace gardens. Heralds announce that no one is to sleep and that death will be the penalty unless the Prince's name is revealed before dawn. Timur and Liu are brought in and they are ordered to tell the name of the Prince. Liu declares that she alone knows the name but will never reveal it. The executioner is ordered to torture her, and she snatches a dagger from one of the officers and stabs herself. Turandot is awed by the girl's heroism. When she and the Prince are alone, he begs her to throw aside her frigid mask and become human. He tears her veil from her face and kisses her passionately. She admits herself beaten, and he tells her his name—Calaf, the son of Timur, King of the Tartars. Turandot's pride returns to her. She has learned his name, and he must die. The last scene shows the outside of the palace at dawn. Turandot leads the Prince before the Emperor and the people. She cries that she knows the name of the stranger. Then she whispers: "His name is Love." She and the Prince embrace and the crowd shouts with joy.

§)&(§

DIE WALKÜRE

See Der Ring des Nibelungen

§)&(§

THE WARRIOR

Bernard Rogers

The Warrior, a one-act opera with music by Bernard Rogers and libretto by Norman Corwin, was first produced at the Metropolitan Opera House, New York, January 11, 1947. The plot is based on the Biblical Story of Samson and Delilah, who are the principal characters—the one a baritone and the other a soprano.

The first scene shows Delilah's betrayal of Samson, and the shearing of his locks while he sleeps. In the second scene Samson is bound and taunted by the Philistines, who blind him with red-hot irons. The third scene shows Samson in prison, hearing the mocking voice of Delilah. In the final episode the Philistines are holding a festival in honor of their God, Dagon. Samson prays to his God for a return of his strength. He asks the little boy who is to lead him before the mob to take him between the main pillars of the temple.

Then he summons his renewed strength and forces the pillars apart. The opera ends with the crashing of the temple and the terrified cries of the people.

§)&(§

WERTHER

Jules Massenet

Three librettists—Edouard Blau, Paul Milliet, and Georges Hartmann—wrote the libretto for Jules Massenet's opera, *Werther,* founding its plot on Goethe's story, *Die leiden des jungen Werther.* The opera was first produced at the Hof-Operntheater in Vienna, February 16, 1892.

The characters include:

WERTHER (*Tenor*)
THE BAILIFF (*Bass*)
CHARLOTTE (*Soprano*), his older daughter
ALBERT (*Baritone*), betrothed to Charlotte
SOPHIA (*Mezzo-soprano*), Charlotte's sister, the Bailiff's younger daughter

The action takes place at Wetzler, during the eighteenth century. The first act shows the terrace in front of the Bailiff's home. Charlotte is getting ready to go to a ball in the village. Werther, a newcomer to the town, calls at the house. He is so impressed with Charlotte that he asks if he may go to the ball with her. Charlotte accepts him as an escort, and they have hardly left when Albert, Charlotte's fiancé, returns from a long journey. Learning that Charlotte is not at home, he leaves. Later in the evening Charlotte and Werther come back from the ball. They have fallen in love with each other, but Charlotte tells Werther that her mother's deathbed wish was that she marry Albert. She must be true to her promise.

The second act shows a square in front of the village inn. Albert and Charlotte, now married, enter the church. Werther watches them and sings of his sorrow at Charlotte's having another man for her husband. When church is over Albert greets Werther understandingly. Albert hints that Werther would be happier if he transferred his affection to Charlotte's younger sister, Sophia. This Werther cannot do, even though Charlotte convinces him that she really loves her husband. Sophia, in turn, is heartbroken because Werther does not love her.

The third act occurs in Albert's and Charlotte's home. Charlotte is reading the love letters Werther has sent her, and has come to realize that she does love him and not her husband. Werther calls on her and he and Charlotte admit that they love each other. She will not leave Albert, however, and she tears herself from Werther's arms. Werther leaves in despair. Albert returns and finds his wife emotionally upset. Soon he receives from a messenger a note from Werther asking for the loan of a pistol. He is going on a journey. Albert gives the pistol to the messenger. The scene changes to Werther's room. Charlotte has guessed the reason for Werther's wanting a pistol and has hurried to prevent a tragedy. She arrives too late, for Werther has already shot himself and is lying on the floor fatally wounded. She takes him in her arms and he dies in her embrace.

§)&(§

WILLIAM TELL

Giaocchino Rossini

Giacchino Rossini's opera *William Tell* is best known today for its overture, which in itself summarizes the principal events of the story—the calm of an Alpine lake, the horns of the hunters and the trumpet call which gives the signal for uprising, and the terrific storm. The libretto of the opera was written by Hippolyte Bis and Victor Etienne de Jouy and was founded on Friedrich von Schiller's play, *Wilhelm Tell*. The work was first produced at the Grand Opéra in Paris, August 3, 1829.

The characters include:

WILLIAM TELL (*Baritone*), a Swiss patriot
HEDWIGA (*Soprano*), his wife
JEMMY (*Soprano*), his son
MELCTHAL (*Bass*), a patriot
ARNOLD (*Tenor*), Melcthal's son
LEUTHOLD (*Bass*), a shepherd
GESSLER (*Bass*), a tyrant, governor of Schwitz and Uri
MATILDA (*Soprano*), Gessler's daughter

The action occurs in thirteenth-century Switzerland. The first act shows the outside of William Tell's house on the shore of Lake Lucerne. A shepherds' festival is in progress. William Tell is plotting with the shepherds and peasants to overthrow the tyrant Gessler. Arnold is dejected. He is in love with Matilda, Gessler's daughter, and he is torn between his love and his patriotism. Leuthold, the shepherd, rushes in with the news that he has killed one of Gessler's guards who tried to abduct his, Leuthold's, daughter. He begs to be rowed across the lake. Tell is the only one who will risk Gessler's wrath. He helps Leuthold into a boat and rows him from the shore just as Gessler's soldiers arrive. They are furious because Leuthold has escaped. They set fire to Tell's house and the other cottages, and seize Arnold's father, Melcthal, as hostage.

The second act opens in a forest. After a party of huntsmen has passed Arnold meets Matilda. He is so much in love with her that he is willing to forget his patriotism and desert his comrades. Tell comes with the news that Gessler's soldiers have killed Arnold's father. Arnold bids farewell to Matilda and rejoins the patriots to avenge his father's death. The scene changes to an open field where Tell and the patriots meet to prepare for their battle against Gessler's troops.

The third act shows an open square at Altdorf. Gessler has placed a cap on the top of a pole and demands that everyone shall bow before it in recognition of his authority. Tell refuses to bow and is arrested. Gessler sneeringly announces to Tell that the only way he can save his life and that of his child, is to place an apple on the boy's head and from a considerable distance shoot an arrow through it. Tell instructs the boy to stand motionless and then walks back, draws his bow, and sends the arrow through the middle of the apple. The boy is untouched. When he is finished Tell's coat opens and shows another arrow that was hidden in his clothing. When asked about it he replies defiantly that he had it ready to shoot at Gessler if the first arrow had touched the child. Tell and the boy are again made prisoners.

The fourth act returns to the shore of Lake Lucerne and the ruined cottages. Hedwiga is grieving for her husband and her son. Matilda comes with the boy, whom she has helped to escape. Tell soon joins them, having made his own escape. He lies in wait for Gessler and when he sees him standing on a rock over the lake, he sends an arrow direct to the tyrant's heart. Arnold enters at the head of the victorious patriots. They have found a hidden cache of arms and have defeated Gessler's soldiers. A storm breaks overhead and the patriots sing in thanksgiving for having won their freedom.

§)&(§

A WITCH OF SALEM

Charles Wakefield Cadman

The libretto of Charles Wakefield Cadman's *A Witch of Salem* was written by Nelle Richmond Eberhart, and its plot deals with the hysteria over witchcraft at Salem, Mass., in 1692. The opera was first produced at the Auditorium in Chicago by the Chicago Civic Opera Company, December 8, 1926.

The cast includes:

ARNOLD TALBOT (*Tenor*)
SHEILA MELOY (*Soprano*)
CLARIS WILLOUGHBY (*Soprano*)

Sheila is in love with Arnold, but he loves instead her cousin Claris Willoughby. When Arnold is cold to Sheila she accuses Claris of witchcraft. Claris is condemned to be hanged, but just before the execution, Sheila confesses her own treachery to Arnold. She offers to save Claris's life if Arnold will kiss her just once. Arnold agrees, and Sheila takes Claris's place on the scaffold, happy in the thought that Arnold has kissed her.

§)&(§

WOZZECK

Alban Berg

Alban Berg was a pupil of Arnold Schoenberg, and in his operas *Wozzeck* and *Lulu* he used the Schoenberg atonal idiom. The results are almost horrifying, but in the case of *Wozzeck* the unrelieved dissonance is altogether appropriate in depicting the tragedy of the psychopathic soldier who murdered his unfaithful mistress. The composer himself wrote the libretto of *Wozzeck*, which he adapted from a drama by George Büchner. The opera was first produced at the Staatsoper in Berlin, December 14, 1925.

The cast includes:

WOZZECK (*Tenor*), a soldier
MARIE (*Soprano*), his mistress
THE CAPTAIN (*Bass*)
A DRUM MAJOR (*Baritone*)
A DOCTOR (*Bass*)
MARGARET (*Contralto*)

The time and place of the opera are not stated. The first act opens in the Captain's room, where Wozzeck is shaving the Captain. The Captain asks Wozzeck about his illegitimate child and delivers a lecture on morals. The second scene shows the open country. Wozzeck and a fellow-soldier are chopping wood. Wozzeck shows a dread of the supernatural. He hears strange noises and is afraid the place is haunted. The scene changes to Marie's room. Marie is standing at the window with her little son, the child of Wozzeck. They watch the military band pass by and Marie flirts with the Drum-Major. Her neighbor Margaret scolds her for being unfaithful to Wozzeck. Wozzeck comes to see Marie. He is disturbed by the voices he heard while he was chopping wood. He frightens Marie with meaningless utterances. The fourth scene shows a doctor's study. To get money for the support of Marie and her son, Wozzeck has offered himself as a subject for medical experiments by a fanatic doctor. The doctor reproves Wozzeck for coughing, for as part of his bargain Wozzeck has promised not to cough. The doctor repeats the rigid, ridiculous diet he has ordered for the wretched Wozzeck. Wozzeck becomes confused and incoherent and the doctor is delighted at his victim's outburst of hallucinatory insanity. He tells Wozzeck he will raise his pay if he obeys his orders. Then the doctor fanatically describes the new scientific theory which will make his name immortal. Scene Five shows the street in front of Marie's house. Marie is talking to the Drum-Major. At first she resists his advances, but she finally yields and the two go into the house in close embrace.

The second act opens in Marie's room. Marie is admiring a pair of earrings which the Drum-Major has given her. As she is trying to put her child to sleep Wozzeck enters. When Marie sees him she covers her ears with her hands. Wozzeck sees the earrings between her fingers and demands to know where she got them. Marie declares that she found them, but Wozzeck is skeptical. Marie manages to soothe Wozzeck and he hands her his weekly wages. When he has gone Marie reproaches herself for her wickedness. The scene changes to a street in the city. The Captain teases Wozzeck with veiled hints about Marie's affair with the Drum-Major. Wozzeck rushes off to learn if the Captain is speaking the truth. The next scene shows the street outside Marie's house. Wozzeck accuses Marie of being intimate with the Drum-Major. He starts to strike Marie, but manages to control himself. She cries: "Don't you dare touch me! Rather a knife in my heart than a hand laid on me!" Wozzeck repeats the words: "Rather a knife . . ."

The following scene is laid in a garden of an inn where Wozzeck discovers Marie dancing with the Drum-Major. In Scene Five Wozzeck is in the barracks, unable to sleep. The Drum-Major passes Wozzeck's bed, and in drunken boldness boasts to Wozzeck that he has stolen his Marie. When Wozzeck refuses to drink with him, the Drum-Major beats him. Wozzeck mutters vengeance as the Drum-Major blusters out of the room.

The third act opens in Marie's room. Marie is repentant and reads in her Bible the story of Mary Magdalene. In the second scene Wozzeck and Marie are walking along a path on the shores of a pond. Wozzeck asks her to sit by him. She is so frightened by his strange utterances that she tries to escape. Wozzeck seizes her and stabs her. The third scene shows a tavern. Wozzeck is drinking heavily. He talks to Margaret who sees blood on his hands. She calls to the others and Wozzeck leaves hurriedly. The fourth scene returns to the shore of the pond. Wozzeck is hunting for the knife with which he stabbed Marie. When he finds it he throws it into the pond. Thinking that it has sunk too near the shore he wades into the water. In a half-crazed fashion he tries to wash the blood from his hands. He goes deeper and deeper and is finally drowned. Meanwhile the doctor and Captain enter. They hear Wozzeck's groans. The doctor wants to investigate but the Captain is filled with superstitious fears and drags the doctor away. The last scene returns to the street in front of Marie's house, where her little son is playing with his hobby-horse. The children tell him about his mother's death, but he does not understand. He follows the children on his hobby-horse as they run toward the pond.

§)&(§

ZAMPA

Louis Hérold

Louis Hérold's *Zampa* is an opera that is known today chiefly for its overture, which is a great favorite with concert bands. The libretto of *Zampa* was written by "Mélesville," which was the pen name of Anne Honoré Duveyrier. The opera was first produced at the Opéra Comique in Paris, May 3, 1831.

The cast includes:

CAMILLE (*Soprano*)
ALPHONSE (*Tenor*), betrothed to Camille
ZAMPA (*Bass*), a pirate chief

Camille is about to marry Alphonse, when Zampa, leading a band of pirates, lands at the Lugano castle on the Mediterranean coast. He captures Camille's father and holds the old man as a hostage. Zampa forces Camille to promise that she will marry him instead of Alphonse. In drunken mockery Zampa puts a betrothal ring on the finger of a statue of Alice, a young girl he seduced and who later died. The statue raises its arm threateningly and will not let Zampa take back the ring. As Camille and Zampa are about to be married, Camille escapes. Zampa pursues her, but the statue of Alice seizes him and drags him into the sea.

§)&(§

ZAZA

Ruggiero Leoncavallo

Zaza was a play in which Mrs. Leslie Carter appeared from 1898 until her final retirement in 1923. It was written by

Pierre Berton and Charles Simon, and when Ruggiero Leoncavallo composed an opera to it, he himself adapted the text for his libretto. The opera was first produced at the Teatro Lirico Internazionale, Milan, November 10, 1900.

The cast includes:

ZAZA (*Soprano*), a music-hall singer
CASCART (*Baritone*), her partner, also a music-hall singer
ANAIDE (*Mezzo-soprano*), Zaza's mother
NATALIA (*Comprimaria*), Zaza's maid
FLORIANA (*Contralto*), a music-hall singer
MILIO DUFRESNE (*Tenor*)
MADAME DUFRESNE (*Comprimaria*), his wife
TOTO, their child
BUZZY (*Baritone*), a journalist

The action occurs in contemporary times at St. Étienne and in Paris. The first act shows the stage of a music hall in St. Étienne. At one side is Zaza's dressing room and at the other the rear of the stage. A performance is in progress. Zaza, the star of the theater, would like to lure Milio Dufresne away from her fellow-singer, Floriana, and she wagers with Buzzy, the journalist, that she can win Dufresne as her lover. Dufresne does not respond at first, but at length yields to Zaza's charms.

The second act is laid at Zaza's house. Zaza is now seriously in love with Dufresne, even though her mother, Anaide, and her singing partner, Cascart, warn that her attachment will ruin her professional career. Dufresne comes to tell Zaza that he must take a long-postponed business trip to the United States, and will be gone for four months. Zaza pleads with him not to leave her for so long. Dufresne promises to give up the journey but says he must go to Paris for a few days. When he has gone Cascart tells

Zaza that he has seen Dufresne at a Paris theater in company with another woman. Zaza decides to investigate and leaves for Paris with her maid, Natalia.

The third act shows a room in Dufresne's Paris home. Zaza comes with her maid, and is admitted to the house through mistaken identity. She finds a letter addressed to Madame Dufresne and she realizes that Dufresne is married. She decides to wait for Madame Dufresne and to expose her husband. While she is waiting, Dufresne's child, Toto, appears. Toto is so charming that Zaza thinks better of her plan to wreck Dufresne's home. She is about to leave quietly when Madame Dufresne returns. Zaza explains her presence by saying that she has called at the wrong house, and leaves hurriedly.

The last act returns to Zaza's home. Cascart tries to comfort Zaza, and tells her of a splendid offer they have both had from a theater in Marseilles. He begs Zaza not to see Dufresne again, but when Dufresne is announced, Zaza insists on receiving him. Dufresne does not know that Zaza has been to his home. He continues his deception until Zaza tells him that she has seen his daughter and knows that he is married. Dufresne is angry, and Zaza pretends that she has told his wife about their relationship. Dufresne is so agitated by this announcement that Zaza realizes that he loves his family very deeply, and that his attachment for herself was only a passing fancy. She assures him that she has told his wife nothing and sends him away.

§)&(§

AMAHL AND THE NIGHT VISITORS

Gian-Carlo Menotti

This one-act opera was commissioned for television by the National Broadcasting Company and was first performed on the NBC-TV network Christmas Eve, 1951. Since then it has been broadcast during every Christmas season. It has also had many stage performances, the first in New York by the New York City Opera Company at the City Center, April 27, 1952.

As in all of his works, the composer wrote his own libretto for the opera. The cast includes:

AMAHL (*Soprano*), a crippled boy of about 12
HIS MOTHER (*Soprano*)
KASPAR (*Tenor*) } the Three Kings
MELCHIOR (*Baritone*) } the Three Kings
BALTHAZAR (*Baritone*) } the Three Kings
THE PAGE (*Baritone*)
SHEPHERDS AND VILLAGERS, DANCERS

The scene is the cottage where Amahl lives with his mother. The star-dotted sky reaches its climax in the brightness of the Eastern Star. Amahl, his crutch lying beside him, sits on a stone as he plays his shepherd's pipe. He answers: "Coming!" when his mother calls him to bed, but he continues to play his pipe. At length he goes to the doorway and tells his mother that a Star as large as a window is hanging over the roof. It has a tail that moves across the sky like a chariot of fire. The mother scolds Amahl for telling lies. She fears that hunger has gone to his head and that unless they go begging they cannot live through tomorrow.

Amahl lies on a pallet of straw beside the fireplace. His mother covers him with his cloak, snuffs out the lamp and lies on a nearby bench. In the distance the figures of the Three Kings and the Page wend their way along the mountain road. Amahl hears their singing and watches from the window as they approach. As they come nearer we see Melchior, bearing the coffer of gold, Balthazar, with the urn of incense, and Kaspar, who carries the chalice of myrrh. The Page brings many bundles and a lantern to light the way. The group sings to the crystal star, asking how far they must follow it.

When they knock at the door Amahl opens it and hobbles to tell his mother that Three Kings have come to see them. Again the mother accuses him of lying, but when she looks for herself and sees that the boy has told the truth she tells the Kings that all she has to offer them is a cold fireplace and a bed of straw. To these they are welcome.

The Kings enter the cottage and make themselves as comfortable as possible. Amahl asks if they are real kings. Kaspar, who is slightly deaf, shows Amahl the jewels they are taking to the Child to which the Star is guiding them. Amahl takes his crutch and hurries out to ask the shepherds to bring whatever they may have to the cottage. He and his mother have nothing to give the visitors.

The mother looks covetously at the gold the Kings have with them. Presently Amahl returns with the shepherds who bring baskets of fruit and vegetables. After they have danced for the Kings and have bid them good-night the Kings settle themselves for sleep. Amahl asks Kaspar if among his magic stones he has one that might cure a crippled boy. The deaf Kaspar does not seem to hear him.

When all are asleep the mother rises from her pallet of sheepskins and touches the gold, whispering: "For my child." The Page is instantly aroused and cries: "Thief!" The Kings awaken and cry: "Shame! Shame!" The Page struggles with the mother for the gold and Amahl hurls himself at him. Kaspar signals the Page to release the mother and says: "Woman, you may keep the gold." The Child they seek does not need gold. He will build his kingdom on love alone.

As the Kings turn to leave the mother begs them to take back their gold. Amahl gives them his crutch as his offering to the Child. As he does so he takes a step towards the Kings and finds that he can walk unaided. He tries further steps and cries: "I can dance, I can jump, I can run!" As the Kings depart Amahl follows them in their stately procession. The mother stands in the doorway waving to Amahl as he disappears in the distance.

§)&(§

ARABELLA

Richard Strauss

Arabella, an opera in three acts, was first produced in Dresden, July 1, 1933. It was not performed in America until it was produced by the Metropolitan Opera Company in New York, February 10, 1955.

The libretto was written by Hugo von Hofmannstahl. The cast includes:

COUNT WALDNER (*Bass*)
ADELAIDE (*Mezzo-soprano*), his wife
ARABELLA (*Soprano*) } their daughters
ZDENKA (*Soprano*) }
MANDRYKA (*Baritone*)
MATTEO (*Tenor*), an officer

COUNT ELEMER (*Tenor*)
COUNT DOMINIK (*Baritone*) } Arabella's suitors
COUNT LAMORAL (*Bass*)

THE FIAKERMILLI (*Soprano*)

A FORTUNE-TELLER (*Soprano*)

MANDRYKA'S SERVANTS, GAMBLERS, COACHMEN, GUESTS AT THE BALL, HOTEL RESIDENTS, WAITERS

The story is laid in Vienna, in the year 1860. The first act shows the hotel suite of the impoverished Count Waldner, a retired Army captain. His wife, Adelaide, is consulting a fortune-teller, hoping to find some solution to the family's financial situation. Meanwhile the younger daughter, Zdenka, is stalling insistent creditors. Zdenka masquerades as a boy, for the family can afford feminine finery for only one of the daughters, the beautiful Arabella. The fortune-teller brings hope by foreseeing a wealthy marriage for Arabella. Zdenka is left alone in the room and receives Matteo, an Italian officer, who is very much in love with Arabella. He begs Zdenka to intercede for him, for while he had a most encouraging letter from Arabella a few days ago, she hasn't even looked at him when he has been near her. He leaves a bouquet for Arabella. When he is gone Zdenka confides to the audience that she herself is in love with Matteo, and that it is she who wrote the encouraging letter to him, letting him believe it was from her sister. Arabella comes in to find gifts from three of her suitors, the Counts Elemer, Dominik, and Lamoral. Zdenka keeps her promise and pleads for Matteo. Arabella replies that the right man has not yet appeared, and she urges Zdenka to stop disguising herself as a boy and to get a man for herself. Secretly Arabella is impressed by a tall stranger she has just seen, but she must now get ready for a sleigh-ride with Count Elemer.

Count Waldner returns from a card game, disgusted

with his bad luck and the increasing number of unpaid bills. He confides to his wife Adelaide that he has sent Arabella's picture to a wealthy friend and former fellow-officer, Mandryka. He has not known that Mandryka is dead, and that his wealth has gone to a nephew and namesake. It is this nephew, the younger Mandryka, who now appears to tell Count Waldner that he has read the letter to his deceased uncle, has fallen in love with the picture of Arabella, and will be delighted to marry her. As a token of his good faith he gives Waldner a thousand gulden. Waldner is delighted, and shows the money to Zdenka. Arabella is now ready for the sleigh-ride. She sings of the men she does not want to marry, including Count Elemer, and mentions the mysterious stranger she has seen. She does not know that he is Mandryka who has already interviewed her father. She thinks too of the ball where tonight she will be queen.

The second act shows the ball. As Arabella turns down a series of suitors who ask her to dance, Waldner and Mandryka stand at the entrance to the ballroom. Presently Waldner presents Mandryka to Arabella and she discovers that he is the mysterious stranger, the "right man" she has been waiting for. Mandryka is fascinated with her and tells her of his dead wife, his vast estates in Slavonia, and most important, of his love for her. Arabella accepts him immediately, but asks permission to bid farewell to her youth and to dismiss her other suitors. The Fiakermilli, in charge of ceremonies, declares Arabella queen of the ball, and Mandryka orders champagne for everybody. Arabella gently dismisses Dominik and Elemer and saves a last dance for Lamoral. Matteo pleads once more with Zdenka, still thinking that she is Arabella's brother. Zdenka is afraid that Matteo, whom she herself loves, will commit suicide. She gives Matteo a key, letting him think it will fit the door of Arabella's room. She says that it will open the door of the person who sent it.

Mandryka overhears the conversation and immediately concludes that Arabella is already unfaithful. Cynically he flirts with the Fiakermilli, with Arabella's mother, and others of the guests.

The last act takes place in the open hall of the hotel. Matteo appears at the top of the staircase. He has used the key and has been spending an hour with a lady he thought was Arabella. When he sees Arabella enter the lobby he cries: "I cannot believe it!" and when she is cold to him he accuses her of make-believe. They are interrupted by the coming of Adelaide, Walther and Mandryka. The latter, believing Arabella unfaithful, tells Waldner the betrothal is broken. Waldner challenges Mandryka and the two prepare for a duel. Suddenly Zdenka appears on the staircase, no longer a boy but a beautiful girl. She is filled with shame for having given herself to the unsuspecting Matteo and she threatens to commit suicide. Forgiveness by her parents comes readily when Matteo, entranced by her beauty, realizes that he loves her and not Arabella. Arabella praises Zdenka for her kindness, and approaches Mandryka. She offers him a drink and tells him that if he smashes the glass she will know that she is forgiven. He drains the glass, smashes it on the steps, and takes Arabella into his arms. She breaks away from him and runs up the stairs as her lover looks after her.

§)&(§

THE BALLAD OF BABY DOE

Douglas Moore

This opera was first produced at Central City, Colorado, July 7, 1956, and was given sixteen performances during the town's opera festival in July and August. The libretto by John La Touche portrays real characters—Horace Tabor, the silver king who was at one time the richest man in Colorado, and Baby Doe, for whom he divorced his wife. The characters include:

HORACE TABOR (*Bass-baritone*)
AUGUSTA TABOR (*Mezzo-soprano*), his wife
ELIZABETH (*Soprano*), Baby Doe
WILLIAM JENNINGS BRYAN (*Bass*)
MAMA MC COURT (*Contralto*), Baby Doe's mother
AN OLD MINER (*Tenor*)
HOTEL CLERK (*Tenor*)
PRIEST (*Tenor*)
MAYOR (*Tenor*)
STAGE-DOORMAN (*Tenor*)
BOUNCER (*Baritone*)
POLITICIAN (*Baritone*)
BELLBOY (*Baritone*)
SILVER DOLLAR (*Mezzo-soprano*)
MAG (*Soprano*)
KATE (*Mezzo-soprano*)

The first act occurs on a summer evening in 1879. The opening scene shows the exterior of the Tabor Opera House in Leadville, Colorado. On one side of the entrance is the front of a saloon; on the other the doorway of a hotel. From the saloon comes the sound of men singing. Pistol shots are heard and the Bouncer throws an Old Miner out of the door. The Miner holds a pot of silver ore in one hand and waves a pistol with the other. The Bouncer tells him not to shoot again. A concert is going on in Tabor's new opera house. Girls on the street remark that Tabor owns the opera house, the saloon, the hotel, the grocery store, the bank, the "whole damn town." Tabor enters with a group of his friends. He boasts about the opera house, "a fittin' place for art and culture," which, he adds, is much needed in Colorado. Tabor and his cronies sing a rowdy miners' folk song and dance with the girls. His wife Augusta appears at the entrance of the opera house and demands to know why he and his friends have left the concert and are cavorting with these "harrigans" and dancing with these "jezebels."

Tabor answers that he just stepped outside for a cigar while the string quartet was playing. He adds that dollars from the saloon where the "jezebels" entertain the customers have built the opera house just as much as did the dollars from the silver mines. As the concert audience returns to the auditorium Tabor is approached by Baby Doe. She has just arrived from Central City and asks Tabor the way to the hotel. After he has introduced himself he heeds his wife's command to return to the concert. Baby Doe looks after him and remarks "I'm sure we'll meet again."

After a short interlude the audience comes from the concert. Tabor sits alone in the hotel lobby while outside Kate and Mag talk about Baby Doe, and her recent arrival. Apparently she is well known to the miners. The girls agree that she is no better than they are and that Tabor had better watch out. Presently Baby Doe sits at the piano in the hotel and sings and plays a sentimental song. Tabor is fascinated and again introduces himself. His wife calls him from an upstairs window.

The next scene takes place in the Tabor's hotel apartment. Augusta finds a pair of silk gloves with a card addressed to "my dearest Baby Doe." When Tabor appears she accuses him of carrying on with Baby Doe. Tabor retorts that in her he finds the warmth that Augusta has denied him. Augusta declares that she will drive Baby Doe out of town even though it means the ruin of them both.

The fourth scene is the lobby of the hotel. Baby Doe comes down the stairs, following a bellboy who is carrying her bags. She tells the clerk she is leaving to visit her family in Oshkosh. While waiting for train-time she sits at a desk and writes a letter to her mother, telling her that her husband, Harvey, has left her, and that now she has found her real love. She must, however, give him up. Augusta approaches Baby Doe and tells her she knows about her attachment to her husband and warns that there will be serious trouble. Baby Doe tells her she is leaving. As soon as Augusta has left the room Baby Doe tears up the letter. Tabor enters hurriedly and Baby Doe tells him she is staying. They embrace and declare their love for each other.

The scene changes to Augusta's room. Her friends are asking her what she intends to do about the situation. One of them says she has heard that Tabor has already divorced Augusta in another county. Augusta declares that if Tabor divorces her he will rue the day he was born.

The last scene of the first act takes place in a private room in the Willard Hotel in Washington, in 1883. The occasion is the wedding of Horace Tabor and Baby Doe. Her mother, Mama McCourt, her father, and various State Department dandies are waiting for the bride and groom. Mama McCourt is boasting about the cost of Lizzie's (Baby Doe's) wedding dress. Presently the footman announces Senator and Mrs. Horace Tabor. Glasses are filled and Tabor asks for the news from Capitol Hill. The dandies reply "bimetalism" and predict that gold is going sky-high and silver is doomed. Tabor answers "Rubbish!" and to show what silver can do opens the box of jewels that is his wedding present to Baby Doe. Mama McCourt grows talkative and remarks that she wishes Harvey, Lizzie's first husband, was here tonight to see how well her daughter was doing. The Priest is shocked to learn that Baby Doe's first husband is still living, and when he hears further that Tabor is a divorced man he walks out of the room. The other guests leave murmuring "scandal, scandal."

Act Two occurs ten years later, in 1893. Baby Doe is being snubbed by the women of Denver at a ball in the Windsor Hotel. The womens' husbands protest that Tabor may be chosen the next governor of Colorado but they reply that he never will with Baby Doe as his wife. Baby Doe confides to her mother that although she is sneered at and snubbed she really loves Tabor. When she first met him she wanted his money and his power but when he first kissed her she knew what true love was. Augusta comes to the balcony and insists on talking to Baby Doe. She claims that she has had no part in making Baby Doe an outcast and she is glad Baby and Tabor are happy. Now she wants to warn them that silver is done for. She has heard that tomorrow the President will sign a bill to finish it forever. She knows too that Tabor's fortune is mortgaged. Baby Doe must persuade him to sell the Matchless Mine before it is too late. When Augusta has left Tabor joins Baby Doe. He assures her that silver will rise again and makes her promise that no matter what happens she will always hold on to the Matchless Mine.

The second scene shows four of Tabor's cronies playing poker. They talk about Tabor's stubbornness in relying on silver. Tabor comes to join the game. He admits that he is in a squeeze at the moment but he still has the Tabor Block, three hotels, stores and railroad stocks. And, he adds, William Jennings Bryan is going to save them. The cronies tell Tabor he must be crazy.

The third scene shows the exterior of the Matchless Mine. William Jennings Bryan addresses the people of Leadville and promises that the free coinage of silver will save them. Scene Four, a few weeks later, shows Augusta Tabor's home in California. Newsboys are crying the defeat of Bryan and the Republican landslide. Augusta is moved by the news and presently her maid announces Mama McCourt, Baby Doe's mother. Mama McCourt tells Augusta that Tabor is penniless. Bryan was his last hope and everything is gone except a worthless mine or two. He is working as a laborer and Mama McCourt thought that perhaps Augusta might like to help him. Augusta replies that if Tabor wants help he must come himself and ask for it. Mama McCourt protests that this is impossible; Tabor does not know that she is asking Augusta for help. When Mama McCourt has gone Augusta sings that she should go to Tabor but that she cannot.

The fifth scene shows the stage of the Tabor Opera House in 1899. It is deserted except for an old stage-doorman. Tabor, dressed as a laborer, comes to have a look at the old place. In a vision he sees a politician giving him a watch-fob on the opening night, and then his life passes in review—his meeting Augusta, his finding silver in the West, his glorious successes, and his meeting Baby Doe. A half-naked woman impersonating a Silver Dollar dances drunkenly. As the phantoms disappear Baby Doe herself is shown in by the stage-doorman. She takes the exhausted Tabor into her arms and as he sinks to the floor she throws her cloak over him.

The scene fades and the Matchless Mine comes into view. Baby Doe, now a white-haired old woman, sits by the mine-shaft as the snow begins to fall.

§)&(§

THE CONSUL

Gian-Carlo Menotti

The Consul was Menotti's first full-length opera. It was first produced in Philadelphia, March 1, 1950, and was then brought to the Ethel Barrymore Theatre in New York where it enjoyed a run of several months. It was awarded the Pulitzer Prize for 1950 and the New York Drama Critics Circle citation as the best musical play of the season.

Menotti wrote the libretto as well as the music. The cast includes:

<table>
<tr><td colspan="2">JOHN SOREL (Baritone)</td></tr>
<tr><td colspan="2">MAGDA SOREL (Soprano), his wife</td></tr>
<tr><td colspan="2">HIS MOTHER (Contralto)</td></tr>
<tr><td colspan="2">SECRET-POLICE AGENT (Bass)</td></tr>
<tr><td colspan="2">THE SECRETARY (Mezzo-soprano)</td></tr>
<tr><td>MR. KOFNER (Bass-Baritone)</td><td rowspan="5">applicants in the Consul's office</td></tr>
<tr><td>THE FOREIGN WOMAN (Soprano)</td></tr>
<tr><td>ANNA GOMEZ (Soprano)</td></tr>
<tr><td>VERA BORONEL (Contralto)</td></tr>
<tr><td>NIKA MAGADOFF (Tenor), a magician</td></tr>
<tr><td colspan="2">ASSAN (Baritone), a friend of John Sorel's</td></tr>
</table>

The time is after World War II; the place somewhere in Europe. The first scene of Act One shows an empty room in the rather forlorn home of John Sorel, a man who is working for an underground group. As the curtain rises a phonograph in a neighboring house is playing a French jazz song, *Tu Reviendras* ("You will return"). Sorel comes in limping, and explains to his wife Magda and to his mother that he was shot by the police as he was escaping from a meeting. As Magda is bandaging his leg she looks through the window and sees the police coming. John barely has time to climb from the window to an overhanging ledge. As the Police Agent questions Magda the mother sings a lullaby to the child in the cradle. The Agent is scrupulously polite but throughout the questioning there is an atmosphere of veiled threats. Magda parries the questions and gives no important information. When the police have left John climbs in from the window. He realizes that he must leave immediately and he tells Magda that any message from him will come by someone's breaking a window of the house. She is then to send for his friend Assan, a glass cutter.

The second scene takes place in the antechamber of the consulate. Various applicants are waiting in the room, hoping to obtain visas. All of them have to go through endless forms of red tape, filling in forms, getting photographs, and being told by the Secretary that they must wait. Magda is given blank forms and is told that she cannot see the Consul. One of the applicants, Magadoff, is a conjuror who tries to win the favor of the Secretary by performing a few tricks. He is wasting his time, however, and the applicants join in singing of their frustration.

The second act opens in Sorel's room where the strains of *Tu Reviendras* are again coming through the window. Magda and Sorel's mother are talking about the difficulty of getting a visa. The child in the cradle is alarmingly quiet, and the mother sings it a lullaby. Magda falls asleep in a chair and in a nightmare has a vision of a dead child. She is suddenly wakened by a stone crashing through the window. She telephones for Assan and has scarcely finished when the Police Agent returns. He tells Magda that if she will give him the names of some of John's associates, she may be allowed to join him. Magda hysterically threatens to kill the Police Agent if he comes again.

While she is still talking to the Police Agent Assan

comes to fix the window. When he and Magda are alone he tells her that John is hiding in the mountains, waiting for her. He refuses to leave the country until he knows that she has a visa and can join him. Magda and Assan agree that it is necessary to pretend to John that Magda has a visa, so that he will escape and save his own life. When Assan has left Magda finds that the child has died in its grandmother's arms. She is too stunned even to cry.

The second scene is in the waiting room of the consulate. The Secretary is still giving the applicants forms to fill out. Magadoff again tries his magic tricks and this time hypnotizes his fellow applicants so that they join in a trance like dance. The Secretary orders Magadoff to break the spell. Magda once more demands to see the Consul. Again she is refused and she launches a tirade against official red tape and the endless forms and applications. The Secretary replies that she is being most unreasonable but promises to see what can be done. Presently she tells Magda that the Consul will see her. His shadow appears on the glazed panel of his office door, shaking hands with a man. When this man appears in the outer office, Magda discovers that he is the Police Agent. Shocked, she falls in a faint.

The third act opens in the waiting room. Magda is there again, still hoping to see the Consul. The Secretary tells her that there is little chance, for the office is due to close in ten minutes. One of the applicants has good news, her application has been approved. Assan comes with bad news for Magda. John has learned that both his baby and his mother are dead, and he is recrossing the border to rescue Magda. Magda hurriedly writes a note for Assan to take to John. The applicants and Magda and Assan leave the office. The Secretary, now alone, sings a solo aria that shows that underneath her business-like exterior she has a warm sympathy for the unfortunate people she must deal with. When she has finished her soliloquy John enters hurriedly, looking for Magda. He is followed by the police, who arrest him. As soon as they leave the Secretary starts to dial the telephone.

Scene Two returns to the Sorel home. The telephone is ringing, but stops just before Magda enters. She goes to the stove, turns on the gas, and sits beside it as she covers her head with a shawl. As she loses conciousness the audience sees the walls of the room disappear as the scene changes to the consulate where the applicants, together with John and his mother, in a wedding dress, perform a strange dance. Magda tries to talk to them but there is no answer. As they slowly disappear Magda's deep breathing becomes audible. The phone starts ringing again. Magda seems to hear it and makes an effort to reach it. She is too far gone to succeed, and falls as the ringing continues.

§)&(§

DIALOGUES OF THE CARMELITES

Dialoghi delle Carmelitane

Francis Poulenc

This three-act opera was first produced at La Scala in Milan, January 26, 1957. It was performed at Cologne the following July 15, and in San Francisco September 20. On December 8, 1957 it was given a television production, in English, by the NBC-TV Opera Theatre. The libretto was adapted from a play by Georges Bernanos that had been inspired by a novel by Gertrude von Le Fort and a scenario by Philippe Agostini and the Rev. Fr. Bruckberger.

The characters include:

THE MARQUIS DE LA FORCE (*Baritone*)
BLANCHE (*Soprano*), his daughter
THE CHEVALIER (*Tenor*), his son
MADAME DE CROISSY (Mother Henriette) (*Contralto*), Prioress of the Carmelite Convent
MADAME LIDOINE (Mother Marie of St. Augustine) (*Soprano*), the new Prioress
MOTHER MARIE OF THE INCARNATION (*Mezzo-soprano*), Assistant Prioress
SISTER CONSTANCE OF ST. DENIS (*Soprano*), a very young nun
MOTHER JEANNE OF THE CHILD JESUS (*Contralto*), Dean of the Community
SISTER MATHILDE (*Mezzo-soprano*)
THE CHAPLAIN OF THE CONVENT (*Tenor*)
FIRST COMMISSIONER (*Tenor*)
SECOND COMMISSIONER (*Baritone*)
OFFICER (*Baritone*)
JAILER (*Baritone*)
THIERRY (*Baritone*)
M. JAVELINOT (*Baritone*), a doctor
CHORISTERS INCLUDING THREE OLD NUNS AND EIGHT SISTERS, OFFICIALS OF THE MUNICIPALITY, OFFICERS, POLICEMEN, PRISONERS, GUARDS, TOWNSFOLK

The action opens in April, 1789, at the beginning of the French Revolution. The first scene of the first act is in the library of the Marquis de la Force. The Marquis and his son, the Chevalier, are talking about Blanche, the Marquis's daughter and the Chevalier's sister. Blanche is a maladjusted girl who cannot conquer her fear of life. While her father and brother are discussing her she comes in completely shaken by having had her carriage stopped by an angry mob. Even the unexpected entrance of a servant upsets her and throws her into a panic. Suddenly she resolves to do what she has long been planning. She will be a nun and stop struggling with a life she cannot master. The second scene shows the parlor of the Carmelite Convent at Compiegne, where Blanche talks to the Mother Superior. The Mother explains that the Order is not a refuge from life. The courage Blanche seeks can be gained only through self-discipline. In the third scene, in the workroom of the Convent, Blanche has become a nun and is working with the young Sister Constance. Blanche rebukes Sister Constance for being unconcerned while the Mother Superior lies dangerously ill. Constance tells Blanche about a strange premonition she has had, that she and Blanche will die together. In the fourth scene the Mother Superior lies dying in the infirmary of the Convent. She confesses to Mother Marie of the Incarnation, the assistant Prioress, that even though she has thought about death throughout her life, she is now afraid. As she dies she turns Blanche over to the care of Mother Marie.

The second act opens in the Chapel, where Blanche and Constance watch by the bier of the Mother Superior. During a moment when Constance leaves to get the nuns who will relieve them, Blanche is afraid to be alone and goes to the door. Mother Marie enters. Even though Blanche has neglected her duty she is so upset emotionally that Mother Marie takes her to her cell. In an Interlude Blanche and Constance talk about the Mother Superior's death. Blanche cannot understand why anyone who has lived a life of such devotion could die with such fear. Constance replies that even though God grants to everyone a fitting death, sometimes he may make a mistake. Inasmuch as the Mother Superior was given a death that was unworthy of her, some little person will have a much more noble death than he deserves and will be astonished at how bravely he meets it. In the second scene the sisters meet their new Prioress, Mme. Lione, and in the following Interlude the Chevalier, forced to leave France, comes to the Convent to say goodbye to his sister Blanche. They meet in the parlor of the Convent. He tells her that their father will now be alone and he urges her to return to him. Blanche replies that although she has a duty to her father she now has a higher loyalty and must stay in the Convent. In Scene Four the Chaplain talks to the nuns in the Sacristy. He has been relieved of his duties by the revolutionary regime. Outside a mob demands admittance. An official enters to read a decree of the Legislative Assembly. All religious orders are to be disbanded. An old nun hands Blanche the statue of the Little King. Blanche is so frightened that she drops it. It is smashed to pieces on the stone floor.

The third act opens in the Chapel. The Convent has been pillaged. The nuns greet the Chaplain who has been secretly returned to them. The new Prioress is absent and Mother Marie of the Incarnation takes charge. She urges the nuns to take the vow of martyrdom which can be binding only if it is unanimous. Each nun will pass behind the altar where she will give her decision to the Chaplain. As Blanche comes from the interview her face is drawn and frightened. When the Chaplain tells Mother Marie that there is one dissenting vote the nuns assume that it was Blanche who cast it, but Sister Constance declares that it was she herself who was afraid and would now like to reverse her decision. The nuns come forward in pairs to take the vow, Blanche and Constance, as the youngest, leading the procession. In the next Interlude the nuns are divested of their garb and leave the Convent. The second scene is in the library of the Marquis, now ravaged and pillaged. The Marquis has been guillotined. Blanche, dressed as a civilian, works as a servant in her father's former home. Mother Marie, also dressed in ordinary clothes, comes to Blanche and urges her to return to the nuns. Blanche feels safer where she is and refuses. In the Interlude Blanche learns from an old woman on a street near the Bastille that the nuns have been arrested. The next scene is in the Conciergerie where the Sisters have spent their first night in prison. Sister Constance is confident that Blanche will rejoin them. The jailer announces that they are all sentenced to death for their crimes against the Republic. The Mother Superior gives them her blessing. In the last Interlude Mother Marie learns from the Chaplain of the nuns' sentence. She feels that she should go back to the Sisters but the Chaplain replies that God decides who shall live and who shall die. In the last scene, in the Place de la Revolution, the Carmelites, led by the Mother Superior, chant the *Salve Regina* as they go to the guillotine. As each mounts the scaffold one less voice is heard. At last only one is left, that of Sister Constance. Blanche appears, making her way through the crowd. As Constance's voice stops chanting Blanche continues the hymn. She mounts the scaffold with head erect, proud that she has conquered the fears that have dominated her life.

§)&(§

DIE FLEDERMAUS

(The Bat)

Johann Strauss, the younger

Die Fledermaus was first produced in Vienna, April 5, 1874, and within a few years became famous throughout the world. Its first New York production (November 21,

1874) was in German and on March 16, 1885 the city heard an English version. In addition to the original, the work has been known in such American adaptations as *The Merry Countess, Champagne Sec,* and in 1942 as *Rosalinda,* the latter adapted from a version by Max Reinhardt. In 1950 Rudolf Bing commissioned Howard Dietz and Garson Kanin to prepare an English version that is now used at the Metropolitan Opera House.

The story was originally a German play by Roderich Benedix, *The Prison.* The French playwrights, Henri Meilhac and Ludovic Halévy, librettists of Bizet's *Carmen,* made it into a French comedy, *Le réveillon.* From this Carl Haffner and Richard Genée wrote the libretto of *Die Fledermaus* expressly for Johann Strauss.

The cast includes:

GABRIEL VON EISENSTEIN (*Tenor*), a rich Austrian
ROSALINDA (*Soprano*), his wife
ADELE (*Soprano*), her maid
ALFRED (*Tenor*), a profligate
DR. FALKE (*Baritone*)
DR. BLIND (*Tenor*), Eisenstein's lawyer
FRANK (*Baritone*), prison governor
PRINCE ORLOFSKY (*Traditionally sung by a Mezzo-soprano, sometimes by a Tenor*)
IDA (*Speaking part*), Adele's sister
FROSCH (*Speaking part*), a jailer

The place is Bad Ischl and the time 1874. The first act shows the morning room of von Eisenstein's house. From the outside we hear the voice of Alfred, serenading his former love Rosalinda. Adele, the maid, comes in with a letter she has received from her sister Ida, a dancer. Ida's ballet-company is having a party that night and her letter urges Adele to borrow an evening dress and join them.

Adele's mistress, Rosalinda, will not allow it, for her husband, von Eisenstein, is sentenced to start tonight a five-day term in prison for having insulted an officer. Rosalinda is considerably disturbed, but she is for the moment diverted by the entrance of the serenader, Alfred. He had once loved her unsuccessfully but he hopes he will be more successful now that she is married. He refuses to leave the house unless Rosalinda promises that she will see him while her husband is in jail. Fascinated by his singing, Rosalinda agrees.

Eisenstein enters with Dr. Blind, his lawyer. He is furious with the attorney for his bungling of the court hearing so that Eisenstein's sentence was increased from five days to eight. While Rosalinda is finding some old clothes for Eisenstein to wear in jail, his friend Dr. Falke comes to see him. Falke is secretly anxious to revenge himself on Eisenstein for a practical joke Eisenstein once played on him when he forced Falke to march through the town in a carnival costume, as a bat. Falke invites Eisenstein to attend a party tonight. In the morning he can turn himself in at the prison and his wife need know nothing about it. Eisenstein is delighted to accept and asks Rosalinda for evening clothes as his prison suit. He explains that it is a very distinguished prison and Rosalinda is too much occupied with thoughts of her coming rendezvous with Alfred to question the logic of such a costume. She has also changed her mind about Adele's request and has agreed to lend her an evening gown and give her the evening off. As soon as she is rid of her husband and her maid she receives Alfred. As they start their rendezvous they are interrupted by Frank, governor of the prison, who has come to take Eisenstein into custody. Something of a gay blade himself, Frank is eager to have the business over with as soon as possible. He too is planning to attend the party. Rosalinda pretends that Alfred is Eisenstein, so Frank leads him off to jail. Alfred's only reward is a kiss from Rosalinda.

The second act takes us to the party, given by the Russian Prince Orlofsky. Dr. Falke has taken over most of the arrangements and he introduces everyone as someone else. Adele the maid is an actress, Olga. Eisenstein is the Marquis Renard. Frank, the prison governor, is announced as Chevalier Chagrin, and finally Rosalinda, wearing a mask, appears as a Hungarian countess. They all become close friends as the champagne flows freely. Flirting with her own husband, Eisenstein, Rosalinda manages to take his watch. At six in the morning, the party breaks up and Frank and Eisenstein each remembers that he has important business on hand.

The third act shows the front office of the jail where Frosch the jailer has been in charge in Frank's absence. From one of the cells we hear the voice of Alfred, demanding a lawyer. Dr. Blind has been summoned. Frank returns from the party, dressed in evening clothes and well fortified by champagne. Adele and her sister Ida come to visit the jail and Adele admits she is only a chambermaid. When Eisenstein arrives he is astounded to learn that Eisenstein is already in jail. He hurriedly disguises himself as a lawyer and is ready for the coming of Rosalinda to question her and Alfred about their rendezvous. When he has learned the story he takes off his disguise and scolds them angrily. Rosalinda shows Eisenstein his watch and retorts that it is not only she who has been flirting. It is then explained that the whole party was arranged by Falke as revenge for the Bat joke Eisenstein had once played on him. Prince Orlofsky joins the gathering and announces that Adele acted her part so well that he will promote her as an actress. The opera ends with a chorus extolling the virtues of Champagne.

§)&(§

MACBETH

Giuseppe Verdi

Verdi's *Macbeth* was first produced in Florence, March 14, 1847. Its first American performance was given in New York, April 24, 1850. The libretto, based on Shakespeare's tragedy, was written by Francesco Maria Piave and Andrea Maffei. The cast includes:

DUNCAN (*Silent role*), King of Scotland
MACBETH (*Baritone*) } Generals of Duncan's army
BANQUO (*Bass*) }
MALCOLM (*Tenor*), Duncan's son
FLEANCE (*Silent role*), Banquo's son
LADY MACBETH (*Soprano*)
MACDUFF (*Tenor*), Thane of Fife
DOCTOR (*Bass*)
GENTLEWOMAN TO LADY MACBETH (*Mezzo-soprano*)
WITCHES, SOLDIERS, ASSASSINS, MESSENGERS, ATTENDANTS

The first act opens in a wood. Macbeth and Banquo, returning from a victory over a rebel army, come upon the three witches. The witches hail Macbeth as Thane of Glamis (his present title), as Thane of Cawdor, and as the future King of Scotland. They tell Banquo that his sons will be Kings of Scotland. Almost immediately messengers arrive to tell Macbeth that the King has appointed him Thane of Cawdor.

The second scene shows a hall in Macbeth's castle. Lady Macbeth reads a letter from her husband, telling her of the witches' prophecy and of the immediate fulfillment of the first part of it. When messengers announce that King Duncan is coming to the castle with Macbeth, Lady Macbeth resolves that there shall be no delay in realizing the rest of the prophecy. When Macbeth arrives she urges him to murder the King that very night. Macbeth steels himself, crying: "Is this a dagger that I see before me, the handle towards my hand?" and enters the King's bedchamber. As he returns from the bedroom with a blood-stained dagger he meets Lady Macbeth. She urges him to take the dagger and smear the blood on it over the sleeping guards of the dead King. Macbeth is terrified at the thought of returning to the King's bedroom, so Lady Macbeth takes the dagger and places it by the guards. A loud knocking is heard at the gates. Macduff and Banquo are coming for the King. The murder is discovered and the household aroused.

The second act opens in the castle, where Macbeth, now King of Scotland, is frightened and conscience-stricken. Lady Macbeth persuades him that Banquo knows too much and that he and his son Fleance must be killed. Had not the witches prophesied that Banquo's sons would rule after Macbeth? In the second scene assassins hired by Macbeth attack Banquo and Fleance in a wood near the castle. Banquo is murdered but Fleance escapes. The third scene shows a banquet where Macbeth is entertaining his nobles. Banquo's ghost appears to Macbeth who is so frightened that he resolves to consult the witches again.

The third act is laid in the witches' cavern. Although

they tell Macbeth to beware of Macduff they assure him that he need fear no man born of woman. They tell him also that he is safe until Birnam wood shall come to Dunsinane, his castle. Macbeth persists in his questioning and asks if Banquo's sons will become kings. In answer the witches conjure various apparitions from their cauldron. One of them is the ghost of Banquo. Terrified, Macbeth attacks it with his sword. He falls in a faint as the witches dance around him and vanish. As Macbeth regains consciousness Lady Macbeth enters and persuades him that Macduff and all his family should be murdered.

Act Four opens in desert country near the forest of Birnam. Refugees from Macbeth's tyranny are lamenting their exile. Macduff vows revenge for the murder of his family. Malcolm comes at the head of an English army and orders the soldiers to cut branches from the trees of Birnam wood and hold them in front of them as they march on Macbeth's castle at Dunsinane. In this way they will hide their numbers. In the second scene, in the castle, a doctor and Lady Macbeth's gentlewoman watch outside Lady Macbeth's bedroom. In her sleep she enters the room and reenacts the scene that occurred after Duncan's murder. She tries to wash bloodstains from her hands. The scene changes to another part of the castle where Macbeth is repeating to himself the witches' prophecy that none born of woman can harm him. Cries are heard outside and Lady Macbeth's gentlewoman comes to tell Macbeth that his wife is dead. Macbeth's soldiers rush in with news that Birnam wood is moving towards the castle. The scene changes to the battlefield where the English soldiers are advancing, each holding before him a leafy branch. Macbeth enters, followed by Macduff. Macduff cries: "At last I have met thee, murderer of my children." Macbeth answers that he bears a charmed life. "Thou canst in no way harm me," he tells Macduff, "thou who wert born of woman." Macduff replies that he was not born; he was "untimely ripped" from his mother's womb. Macbeth is killed and Malcolm, son of Duncan, is proclaimed King.

§)&(§

THE MIGHTY CASEY

William Schuman

The libretto of this baseball opera in three scenes was written by Jeremy Gury and was adapted from the poem "Casey at the Bat" by Ernest L. Thayer. The work was first performed May 4, 1953 by Julius Hartt Opera Guild at Hartford, Connecticut.

The cast includes:

MERRY (*Soprano*), Casey's girl
THE WATCHMAN (*Baritone*)
THATCHER (*Baritone*), Centerville catcher
FIREBALL SNEDEKER (*Baritone*), Centerville pitcher
CHARLIE (*Boy soprano*)
CASEY (*Silent role*)
UMPIRE BUTTENHEISER (*Baritone*)
CONCESSIONAIRE (*Baritone*)
MANAGER (*Baritone*)
MEMBERS OF THE MUDVILLE TEAM, HAWKERS, FANS

Scene One opens on Main Street, Mudville, U.S.A., a few minutes before noon on the day of the state championship game between Mudville and Centerville. As people pass, the town band assembles to lead the march to the Mudville Stadium. The scene changes to the outside of the Stadium where Merry, Casey's girl, and the Watchman discuss Casey's prowess at the bat. Charlie, a nine-year-old boy, is looking for a hole in the fence. Thatcher, the Centerville catcher, confers with Snedeker, its pitcher. Thatcher tells Snedeker a Centerville spy has reported that Casey cannot resist swinging at a ball that is inside and high. Thatcher will signal for it by scratching his ear. The Concessionaire and the Hawkers bring in their supplies. Charlie shows the Watchman a birthday present he has received, a book entitled *Famous Men of Baseball.* Charlie wonders if Casey will autograph it for him, and the Watchman thinks he will, for he may be in it some day. The Fans and the Mudville team wander in and when Casey appears with Merry the crowd cheers him wildly. Charlie breaks through and asks Casey for his autograph. Casey is delighted at this tribute but Charlie is pushed aside as the crowd gathers around their hero. As the players go to the field and the Fans to the stands the Watchman tells Merry that Casey is a lucky man to have a girl like her. He has heard that Big League scouts are there today with contracts in their hands.

The Second Scene shows the inside of the Stadium. It is the last half of the ninth inning and the score stands four to two in favor of Centerville. Cooney and Barrows of the Mudville team have each been thrown out at second. As Flynn comes to bat Merry sings a prayer, asking that he and then Blake get to base so that Casey will have a chance to bring them home. For the moment her prayer is answered: Flynn gets to first and Blake hits a double which brings him to second and Flynn to third. The crowd roars as Casey comes forward, deliberately hitches his pants, adjusts his cap and lightly swings a couple of bats. He knocks the dirt out of his spikes.

Thatcher and Snedeker confer. Thatcher says: "You're

doin' fine, kid," and Snedeker hurls the first pitch. "Strike one!", calls the Umpire. The crowds cry: "Kill the Umpire," and when the Mudville Manager protests the Umpire answers: "I call 'em as I see 'em." The crowd throws pop-bottles at him. Casey raises his hand for silence. He ignores the second pitch and when the Umpire calls "Strike two," and the crowds yell "Fraud!", Casey again silences them. The Centerville catcher scratches his ear and Snedeker sings to himself: "History hangs on a slender thread." He hurls the ball, high and inside, and the air is shattered by the force of Casey's swing.

As Casey and the other players disappear the fans move out of the stands and sing the concluding lines of Thayer's poem:

Oh, somewhere in this favored land, the sun is shining bright,
The band is playing somewhere, and somewhere hearts are light,
And somewhere men are laughing, and somewhere children shout,
But there is no joy in Mudville; Mighty Casey has struck out.

The third scene shows the Stadium again. Merry stands waiting for Casey. Casey enters, dressed in street clothes, miserable and dejected. Charlie approaches him and again asks for his autograph. Casey's spirits rise as he signs the boy's book and he takes a bat and re-enacts his last appearance in the game. As he swings at the imaginary third pitch a mighty crack is heard and he starts running around the bases. As he passes third and starts for home he sees Merry. He stops and takes her in his arms.

§)&(§

LA PÉRICHOLE

Jacques Offenbach

La Périchole was first produced at the Varietiés in Paris, October 6, 1868. It was first performed in New York, January 4, 1869. The libretto was written by Henri Meilhac and Ludovic Halévy. When the work was revived by the Metropolitan Opera House in New York in 1956 an English translation by Maurice Valency was used.

The characters include:

LA PÉRICHOLE (*Soprano*)
PAQUILLO (*Baritone*), her lover
DON ANDRÉS DE RIBEIRA (*Baritone*), Viceroy of Peru
DON PEDRO DE HINOYOSA (*Baritone*), Governor of Lima
THE COUNT OF PANATELLAS (*Tenor*), First Gentleman of the Bedchamber
THE MARQUIS DE TARAPOTE (*Bass-baritone*), Lord Chancellor
THE OLD PRISONER (*Tenor*)
GUADALENA (*Soprano*)
ESTRELLA (*Soprano*) } the Three Cousins
VIRGINELLA (*Mezzo-soprano*)
LADIES IN WAITING, COURTIERS, DRAGOONS, PEOPLE OF THE CITY

The action takes place in Lima, Peru, in mid-eighteenth century. The first act shows the front of the Cafe of the Three Cousins in the Public Square. On this Spring afternoon the people are celebrating the birthday of the Viceroy, Don Andrés. The Governor of the city, Don Pedro, is in charge of the festivities and is seeing to it that the people make at least a show of enthusiasm. He has learned that Don Andrés, the Viceroy, is prowling about the city incognito, trying to learn what people think of Don Pedro's administration. Pedro makes sure that everyone Don Andrés questions knows who he is and gives satisfactory answers. Two street singers, Paquillo and La Périchole sing a ballad for the crowd. This hungry pair are very much in love with each other but do not have enough money to buy a marriage license. The girl, La Périchole, is so exhausted that she falls asleep on a bench while her lover leaves for the moment to follow the crowd.

Don Andrés sees La Périchole on the bench and immediately falls in love with her. He awakens her and invites her to dinner, after which he will take her to the palace to become lady-in-waiting to his wife, long-since deceased. Even though La Périchole is devoted to Paquillo she is practical enough to realize that the proposed arrangement will at least keep her fed. She writes Paquillo a letter telling him they must part. Meanwhile Don Andrés' henchmen tell him that the laws of the country prohibit the Viceroy from having an unmarried mistress. Don Andrés orders the Count of Panatellas to find a suitable husband for La Périchole.

When Paquillo is handed La Périchole's letter he decides to hang himself, but even though Panatellas tries to help him his attempt is not successful. Instead of dying he accepts the offer of a suitable fee to become the husband of an unnamed lady who must be married. Panatellas does not know that Paquilla is even acquainted with La Périchole. Meanwhile Don Andrés, with the aid of liquor, has been trying to persuade La Périchole to consent to a marriage. She continues to refuse until she sees who it is that Don Andrés wants her to marry. Paquillo is so filled with wine that he does not recognize La Périchole. Notaries come to perform the ceremony and as soon as it is completed the bride and groom are led away in opposite directions.

The second act occurs the next morning and shows a hall in the Viceroy's palace. Paquillo enters. He has been made Baron of Tobago but is outraged to learn that he was tricked into a dishonorable marriage while he was drunk. Before he can be paid his promised fee he must present his wife formally to the Viceroy. La Périchole, now Baroness of Tobago, appears and Paquillo discovers that it is she he has married for the Viceroy's convenience. He flings La Périchole at the Viceroy's feet. Don Andrés orders him sent to the dungeon for recalcitrant husbands.

The third act opens in the dungeon. La Périchole enters through a tunnel an old Prisoner has made, bringing with her a bag of jewels for bribing the Turnkey. The Turnkey proves to be Don Andrés in disguise. He commands that La Périchole be chained in the dungeon opposite her husband. The old Prisoner returns through the tunnel and helps the pair to capture Don Andrés. They escape and leave the Viceroy in chains.

The next scene returns to the Public Square where royal dragoons are searching for the escaped pair. They are hiding in the Cafe of the Three Cousins. The clocks of the city strike the dinner hour and all operations must be suspended while the dragoons seat themselves at tables. The Viceroy takes his place on the balcony of the hotel. While they all are eating Paquillo and La Périchole appear and sing so beautifully of their love that Don Andrés forgives them. He confirms their newly-appointed titles and estates and the couple departs, rich and married.

§)&(§

THE RAKE'S PROGRESS

Igor Stravinsky

The libretto of *The Rake's Progress* was written by W. H. Auden and Chester Kallman and is based on a series of lithographs by the eighteenth-century English artist, William Hogarth. The opera was first performed at Venice, Italy, September 11, 1951. Its American première was given at the Metropolitan Opera House, New York, February 14, 1953.

The cast includes:

TOM RAKEWELL (*Tenor*)
NICK SHADOW (*Baritone*)
TRULOVE (*Bass*)
SELLEM (*Tenor*), an auctioneer
A KEEPER
ANNE (*Soprano*), Trulove's daughter
BABA THE TURK (*Mezzo-soprano*)
MOTHER GOOSE (*Mezzo-soprano*), madame of a brothel
ROARING BOYS, WHORES, SERVANTS, CITIZENS, MADMEN

The first scene of the first act takes place in the garden of Trulove's English cottage. The time is a Spring afternoon in the eighteenth century. Tom Rakewell and Anne Trulove are singing of their love for each other and are interrupted by Anne's father who tells Tom he has obtained for him a position in a friend's banking house. Tom turns down the offer. He has other prospects in view. Left alone Tom declares he will never be a drudge, he will entrust himself to fortune. As he makes a wish for money Nick Shadow appears at the garden gate to tell him that his former master, an unknown uncle of Tom's, has recently died and left his nephew all of his money. Tom exclaims that he was justified in his belief that fortune would favor him. In gratitude to Shadow he engages him as his own servant. Instead of marrying Anne immediately, Tom must go with Shadow to London to make arrangements for settling his affairs. When Tom asks Shadow what wages he will expect Shadow says that a year and a day hence Tom shall pay him whatever his services shall have been worth. Tom tells Anne he will send for her and marry her as soon as his affairs are arranged. Trulove gives his blessing but remarks to himself that "fortune so swift and so easy" may only encourage Tom's sins.

The second scene of the first act is laid in Mother Goose's London brothel. Tom, expensively dressed, is sitting at a table with Shadow and Mother Goose. After the Roaring Boys have sung of the joys of brawling and the Whores of winning gold by practicing the arts of love, Shadow tells Tom to show Mother Goose how well he has been prepared for the delights of his newly-found state of manhood. In a mock catechism on the essence of Nature, Beauty, and Pleasure, Tom gives worldly and cynical answers, but when he is asked what Love is, he remembers Anne and wants to go to her immediately. Shadow makes a sign and the cuckoo clock on the wall turns backward. "Time is yours," he says to Tom. "The hours obey your pleasure. You may repent at leisure." Tom sings of the love he has betrayed, and the whores are so attracted by his sadness, and his wealth, that they gather around him. Mother Goose asserts her elder right and claims Tom as her prize.

The third scene of the first act returns to Trulove's garden, on an Autumn night. Anne has not heard from Tom. She prays for his happiness, and is so sure that he needs her help that she decides to leave immediately for London.

The second act opens in the morning room of Rakewell's London house, on an Autumn morning. Tom is tired and disgusted with his life of pleasure. He makes his second wish, not for money, but to be happy. Shadow enters immediately with a circus handbill advertising Baba the Turk. He urges Tom to marry her, and when Tom protests he explains that freedom alone can bring happiness. The only way freedom may be gained is by ignoring passion and reason. To marry Baba, to whom he is neither attracted nor obligated, would be altogether unemotional and irrational. Such an act would prove Tom's freedom. Tom is delighted with this reasoning and sets forth to woo Baba the Turk.

The second scene shows the street in front of Tom's house. Anne is about to knock at the door when she sees a procession of servants carrying curiously shaped packages. As they enter the house a sedan chair is brought in. Tom steps from it and on seeing Anne is embarrassed and confused. He asks Anne to forget him, but she refuses. Baba's head, heavily veiled, appears at the window of the sedan. Anne learns that this is Tom's wife and leaves. Tom leads Baba toward the house and asks her to unveil. Baba obeys him and shows that she has a full black beard.

The third scene returns to the morning room of Tom's house, in the Winter. Tom and Baba are quarreling. When he repulses her advances she starts a violent harangue which Tom cuts short by putting an enormous wig over her face. When Tom lies down to rest Shadow enters pushing a strange looking machine. As Tom continues to sleep Shadow explains that the contrivance is a false-bottomed mechanism that seems to turn stone into bread. In his sleep Tom utters his third wish: that the dream he is having come true. On awakening he tells Shadow that he has dreamed of a machine that will save the world from poverty. When he sees the contrivance Shadow has brought with him he believes that he himself has invented it and that he has a means of benefiting mankind that will make him again worthy of Anne. He and Shadow will immediately sell shares of stock in the enterprise. As the two are leaving the house Shadow asks Tom about Baba. Tom replies that he has buried her.

The third act opens on a Spring afternoon in the morning room of Rakewell's house, now dusty and dilapidated. Tom and all the shareholders in the machine are bankrupt, and a crowd is gathered for an auction. Anne enters, looking for Tom, but no one will tell her where he is. After the auction the crowd clamors for the sale of an unknown object that proves to be Baba herself. On being aroused from a trance she accuses the auctioneer and the crowd of theft. While Tom and Shadow are heard singing in the street Anne returns and meets Baba. Knowing that she herself is ruined financially Baba begs Anne to save Tom, but to beware of Shadow. Baba can reestablish herself by returning to the stage.

In the second scene, in a churchyard the year and a day have elapsed and Shadow reveals himself as an agent of the devil. His payment will be Tom's soul and he orders Tom to kill himself at midnight. A clock starts to chime twelve, and after it has struck nine times Shadow again shows his power to arrest time. The striking stops and Shadow proposes a card game with Tom's soul as the stake. Shadow will cut three cards and Tom must guess what they are. Tom calls the first card correctly, and the clock sounds the tenth chime. He is again lucky on the second card and the eleventh chime is struck. As he is about to call the third card he cries: "Return, O love!" and Anne's answering voice makes him sure that the answer is the Queen of Hearts. The twelfth chime sounds and Tom falls in a faint. Shadow has been thwarted but he can still take Tom's reason from him. As dawn appears Shadow sinks into the ground, and Tom, demented, imagines he is Adonis.

The final scene is in Bedlam. The inmates taunt Tom for believing that Venus will come to visit him, her Adonis. Presently Anne comes to see Tom and when the keeper tells her of Tom's delusion she pretends to be Venus and tries to comfort him. She sings him to sleep and the mad folk join in the song. Trulove, Anne's father, comes to take her away. She bids the sleeping Tom farewell and as she leaves he wakes with a start, sees that she is gone, and accuses the inmates of having stolen her. When they reply that no one has been there Tom tells them to mourn Adonis, whom Venus loves. As they sing he falls upon his pallet.

In the Epilogue, all the characters come before the curtain and sing: "For idle hands and hearts and minds, the Devil finds a work to do."

§)&(§

THE RAPE OF LUCRETIA

Benjamin Britten

This two-act chamber opera was first performed at Glyndebourne, England, July 12, 1946. The libretto by Ronald Duncan is based on a play by André Obey, *Le Viol de Lucrèce.*

The cast includes:

MALE CHORUS (*Tenor*)
FEMALE CHORUS (*Soprano*)

COLLATINUS (*Bass*), a Roman General
JUNIUS (*Baritone*), a Roman General
TARQUINIUS SEXTUS (*Baritone*), an Etruscan Prince
LUCRETIA (*Contralto*), wife of Collatinus
BIANCA (*Mezzo-soprano*), Lucretia's aged nurse
LUCIA (*Soprano*), a maid

The time of the opera is 500 B.C. As the house curtain rises the Male and Female Choruses explain that Rome is now ruled by the Etruscan upstart, Tarquinius Superbus, a man who reached the throne by means of murder and evil deeds. His son, Tarquinius Sextus, is now at the head of the Roman army, once more moving against the Greeks. The inner curtain rises and the first scene of Act One shows the Generals' tent in the army camp outside Rome. Prince Tarquinius and the two generals, Collatinus and Junius, are making merry in the tent. They talk about the secret visits several officers had made to their homes to see how their wives were behaving during their absence. Only one of the wives proved faithful to her husband, and that was Lucretia, the wife of Collatinus. Lucretia's chaste fidelity is acclaimed. Tarquinius taunts Junius for being a cuckold, one whose wife is unfaithful. Junius returns the compliment by saying that although Tarquinius is a bachelor, he too is a cuckold since none of the many loose women with whom he has been intimate have ever been faithful to him. The quarrel is interrupted by Collatinus who reminds them that they are to march tomorrow. He begs them to drink a toast instead of brawling. Tarquinius proposes a toast to the chaste Lucretia.

When Tarquinius and Junius are left alone they speculate as to whether Lucretia would remain so chaste if she were really tempted. Tarquinius says that he himself will test her chastity. Junius answers that even Tarquinius would not dare attempt such a deed. Tarquinius, determined to conquer Lucretia, by force if necessary, mounts his steed and rides towards the lights of Rome.

The second scene shows a room in Lucretia's house, the same evening. Lucretia is spinning with her maid Lucia and her old nurse Bianca. As they prepare to retire a loud knocking is heard at the door. Tarquinius stands there saying that his horse has gone lame and asking Lucretia for a night's shelter. Lucretia cannot refuse the Prince of Rome. She invites him in and offers him wine. She asks eagerly about the health of her husband Collatinus. With her servants she conducts Tarquinius to his bedchamber and retires to her own couch.

The second act opens in Lucretia's bedroom. Tarquinius steals in and gazes at the sleeping woman, lying unprotected and helpless. He awakens her with a kiss. Lucretia is terrified and begs her attacker to spare her virtue. The lustful Tarquinius threatens her with his sword, and as she shrinks from him he blows out the candle and attacks her.

The second scene shows the outer room in Lucretia's house, the next morning. Lucia and Bianca are arranging flowers. Lucia wonders how long Tarquinius will be staying, and Bianca replies that he may have left already for she was awakened early in the morning by the sound of a horse in the courtyard. Lucretia enters, a tragic figure. She is repelled by the orchids Bianca hands her to arrange for her husband and orders Lucia to send a messenger to the camp begging her husband to come at once. She hands Lucia an orchid for the messenger telling her it is a gift to Collatinus "from a Roman harlot." She asks Bianco for the remaining orchids and arranges them as a wreath. Before the messenger has time to leave Collatinus arrives, accompanied by Junius. Junius hears some pertinent remarks of Bianca's and guesses what has happened. He sadly repeats what he has heard to Collatinus. Lucretia enters wearing purple as a sign of mourning for her lost virtue. Collatinus assures her that Tarquinius's foul deed does not affect his own deep love for her. Lucretia is too distraught to respond to her husband's assurances. She draws a dagger from the folds of her gown and stabs herself through the heart.

§)&(§

THE RUBY

Norman Dello Joio

The libretto of this one-act opera was written by William Mass, and is based on Lord Dunsany's story, *A Night at an Inn.* The work was first produced at the University of Indiana, May 13, 1955.

The characters are:

SCOTT (*Baritone*)
LAURA (*Soprano*), his wife
ALBERT (*Tenor*)
SNIGGERS (*Tenor*)
BULL (*Bass*)
THREE INDIAN PRIESTS (*Silent roles*)
THE IDOL (*Silent role*)

The time of the action is about the turn of the last century. The scene is the interior of a lonely house on the English moors that has not been used or lived in for some time. Sniggers and Bull are playing cards by the light of a candle. Lightning flashes outside and Sniggers is frightened. He has been dreaming of menacing figures with knives in their mouths. Albert comes in from the storm exclaiming: "I saw them—in town." Scott appears at the head of the staircase and asks why the three are making such a racket. They answer that they want to run while there is still time.

It then develops that the four Englishmen have stolen from an Indian idol the ruby that was its giant eye. They have made their way back to England and have taken refuge in this deserted house that once belonged to Scott. During their flight the thieves have been relentlessly followed by the three priests who guarded the idol. Now Albert has seen them in a nearby town.

Scott arrests the others' panic by telling them that for months he has purposely dropped clues for the priests to follow so that they could be appropriately dealt with at the proper time and place. Although the men are furious at Scott's recklessness they are not sure enough of themselves to do anything but agree to whatever he is planning.

Scott's wife, Laura, has left him because of his many evil deeds even though she loves him deeply and has always hoped that his better nature might someday prevail. For this reason she answers his latest appeal and comes to the house. He pleads with her to resume their once happy life and she agrees on condition that he choose between her and his crimes.

As she finishes her statement a priest's shadow passes on the wall of the room. Quickly Scott tells his accomplices what they must do. Each of the priests is murdered as Laura watches in horror. As the three associates drink a toast to Scott Laura runs sobbing from the house. Soon she rushes back into the room, speechless with fright. She points through the open door. A monstrous roar is heard from outside calling three Hindu words meaning Vengeance, Retribution, Death. One by one, Sniggers, Bull and Albert are drawn through the door as by a magnet. Scott bolts the door as the shrieks of the three conspirators are heard. Suddenly the door crashes. The Idol stands there, its face smeared with blood. It gropes its way to the box that holds the ruby. It screws the jewel into the empty socket on its forehead and walks back to the door. Slowly it turns and beckons Scott to follow. While Laura clings to him Scott is drawn irresistibly. At the foot of the door Laura collapses as Scott walks slowly through the door.

§)&(§

THE SAINT OF BLEECKER STREET

Gian-Carlo Menotti

This three-act opera was first performed at the Broadway Theatre, New York, December 27, 1954. Its libretto was written by the composer, and the cast includes:

ASSUNTA (*Mezzo-soprano*)
CARMELA (*Soprano*) } friends of Annina
DON MARCO (*Bass*), a priest
ANNINA (*Soprano*)
MICHELE (*Tenor*), her brother
DESIDERIA (*Mezzo-soprano*), in love with Michele
MARIA CORONA (*Soprano*), a newsstand vendor
HER DUMB SON

The action of the opera occurs in New York's "Little Italy" and concerns the sickly girl Annina. Her neighbors believe that she is a saint and hope that her religious visions will enable her to cure sickness.

The first scene of the first act shows a room in a cold-water flat in the tenements of Bleecker Street. It is the afternoon of Good Friday. A group of neighbors are grouped around Assunta, who is chanting the Litany. The visitors face the half-opened door of Annina's bedroom, waiting impatiently until she may be brought in. Maria Corona hopes that her dumb child may be given the power to speak, and another woman has brought her idiot son who clings to her skirt. The suspense leads to bickering and an open quarrel between Maria Corona and a young woman. As they are about to come to blows Don Marco, the priest, appears in the doorway. He announces that Annina will be carried in but she is very ill and the visitors must be gentle with her. If she should again be blessed with the stigmata, he, the priest, will throw anyone out who tries to touch her bleeding wounds. Annina is brought in, half-conscious. Her pale face shows the marks of suffering. She is placed in a chair as the neighbors kneel and chant: "Salve Virgo florens." When they have finished Annina has a vision of the Crucifixion and actually receives the stigmata. As her wounds bleed the neighbors crowd around her, trying hysterically to touch her. Suddenly Annina's brother Michele appears in the doorway. Angrily he drives the people from the flat, threatening to call the police. He warns the priest to keep away from Annina. He, her brother, will guide her and save her from fanaticism. Don Marco tells Michele that it is not he but God himself who is Michele's rival for his sister's affections.

The second scene is an empty lot on Mulberry Street, flanked by tenement houses. It is Saint Gennaro Day, when the image of the patron saint of Naples is carried through the streets. Michele has forbidden his sister to take part in the procession but the enraged Sons of San Gennaro beat him and tie him to a gate. They take Annina and carry her in the wake of the image. When the procession has passed Michele is freed by Desideria, a girl who loves him.

The second act is laid in an Italian restaurant, the following May. Carmela, Annina's dearest friend, is celebrating her wedding. Although Desideria is uninvited, she comes to the restaurant and pleads with Michele for his love. He admits that he is fond of her but he is torn between his love for Desideria and his almost abnormal devotion to his sister. When the guests have arrived Michele harangues them. He scorns their resignation to lives of poverty, he rejects their humility and religious faith, and cries that if he could know what it means to be an Italian and feel Italian soil beneath his feet, he might feel well and strong again. When his tirade is finished Desideria taunts him with having a greater love for his sister than for her, his sweetheart. Stung into fury, Michele stabs Desideria to death and escapes.

The first scene of the third act shows a subway station where the fugitive Michele meets his sister Annina. He begs her not to take the veil. She knows she is going to die, and has fully made up her mind. Michele curses her for being disloyal to him and for failing him when he needs her most.

The final scene shows Annina dying, in her own home. Permission has been granted her to take the veil at home, and Don Marco, with an assisting priest and a nun, performs the rites. Michele arrives and makes one more appeal to Annina, this time more like a lover than a brother. Annina seems not to hear him, and dies before she receives the sacred ring. Don Marco slips it on her lifeless finger.

§)&(§

SUSANNAH

Carlisle Floyd

The plot of this two-act opera is based on the Apochrypha story of Susannah and the Elders. The libretto was written by the composer and the work was given its first performance February, 1955 at Florida State University, Talahassee. It was produced by the New York City Opera Company at the City Center, September, 27, 1956.

The cast includes:

SUSANNAH POLK (*Soprano*)
SAM (*Tenor*), her brother
REVEREND OLIN BLITCH (*Bass-baritone*), itinerant evangelist
LITTLE BAT (*Tenor or spoken*)
THE FOUR ELDERS AND THEIR WIVES
MOUNTAIN FOLK

The first scene shows the yard of the church at New Hope, in the Tennessee Mountains. A square dance is in progress and a fiddler and a caller are putting the mountain folk through the paces of a hoedown. The elders of the church and their wives are watching the dancers as they wait for the coming of the Reverend Olin Blitch, an Evangelist who is to hold a series of revival meetings at New Hope. The Elders' wives are gossiping about Susannah as she dances. She is so beautiful that she makes them jealous. They call her shameless and criticize the cut of her dress. Their husbands are more appreciative and try to cut in on the dance. The Reverend Blitch arrives and is greeted by the chanting of a hymn-like refrain. When the dancing resumes Blitch discovers Susannah and manages to dance with her.

The second scene of the first act shows the front of the rickety farmhouse where Susannah lives with her brother Sam. Little Bat, a shifty-eyed youth who is not over-bright, teases Susannah about dancing with the preacher. Susannah sings a reverie in which she daydreams of places beyond the mountains where "the folks talk nice an' the folks dress nice." Susannah's brother Sam appears and Little Bat runs away in fright. Susannah tells Sam about dancing with the preacher and Sam replies that perhaps she will soon be leaving him to be married. Susannah laughs at such an idea.

The third scene shows a nearby field where four of the Elders are searching for a creek that the Reverend Blitch may use for his baptisms. They discover Susannah bathing nude in the stream. She is unaware of their presence as they whisper to each other that she is a shameless wench who must be punished. As they make these comments they cast lustful glances at her.

Scene Four returns to the churchyard where the church-members are about to have a potluck supper. They all know about Susannah bathing in the stream and when she appears one of the Elders tells her she is not welcome. She does not know why she is shunned and leaves in bewilderment.

In the last scene of the first act Little Bat comes to the Polk farm and tells Susannah what the gossip is about. He tells her also that the people made him say that he himself had been intimate with her. Susannah screams: "Git away, you 'lyin' varmint," and Little Bat runs off, wailing. Sam has overheard the conversation and he tries to console his sister. He says that people are "short on lovin' kindness."

The second act opens several days later, again at the Polk farm. Susannah is distraught at the scorn people have for her and has come almost to believe that she is what people say she is. "Mebbe the devil is in me," she tells Sam. Sam begs her to keep her courage and to face the church-members by attending the revival meeting that evening. He himself has to leave for an overnight hunting expedition.

Scene Two shows the interior of the church. When the choir has finished a gospel song the Reverend Blitch begins his hell-fire sermon. As he reaches the climax of his frenzied exhortation the choir takes up an "invitation" hymn. One by one couples come forward for their confession of faith. Susannah sits on a bench gazing at the preacher. As the congregation watches her she rises and starts to move forward. Suddenly she shakes off her trance and crying "no! no!" rushes from the church.

Scene Three returns to the farm, an hour later. As Susannah is sitting on the porch, singing softly to herself, Blitch appears saying that he is concerned for Susannah's soul. She tells Blitch of her bitterness and of the injustice she has been shown by her fellow-beings. Blitch tells her of his own unhappiness and of his loneliness. He needs so desperately a woman to love. He puts his arm around Susannah and leads her to the house. Susannah sighs that she "jes' cain't fight no more," and enters the house with Blitch.

The next scene shows Blitch alone in the church, praying desperately for his own salvation. He knows that Susannah was innocent and when the Elders and their wives enter the church he pleads with them to ask Susannah to forgive them. Blitch fails to move the Elders and they walk silently out of the church. Alone with Susannah Blitch begs her to forgive him. She answers that she has forgotten what the word "fergive" means.

In the final scene Sam, a bit tipsy, returns from his hunting expedition. Susannah tells him of her affair with the preacher and takes him to task for having left her when she needed him. Sam takes his shotgun and runs off towards the creek where Blitch is conducting baptisms. A shot is heard and Little Bat runs in to tell Susannah that her brother has shot the preacher as he was praying for her blessing. A mob is on its way to run her off her farm and out of the valley. When the mob arrives Susannah faces them with a shotgun. She laughs at them hysterically. After they have backed away and disappeared muttering maledictions Susannah sees Little Bat lurking in the background. Suddenly adopting a seductive manner she invites Little Bat to "come on over and love me up some." As Little Bat puts his arms around her she slaps him viciously across his face. He runs whimpering across the yard as Susannah goes back to the porch. She stands in the doorway as the curtain falls.

§)&(§

THE TAMING OF THE SHREW

Vittorio Giannini

The libretto of this opera was adapted by Dorothy Fee from Shakespeare's comedy, using additional texts from the Sonnets and from *Romeo and Juliet*. The work was first performed in Cincinnati, January 31, 1953 and in November of 1954 it was included in the repertoire of the Chicago Lyric Theater.

The cast includes:

BAPTISTA (*Bass*), a wealthy gentleman of Padua
KATHARINA (*Soprano*), his elder daughter
BIANCA (*Soprano*), his younger daughter
PETRUCHIO (*Baritone*), Katharina's suitor

GRUMIO (*Tenor*) }
CURTIS (*Bass*) } Petruchio's servants

HORTENSIO (*Baritone*), suitor to Bianca, who masquerades as Licio, a music teacher

GREMIO (*Tenor*), suitor to Bianca

LUCENTIO (*Tenor*), suitor to Bianca, who masquerades as Cambio, a Latin teacher

TRANIO (*Baritone*), Lucentio's servant who masquerades as his master

BIONDELLO (*Bass*), servant to Lucentio

VINCENTIO (*Bass*), Lucentio's father

A PEDANT (*Tenor*), who masquerades as Vincentio

A TAILOR (*Tenor*)

The first act shows a street in Padua. At the right is Signor Baptista's house, showing a corner of its garden. Signor Hortensio's house is at the left. Lucentio and his servant Tranio arrive from Pisa. Lucentio has come to study and increase his knowledge. Baptista enters with his two daughters, Katharina and Bianca, as well as two of Bianca's suitors, Gremio and Hortensio. Baptista announces that Bianca may not marry before he has found a husband for her elder sister, Katharina. Katharina shows her shrewish disposition by calling them all fools and devils. Lucentio and Tranio stand in the background remarking that the older daughter is stark mad but that the younger is mild and sober in her behavior. Baptista tells Bianca to go into the house. She obeys meekly saying that music and poetry shall be her company. Her father promises her he will engage masters to teach her.

Hortensio and Gremio agree that although they are rivals for Bianca's hand, neither of them will have her unless they can find a husband for Katharina. When they have left, Lucentio exclaims to Tranio that he has already fallen in love with Bianca. Instead of studying in

Padua he will devote himself to winning the girl. Since her father wants masters to teach her he will assume Tranio's clothes and will become Cambio, a Latin teacher. Tranio will become Lucentio and wear his master's clothes. Biondello, a second servant to Lucentio, will now be the servant of Tranio. As the three leave, Petruchio, a young man of Verona, enters with his servant Grumio. Knocking at his friend's, Hortensio's, door he explains that his father has died and left him his wealth. He now seeks a wife in Padua. Hortensio remarks that he can find him a wealthy and beautiful wife but that her disposition is devilish. Petruchio is delighted, particularly when he learns that the lady is the daughter of his father's wealthy friend Baptista. Hortensio offers to take Petruchio to Baptista and asks his friend to introduce him as a music master, so that he may have opportunity to make love to Bianca. Lucentio, disguised as a Latin teacher, enters with Gremio, and promises Gremio that he will plead his cause for him to Bianca. They all knock at Baptista's door. The servant shows Gremio and the others to the garden while Petruchio introduces himself to Baptista as the son of the late Antonio. Petruchio introduces Hortensio as a music teacher. Gremio and Lucentio are introduced as teachers and are welcomed by Baptista. Tranio announces himself as Lucentio, the son of Vincentio of Pisa, and offers himself as a suitor to Bianca. Petruchio asks Baptista what dowry he will give Katharina and Bianca's suitors, eavesdropping, are delighted to learn that the lands and money he will give his older daughter will be matched by an equal amount for Bianca. During this discussion a commotion is heard from the house and Hortensio rushes out with a broken lute hanging about his neck. Petruchio is delighted to learn that Katharina has disposed thus of the music master, and he waits for her eagerly as the others leave. He will conquer her spirit. Katharina comes from the house and retorts scornfully to every remark Petruchio makes to her. He stands his ground and parries every insult. Then he takes her in his arms and kisses her forcibly. He is born to tame her, he exclaims, and he must have her for his wife. The others return and are amazed to hear Petruchio cry "Kiss me Kate, we shall be married on Sunday!" Katharina calls him a ruffian, lunatic, fool, and says she'll see him hanged on Sunday first. Her father, however, has noticed that she was moved by Petruchio's kiss.

The first scene of the second act shows the garden of Baptista's house on the afternoon before the wedding. Hortensio is tuning his lute while Lucentio, supplied with books, scrolls, and quills, is trying to distract him. Bianca is waiting to begin her lessons. She tells Hortensio to finish tuning his instrument while Lucentio gives her a Latin lesson. Between phrases Lucentio whispers that he is really not a tutor but a nobleman disguised so that he may win her love. When he has received partial encouragement he pretends to leave, but watches from the doorway to see how Hortensio makes out. Hortensio, too, tries to woo Bianca during his lesson but she will have none of it. Petruchio enters with Grumio. Both of them are dressed in old, ragged clothes. Petruchio bawls for Kate at the top of his voice. Katharina appears and declares that she will not marry Petruchio dressed in so ridiculous a fashion. Petruchio declares she will indeed and struts off with Grumio. Lucentio, alone with Bianca, urges her to elope with him.

The next scene is the garden on the wedding morning. Inside the house Katharina is calling for her hair-dresser, her shoes, her gown and her jewels. While servants are rushing back and forth Hortensio confides in Tranio (disguised as his master Lucentio) that Bianca loves Cambio the Latin teacher. They watch Lucentio and Bianca as they embrace. Katharina is furious that Petruchio has not yet appeared. She exclaims that she has been forced to wed a man who wooed in haste and intends to marry at leisure. Biondello comes with a note from Petruchio. It tells Baptista that business has detained him. He says he will be at the church at noon and that if Katharina is as much as one minute late he will depart immediately. Baptista is insulted and roars that there will be no wedding. Hortensio encourages Baptista's anger, but Lucentio urges him to relent. Baptista drags Kate from the house and as the others follow takes her off to the church.

The third act shows a room in Petruchio's house, a few days after the wedding. Grumio is telling his fellow-servant Curtis of their master's rough treatment of Katharina. Petruchio enters and demands his dinner. He commands Kate to come and sit at the table and then proceeds first to abuse his Tailor for the quality of a cap he has made (which Katharina says she likes) and then complains that the meat served for dinner is not fit for dogs. Katharina is ravenously hungry but Petruchio throws the food on the floor and rushes out to deal with the cook. As Katharina is singing of her unhappiness and her need for comfort and love Lucentio and Bianca appear. They have been secretly married and Lucentio explains that he is not really the Latin teacher Cambio. Petruchio calls from outside that they have a guest and as the newlyweds hide in a side room he brings in Vincentio who announces that he is looking for his son, Lucentio. Petruchio says that he knows Lucentio, he has married his sister-in-law. Baptista enters with Lucentio's two servants, Tranio and Biondello. They have with them the Pedant, dressed to look like Lucentio's father, Vincentio. A series of mixed identities follows. Baptista says that Bianca has eloped with that rascal Cambio. Vincentio and the Pedant both claim to be Lucentio's father and chaos prevails until Katharina brings in the real Lucentio and Bianca and matters are straightened out and explained. Katharina by this time has softened and when she and Petruchio are left alone they speak tenderly to each other and sing a love duet.

§)&(§

THE TENDER LAND

Aaron Copland

This two-act opera was first performed by the New York City Opera Company at the City Center, April 1, 1954. Its libretto was written by Horace Everett. The cast includes:

LAURIE MOSS (*Soprano*), the older sister
MA MOSS (*Contralto*)
BETH MOSS (*Speaking role*), the younger sister
GRANDPA MOSS (*Bass*)
MARTIN (*Tenor*) } drifters
TOP (*Baritone*) }
MR. SPLINTERS (*Tenor*), the postman
MRS. SPLINTERS (*Mezzo-soprano*)
MR. JENKS (*Baritone*) } a neighboring couple
MRS. JENKS (*Soprano*) }
PARTY GUESTS

The action takes place on a lower-middle-class farm in the midwest. It is June, in the early 1930's. The first act shows the outside of the Moss farmhouse, with the yard. Beth, a child of from eight to ten years, is playing with her doll. Ma Moss is sewing on the porch. The postman, Mr.

Splinters, arrives with a package that contains Laurie's graduation dress, ordered from Chicago. Ma Moss invites Mr. Splinters to the graduation party the family is giving for Laurie tonight, and asks him to bring his fiddle. Mr. Splinters tells Ma Moss the latest news. A neighbor's girl met a "strange fellar" in the fields. He is probably one of two that are travelling together, no doubt the ones who attacked another girl a couple of months ago. Ma goes into the house with the dress and Beth races off with her doll. Laurie comes in with her schoolbooks. She reveals some of her thoughts about graduating from school and her uncertainty about her future place in the world. She feels that there must be a larger life than the one she has known. As she starts up the steps of the porch two itinerant youths, Martin and Top, appear. Laurie hides behind the porch. The boys talk about their vagabond existence. They are hungry and Top, the older, says he can almost smell his ex-wife's stew. They discover Laurie and talk to her. She is frightened but fascinated by their account of all the places they have been and to which they are going. Laurie introduces the two to Grandpa Moss. He is suspicious of strangers but he needs more men on the farm so he hires them to help with the crop. He tells Ma Moss to set two more places for supper and Laurie asks the boys to her party tonight.

The second act shows the party in progress. The family and the guests, Mr. and Mrs. Splinters and Mr. and Mrs. Jenks, and the two drifters, Top and Martin, are seated around a large table. They have finished supper and as Grandpa passes around the berry wine Top becomes talkative and tells how many jails he has been in. A toast is proposed to Laurie and she answers by wondering what the day after tomorrow will be, and what other lands are like. Grandpa and Top start drinking in earnest as the dancing starts. Ma Moss is suspicious of the strangers; she thinks they may be the ones who attacked the neighbors' girls. She asks Mr. Splinters to go for the sheriff. As the dancing continues and Top sings ribald songs to Grandpa, Martin and Laurie dance together and go to the porch to look at the moon. Martin tells Laurie he is tired of travelling. He is in love with her and would like to settle down. Laurie says that she loves him and is ready to marry him if he wants her. As they embrace Grandpa Moss staggers to the porch looking for Laurie. He cries "no good dirty bums!" and rushes at Martin. The guests come from the house and hold Grandpa back. Ma Moss cries hysterically: "They're the men!" Mr. Splinters returns. The sheriff has not come with him, for he has told Mr. Splinters that two men just caught in the next county have confessed to attacking the girls. The guests shamefacedly take their leave and Grandpa, now sober, tells the boys that while they have done no real harm they must leave at daybreak. In the next scene Martin comes from the shed where he and Top are spending the night. He calls Laurie. She appears at the window and they plan to elope as soon as morning comes. When Laurie has gone back into her room Top appears from the shed. Martin tells him that Laurie is leaving with them. Top tells him he is crazy. Could Laurie "hop a freight; sleep in a railroad crate?" He gets their bundles from the shed and leads the dazed Martin away.

The last scene occurs at daybreak. Laurie comes down the steps carrying a small satchel. When she finds that Martin has gone she weeps hysterically. Heartbroken, she decides that she must go away, even if she goes alone. Her mother tries to dissuade her, reminding her she is to graduate today. Laurie does not heed her but goes off down the road. Ma Moss, beginning to understand, turns to Beth, and seems to see her for the first time.

TROILUS AND CRESSIDA

William Walton

Sir William Walton's three-act opera was first produced in London, December 3, 1954. In the autumn of 1955 it received two productions in the United States, by the San Francisco Opera Company October 7, and by the New York City Opera Company at the City Center October 21.

The legend of Troilus and Cressida has been developed and treated by many authors. Homer, in the 24th book of the *Iliad* mentions Troilus as the son of Priam, and several Greek and Latin authors make him a prominent hero in their writings. Sometime before 1340 Giovanni Boccaccio wrote his novel *Filostrato* in which the chief characters were Troilo and Criseida. From this work of Boccaccio Geoffrey Chaucer adapted his poem, *Troilus and Criseyde,* about 1380. Sometime around 1600 Shakespeare wrote his play *Troilus and Cressida,* and in 1678 John Dryden wrote a play of the same name.

The libretto of the Walton opera was written by Christopher Hassall, who acknowledges as his sources Boccaccio and Chaucer rather than Shakespeare or Dryden.

The cast includes:

CALKAS (*Bass*), a High Priest
CRESSIDA (*Soprano*), his daughter
PANDARUS (*Tenor*), his brother
ANTENOR (*Baritone*), a Trojan captain
TROILUS (*Tenor*), a Trojan prince
EVADNE (*Mezzo-soprano*), Cressida's servant
HORASTE (*Baritone*), a friend of Pandarus
DIOMEDE (*Baritone*), Prince of Argos

The action takes place in Troy during the 12th century, B.C. The first act shows the Temple of Pallas. The Greeks are besieging the city and the citizens are complaining that the prayers and sacrifices of the priests and priestesses have been useless. Calkas, the High Priest, tells the people that the Oracle of Delphi advises them to arrange a peace with the Greeks. Antenor, a Captain, publicly accuses Calkas of being a traitor. He claims that Calkas has himself invented the counsel of the Oracle and that he is in the pay of the enemy. Prince Troilus, son of the Trojan king Priam, drives the threatening crowd away. He tells Antenor that he will watch Calkas and although Antenor accepts this assurance, he guesses that it will be Calkas's daughter Cressida who gets the most attention from Troilus. We soon learn that Antenor has guessed shrewdly for as soon as Troilus is alone he sings passionately of his love. Cressida appears on the steps of the Temple but since she is a recent widow and still wears the pure white of mourning she sorrowfully returns to the Temple without encouraging Troilus. The effeminate Pandarus is borne in on a litter. He is a brother of the priest Calkas and Cressida's uncle. He feels that he is an expert at arranging other people's affairs and he offers to help Troilus in wooing Cressida. As Cressida enters with her father Calkas, Pandarus hides so that he can hear what they say to each other. Calkas is planning to go over to the Greeks. In vain Cressida and her maid Evadne try to dissuade him. Calkas leaves, followed by Evadne and then by Pandarus. Cressida, in a soliloquy, calls her father a traitor. She confesses her love for Troilus and does not want to involve him with her father's perfidy. Evadne and Pandarus return to discuss Calkas's desertion and Pandarus, realizing that the family's only hope lies in royal favor starts in earnest to persuade Cressida to marry Troilus.

A small army patrol comes from a skirmish with the Greeks. Antenor has been taken prisoner and Troilus decides that they must arrange an exchange of prisoners so that Antenor may be returned to them. Calkas, the priest, would normally be the one to arrange the exchange but they cannot find him. Everyone goes to look for him but Pandarus and Cressida. Pandarus invites Cressida to a party he is giving at his house the next evening. He persuades Cressida to let him have her red scarf which he will give to Troilus as a token of her favor. As the act ends Troilus is delighted to receive Cressida's scarf from Pandarus.

The first scene of the second act shows the party at Pandarus's house. Cressida is playing a game with one of the guests as Pandarus sends a messenger for Troilus. It is decided that because a storm is gathering the party should disband. Cressida and her maid Evadne accept Pandarus's invitation to spend the night. Evadne and her assistants help Cressida prepare to sleep in a bed that has been placed in an alcove of the room. When Cressida is alone she sings of her love for Troilus. Suddenly Pandarus comes to tell her that Troilus has arrived, jealous of her spending the night at Pandarus's house. Troilus bursts into the room and Pandarus leaves them to their love-making.

In the next scene morning has come and the lovers have time for only a few more words before Pandarus interrupts to tell them that a party of Greek soldiers is entering his yard. He hides the lovers just before Diomede, Prince of Argos, enters. He offers to exchange Antenor for Cressida. Inasmuch as it has been Troilus who had a couple of days before suggested an exchange of prisoners, Diomede believes that the exchange of Antenor for the daughter of the traitor Calkas, who is now serving the Greeks, should be pleasing to all concerned. Troilus has to comply with what has already been agreed upon between the Trojan and Greek kings. Although Cressida receives from Troilus the red scarf she had given him she tells him she is his forever.

The third act takes place in the Greek camp. Calkas and his daughter Cressida are housed in a pavilion. Cressida has been waiting for a message from Troilus but Evadne comes from the direction of the Trojan plains to tell her, as she has on previous occasions, that there is no word from him. Evadne urges Cressida to forget Troilus and to marry Prince Diomede. Cressida orders Evadne to try once more to find a message from Troilus. Calkas also tries to persuade his daughter to marry Diomede. When Diomede comes to plead his own cause Cressida weakens. She gives him her red scarf. Evadne returns and signals to Cressida that there still is no message from Troilus, and Diomede leaves to tell his troops that Cressida will become Queen of Argos. When Evadne is alone for a few minutes she takes out and burns a whole package of messages that she has received from Troilus but has not delivered to Cressida, murmuring that her mistress will thank her some day. Pandarus and Troilus enter. Troilus's father, the Trojan King Priam, is arranging a ransom for Cressida and Troilus wants to take her away at once. As the Greek troops from the distance hail her as "Bride of Argos" Cressida cries "too late!" Diomede comes in wearing the red scarf, and when Troilus steps forward and sings of woman's perfidy, the other five join him in a sextet. Diomede sings of Troy's falsehood, Cressida of her tragic love that is now doomed, Pandarus of the futility of trying to arrange matters, Calkas of the uselessness of defying fate, and Evadne of her hope that Diomede will kill Troilus. It is not Diomede who kills Troilus, it is Calkas, who stabs him in the back while he is fighting a duel with Diomede.

Diomede is outraged at such treachery. He orders Calkas to be sent back to Troy in chains, he ignores the crafty Pandarus, and he orders Cressida to be confined in the army camp as a prostitute. He commands that the dying

Troilus be treated with high honors. Cressida picks up Troilus's sword, wraps it in the red scarf, and, singing a last farewell to her lover, stabs herself.

§)&(§

THE TURN OF THE SCREW

Benjamin Britten

This opera, in two acts of eight scenes each, was first performed at Venice, Italy, September 14, 1954. The libretto by Myfanwy Piper is based on a novel of the same title by Henry James.

Musically and dramatically the action of the opera is circular. Its continuous orchestral interludes connect the scenes that portray the struggle between the governess of two children and the spirits of a former governess and manservant who when alive exercised a sinister, unwholesome influence over the children, and who return from the dead to gain possession of their souls.

The action takes place during the middle of the 19th century at an English country house named Bly. The characters are:

THE PROLOGUE (*Tenor*)
THE GOVERNESS (*Soprano*)
MILES (*Treble*) } the children
FLORA (*Soprano*) } the children
MRS. GROSSE (*Soprano*), the housekeeper
MISS JESSEL (*Soprano*), the former governess
QUINT (*Tenor*), the former manservant

The Prologue opens the opera by explaining that the Governess is to have sole responsibility for the childrens' well-being. Under no circumstances is she to trouble their guardian, not even with a letter.

Scene One shows the Governess on her journey to Bly. She is fearful of her ability to take proper care of the orphan children, and wonders to whom she may turn if things go wrong. In the second scene the Governess is warmly welcomed by Mrs. Grosse, the housekeeper, and by the children. She is charmed by the beauty of the house and its surrounding park. Mrs. Grosse tells the Governess that the children are clever and wonderful at their lessons. They will do better now that the Governess is here to teach them and to play games with them.

In the third scene, on the porch at Bly, Mrs. Grosse brings the Governess a letter dismissing Miles from his school. Mrs. Grosse tells the Governess that she has never known Miles to be really bad, or, as the letter states, "an injury to his friends." When the two of them look through the window and see Miles and Flora playing quietly together they decide that they will do nothing about the letter. The fourth scene shows the tower of Bly. The Governess soliloquizes about the beauty of the place and of her fondness for the children. Her fears have vanished. Suddenly she sees the shade of Quint on the tower. At first she thinks it must be the childrens' guardian, but she soon realizes that it is some strange intruder who has broken into the house. In the fifth scene, in the hall, as the children are acting out a nursery rhyme, Quint appears at the window long enough to meet the stare of the Governess. She is terrified and tells Mrs. Grosse about the man on the tower and at the window. Mrs. Grosse recognizes him as the dead Quint, a former manservant at Bly who was excessively intimate with young Miles, as well as with the former Governess, Miss Jessel. Miss Jessel went away from Bly and died, and Quint was killed by a fall on an icy road. "Is there no end to his dreadful ways?" Mrs. Grosse exclaims. The Governess determines that the children shall not know of the evil spirit's presence and Mrs. Grosse promises to keep silent on the subject. In the seventh scene the Governess is teaching Miles his Latin nouns. After reciting them the boy begins to chant: "Malo, malo, malo." The scene changes to the shore of the lake. As the Governess is playing with Flora Miss Jessel appears on the other side. Although Flora runs off the Governess realizes that the girl has seen Miss Jessel and that both children are aware of the ghosts, even though they keep their knowledge secret. In the last scene of the act, at night, Miles is in the garden under the tower. Quint stands on the tower and Flora is in the window talking to Miss Jessel, who stands by the lake. The ghosts beg the children to come to them. As the Governess comes to the porch and Mrs. Grosse appears behind Flora at the window they hear the children promise that they will come without fail. The ghosts disappear and Miles cries to the Governess: "You see, I am bad, aren't I?"

In the opening scene of the second act Miss Jessel accuses Quint of having betrayed her in life. She now offers herself to him as the friend he says he needs but he refuses her, saying he must possess some soul that will be wholly obedient and compliant. Miss Jessel realizes that she too must have a soul to share her woe. As Quint and Miss Jessel disappear the Governess despairs of her inability to protect the children. In the second scene Miles and Flora are on their way to church with the Governess and housekeeper. They sit on a tombstone and pretend to chant religious phrases. Mrs. Grosse is impressed but the Governess knows that they are talking blasphemy and in spirit are not with them but with Quint and Miss Jessel. Miles subtly reveals that he and his sister are aware of what the Governess knows and he challenges her to do anything about it. In Scene Three the Governess comes on the spectre of Miss Jessel in the schoolroom, sitting at her desk. This sight shocks her into disobeying her instructions. She writes a letter to the children's guardian. In Scene Four the Governess tries in vain to win Miles's confidence, while Quint, lurking in the background of the boy's bedroom, urges him to steal the letter the Governess has written to his guardian. In the fifth scene Miles takes the letter. In Scene Six, in the schoolroom, Miles so diverts the attention of the Governess and Mrs. Grosse with his brilliant piano playing that Flora is able to disappear in search of Miss Jessel. The seventh scene shows her by the lake with Miss Jessel, but when the Governess and Mrs. Grosse find her she will not admit that the ghost is even present. She turns violently upon the Governess and convinces Mrs. Grosse of her innocence. By Scene Eight, however, Mrs. Grosse has heard Flora talking in her dreams, and she knows that everything the Governess has told her is true. She offers to take Flora to her guardian, and tells the Governess that her letter to him was never sent.

Then follows the climax of the opera, in which the Governess battles with Quint for Miles's soul. The Governess pleads with Miles to tell her what is troubling him, while Quint in the background commands him to be silent. Finally Miles yields to the Governess and cries: "Peter Quint, you devil." Quint disappears and Miles collapses in the arms of the Governess. She holds him until she realizes he is dead and then tenderly lays him on the ground, singing: "Malo, malo, what have we done between us?"

§)&(§

THE UNICORN, THE GORGON AND THE MANTICORE
(or The Three Sundays of a Poet)
Gian-Carlo Menotti

The composer has characterized this work as a Madrigal Fable for Chorus, Ten Dancers and Nine Instruments. It is not strictly an opera; the dancers act in pantomime while the Chorus sings the narration. The libretto was written by the composer, and the work was commissioned by the Elizabeth Sprague Coolidge Foundation in the Library of Congress and was first performed at the Library, in Washington, December 12, 1956, during the Foundation's Twelfth Festival of Chamber Music. The following January 15 (1957) it was performed by the New York City Ballet at the City Center.

The characters, all portrayed in pantomime, include:

THE MAN IN THE CASTLE, a poet
THE COUNT
THE COUNTESS
THE DOCTOR
THE DOCTOR'S WIFE
THE MAYOR
THE MAYOR'S WIFE
THE UNICORN, a creature no hunter can trap, but which may be caught by a virgin girl, sitting by herself in the wood. It symbolizes the poet's youth.
THE GORGON, a beast with scales like a dragon, fearless and wild, symbolizing the poet's manhood.
THE MANTICORE, having a three-fold row of teeth and a tail like the sting of a scorpion. It symbolizes the poet's old age.

The work is divided into twelve madrigals, with introduction and interludes. In the Introduction the Chorus tells of the Man in the Castle. He shuns the Countess's parties, yawns at town meetings and does not go to church on Sundays. We meet him in the first Interlude, and in the First Madrigal we hear the meaningless gossip of the ladies and gentlemen of the town. In the Second Interlude and Madrigal the Man in the Castle takes his Sunday walk leading his pet Unicorn. The townsfolk look on in amazement and ask each other why a rich and well-born man should raise such a creature when he could have a dog or a cat. In the Third Madrigal the Man in the Castle pets his Unicorn and tells it to beware of the virgin sleeping under the lemon tree. In the Fourth Madrigal the Countess begs the Count to get her a Unicorn. In the following Interlude the Count and the Countess appear with one. The townspeople stare but soon every couple imitates them and gets its own Unicorn.

The Fifth Madrigal occurs on the next Sunday. The Man in the Castle now has a Gorgon that slowly sarabands down the street. In the Sixth Madrigal the townsfolk ask the Man in the Castle what he did with the Unicorn. The Man answers that he grew tired of him and killed him. The people believe him and call him wicked for destroying so gentle a creature. In the seventh Madrigal the Countess has secretly poisoned her Unicorn and begs her husband to get her a Gorgon. In the next Interlude the Count and Countess appear at a picnic with a Gorgon and soon all the Unicorns in town are killed and every respectable couple parades a Gorgon. In the Eighth Madrigal, on the third Sunday, the Man in the Castle has a Manticore, a shy creature that loves mankind but inadvertently kills the people he loves best. In the Ninth Madrigal the people ask about the Gorgon and the Man in the Castle tells them he died of murder. Again the people believe him and call him unkind and ungrateful. The Countess secretly stabs her Gorgon in the next interlude and in Madrigal Ten asks her husband for a Manticore. He protests vainly and calls her a Medusa and Xantippe, but he finally agrees. The Count and Countess appear with a Manticore in the following Interlude and although the townspeople stare at them in surprise they kill all their Gorgons and soon appear with Manticores. In the Eleventh Madrigal the people wonder why they have not seen the Man in the Castle recently. They decide to go to the castle and find out what he has done with his Manticore. During the March to the Castle they say that they, the elect, must condemn everything except that which is blest by fashion and seems clever, whether evil or good. In the Twelfth Madrigal they enter the castle and find the Man lying on his deathbed, surrounded by his three pets, the Unicorn, the Gorgon and the Manticore. He tells the people that it is they, not he, who are "the indifferent killers of the Poet's dreams," the "foolish people who feign to feel what others have suffered." Turning to the pets that symbolize his youth, his middle age, and now his old age, he sighs: "not even death do I fear as in your arms I die."

§)&(§

VANESSA

Samuel Barber

This four-act opera was first produced at the Metropolitan Opera House, New York, January 15, 1958. Its libretto was written by the composer Gian-Carlo Menotti.

The cast includes:

VANESSA (*Soprano*)
ERIKA (*Mezzo-soprano*), her niece
THE OLD BARONESS (*Contralto*), her mother and Erika's grandmother
ANATOL (*Tenor*)
THE OLD DOCTOR (*Baritone*)
NICHOLAS (*Bass*), the Major-Domo
FOOTMAN (*Bass*)
THE YOUNG PASTOR, SERVANTS, GUESTS, PEASANTS

The action takes place at Vanessa's country house in a northern country, about 1905. The first act is laid in the richly appointed drawing room of Vanessa's house. Vanessa and the Baroness are sitting by the fire. The Baroness will speak to no one but Erika, who is giving orders to the Major-Domo and a group of servants. She is ordering a sumptuous dinner which we learn is to be served in honor of an expected guest. When the servants have left Vanessa wonders why the guest has not yet arrived, she fears he may have been lost in the snowstorm. Erika vainly tries to calm her aunt's nervousness by reading to her. After the Old Baroness is led away to bed the tower bell rings. Vanessa cries hysterically: "He has come!" and sits by the fire with her back to the door. Anatol appears in the doorway. Without looking at him Vanessa bids him not to utter a word. For over twenty years, she says, she has waited for him. Unless he still loves her she does not want him to see her. Anatol replies that he believes he shall love her and Vanessa turns to look at him. She screams: "It is not he!" and demands that he be put out of the house. She asks Erika to help her upstairs.

Erika returns to ask Anatol who he is. He explains that he is Anatol, the son of Vanessa's lover. All his life he has heard from his father about Vanessa, a name that "used to scorch his mother's lips and light my father's eyes with longing." Now that his father is dead he has come to meet the woman who haunted his house. He asks Erika who she is, and she says that sometimes she is Vanessa's niece but mostly her shadow. She tells Anatol he must leave but he asks her not to send him out into the storm again but to allow him to spend the night. He sees the table laid for supper and remarks that his father loved good wines. He lost his fortune dreaming, while his wife, the young Anatol's mother, "bought subtle poisons to destroy his dreams." Now the son can drink only other people's wines. He persuades Erika to join him at the supper table.

The scene of the second act is the same. It is a month later. Erika is confiding to her grandmother. She drank too much wine with Anatol the night he came and spent the night with him in his room. Answering the Baroness's question as to what Anatol intends to do about it Erika replies that he will marry her if she wants him, but she does not want his honor so that hers may be saved. He says he loves her but Erika feels that he is incapable of real love. Moreover, since Vanessa has learned who he is she herself has come to love him blindly. Erika does not feel she has the right to break her aunt's heart. Vanessa and Anatol enter. They have been skating and Vanessa is radiant. She has ordered the servants to remove the covers that have hidden the mirrors for twenty years. As they have breakfast in the adjoining winter garden the Old Doctor comes to call. He remarks that it is good to see the house alive again. Left alone with Erika, Vanessa explains that now she realizes it was the young Anatol she was waiting for. Her old lover has sent her his younger self and she has kept her youth for him. As the household prepares to leave for the Sunday morning chapel service with the young pastor, the Old Baroness warns Erika that she must speak at once or she will lose Anatol. Erika replies that it is his love she wants, not his capture. When Anatol enters Erika asks him if he intends to marry Vanessa. Anatol replies that he would like to marry Erika but that if she refuses him he has no intention of slashing his throat. If he and Erika were married they could enjoy Paris, Rome, Budapest and Vienna, and perhaps, who knows, his love might last forever. Just as he is asking Erika for her answer the others come in on their way to the chapel. Erika lingers behind, with her grandmother. As the sounds of a hymn come from the chapel, Erika cries to herself: "No, Anatol, my answer is no. Let Vanessa have you, she who for so little had to wait so long."

The third act takes place on New Year's eve in the entrance hall to the Castle. Guests are arriving for a party to announce the engagement of Vanessa and Anatol. Vanessa approaches the Doctor and asks him why her Grandmother and Erika will not come downstairs for the announcement. As Anatol assures Vanessa that Erika has promised him she will join them, the Doctor comes from Erika's room and explains that she is a little frightened and will come later. They all go into the ballroom and as the Doctor's voice is heard announcing the betrothal Erika appears at the head of the stairs and faints on the steps. The Major-Domo finds her and goes for the Doctor. As she revives Erika gasps: "His child, it must not be born." She gropes her way down the stairs, makes her way to the entrance door and goes out into the night. The Baroness, dishevelled, appears at the top of the stairway. She goes to the open door and looking out of it calls "Erika, Erika!"

The fourth act opens in Erika's bedroom. The Old Baroness sits by the fire, the Old Doctor stands by a window, and Vanessa nervously paces the room. A party of servants and peasants, headed by Anatol, is searching outside for Erika. At length they return carrying Erika, still wearing her ball dress. As the Doctor sends the others from the room assuring them that Erika seems to be all right, Anatol tells Vanessa that they found Erika in a small ravine on the path to the lake. Vanessa asks Anatol if he knows why Erika did this strange thing. Does she love him? Anatol swears that she does not and Vanessa begs him to take her away at once. The Doctor comes from Erika's bed and says there is nothing to worry about. After the others have left the Grandmother asks Erika about her child. When Erika replies that he will not be born, the Grandmother silently leaves the room.

The second scene of the act is in the drawing room. Anatol and Vanessa have been married and are preparing to leave for Paris. Alone with Erika, Vanessa asks her if it was because of Anatol she went out on New Year's Eve. Erika says it was not because of Anatol but admits that it may have been because of some man she now knows is not the man for her. Vanessa tells her that she may live here as long as she wishes. The house is willed to her. Anatol has a moment alone with Erika and tells her there was a time when he hoped it would be with her that he left this house. Erika replies that he is to forget her and begs him to make Vanessa happy. When Vanessa and Anatol have gone Erika cries "Anatol!" and then adds that she must never say that name again. She turns to her Grandmother and learns that the old lady will not speak to her either any more. She summons the Major-Domo and orders him to cover the mirrors again. From now on she will receive no visitors. It is her turn to wait.

§)&(§

LA VIDE BREVE
A Short Life
Manuel de Falla

De Falla's two-act opera, composed in 1905, was first produced at the Casino Municipal in Nice, April 1, 1913. It was introduced to the United States by the Metropolitan Opera Company, New York, March 7, 1926.

The libretto was written by Carlos Fernández-Shaw and the cast includes:

SALUD (*Soprano*)
HER GRANDMOTHER (*Mezzo-soprano*)
SARVAOR (*Bass-baritone*), her uncle
PACO (*Tenor*), her lover
CARMELA (*Mezzo-soprano*), Paco's bride
MANUEL (*Baritone*), Carmela's brother
A VOICE IN THE FORGE (*Tenor*)
FOUR STREET VENDORS

The first act opens in the gypsy home of Salud and her grandmother, in the Albaicin quarter of Granada. At the rear is a forge from which the voices of the smiths sing about the wretchedness of those who have been born under an evil star. Salud is disturbed because her aristocratic lover Paco has not yet arrived. He is late, and Salud says that she would rather die than lose him. The grandmother's reassurances prove to be correct, for Paco arrives and Salud's despair turns to joy. As she and Paco are telling each other of their love Uncle Sarvaor comes to the house intending to kill Paco on the spot. He tells the grandmother that Paco has already betrayed Salud and tomorrow is marrying a rich girl named Carmela. The grandmother begs Sarvaor to let the girl have a few more moments of happiness, and the old lady and the uncle leave the lovers alone, dreading the time when Salud will learn the truth.

As the first tableau ends the stage becomes dark. When the light returns the scene is the same but a curtain at the back has been dropped to reveal a panoramic view of Granada from Sacro Monte. Twilight falls as voices are heard in the distance. Salud and Paco are seen leaving the house. They walk to a fork in the road and silently bid each other adieu. As it becomes darker the distant voices and songs become fainter. The grandmother and Sarvaor come from the forge. She is struggling to restrain him.

The first tableau of the second act shows an alley. Through open windows we see the courtyard of the house where Carmela lives with her brother Manuel. A gay party is in progress celebrating the betrothal of Paco and Carmela. Salud comes into the alley followed by her grandmother and Uncle Sarvaor. She knows now that she has been betrayed. She curses her lover and upbraids her grandmother and uncle for hiding the truth from her. She sees Paco through the window and resolves to meet him once more. She creeps to the window and sings:

> Never ask after her again,
> Nor go down to her house!
> She is dead. The very stones
> Would rise against you!

Paco hears her voice and turns pale. The scene changes to the courtyard. Paco is trying to appear unconcerned. Salud confronts him as he sits beside Carmela. At first the guests think the gypsy girl has come to dance for them but they soon learn the truth. Caught off guard, Paco calls her by name. Salud denounces him. Paco cries: "Put her out!" As Salud takes a step towards him she sways and falls lifeless. The grandmother calls Paco a Judas and the Uncle curses him.

§)&(§

APPENDIX

APPENDIX 1

Composers of the Operas

(Dates of operas in parentheses indicate years of first performances)

ADAM, Adolphe (Born, Paris, 1803—Died, Paris, 1856). A prolific French composer of fifty-three stage works. His work is marked by elegance and grace, but not by great dramatic depth. He was most effective in the field of comedy-opera.

The Postillion of Longjumeau (1836) 316

D'ALBERT, Eugène (Born, Glasgow, 1864—Died, Riga, 1932). A celebrated pianist-composer. Known today chiefly for his piano transcriptions of the organ works of Bach. Composed sixteen operas.

Tiefland (1903) 409

AUBER, Daniel François (Born, Caen, Normandy, 1782—Died, Paris, 1871). A French operatic composer whose *Masaniello,* together with Meyerbeer's *Robert the Devil,* is credited with laying the foundations of French grand opera. Auber composed more than forty operas.

Masaniello (1828) 248
Fra Diavolo (1830) 134

BALFE, Michael William (Born, Dublin, 1808—Died, Rowney Abbey, Hertfordshire, 1870). An Irish composer of light operas.

The Bohemian Girl (1843) 42

BARBER, Samuel (Born, West Chester, Pa., 1910—). A composer chiefly of symphonic works and songs.

Vanessa (1958) 507

BEETHOVEN, Ludwig van (Born, Bonn, 1770—Died, Vienna, 1827). One of the greatest symphonists of all time, who composed but one opera, *Fidelio.* This, however, has been termed the one opera of its period (1805) that still remains intensely alive.

Fidelio (1805) 126

BELLINI, Vincenzo (Born, Catania, Sicily, 1801—Died, Puteaux, near Paris, 1835). One of the three Italian composers of opera (Bellini, Donizetti, and Verdi) who carried on the *bel canto* tradition of Rossini. Bellini was not as gifted in comedy, or in the grand manner, as was Rossini, but he had a fine gift of pure and elegiac melody. His orchestration was thin and has been likened to a "big guitar," and the chief interest of his operas had to be maintained by the singers.

La Sonnambula (1831) 392
Norma (1831) 276
I Puritani (1835) 323

BERG, Alban (Born, Vienna, 1885—Died, Vienna, 1935). A German "atonalist," pupil of Arnold Schoenberg, who used the twelve-tone, or atonal, technique in his opera *Wozzeck* and in an unfinished opera, *Lulu*.

BERLIOZ, Hector (Born near Grenoble, France, 1803—Died, Paris, 1869). A composer whose works are regarded as the culmination of French musical romanticism. Known chiefly for orchestral tone-poems which are often extravagant in musical proportions and expressiveness, Berlioz was one of the great masters of instrumentation and did much to develop the modern orchestra. He composed four operas, and a dramatic oratorio (*The Damnation of Faust*) which was later presented as an opera, and is known as such today.

BIZET, Georges (Born, Paris, 1838—Died, Bougival, near Paris, 1875). A French composer with a sparkling melodic gift and a thorough understanding of stage requirements. He is known best by his opera *Carmen*, and by the incidental music he composed for Daudet's play. *L'Arlésienne,* now known in the form of two orchestral suites. It has been said of *Carmen* that inexperienced listeners are fascinated by it, and that the most sophisticated musicians never tire of it.

BOÏTO, Arrigo (Born, Padua, Italy, 1842—Died, Milan, 1918). An Italian composer and poet who is known today chiefly as a librettist for Ponchielli's *La Gioconda* and Verdi's *Otello* and *Falstaff*. Boïto was himself a prolific composer, and composed works which are distinguished in style and profoundly thoughtful.

BORODIN, Alexander (Born, St. Petersburg, 1833—Died, St. Petersburg, 1887). A Russian composer who was an ardent exponent of Russian nationalism. He composed symphonic works, chamber music, one complete opera, and another which was unfinished at the time of his death (*Prince Igor*). This work was completed by Rimsky-Korsakoff and Alexander Glazounov.

BOUGHTON, Rutland (Born, Aylesbury, England, 1878—). An English composer of opera who was a protagonist of Wagnerian ideas and tried to establish an English "Bayreuth" at Glastonbury for the production of music-dramas based on Arthurian legends.

BREIL, Joseph Carl (Born, Pittsburg, Pa., 1870—Died, Los Angeles, Cal., 1926). American composer of comic and serious operas.

BRITTEN, Benjamin (Born, Lowenstoft, Suffolk, England, 1913—). English composer of orchestral music, chamber music, film music, and operas.

The Turn of the Screw (1954) 500

CADMAN, Charles Wakefield (Born, Johnstown, Pa., 1881—Died, Los Angeles, Cal., 1946). Prolific American composer of orchestral works, piano music, concert songs, operettas, and grand operas.

Shanewis (1918) 385
A Witch of Salem (1926) 435

CHARPENTIER, Gustave (Born, Dieuze, Lorraine, 1860—Died, Paris, 1956). A French composer who was a pioneer in bringing realism and social idealism to the stage.

Louise (1900) 207

CIMAROSA, Domenico (Born near Naples, 1749—Died, Venice, 1801). An early Italian composer of at least seventy-six operas, whose works became the models for the operas of Rossini. Although Cimarosa composed serious operas, he was at his best in comedy, where the verve and sparkle of his melodies combined with his patter songs and his chattering ensembles to make effective and amusing entertainment.

Il Matrimonio Segreto (1792) 252

CONVERSE, Frederick Shepherd (Born, Newton, Mass., 1871—Died, Westwood, Mass., 1940). American composer and teacher. His *The Pipe of Desire* was the first American opera to be produced at the Metropolitan Opera House in New York (1910).

The Pipe of Desire (1906) 309

COPLAND, Aaron (Born, Brooklyn, N.Y., 1900—). One of the leading contemporary American composers. His music includes symphonic works, piano pieces, chamber music, and scores for motion pictures.

The Tender Land (1954) 493

CORNELIUS, Peter (Born, Mayence, 1824—Died, Mayence, 1874). A minor German composer who was an early champion of Richard Wagner. He composed songs, instrumental pieces, and three operas.

The Barber of Bagdad (1858) 28

DAMROSCH, Walter (Born, Breslau, Germany, 1862—Died, New York, 1950). Came to America at the age of nine, and became one of our leading orchestral conductors. Composer of several operas, choral works and songs.

The Scarlet Letter (1896) 374
Cyrano de Bergerac (1913) 74
The Man Without a Country (1937) 230

DEBUSSY, Claude Achille (Born, St. Germain-en-Laye, 1862—Died, Paris, 1918). Founder of the French school of Impressionism in music. He composed orchestral and chamber music, instrumental pieces and songs, and the opera, *Pelléas et Mélisande,* which made a complete break with all the operatic traditions of the past and represented a deliberate reaction against the Wagnerian style.

Pelléas et Mélisande (1902) 297

DE KOVEN, Reginald (Born, Middletown, Conn., 1859—Died, Chicago, 1920). American composer best known for his light operas (*Robin Hood,* etc.). He composed two grand operas which were produced with moderate success.

The Canterbury Pilgrims (1917) 50
Rip van Winkle (1920) 348

DELIBES, Léo (Born, St. Germain-du-Val, 1836—Died, Paris, 1891). French composer of vivacious, melodious, ballet music. He also composed four operas.

Lakmé (1883) 195

DELLO JOIO, Norman (Born, New York City, 1913—). Composer of orchestral music, piano sonatas, chamber music, and several operas.

The Ruby (1955) 480

DONIZETTI, Gaetano (Born, Bergamo, Italy, 1797—Died, Bergamo, 1848). One of the brilliant triumvirate (Donizetti, Rossini, and Bellini) who developed Italian opera in the first half of the nineteenth century. Donizetti's operas belong to a period when opera was designed to show off the voices of singers. Today these works seem flashy and empty in style, lacking the musical emotional depth that is demanded by tragic subjects. Hence his comedy operas—*L'Elisir d'Amore, The Daughter of the Regiment, Don Pasquale,* etc., are his happiest expression. Although Donizetti lived for little more than a half-century, he composed sixty-seven operas.

L'Elisir d'Amore (1832) 101
Lucrezia Borgia (1833) 215
Lucia di Lammermoor (1835) 212
The Daughter of the Regiment (1840) 81
La Favorita (1840) 122
Linda di Chamounix (1842) 199
Don Pasquale (1843) 91

DUKAS, Paul (Born, Paris, 1865—Died, Paris, 1935). A French composer, chiefly of orchestral works. His only opera, *Ariane and Bluebeard,* is often ranked with Debussy's *Pelléas et Mélisande* as a masterpiece of the French twentieth-century lyric stage.

Ariane and Bluebeard (1907) 23

FALLA, Manuel de (Born Cádiz, Spain, 1876—Died, Alta Gracia, Argentine, 1946). One of Spain's leading composers. His works include colorful symphonic works, ballets, piano music, and songs.

La Vide Breve (1913) 511

FÉVRIER, Henri (Born, Paris, 1875 —). French composer, pupil of Massenet.

Monna Vanna (1909) 271

FLOTOW, Friedrich von (Born, Teutendorf, Mecklenburg, Germany, 1812—Died, Darmstadt, 1883). German composer of eighteen operas which were once highly popular. Only *Martha* is frequently heard today.

Alessandro Stradella (1844) 9
Martha (1847) 245

FLOYD, Carlisle (Born, Latta, S.C., 1926—). An American composer of operas. Since 1947 he has taught at Florida State University.

Susannah (1955) 485

GERSHWIN, George (Born, Brooklyn, N. Y., 1898—Died, Hollywood, Cal., 1937). An American composer who did more than any musician up to his time to merge the popular elements in contemporary American music with the so-called serious music of the opera house and the concert-hall. Known first as a writer of gay tunes for musical comedies, he took jazz patterns and other devices of current popular songs to concert works of larger dimensions

—*Rhapsody in Blue, An American in Paris,* etc. In his one grand opera, *Porgy and Bess,* Gershwin used the spirit and idiom of the Negro folk-song, both spirituals and the blues, to create a genuine folk-opera.

Porgy and Bess (1935) 313

GIANNINI, Vittorio (Born, Philadelphia, Pa., 1903—). His operas have been produced both in the United States and abroad.

The Taming of the Shrew (1953) 488

GIORDANO, Umberto (Born, Foggia, Italy, 1867—Died, Milan, Italy, 1948). An Italian composer who has followed the "verismo" or realistic school of Mascagni's *Cavalleria Rusticana* and Leoncavallo's *Pagliacci.*

Andrea Chenier (1896) 19
Fedora (1898) 124
Madame Sans Gêne (1915) 220

GLINKA, Michael Ivanovitch (Born, Smolensk, Russia, 1804—Died, Berlin, 1857). Generally considered the founder of distinctively Russian music. The themes in his operas were based on Russian folk-songs which he clothed with characteristic harmonies and setting. The music of *Russlan and Ludmilla* was considered so true to the humbler classes of Russian society that a group of noblemen sneeringly called it "the music of coachmen."

A Life for the Czar (1836) 198
Russlan and Ludmilla (1842) 363

GLUCK, Christoph Willibald (Born, Erasbach, Upper Palatinate, 1714—Died, Vienna, 1787). A German composer who learned to write operas in Italy. He became one of the great reformers in music history, and because he was dissatisfied with Italian works which were composed merely for vocal display, he made music a medium for expressing the meaning of the text, and for furthering the action of the drama without interrupting and weakening it with superfluous ornaments designed solely to display the agility of fine voices.

Orfeo ed Euridice (1762) 283
Alceste (1767) 8
Iphigenia in Aulis (1774) 166
Armide (1777) 25
Iphigenia in Tauris (1779) 167

GOLDMARK, Karl (Born, Keszthely, Hungary, 1830—Died, Vienna, 1915). Composer of orchestral music, chamber music and operas.

The Queen of Sheba (1875) 325
The Cricket on the Hearth (1896) 70

GOUNOD, Charles-François (Born, Paris, 1818—Died, Paris, 1893). Distinguished French composer, largely of church music. Composed also twelve operas.

Faust (1859) 119
Philémon et Baucis (1860) 307
Mireille (1864) 268
Romeo and Juliet (1867) 355

GRANADOS, Enrique (Born, Lérida, Spain, 1867—Died at sea, 1916). Spanish pianist and composer of piano works and songs which are filled with the spirit of Spanish folk-songs and dances.

Goyescas (1916) 147

GRUENBERG, Louis (Born, Brest Litovsk, Poland, 1884—). Naturalized American composer of orchestral works, film music and operas.

The Emperor Jones (1933) 103

HADLEY, Henry Kimball (Born, Somerville, Mass., 1871—Died, New York, 1937). Prominent American composer who wrote successfully in all forms.

Azora (1917) 27
Cleopatra's Night (1920) 65

HAGEMAN, Richard (Born, Leeuwarden, Holland, 1882—). Naturalized American conductor, pianist and composer. Author of successful concert songs, now engaged in composing background music for motion pictures.

Caponsacchi (1932) 51

HALÉVY, Jacques (Born, Paris, 1799 —Died, Nice, 1862). French composer of many operas, of which *La Juive* is the only work to survive.

La Juive (1835) 184

HANSON, Howard (Born, Wahoo, Nebraska, 1896—). American composer, conductor, and educator, director of the Eastman School of Music, Rochester, New York.

Merry Mount (1934) 260

HERBERT, Victor (Born, Dublin, 1859—Died, New York, 1924). Naturalized American composer of tuneful operettas. Composed also two grand operas.

Natoma (1911) 273
Madeleine (1914) 224

HÉROLD, Louis Joseph (Born, Paris, 1791—Died, Les Ternes, 1833). Prolific composer of operas, none of which is generally performed today.

Zampa (1831) 439

HOLST, Gustav (Born, Cheltenham, England, 1874—Died, London, 1934). English composer of orchestral and choral music, and of several operas.

The Perfect Fool (1923) 299

HUGO, John Adam (Born, Bridgeport, Conn., 1873—Died there, 1945). American composer of orchestral music and two operas.

The Temple Dancer (1919) 405

HUMPERDINCK, Engelbert (Born, Siegburg, Germany, 1854—Died, Neusterlitz, 1921). German composer of six operas, and of incidental music for plays.

Hänsel and Gretel (1893) 154
Die Königskinder (1910) 191

KIENZL, Wilhelm (Born, Waizenkirchen, Austria, 1857—Died, Vienna, 1941). German composer, disciple of Wagnerian principles.

Der Evangelimann (1895) 113

KORNGOLD, Erich Wolfgang (Born, Brünn-Brno, 1897—Died, Hollywood, Cal., 1957). Naturalized American composer and conductor, once active in Hollywood as composer of background music for motion pictures.

Die Tote Stadt (1920) 414

KŘENEK, Ernst (Born, Vienna, 1900 —). Austrian-born composer, now resident in the United States.

Jonny spielt auf (1927) 180

LALO, Édouard (Born, Lille, 1823—Died, Paris, 1892). French composer of Spanish descent, who is best known for his *Symphonie Espagnole* for violin and orchestra.

LEONCAVALLO, Ruggiero (Born, Naples, 1858—Died, near Florence, 1919). Italian composer whose *Pagliacci* was a masterpiece he never surpassed, nor equalled. This work followed Mascagni's *Cavalleria Rusticana* as a type of opera employing crude realism. This genre has had many imitations, most of them of short-lived success.

LEONI, Franco (Born, Milan, 1864—Died, London, 1949). Another Italian composer of the realist school.

LORTZING, Gustave Albert (Born, Berlin, 1801—Died, Berlin, 1851). Minor German composer of grand and light operas.

MARSCHNER, Heinrich (Born, Zittau, Saxony, 1798—Died, Hanover, 1861). Early nineteenth-century German opera composer.

MASCAGNI, Pietro (Born, Leghorn, Italy, 1863—Died, Rome, 1945). Italian composer whose *Cavalleria Rusticana* ranks with Leoncavallo's *Pagliacci* as a leading product of the Italian *verismo* or realist school.

MASSENET, Jules (Born, near St. Etienne, France, 1842—Died, Paris, 1912). French composer of thirty-one operas. His style was typical of French elegance and grace. His music inclined toward sentimentality, and was composed with delicate craftsmanship. Massenet attempted to use the Wagnerian *leit-motif* system, but in a thoroughly French, rather than German, manner.

MENOTTI, Gian-Carlo (Born, Cadegliano, 1911—). Resident American composer of operas in the Italian tradition, some in the opera-bouffe manner, and others tragic.

MEYERBEER, Giacomo (Born, Berlin, 1791—Died, Paris, 1864). German-born composer whose life was passed mostly in France. Composed seventeen operas in which he introduced a synthesis of musical and dramatic elements. His innovations fixed the course of French opera over a long period of years. Musically his works are somewhat shallow, and only a few of them have survived in the active repertoire of opera houses.

Robert the Devil (1831) 350
The Huguenots (1836) 161
Le prophète (1849) 321
Dinorah (1859) 84
L'Africaine (1865) 3

MONTEMEZZI, Italo (Born, near Verona, Italy, 1875—Died, Vigasio, Italy, 1952). Italian opera composer, known chiefly for *L'Amore dei Tre Re.*

L'Amore dei Tre Re (1913) 15

MOORE, Douglas (Born, Cutchogue, New York, 1893—). American composer of orchestral works and chamber music.

The Devil and Daniel Webster (1939) 83
The Ballad of Baby Doe (1956) 448

MOUSSORGSKY, Modeste Petrovitch (Born, Karevo, Russia, 1839—Died, St. Petersburg, 1881). A great Russian nationalist composer, musically uncouth and rugged, whose work stemmed not from the Italian and German schools in vogue in his youth, but from Russian folk-songs and from the modal style of the Greek Catholic Church. Essentially a realist, Moussorgsky created operatic works which are vital and honest dramatically, and which exerted a strong influence on the work of late eighteenth- and early nineteenth-century modernists.

Boris Godounow (1874) 45
Khovantchina (1886) 186
The Fair at Sorochintzky (1923) 114

MOZART, Wolfgang Amadeus (Born, Salzburg, 1756—Died, Vienna, 1791). A composer who wrote masterpieces in every musical form, and for every instrumental and vocal combination. Many feel that Mozart's greatest achievements were his operas. In writing them he used a symphonic technique in building a stage scene along the lines of an orchestral work. *The Marriage of Figaro* and *Don Giovanni* are considered the foundations of all later comic operas, of every nation. Mozart developed and perfected the comic ensemble and the comic finale, and he endowed everything he wrote with a wealth of melody that seems inexhaustible. Altogether Mozart composed twenty-two operas.

Die Entführung aus dem Serail (1782) 105
The Marriage of Figaro (1786) 242
Don Giovanni (1787) 87
Cosi Fan Tutte (1790) 69
The Magic Flute (1791) 225

NESSLER, Viktor (Born, Baldeheim, Alsace, 1841—Died, Strasbourg, 1890). An Alsatian composer of eleven operas.

The Trumpeter of Säkkingen (1884) 425

NICOLAI, Otto (Born, Königsberg, Germany, 1810—Died, Berlin, 1849). A German composer of five operas, whose fame rests largely on one of them—*The Merry Wives of Windsor.*

The Merry Wives of Windsor (1849) 263

OFFENBACH, Jacques (Born, Offenbach-on-Main, near Cologne, 1819—Died, Paris, 1880). A supreme master in the field of light, satirical operettas. Only one of his works, however

(*The Tales of Hoffmann*), is considered a "grand" opera.

La Périchole (1868) 470
The Tales of Hoffmann (1881) 399

PADEREWSKI, Ignace Jan (Born, Kurylowka, Poland, 1860—Died, New York City, 1941). World-famous Polish pianist and statesman. His compositions include piano pieces, orchestral works, and one opera, *Manru*.

Manru (1901) 239

PARKER, Horatio William (Born, Auburndale, Mass., 1863—Died, Cedarhurst, N. Y., 1919). American composer, best known for choral works and church music.

Mona (1912) 269

PERGOLESI, Giovanni Battista (Born, near Ancona, Italy, 1710—Died, near Naples, 1736). An early Italian composer, whose *La Serva Padrona* was once considered the model of Italian "opera buffa," or comic opera.

La Serva Padrona (1733) 383

PFITZNER, Hans (Born, Moscow, 1869—Died, Salzburg, Austria, 1949). A German composer who derives from the romantic era of Schumann and Wagner.

Palestrina (1917) 290

PONCHIELLI, Amilcare (Born, near Cremona, Italy, 1834—Died, Milan, 1886). Italian composer of ballets and opera.

La Gioconda (1876) 141

POULENC, Francis (Born, Paris, France, 1899—). French composer who became a member of the famous "Les Six" at the age of 18. His works were influenced by Satie and Ravel, and include orchestral and chamber music.

Dialogues of the Carmelites (1957) 456

PROKOFIEFF, Serge (Born, Sontsovka, Russia, 1891—Died, Moscow, 1953). One of the leading twentieth-century Russian composers. As a modernist, his works belong to the neo-classic school. He has produced compositions in almost every form and for almost every medium.

The Love for Three Oranges (1921) 210

PUCCINI, Giacomo (Born, Lucca, Italy, 1858—Died, Brussels, 1924). The most successful composer of operas since Verdi, and a leading exponent of the *verismo* or realist school. He was possessed of fine technical craftsmanship and a gift for writing languishing melodies which are admirably suited to the voice. He had a keen sense of theatrical effectiveness, and his work has appealed alike to the masses and to the cultured sections of the public.

Manon Lescaut (1893) 236
La Bohéme (1896) 40
Tosca (1900) 411
Madame Butterfly (1904) 217
The Girl of the Golden West (1910) 144
La Rondine (1917) 357
Il Tabarro (1918) 398
Suor Angelica (1918) 397
Gianni Schicchi (1918) 139
Turandot (1926) 427

RABAUD, Henri (Born, Paris, 1873—Died there, 1949). French composer and conductor.

Marouf (1914) 240

RAVEL, Maurice (Born, Ciboure,

France, 1875—Died, Paris, 1937). Generally considered the greatest French composer since Debussy. Although Ravel used methods that have characterized the impressionists, he remained fundamentally a classicist. Some of his works foreshadowed the polytonalism that later became a much-used device of many of the modernists.

L'Heure Espagnole (1911) 159

RESPIGHI, Ottorino (Born, Bologna, Italy, 1879—Died, Rome, 1936). One of the most talented of twentieth-century Italian composers. Known chiefly for his orchestral suites—*The Fountains of Rome* and *The Pines of Rome.*

The Sunken Bell (1927) 394

RICCI, Federico (Born, Naples, 1809—Died, Conegliano, 1877).

RICCI, Luigi (Born, Naples, 1805—Died, Prague, 1859). Italian composers who wrote numerous operas, some alone, and many in collaboration.

Crispino e la comare (1850) 72

RIMSKY-KORSAKOFF, Nicolas Andreivitch (Born, Tikhvin, Russia, 1844—Died, Lyubensk, 1908). A Russian composer whose work provides a link between the music of the nineteenth and twentieth centuries. He had a fine gift for writing characteristic Russian melodies, many of which were blended with an Oriental influence. He had also a masterly command of orchestration, and was at his best in works that were based on legends and fairy-tales, such as his orchestral *Scheherazade.*

Snegurotchka (1882) 390
Sadko (1898) 364

Le Coq d'Or (1909) 66

ROGERS, Bernard (Born, New York, 1893—). American composer and teacher.

The Warrior (1947) 430

ROSSINI, Gioacchino (Born, Pesaro, Italy, 1792—Died, Paris, 1868). One of the great Italian composers of opera, who had a gift for both the grand manner and for comedy. He followed Mozart in using the orchestra in symphonic style, and he continued to develop the art of *bel canto.* A few of his operas, notably *The Barber of Seville,* are still in the active repertory of opera houses, and those that are no longer performed in their entirety are still known for numerous of their arias and for their overtures. Rossini composed thirty-eight operas.

L'Italiana in Algeri (1813) 173
The Barber of Seville (1816) 30
La Cenerentola (1817) 62
Semiramide (1823) 381
William Tell (1829) 433

SAINT-SAËNS, Charles Camille (Born, Paris, 1835—Died, Algiers, 1921). One of the most prolific of French composers, who wrote in almost every form. He was an excellent craftsman and his style was marked by a typically French elegance. He composed twelve operas, of which *Samson and Delilah* alone remains in the active repertoire.

Samson and Delilah (1877) 370

SCHUMAN, William (Born, New York City, 1910—). Composer of symphonic works and chamber music. Since 1954 president of the Julliard School of Music.

The Mighty Casey (1953) 467

SEYMOUR, John Lawrence (Born, Los Angeles, 1893—). American composer of operas and musical comedies.

SMETANA, Bedřich (Born, Litomyschl, Bohemia, 1824—Died, Prague, 1884). A Bohemian composer who is generally regarded as the founder of the Czech nationalist school in music.

STRAUSS, Johann, the younger (Born, Vienna, 1825—Died there, 1899). Known as the waltz-king he wrote almost 500 pieces, among them *The Blue Danube*. He also composed many operettas.

STRAUSS, Richard (Born, Munich, 1864—Died, Garmish-Partenkirchen, Germany, 1949). One of the most prominent of late nineteenth- and early twentieth-century German composers. His early works were written in a classic-romantic style, which then developed into a realism which was considered daring and revolutionary in the closing years of the nineteenth century. Strauss is one of the great masters of orchestration, and his tone-poems became the most widely played of contemporary works in the symphonic repertoire. As a composer of operas he has gained equal distinction, although his later works do not rank with his earlier *Salome, Elektra* and *Der Rosenkavalier*.

STRAVINSKY, Igor (Born, near St. Petersburg, Russia, 1882—). One of the leading innovators in twentieth-century music. His career represents a definite series of developments which are characteristic of the course of modern music. In his mature years Stravinsky has passed from primitivism (expressed in the tone-poem, *Rite of Spring*), to neoclassicism. Most of his stage works are ballets, but some of them are classed as operas.

TAYLOR, Deems (Born, New York City, 1885—). American composer of successful orchestral works and operas.

TCHAIKOWSKY, Peter Ilich (Born, Votinsk, Russia, 1840—Died, St. Petersburg, 1893). The great Russian post-romanticist, whose operas have the lyric charm of his songs rather than the emotional stress of his orchestral works.

THOMAS, Ambroise (Born, Metz, 1811—Died, Paris, 1896). French composer of melodious, effective operas.

THUILLE, Ludwig (Born, Bozen, Germany, 1861—Died, Munich,

1907). A German composer who was once considered the leader of the romantic school of Munich composers.

VAUGHAN WILLIAMS, Ralph (Born, Down Ampney, England, 1872—Died, London, 1958). A leader among the English composers of his generation. His style is typically British, and yet highly individual.

VERDI, Giuseppe (Born, Le Roncole, Italy, 1813—Died, Milan, 1901). One of the great opera composers of all times. In his youth he was a frankly commercial composer, at a time when Italian opera had become commercialized and the tuneful works of Rossini, Donizetti and Bellini were coming into vogue. Verdi's early operas were tuneful and melodious, with the guitar-like orchestral accompaniment of the "um-pah" variety. Nevertheless, many of Verdi's works of this period are still top favorites in opera houses—*Rigoletto* (1851), *Il Trovatore* (1853), *La Traviata* (1853), and others. With *Aïda* (1871) Verdi came into a new stage in his development. He composed fewer operas, but they were of greater substance, and culminated in the masterpieces, *Otello* (1887) and *Falstaff* (1893).

WAGNER, Richard (Born, Leipzig, 1813—Died, Venice, 1883). One of the towering masters in the history of music. He developed the music-drama, in which music and drama are closely unified and in which set numbers and arias are dispensed with. Greater continuity is thus achieved and the symbolic meaning of the work is made more clear. In effect, music drama is a super-art form in which all the arts merge. Wagner developed also a system of *leit-motifs,* musical themes which are each connected with a particular character or ideal, and which recur in accordance with their recurrence in the action. Wagner was his own dramatist and librettist. As a musician, he represented the culmination of the romantic era, and his musical style and his idea of continuous melody influenced dozens of composers of the late nineteenth century. This influence was so powerful that it produced a reaction that became anti-Wagnerian and was represented by such works as Debussy's *Pelléas et Mélisande.*

WALTON, Sir William (Born, Oldham, England, 1902—). Composer of orchestral and chamber music, ballets, and numerous film scores.

WEBER, Carl Maria von (Born, Eutin in Oldenburg, Germany, 1786—Died, London, 1826). The leader of the German romantic movement in music. As an opera composer he lacked a dramatic sense, but he brought about a new principle of unity in German opera, largely by means of ingenious orchestral coloring.

WEINBERGER, Jaromir (Born, Prague, 1896—). Czech nationalist composer, now living in the United States.

WILLIAMS, Ralph Vaughan
See VAUGHAN WILLIAMS

WOLF-FERRARI, Ermanno (Born, Venice, 1876—Died, Venice, 1948). Italian composer of twelve operas, several of them widely performed in the current repertoire.

WOLFF, Albert Louis (Born, Paris, 1884—). French conductor and composer.

ZANDONAI, Riccardo (Born, Sacco, Trentino, 1883—Died, Pesaro, Italy, 1944). Italian composer, pupil of Mascagni.

APPENDIX 2

Librettists of the Operas

(Note: coll.—collaborator, transl.—translator)

Librettists of the Operas

APPENDIX 3

Sources and Derivations of the Plots

ANCELOT, F.
I Puritani (coll.) (Pepoli-Bellini) 323

ANDERSEN, Hans Christian
Rossignol (Stravinsky & Mitousoff—Stravinsky) 360

ANELLI, A.
Don Pasquale (Ruffino—Donizetti) 91

ANNUNZIO, Gabriele D'
Francesca da Rimini (Ricordi—Zandonai) 136

ARABIAN NIGHTS
Marouf, the Cobbler of Cairo (Népoty—Rabaud) 240

BACULARD-DARNARD
La Favorita (Roger & Vaëz—Donizetti) 122

BAILEY, Chester
L'Oracolo (Zanoni—Leoni) 281

BEAUMARCHAIS, Pierre-Augustin-Caron de
The Barber of Seville (Sterbini—Rossini) 30
The Marriage of Figaro (da Ponte—Mozart) 242

BELASCO, David
The Girl of the Golden West (Civinini & Zangarini—Puccini) 144
Madame Butterfly (Illica & Giacosa—Puccini) 217

BENEDIX, Roderich
Die Fledermaus (Haffner & Genée—J. Strauss) 460

BENÉT, Stephen Vincent
The Devil and Daniel Webster (Moore—Moore) 83

BERNANOS, Georges
Dialogues of the Carmelites (Poulenc) 456

BERTATI, Giovanni
Don Giovanni (da Ponte—Mozart) 88

BERTON, Pierre
Zaza (coll.) (Leoncavallo—Leoncavallo) 439

BIBLE, Apochrypha
Susannah (Floyd) 485

BIBLE, New Testament
Hérodiade (Milliet & Grémont—Massenet) 156
Salome (Wilde—Strauss) 368

BIBLE, Old Testament, Book of Judges
The Queen of Sheba (Mosenthal—Goldmark) 325
Samson and Delilah (Lemaire—Saint-Saëns) 370
The Warrior (Corwin—Rogers) 430

BOCCACCIO, Giovanni
Troilus and Cressida (Hassall—Walton) 496

Sources and Derivations of the Plots

APPENDIX 4

Characters in the Operas

ABIMELECH
Samson and Delilah (Basso) 370

ABUL HASSAN ALI EBE BEKAR
The Barber of Bagdad (Basso) 28

ACHILLES
Iphigenia in Aulis (Tenor) 166

ADALGISA
Norma (Contralto) 276

ADELAIDE
Arabella (Mezzo-soprano) 444

ADELE
Die Fledermaus (Soprano) 460

ADINA
L'Elisir d'Amore (Soprano) 101

ADMETES
Alceste (Tenor) 8

ADOLAR
Euryanthe (Tenor) 110

ADORNO, Gabriele
Simon Boccanegra (Tenor) 387

ADRIANO
Rienzi (Contralto) 329

AEGHISTUS
Elektra (Tenor) 99

AELFRIDA
The King's Henchman (Soprano) 189

AETHELWOOD
The King's Henchman (Tenor) 189

AFRON, Prince
Le Coq d'Or (Baritone) 67

AGAMEMNON
Iphigenia in Aulis (Baritone) 166

AGNES
The Bartered Bride (Contralto) 33
Der Freischütz (Soprano) 137

AH-YOE
L'Oracolo (Soprano) 282

AÏDA
Aïda (Soprano) 6

AITHRA
The Egyptian Helen (Soprano) 97

ALAIN
Grisélidis 148

ALBERICH
Die Götterdämmerung (Baritone) 345
Das Rheingold (Baritone) 336
Siegfried (Baritone) 342

ALBERT
The Ruby (Tenor) 480
Werther (Baritone) 431

ALBIANI, Paolo
Simon Boccanegra (Basso) 387

ALCESTE
Alceste (Soprano) 8

ALCINDORO
La Bohème (Basso) 40

ALESSANDRO
Alessandro Stradello (Tenor) 10

Characters in the Operas

MODERN LIBRARY GIANTS

A series of sturdily bound and handsomely printed, full-sized library editions of books formerly available only in expensive sets. These volumes contain from 600 to 1,400 pages each.

THE MODERN LIBRARY GIANTS REPRESENT A SELECTION OF THE WORLD'S GREATEST BOOKS

G76 ANDERSEN & GRIMM: *Tales*
G74 AUGUSTINE, ST.: *The City of God*
G58 AUSTEN, JANE: *Complete Novels*
G70 BLAKE, WILLIAM & DONNE, JOHN: *Complete Poetry*
G2 BOSWELL, JAMES: *Life of Samuel Johnson*
G17 BROWNING, ROBERT: *Poems and Plays*
G14 BULFINCH: *Mythology* (ILLUSTRATED)
G35 BURY, J. B.: *A History of Greece*
G13 CARLYLE, THOMAS: *The French Revolution*
G28 CARROLL, LEWIS: *Complete Works*
G15 CERVANTES: *Don Quixote*
G33 COLLINS, WILKIE: *The Moonstone* and *The Woman in White*
G27 DARWIN, CHARLES: *Origin of Species* and *The Descent of Man*
G43 DEWEY, JOHN: *Intelligence in the Modern World: John Dewey's Philosophy*
G70 DONNE, JOHN & BLAKE, WILLIAM: *Complete Poetry*
G36 DOSTOYEVSKY, FYODOR: *The Brothers Karamazov*
G60 DOSTOYEVSKY, FYODOR: *The Idiot*
G51 ELIOT, GEORGE: *Best-Known Novels*
G41 FARRELL, JAMES T.: *Studs Lonigan*
G82 FAULKNER, WILLIAM: *The Faulkner Reader*
G39 FREUD, SIGMUND: *The Basic Writings*
G6, G7, G8 GIBBON, EDWARD: *The Decline and Fall of the Roman Empire* (COMPLETE IN THREE VOLUMES)
G25 GILBERT & SULLIVAN: *Complete Plays*
G76 GRIMM & ANDERSEN: *Tales*
G37 HAWTHORNE, NATHANIEL: *Compl. Novels & Selected Tales*
G78 HOLMES, OLIVER WENDELL: *The Mind and Faith of Justice Holmes*
G19 HOMER: *Complete Works*
G3 HUGO, VICTOR: *Les Miserables*
G18 IBSEN, HENRIK: *Eleven Plays*
G11 JAMES, HENRY: *Short Stories*
G52 JOYCE, JAMES: *Ulysses*
G4 KEATS & SHELLEY: *Complete Poems*
G24 LAMB, CHARLES: *The Complete Works and Letters*
G20 LINCOLN, ABRAHAM: *The Life and Writings of Abraham Lincoln*
G84 MANN, THOMAS: *Stories of Three Decades*
G26 MARX, KARL: *Capital*
G57 MELVILLE, HERMAN: *Selected Writings*
G38 MURASAKA, LADY: *The Tale of Genji*
G30 MYERS, GUSTAVUS: *History of the Great American Fortunes*
G34 NIETZSCHE, FRIEDRICH: *The Philosophy of Nietzsche*
G88 O'HARA, JOHN: *49 Stories*

G55 O'NEILL, EUGENE: *Nine Plays*
G68 PAINE, TOM: *Selected Work*
G86 PASTERNAK, BORIS: *Doctor Zhivago*
G5 PLUTARCH: *Lives* (The Dryden Translation)
G40 POE, EDGAR ALLAN: *Complete Tales and Poems*
G29 PRESCOTT, WILLIAM H.: *The Conquest of Mexico* and *The Conquest of Peru*
G62 PUSHKIN: *Poems, Prose and Plays*
G65 RABELAIS: *Complete Works*
G12 SCOTT, SIR WALTER: *The Most Popular Novels* (Quentin Durward, Ivanhoe & Kenilworth)
G4 SHELLEY & KEATS: *Complete Poems*
G32 SMITH, ADAM: *The Wealth of Nations*
G61 SPAETH, SIGMUND: *A Guide to Great Orchestral Music*
G92 SPENGLER, OSWALD: *The Decline of the West* (one volume)
G91 SPENSER, EDMUND: *Selected Poetry*
G75 STEVENSON, ROBERT LOUIS: *Selected Writings*
G53 SUE, EUGENE: *The Wandering Jew*
G42 TENNYSON: *The Poems and Plays*
G23 TOLSTOY, LEO: *Anna Karenina*—tr. revised
G1 TOLSTOY, LEO: *War and Peace*
G49 TWAIN, MARK: *Tom Sawyer* and *Huckleberry Finn*
G50 WHITMAN, WALT: *Leaves of Grass*
G83 WILSON, EDMUND: *The Shock of Recognition*

MISCELLANEOUS

G77 *An Anthology of Famous American Stories*
G54 *An Anthology of Famous British Stories*
G67 *Anthology of Famous English and American Poetry*
G81 *An Encyclopedia of Modern American Humor*
G47 *The English Philosophers from Bacon to Mill*
G16 *The European Philosophers from Descartes to Nietzsche*
G31 *Famous Science-Fiction Stories*
G85 *Great Ages and Ideas of the Jewish People*
G89 *Great Classical Myths*
G72 *Great Tales of Terror and the Supernatural*
G9 *Great Voices of the Reformation*
G87 *Medieval Epics*
G48 *The Metropolitan Opera Guide*
G46 *A New Anthology of Modern Poetry*
G69 *One Hundred and One Years' Entertainment*
G93 *Parodies: An Anthology from Chaucer to Beerbohm and After*
G90 *Philosophies of Art and Beauty: Readings in Aesthetics from Plato to Heidegger*
G21 *Sixteen Famous American Plays*
G63 *Sixteen Famous British Plays*
G71 *Sixteen Famous European Plays*
G45 *Stoic and Epicurean Philosophers*
G22 *Thirty Famous One-Act Plays*
G66 *Three Famous Murder Novels, Before the Fact,* FRANCIS ILES, *Trent's Last Case,* E. C. BENTLEY, *The House of the Arrow,* A. E. W. MASON
G10 *Twelve Famous Plays of the Restoration and Eighteenth Century* (1660–1820): Dryden, Congreve, Wycherley, Gay, etc.
G56 *The Wisdom of Catholicism*
G59 *The Wisdom of China and India*
G79 *The Wisdom of Israel*

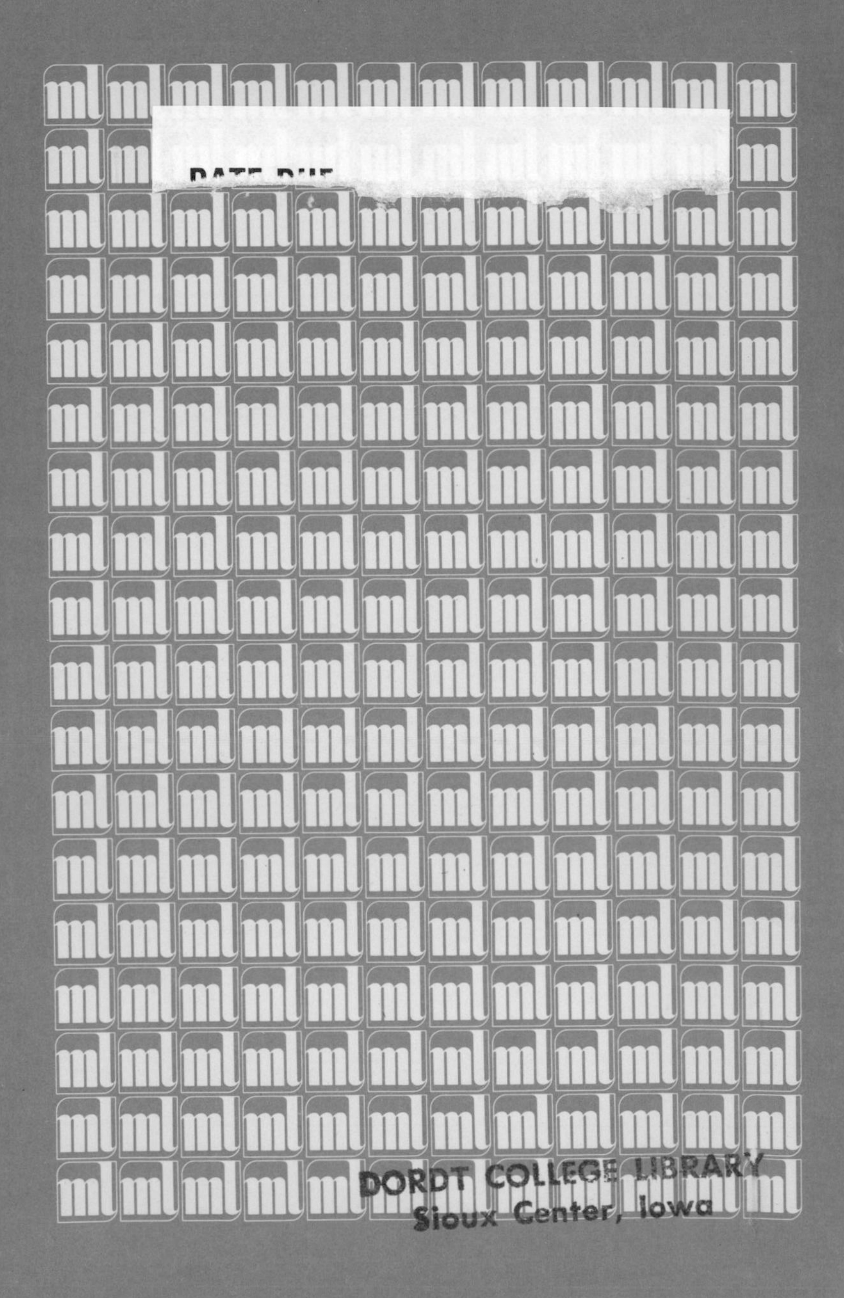